CONTEMPORARY CHILD PSYCHOTHERAPY

CONTEMPORARY CHILD PSYCHOTHERAPY
Integration and Imagination in Creative Clinical Practice

Edited by

Roz Read and Jeanne Magagna

PHOENIX
PUBLISHING HOUSE
firing the mind

First published in 2022 by
Phoenix Publishing House Ltd
62 Bucknell Road
Bicester
Oxfordshire OX26 2DS

British Library Cataloguing in Publication Data

A C.I.P. for this book is available from the British Library

ISBN-13: 978-1-912691-96-8

Typeset by Medlar Publishing Solutions Pvt Ltd, India

www.firingthemind.com

Contents

Acknowledgements

The idea of "Team Around the Child" could be said of producing this work with "Team Around the Book". It's only when putting together a work like this, one realises how dependent we are upon others. Jeanne and I would like to thank our publisher, Kate Pearce, for her enthusiastic support and for staying the course over numerous delays through the Covid-19 pandemic. We would also like to thank all the authors for their tremendous chapters and Dan Hughes for his Foreword. We are very appreciative of Zack Eleftheriadou, Griselda Kellie-Smith, Jane O'Rourke, and Peter Wilson who read drafts and gave us feedback. Finally, we'd like to make a special mention of Dr Margot Sunderland, the principal of the Institute for Arts in Therapy & Education (IATE) who continues to inspire this training.

Roz would like to add: a special thank you to my sister, Philippa Thackrah who helped me recognise that siblings can share the same events but have different experiences. I would also like to thank my greatest friend Elizabeth Ronan for keeping me going over countless Friday night phone chats. I am grateful for my supervisors, Julie Hudson, Dr Daniel Hughes, and Dr Renee Marks who read drafts and continue to guide me as I navigate the often painfully slow terrain in developing as a therapist. They are masters at their craft, and I am privileged to continue to be a student at their feet. Finally, I would like to mention my clients: the children and parents who have taught me so much over the years and challenge me with what I don't yet know.

A note on the text

The case studies included are either composites drawn from similar examples or have direct permission from the clients to be included. Some identifying details have been changed in order to preserve confidentiality.

About the editors and contributors

Irene Alberione originally trained as a teacher and holds an MA in philosophy and political studies from her education in Italy and France. She worked extensively with children, teenagers, and refugees within multicultural humanitarian aid, education, community services, and voluntary sectors. After relocating to the UK she retrained in play therapy (PTUK, PTI) and specialised in working with children who had experienced trauma in inner London schools. She works in gender violence therapeutic services supporting youth impacted by domestic violence. Irene is also currently working towards completing her MA in integrative child psychotherapy at the Institute for Arts in Therapy & Education (IATE).

Celine Allder qualified as an integrative child psychotherapist in 2019 after completing her MA at the Institute for Arts in Therapy & Education. She is currently working towards her UKCP registration. Celine has previously worked as a primary school teacher (with a specialism in PSHE) and as a special needs teacher, working with autistic children and adolescents. It was early in her teaching career that she felt the need to learn and understand more around supporting children with their emotional and mental health and decided to retrain as a child psychotherapist, with a focus on the arts. Now qualified, Celine works in Dorset for an organisation which receives referrals from social care and other bodies for therapeutic work with children and adolescents across the county. She predominantly works with looked-after children, providing psychotherapy sessions in schools. Celine also works directly with schools, supporting teaching staff in their work with children.

Neela Basu is a UKCP-registered integrative child psychotherapist who works in a CAMHS neurodevelopmental team and has experience of providing psychotherapy for children with severe trauma and disability. Neela's special area of interest is early intervention for children, including working with parents and professionals. She is part of the teaching faculty at the Institute for Arts in Therapy & Education (IATE). Her training in fine art at the Ruskin School and later studying at IATE have informed her interest in observation, expression, and communication. She is an advisory member for EI-SMART, a multidisciplinary approach to early intervention for infants at risk of developmental delays. Neela has experience of providing psychotherapy support and follow-up community care as part of the team at the Homerton Hospital Neonatal Intensive Care Unit for families and pre-term infants. She has facilitated parent groups and reflective practice for neonatal doctors as well as providing psychotherapeutic support for families. Neela is passionate about the importance of family-centred and trauma-informed care.

Adina Belloli is the founder of the international UK-registered charity In-Visible fighting global poverty. For over eighteen years she has worked with women and disadvantaged children as a volunteer and in paid work with women and disadvantaged children in organisations such as the World Health Organization, Heart House, Kids Company, and Cure2Children Foundation. Adina has dedicated her life to protecting and defending children's rights and has received awards for her philanthropic work which has been featured by BBC, CNN, PhilStar, *Wandsworth Guardian*, and GMA. With over twelve years of meditation, mindfulness, and yoga practice, Adina is also a children's mindfulness teacher. Hoping that psychotherapy will one day be accessible to all children, Adina is passionate about making a child's emotional well-being as important as a child's academic achievement. Adina trained at the Institute for Arts in Therapy & Education (IATE) and is a UKCP-registered integrative child psychotherapist for a London independent school.

Jane Brinson is a UKCP-registered integrative child psychotherapist whose work includes supporting adopted children and their families at PAC-UK. Formerly a teacher, Jane has worked therapeutically in a range of education settings, developing whole school programmes for well-being which include training school staff in trauma-informed approaches. Jane was awarded a Winston Churchill Fellowship in 2020 to research models of clinical supervision for teaching staff with safeguarding responsibilities.

Kate Clark is a UKCP-registered integrative child and adolescent psychotherapist who graduated from the Institute for Arts in Therapy and Education in 2009. She has over ten years' experience offering therapy in schools, community, wilderness, and clinical settings for children and young people who have a range of social, emotional and behavioural difficulties. Kate has spent the last eight years setting up and managing counselling departments in schools, including Place2Be where she managed teams of trainee counsellors, providing clinical supervision. Today she runs a counselling department in a Hackney secondary school. Her broader interests include using mindfulness approaches to support her clients. Kate hopes to pursue further training in mentalization and wilderness therapy.

Maria Furlong completed her MA in integrative child psychotherapy at the Institute for Arts in Therapy & Education (IATE) and is currently working as a school-based psychotherapist. Prior to completing her psychotherapy training Maria worked with children and families as a coordinator for Home-Start UK and previous to that, in education welfare and residential care. Maria graduated from Durham University with an honours degree in psychology and an MA in counselling.

Megan Holland is a senior child psychotherapist at Family Futures adoption agency. She is also a clinical supervisor and an academic tutor for two counselling psychology courses, two art therapy courses, and the Institute for Arts in Therapy & Education (IATE). Previously she worked in an NHS paediatric liaison service and ran a school-based psychotherapy service. Megan is a UKCP-registered integrative child psychotherapist.

Daniel Hughes, PhD, is a clinical psychologist living in Maine, USA, who founded and developed Dyadic Developmental Psychotherapy (DDP), the treatment of children who have experienced abuse and neglect and demonstrate ongoing problems related to attachment and trauma. This treatment model has expanded to become a general model of family treatment. For the past twenty years Dan has conducted seminars, workshops, and spoken at conferences throughout the US, Europe, Canada, and Australia. He is also engaged in extensive training and supervision in the certification of therapists in his treatment model, along with ongoing consultation to various agencies and professionals. He is the founder of DDPI, a training institute which is responsible for the certification of professionals in DDP. Dan is the author of many books and articles. These include *Building the Bonds of Attachment, 3rd Ed.* (2017), *Attachment-Focused Family Therapy Workbook* (2011), and, with Jon Baylin, *Brain-Based Parenting* (2012) and *The Neurobiology of Attachment-Focused Therapy* (2016). Along with Kim Golding and Julie Hudson, Dan has recently completed *Healing Relational Trauma with Attachment-Focused Interventions: Dyadic Developmental Psychotherapy with Children and Families* (W. W. Norton, 2019). Most recently he and Ben Gurney-Smith have published *The Little Book of Attachment* (W. W. Norton, 2020). His website is www.danielhughes.org.

Clair Lewoski is an integrative child and adolescent psychotherapist, attachment based psychoanalytic adult psychotherapist and dramatherapist. She has MAs from both the Tavistock Clinic and IATE. She has been working as a therapist since 1997. She set up a schools-based therapy service in 2003, across primary schools in the north of England, as well as working for a trauma-based arts therapies service, specialising in work with looked after and adopted children. Her work in Manchester led to the adoption of standards for therapeutic work in schools employing therapists. In recent years, she has been working in private practice as a psychotherapist with adults, young people and families and is a UKCP-registered supervisor and trainer. She is a senior trainer and examiner at IATE and for seven years she was a tutor at Cambridge University, teaching on the UKCP-registered child and adolescent counselling training. She is a Mentalization Based Family Treatment practitioner and is interested in relational ways of working and how these build upon both attachment and psychoanalytic thinking.

Jeanne Magagna, PhD, worked for twenty-four years in the Eating Disorder Team and became head of psychotherapy services at Great Ormond Street Hospital for Children, London. Through the London-based Tavistock Clinic, she received professional qualifications as a child, adult, and family psychotherapist as well as obtaining a doctorate in psychotherapy in conjunction with the University of East London. Jeanne has held roles as vice-president and joint coordinator of the child psychotherapy Tavistock-model trainings in the Centro Studi Martha Harris in Florence and Venice, Italy. Her edited books include: *A Psychotherapeutic Understanding of Children and Young People with Eating Disorders* (2021), *Universals of Psychoanalysis* (1994), *The Silent Child: Communication without Words* (2012), *Creativity and Psychotic States* (2014), and her jointly edited books include: *Intimate Transformations: Babies with Their Families* (2005), *Psychotherapy with Families* (1987), *and Crises in Adolescence* (1994). She both publishes and teaches in person and through video-links in many continents.

Sarah Marx initially trained as a psychodynamic and cognitive analytic psychotherapist, supervisor and MBCT/MBSR group facilitator. Seeing that so many of the adults she worked with were carrying the legacy of childhood trauma, Sarah went on to train at the Institute for Arts in Therapy and Education (IATE) and is a UKCP-registered integrative child psychotherapist. Sarah has a special interest in working with children and young people who have suffered developmental trauma and works at Beacon House Therapeutic Service in the Trauma Team where she offers a variety of interventions to adopted children and their families including creative arts based psychotherapy, EMDR and therapeutic parenting. Sarah has also trained in Dyadic Developmental Psychotherapy and Theraplay®. Alongside clinical work Sarah is passionate about the need for trauma informed education and is a trainer and home group tutor with Trauma Informed Schools UK. Sarah is also part of the teaching faculty at IATE.

Liz Murray-Bligh is a UKCP-registered integrative child and adolescent psychotherapist with extensive experience of independently setting up and providing therapeutic provision within a number of local authority primary schools. She uses a psychodynamic and systemic approach with her clients, developing close working relationships with families, school staff, and external agencies. She also supervises trainee child psychotherapists and counsellors and is closely involved in assessing students' work as they progress through their training at the Institute for Arts in Therapy & Education (IATE).

Graham Music, PhD, is a consultant child psychotherapist at the Tavistock Centre and adult psychotherapist in private practice. His publications include *Respark: Igniting Hope and Joy After Trauma and Depression* (2022), *Nurturing Children: From Trauma to Hope Using Neurobiology, Psychoanalysis and Attachment* (2019), *Nurturing Natures: Attachment and Children's Emotional, Sociocultural and Brain Development* (2016, 2010), *Affect and Emotion* (2001), and *The Good Life* (2014). He has a passion for exploring the interface between developmental findings and clinical work. A former associate clinical director at the Tavistock, he has managed and developed many services working with the aftermath of child maltreatment. He works clinically with forensic cases at the Portman Clinic, and teaches, lectures, and supervises in Britain and abroad.

Jessica Olive trained as an integrative child psychotherapist at the Institute for Arts in Therapy & Education (IATE) and is registered with UKCP and BACP. She works as a child & adolescent psychotherapist in private practice and leads the therapeutic provision within a North London primary school. She has a particular interest in neurodiversity in children and adolescents, working together with individuals, families and schools to support each child to reach their potential.

Roz Read is the programme director of the integrative child psychotherapy MA training at the Institute for Arts in Therapy & Education (IATE) validated by UEL where she teaches and designs the curriculum. With a background working in the arts, for over 30 years Roz has worked extensively with children and teenagers in multi-cultural inner-city community projects, schools and multi-disciplinary teams. Roz trained at IATE, and is a UKCP-registered integrative child psychotherapist, a Dyadic Developmental Psychotherapy (DDP) certified practitioner, and a Somatic Experiencing® practitioner. She has a PG diploma in psychoanalytic observational studies from the Tavistock Clinic. Roz has specialised in working with adopted children and their families, initially with Family Futures and then for eleven years she was part of the child and family team at PAC-UK. Today she works with adoptive families privately. Alongside Graham Music, she has also been co-convenor of the Tavistock Clinic Neuroscience and Attachment Workshop.

Karlien Smith-Claassens is a UKCP-registered integrative child and adolescent psychotherapist. She has experience working in schools as well as private practice supporting children, young people, and their families with a variety of emotional and behavioural issues. She currently works as a senior psychotherapist at Family Futures, a not-for-profit, London-based independent adoption agency, where she is part of the assessment and treatment team. As a former lawyer, Karlien brings her passion for advocacy to her therapeutic work, looking out for her clients' rights alongside their well-being.

Foreword

Daniel Hughes

John, aged nine, did not talk with his therapist over the first four sessions. He played with the clay figures, the puppets, and he increasingly settled into drawing. Sarah—his therapist and the therapist for each of the three children being briefly described—settled in with him, and spoke little herself. During the fifth session John drew a series of figures in various action poses, each with strong facial expressions and done in brilliant colours. Without words, Sarah made sounds with her throat that represented her experience of the drawings that John was making. John suddenly stopped, staring at a distance. Then he looked at Sarah and said quietly, "I feel sad when you speak like that." In subsequent sessions John had much more to say, most often within the context of his complex drawings.

Jenny, aged thirteen, spoke loudly with disagreements and defiance, while being dismissive of both her therapist's initiatives and responses no matter how benign they might be. For Sarah, getting to know her life of relationship traumas was clearly not possible. Getting to know her anger was possible, but only if the reasons for her anger were not explored. Sarah repeatedly accepted her anger, primarily by joining her affective expressions with a similar level of intensity, welcoming whatever expressions Jenny made as her statement about her life and the people who had been in it. Only when Jenny knew that her experience was accepted—fully accepted—did she begin to reveal other aspects of her life. These expressions were initially factual and seemingly routine. Gradually they contained emotional meanings beyond anger—her confusion, worries, wishes, and sadness. And then her mistrust and her shame along with her regular returns to her anger. Sarah accepted it all.

Nathan, aged seven, was an active boy, with his continuous chatter alongside his seemingly unconnected actions and his numerous fleeting bits of attention. Sarah provided the continuity of experience that Nathan lacked through her flowing interest in whatever he manifested in his mind and body. To Sarah, Nathan's expressions represented disorganised pieces of self, which, through her unwavering attention to his words, actions and bodily expressions gradually began to reflect their deeper meanings. Her mind and heart held Nathan's thoughts and emotions as they gradually developed into a more coherent whole. Her presence created the safety that he needed to begin to discover and share his poorly formed story.

John, Jenny, and Nathan struggled with the integration of their reflective, emotional, relational, and physical developmental tasks, often rigidly adhering to one or more of these tasks while remaining disconnected or dysregulated in their remaining areas of functioning. They also struggled with finding ways of engagement that are able to resonate with the other person in synchronised communications that enable the intentions and experiences of the therapist to become integrated with their own.

Their therapist, regardless of her specific therapeutic model and interventions, needed to facilitate the integration of both the child's unique psychological and bodily states as well as the child's ability to join her in reciprocal interactions and intentions. To do so well, their therapist needed to have attained her own high level of intrapersonal and interpersonal integrative functioning upon which the child would be able to rely. The process of integration permeates both the therapeutic goals as well as the manner of attaining these goals by relying heavily upon the therapeutic relationship.

We are increasingly aware of the need for psychological integration within and between individuals in order to maximise human development within relationships that thrive. Such integrative processes have become evident in studies of human development, with attachment theory and research being a primary example of this. Within a secure attachment relationship, the child develops a pattern of organised attachment processes that are central in the child's development of a life story that leads to a coherent autobiographical narrative. The ability of a child's developing identity to consolidate with integrative and flexible features is greatly enhanced by the presence of ongoing safe relationships in the child's life.

In a similar manner, the child's neurological development is characterised by the successive integration of the structures and functions of the child's neurological system. This integrative process is dependent upon safe, reciprocal, persistent relationships being actively present in the child's life. This awareness has led to the field of interpersonal neurobiology (Allan Schore and Dan Siegel) as well as the social baseline theory of neurological functioning (James Coan).

The integration of the functioning of two individuals in the moment involves the synchronisation of their affective, reflective, and intentional states in a manner that leads to interwoven subjective experiences. These are known as intersubjective experiences since they lead to the reciprocal development of the subjective experiences of each member of the dyad. These intersubjective experiences are most evident in the moment-to-moment infant–parent interactions that enhance the neuropsychological development of both infant and parent.

The parent–infant relationship has been seen by many to be a template for the essential characteristics of the therapeutic relationship (Winnicott, Stern, Beebe, Schore). These characteristics include forming an alliance, developing collaboration and goal consensus through qualities such as obtaining feedback and providing repair, as well as empathy, affirmation, and positive regard (Norcross & Lambert, 2018). These authors conclude:

> These relationship behaviors are robustly effective components and predictors of patient success. We need to proclaim publicly what decades of research have discovered and what hundreds of thousands of practitioners have witnessed: The relationship can heal.
>
> (p. 311)

It is within these moment-to-moment reciprocal, synchronised inter-actions that the integration of the affective states, reflective processes, and complementary intentions of both child and therapist are occurring together. When the therapist's regulated affect, comprehensive reflective abilities, and coherent goals are joined with the less integrated states of the child, the child's intrapsychic functioning is likely to become more integrated.

It is crucial that the therapist's psychological state is integrated. It is equally important that the ongoing therapeutic relationship develops the attuned resonance that characterises the parent–infant relationship. This relationship involves a synchronised, non-verbal, body-based state between the members of the dyad and quickly becomes joined by the reflective and intentional qualities that are contained within the thera-peutic conversation.

The therapeutic relationship and process are neurologically both bottom-up and top-down. While for many children, the need to facili-tate their affect regulation skills through joint affective, body-based states take the lead, for other children their need to develop their reflec-tive functioning through engaging in joint conversations that lead to developing and becoming aware of their thoughts and ideas has to be the initial focus. With some children body-based activities or engagement within metaphors greatly aid the process of integration. The therapist's flexible mind and openness to the child's experience as it emerges enable her to become synchronised with the leads of the child in the manner that creates the greatest integration.

The mosaic of chapters in this book are themselves an integration of the knowledge, developing and developed, from student and teacher, young and old, that is characteristic of the Institute for Arts in Therapy & Education (IATE). These chapters demonstrate various therapeutic frameworks and skills, some of which meet the psychological needs of one child, while other ones meet the differing needs of another. In order to maximise the therapeutic relationship and the value of therapy for the individual child, the sensitive therapist integrates specific aspects of their training and their own cultural perspective with the unique psy-chological needs of the child. The sensitive therapist does not prescribe a particular therapeutic technique for all the children she meets, but rather discovers the most appropriate interventions to use as she gets to know each particular person. These ongoing acts of discovery are what create the collaborative, synchronised relationship that joins the affective, reflective, and intentional states of both therapist and child. It is from such a relationship that the integrative processes of healing and psychological development emerge from within the child.

Over the past twenty years I have had the privilege of teaching and consulting with many of the students and staff at IATE. I have been continuously impressed by their curiosity and creativity in finding innovative ways of becoming engaged with troubled and traumatised children in order to assist them on their restorative journeys. Their focus was truly integrative as they developed their understanding and skills from a range of therapeutic schools in order to be able to best treat the complex needs of these children.

Reference

Norcross, J. C., & Lambert, M. J. (2018). Psychotherapy relationships that work III. *Psychotherapy*, *55*: 303–315.

Introduction

In this book, we are presenting work which demonstrates the development of participants on the integrative child psychotherapy MA training at the Institute for Arts in Therapy & Education (IATE) in Islington, London. The MA (validated by the University of East London) is a three-year part-time training, which with the addition of a foundation year, becomes a four-year psychotherapy training validated by the UK Council of Psychotherapy (UKCP).

The training, initiated by Dr Margot Sunderland in 2000, continues with Roz Read as the programme director under Margot's overall leadership of a variety of trainings within IATE's educational programme.

IATE was born over thirty years ago, when Margot with two colleagues began running short trainings for therapists in using a broad range of arts techniques: sand play, art and clay, music, drama, puppetry, poetry, and dance/movement. The arts trainings were a resounding success, and led eventually to a UKCP-validated integrative arts psychotherapy MA which still runs today. The training was the first to bring all the arts together in an integrative way with both humanistic and psychoanalytic theories. It was also one of the first to embrace neuroscience.

This was just the beginning. Having initially trained in child psychotherapy under John Hood-Williams (the last director of studies at Dr Margaret Lowenfeld's Institute of Child Psychology), Margot had always wanted to do something specifically for children. Clinical placements for students on the integrative arts psychotherapy training already included primary schools local to IATE in Islington and children were responding to the multiple, creative ways in which they could express themselves through the arts and metaphor. Finally in 2000, the new training in integrative child psychotherapy was launched at IATE. It became validated by UKCP, and then when it became an MA, it was validated first by London Metropolitan University and subsequently by the University of East London.

Over the last twenty years, the IATE integrative child psychotherapy training has gone from strength to strength, and today graduates are working with children across all sectors—public, private, and voluntary. Some have gone on to management positions within the NHS Child & Adolescent Mental Health Service (CAMHS), while others are working in more specialised services within adoption and fostering, children's homes, therapeutic communities, and charities. Of course, the work in schools continues, the value being increasingly recognised in recent years particularly for those disadvantaged families who neither meet the thresholds for CAMHS nor can engage successfully with statutory services. The IATE training has also inspired new trainings around the country and today it sits proudly alongside others within UKCP.

The foundation year of the training explores the use of multiple art forms in workshops with the student learning from their own experience of engaging expressively with the arts. As students learn to do this themselves, they are then more comfortable to use these tools and engage creatively in their work with children.

Not confined by one particular theory, from the second year the student builds their own theoretical structure with which they work. The choice of theories is not simply eclectic, but linked to the student's own history: what resonates and is meaningful to them. It's also linked to their individual client's needs and so theories and different ways of working may depend on the needs of the specific child engaged in therapy. In this way, an integrative model is a creative, fluid model rather than an established structure imposed from outside.

Working therapeutically with children today acknowledges that the child is within a system including parents, schools, and other professionals and so students also participate in group process where they learn to discuss and share ideas, reflect, and work together. An integrative and creative way of thinking is encouraged from the start and students write a personal learning journal for the first two years, bringing together their learning and reflections from all aspects of the training.

An important part of the training ethos is to hold onto the traditional foundations that have worked while keeping an eye on the horizon for new research and development. It's vital that a training remains relevant and continues to serve those who will benefit—children and families—and that it doesn't become an end product in itself, but rather is up-to-date, modern, and useful practically. Today, bridges have been built with the psychoanalytic community of psychotherapists, many of whom have joined our integrative colleagues in teaching, tutoring, and supervising our students. So it is entirely fitting that twenty years after the training's inception, a psychoanalytic co-editor and integrative co-editor have worked together to publish this book.

The book begins with Chapter 1 by Graham Music, a guest lecturer at IATE, who gives clinical examples demonstrating his way of integrating a wide variety of theories in working therapeutically with children. In his chapter, entitled "Addicted to action, fear of being", Graham brings together psychoanalytical ideas, such as those about defences against difficult feelings, with ideas rooted in body awareness, such as neurobiologically informed mindfulness and trauma therapy, alongside humanistic and integrative skills from play therapy, Gestalt, and person-centred therapies. He emphasises how "tribalism" in the psychotherapies misses how each way of working has important lessons to teach, and paradoxically, given the psychotherapy profession's aims, it has an inability to hear each other's voices. He goes on to suggest that to really understand and help one's clients, especially those who "act out" and have had experiences of stress, trauma, or fear, one must employ and integrate understanding gleaned from many vertices. He feels this is especially the case with children who are dysregulated or impulsive, probably the majority of those who these days come for therapeutic work, who are often referred with issues linked with some form of enactment. Commonly therapists see children who are impetuous, cannot concentrate or be still, can be violent or aggressive, or do other things that create anxiety in the professional system or in their carers. These are children who are "acting" or "doing" what psychoanalysis terms "acting out". He shows in his chapter why such children need a broad-based approach.

Chapter 2, "Experiences of being held: creating a space to think and play within a family", by Neela Basu, narrates her experience of a weekly, hour-long observation of an infant and her family, over two years. Infant observation is now a core feature of many psychotherapy trainings. Often a course is undertaken before any clinical work. In this shorter, integrative training, it's studied alongside the clinical training. It's the one part of the training that is not about pathology but about exploring ordinary "good enough" human development. More than that, however, is the aim of helping the student develop curiosity: to look carefully at the baby, notice, and muse about the smallest of ordinary details. Perhaps they have meaning. In so doing, feelings may be stirred within which may resonate with one's own history. Paying attention to this and teasing out that which belongs to the trainee child psychotherapist and that which belongs to the observation are key. It can be a challenge not to intervene, but to hold these feelings and lend thinking to them. Later when writing up the story of the visit or sharing it in the seminar, the observer may be reminded of forgotten moments, and this may be significant. Did the student dissociate? Was it painful to watch? The learning is as much about what is remembered as what is discounted, missed, or forgotten. In Neela's chapter, the observation allowed her to see both mother and father with the baby as they found ways of sharing parenting and careers, navigating their experiences of becoming part of a family and finding their roles and responses to their child. During the observations, the mother returned to work and later became pregnant again. Neela was able to observe the family as they began to think and explore feelings about the changing dynamic. The focal point remains the young child, following her developing sense of herself in the world that appeared to occur in conjunction with her parents' capacity to hold her, think about and tolerate her feelings.

Karlien Smith-Claassens, in Chapter 3, "The effects of chronic trauma and neglect on attachment security and development", discusses how chronic trauma and neglect can affect a child's attachment security and development. This first-year paper exploring attachment theory and neuroscience grounds students in some of the most fundamental theories of the training. First, Karlien explores what happens when things go well in a parent–child relationship. Using findings from attachment theory as well as neuroscience, she then illustrates how chronic trauma and neglect can have a pervasive and long-lasting effect on a child's neurophysiological development, attachment security, and sense of self. The chapter describes how a child's maladaptive patterns can become ingrained in the child's brain and nervous system, leading to a permanent state of emotional dysregulation. It demonstrates how chronic trauma and neglect in the context of a developing body and mind can have a devastating effect on attachment security and development. Clinical examples are used to illustrate how this might be seen in the therapy sessions.

If Porges and Winnicott were to meet today, would they find a common language? In Chapter 4, "Porges meets Winnicott", Irene Alberione has attempted to integrate two theorists: Porges, a neuroscientist known for his seminal polyvagal theory, and Winnicott, the well-known child psychoanalyst and paediatrician. As integrative child psychotherapists, students need to work at developing a model that integrates psychoanalytic theories with contemporary neuroscience, child development research, and the arts. This first-year paper is presented on the training in a "live" context in small seminars, so that students practise organising and presenting their ideas, critiquing and discussing them together. Irene discusses how the work of Porges offers neuroscientific backing for the experience of heart to heart contact, proving what Winnicott intuitively theorised: that we are primed for relatedness, with an innate bodily energy ready to be plugged into a living relationship. Irene discusses the suggestion that therapy could be a "relating" rather than a "talking" cure, where safety is the treatment and trust is the work. She argues that Winnicott's theoretical and clinical insights might have been "polyvagally" informed ante litteram.

Chapter 5 is "Autism and sensory sensitivity" by Jessica Olive. Integrative child psychotherapists need to have a good working knowledge of the issues around child mental health and psychiatry so that they can feel confident in liaising with statutory services as necessary. In the second year, students are invited to write on any relevant area that engages them, and then consider what integrative child psychotherapy might be able to offer in therapy sessions with a child. Jessica has chosen to write on autism, and in this chapter she explains how many children with autism will experience difficulties when encountering sensory information, often being either under- or oversensitive in response to sensory information, appearing easily distracted, and displaying hypersensitivity to external stimuli. Jessica explores the experience of the autistic child in this respect, considering research that seeks to understand the aetiology of this response. She introduces Joseph, an autistic child with whom she had worked for two years, and how through knowing him she came to a deeper understanding of the experience of an over- or under-whelming response to sensory information. She explores whether the tendency to be quickly distracted by sensory information is a feature of autism itself, or whether it may demonstrate co-morbidity with another disorder, and concludes that such distraction can belong with autism alone. Finally, she gives consideration to how children with sensory issues may best be supported within the therapeutic environment.

Chapter 6, "'Finding Dory': a story of an eight-year-old's journey from loss to hope and strength" by Celine Allder is a case presentation. As with Chapter 4, this second-year assessment was originally presented in a live setting with trainees taking turns to present a clinical case to their colleagues in a small group followed by questions and discussion, linking theory and practice. The sharing and discussing of cases is typically part of the professional life of a child psychotherapist so trainees are encouraged to work in groups and to share their work together. In this chapter, Celine introduces Dee, an eight-year-old girl from London, who was referred for weekly psychotherapy in her school. The case shows the importance of developing a safe therapeutic alliance, and how a trainee might use the arts and bodywork to deepen exploration. The case also shows how a trainee might work with the system around the child which might sometimes bring ethical dilemmas about what can be shared. Highlighted is also the importance of good training supervision to support the risks that a trainee might take. The trainee finishes by reflecting on the learning from the assessment process itself and how it helped shape her own therapeutic framework for practice.

Each of the trainee child psychotherapists spends time working individually with children presenting with different difficulties that impede their development. Long-term cases are written up as dissertations in the final year of the MA. Adina Belloli in Chapter 7, "Making sense of the pieces", describes the therapeutic journey of integrative child psychotherapy with a seven-year-old girl to facilitate deep psychic change over the course of one-and-a-half years. The young girl was referred by her school as she was struggling behaviourally and socially in the classroom. As a result of her early experiences of domestic violence and parental separation, she seemed to be acting out dysregulated feelings and re-enacting her experiences. Adina's initial hypothesis was that the little girl did not have an internal working model of positive human relationships, resulting in a catastrophic aloneness as she tried to manage the unmanageable on her own. The aim of the therapeutic encounter was to create experiences of regulating, empathic, and attuned relating, within which developmental deficits were seen and met. The reader witnesses Adina providing the child with a secure base from which she could explore the various unhappy and painful aspects of her life, past and present. This chapter illustrates different stages of the therapeutic work with the young girl to reflect, hold onto, and process feelings of loss and separation through the use of the therapeutic relationship. Over time, through the use of empathic connection, reciprocity, and trust, the therapeutic relationship becomes a container, providing context for the young girl to understand relationships in a new way. The therapeutic relationship led to a secure attachment, which helped to internalise a message that she deserved love, safety, and hope.

In a similar vein of thinking, Sarah Marx in Chapter 8, "Space rockets and mobile homes: reaching the place of hope by traversing the landscape of trauma and loss", describes two years of integrative child psychotherapy with a nine-year-old girl. Sarah explores how this child's early experiences of neglect, relational trauma, and unresolved loss impacted on her sense of self and her capacity to play and be in relationship. This chapter, originally a dissertation, charts a course through the various stages of the relationship from the child's early avoidance of the therapist through to ambivalence and confusion and finally landing at a place where the child began to feel safe and able to connect. The chapter ends with some reflections on the trainee child psychotherapist's learning.

In Chapter 9, "All in bits: trauma, fragmentation, and the journey of piecing back together", Megan Holland describes two years of integrative child psychotherapy with Mia, a multiply traumatised seven-year-old girl of mixed white British and Ethiopian descent. She explores Mia's presenting issues, examining how her experiences of separation, fragmentation, and loss are held and processed through the different phases of therapy.

Chapter 10, "Safety, trust, and maternal deprivation", by Maria Furlong, explores a twenty-minute verbatim transcript from a recorded psychotherapy session. This final-year qualifying assessment is the culmination of the training. Students work hard to prepare and find recordings that present the trainee's integration of theoretical approaches and use of creative arts to demonstrate their understanding of the child, provide affect regulation, and inform the interventions used throughout the session. A particular theme in this example is the child's fearful responses to intimacy and the connection to early maternal deprivation. Interventions relating to the child's emotionally rich story and use of metaphor are illustrated. The listening of the twenty-minute recording is followed by a close examination of the process by two assessors who ask the student to give an account of what informed their interventions. There is also a discussion of how the use of characters—persecutors, protectors, and the vulnerable—allows exploration of the child's deep feelings, sexually precocious adaptations, and fragmented parts of the self. The chapter further explores the use of the transferential relationship in order to deepen understanding of the child's complex internal and external world. In including this chapter, we thought it important to think about the sexualisation of children who have been traumatised through the sexual lives of their parents and caregivers when there have been multiple partners. This is a subject not discussed nearly enough. Even if the child has not been sexually abused themselves, it's so hard for the young client to stay with their experience of neglect rather than jump into the vicarious excitement of the experience. It becomes almost addictive. Maria shows us in this chapter how she gently helped the client think about the more painful underlying aspects of their unmet attachment needs.

Chapter 11, "The transformer and the measuring tape: using the relationship to help process the trauma of an eight-year-old boy" by Kate Clark is another verbatim transcript of a recording for the final viva exam. On an integrative training, trainees are given opportunity to work in multiple ways as they find their voice and, here, Kate presents a quite different approach of using the arts to work in a more direct way with the child's trauma. In presenting unedited recordings of their work, trainees make themselves vulnerable to show not just their skill, but the risks, the rawness, and mistakes that are made along the way, and are expected to critique and give an account for their interventions. In this moving session, Kate demonstrates how through the regular weekly work, the therapeutic relationship was built up so that the child was able to bring his deepest fears to her. We are aware that he is traumatised and anxious. His worry suggests that he feared his hurt and anger damaged the internalised therapist. Kate's external presence helped him to feel that she could receive his feelings and enable him to repair. She uses toys and metaphor to help the child talk about his trauma for the first time. The twenty-minute recording is a tiny snapshot of the work with one child inside the therapy room, so it is not expected to be comprehensive. In the discussion with the assessors that followed, Kate would have explained its context and the work she was also doing with the child's external world, which involved regular meetings with the family to help them access support, including the mother's own counselling. The chapter ends with some reflections from Kate now that she is qualified and has practised for many years. She discusses her experience of the viva and the recording she presented with fresh insight. In this way, as therapists we continue to be students, often revisiting work we have done to appraise and process it a little bit more.

In Chapter 12, "Working in schools: parents and the system around the child", Liz Murray-Bligh discusses the main areas of environmental influence on the child, drawing on extensive experience of working in primary school settings. She considers the therapists' position in schools and some of the struggles that arise in the holding of professional boundaries when working in a non-clinical setting. She focuses mainly on the roles of parents and schools, and then touches on working with external agencies before taking a brief look at the impact of digital media usage on young children.

Chapter 13, "Building a therapeutic service in schools—the role of an integrative child psychotherapist", by Jane Brinson, explores how integrative child psychotherapists working in schools can promote the development of a therapeutic service and be a part of a programme of whole-school change. It explores how the therapist's relational skills are applied outside the therapy room to establish the therapeutic frame and build relationships within the school community. Over time, and with careful collaboration between clinicians and school staff, a culture can develop where children's emotional needs are central to the day-to-day business of the school, and children can thrive. She illustrates this through the story of a North London school, Highgate Primary, which developed an award-winning pastoral and therapeutic service in partnership with the therapists in the team.

In the psychotherapy training, the trainee child psychotherapists are strongly encouraged to use a wide variety of arts and play materials to facilitate the portrayal of different emotional states. A good example of the therapeutic journey is given by Clair Lewoski in Chapter 14, "Empathising with defences through the use of arts and metaphor". Clair explores an integrative framework to thinking about and working with children's defences. Her aim is to show how a psychoanalytic understanding of defences can be combined with an attachment perspective, which then utilises the arts as a key aspect of technique. Thinking about how a therapist might empathise with the defence is presented as a way of tiptoeing up to what often feels to be the client's very sensitive and tender areas. The chapter ends with examples of using Sunderland's (2015) technique of "big empathy drawings" and therapeutic stories as a method of working with defences.

Subsequently, Roz Read, co-editor and the programme director of IATE's integrative child psychotherapy training, in Chapter 15, "Finding and nurturing the gold: an integrative approach to working with an adopted adolescent and her parent", gives a personal account of the different parts of herself that she brings into play in her work with adopted children. Through her different roles, Roz demonstrates how an integration of the creative arts, work with the body, dissociation, and Dyadic Developmental Psychotherapy can be used to tailor the approach to an individual child and her adoptive family's needs.

Finally, Jeanne Magagna, co-editor, training supervisor, and guest lecturer at IATE, in Chapter 16, "Developing a 'cradle of concern' using transference and countertransference in therapy and supervision", considers how the child has a transference relationship to the psychotherapist that affects how the psychotherapist relates to the child. She then goes on to discuss how the therapist might relate to the child's negative and positive transference towards the therapist through use of the countertransference. Alongside this is a discussion of establishing a "cradle of concern" in the triangular relationship between supervisor, therapist, and the child in therapy which potentially has an effect on the whole system.

The chapters in this book form a collection of coursework from students and graduates that, set alongside chapters written by more experienced therapists, show the depth of understanding, creativity, knowledge, and skill that underpin an integrative child psychotherapist. Rather than a "fixed" model, the reader is introduced to a modern, flexible model that is fluid and evolving, bringing together traditional, long-held ideas with fresh perspectives and research. In bringing together psychoanalytic and humanistic theories, attachment theory, trauma theories, the arts and creativity, neuroscience and the body, a rich framework can be created. The task is that the individual integrative child psychotherapist, in collaboration with parents and schools, can choose to tailor their interventions to understand and foster the development of each specific child and young person.

Reference

Sunderland, M. (2015). *Conversations that Matter. Talking with Children and Teenagers in Ways that Help*. Broadway, UK: Worth.

CHAPTER 1

Addicted to action, fear of being

Graham Music

Introduction

In this chapter I bring together psychoanalytical ideas, such as about defences against difficult feelings, with ideas rooted in body awareness, such as neurobiologically informed mindfulness and trauma therapy, alongside humanistic and integrative skills from play therapy, Gestalt, and person-centred therapies.

"Tribalism" in the psychotherapies misses how each way of working has important lessons to teach, and paradoxically, given the psychotherapy profession's aims, it has an inability to hear each other's voices. To really understand and help our clients, especially those who "act out" and have had experiences of stress, trauma, or fear, I think we must employ and integrate understanding gleaned from a range of vertices.

This is especially the case with children who are dysregulated or impulsive: probably the majority of those who these days come for therapeutic work, often referred with issues linked with some form of enactment. Commonly we see children who are impetuous, cannot concentrate or be still, can be violent or aggressive, or do other things that create anxiety in the professional system or in their carers. These are children who are "acting" or "doing" what psychoanalysis terms "acting out". I hope to show in this chapter why such children need a broad-based approach.

A personal aside

My personal journey as a therapist began doing person-centred play therapy with a maverick therapist called Rachel Pinney who taught us to really stay with a child's actual immediate experience, to follow their play, reflect their actions and feeling back to them, never directly interpret or explain, just stay true to their emotional and bodily experience. The children almost magically seemed to calm when receiving such attention, feeling "held", but also "contained" and having an experience of their experiences being stayed with, rather than being chivvied out of their feelings or being given advice. This "staying with" is also central to mindfulness practice and is at the heart of emotional growth and development in all therapeutic work. I learnt how often it is our own blind spots that take us away from such genuine presence with the other.

My initial formal psychotherapy training mixed analytic and humanistic elements. I soon learnt that empathy and compassion are central, indeed vital, but these attitudes are not about being sweetly "nicey-nice". They require courage and the ability to escort people into dark, uncomfortable places. I learnt that sometimes we need to stay with the unpalatable, to challenge and be challenged, that being a therapist, like being in therapy, can be like being put through a wringer. I have learnt over the years that if we are not challenged or affected we are probably not doing good enough work.

I also learnt from my integrative early training that there are times when it is not helpful to just stay with pain, despair, or difficulty. We also need to help build the more functioning parts of the client's personality, their "ego strength", their belief in an ability to cope and then thrive in the world, to assert themselves and find strength. A constant therapeutic challenge is balancing when it is helpful to stay with vulnerability, difficulties, dependency, anxiety, and when to work with more hopeful aspects of the personality.

Psychoanalysis, with its emphasis on non-conscious and unconscious processes, its ability to bear the harshest of realities, its capacity to understand defensive coping mechanisms, did in time become my bedrock. It enabled me to add an understanding of projection to my armamentarium, and an awareness of countertransference. It was a relief to realise that, when with disturbed children, feelings stirred up in us, whether anger, frustration, inadequacy, are often feelings that the child or young person has known all too well but cannot yet process.

My best work with children and young people who have suffered trauma happens when I am able to use my embodied countertransference as a sounding board, using neurobiologically informed understandings, including of the nervous system, alongside an understanding of attachment, and an awareness that a client's current "problems" often developed as an adaptive way of coping with really difficult early experiences. Such work requires a breadth of therapeutic understandings and an ability to trust when a certain way of working might be helpful or defensive. For me, much of this understanding has come from my own personal therapies but is sustained by my own daily body-based practices, such as mindfulness and yoga, which help me to be present to, and read, the bodily signals that convey understandings of what I might be feeling in a particular moment, and what might be going on in my clients.

As Damasio (1999) has helped us understand, emotions are bodily signals which we can learn to read and make sense of. In the case studies that follow I describe how I try to understand children and young people who are too often out of touch with their body states and feelings, even though it is these very states that drive them to act.

The importance of body awareness

Mick, nine years old, is typical of many traumatised children who are jumpy, hypervigilant, dysregulated, and out of touch with what is going on inside their own skins. In one session with Mick I found myself feeling tense and anxious, worried that he would do something unsafe like climbing a high cupboard or throwing something dangerously. My heart was in my mouth, my body tight and breathing shallow. Just the process of noticing this led to my body relaxing. allowing me to take on a more self-assured easeful stance, stepping outside of a potentially combative enactment (Aron, 2001).

Another time Mick was again restless and edgy, as I was. Noticing my tension, I took a deep breath, trying to stay with my feeling. When I looked up again he was calmly drawing. Whether my simple act of self-regulation had an effect would be hard to prove, but we know how people non-consciously resonate with others' body states, such as via mirror neurons (Rizzolatti et al., 2006) and embodied synchrony (Koole & Tschacher, 2016).

Often, I would simply echo Mick's feelings, letting him know they were understood. He developed confidence that this would happen and began to regulate such feelings for himself. Feeling understood can bring relief and relaxation without the therapist being explicit about what is happening.

We can take a step further and help patients to consciously become aware of, and interested in, what is going on in their bodies. Just bringing awareness to tension, for example, can allow a relaxing. Practice and habit increase such self-regulatory awareness, training our interoceptive self-awareness muscles. Such new psychic muscles are in effect what psychoanalysis thinks of as good internal objects, derived from identification with a "noticing other" (object), enhancing bodily states of softness, ease, and relaxation.

Of course, sometimes insight can make a difference. In one session Paula, aged fourteen, was raging at her new boyfriend's behaviour, and I simply suggested, based on understanding that had developed between us, that her provocative actions might have given him cause to feel jealous. This is the bread and butter of much therapy and made no reference to bodily states. Paula said something like "Oh yeah," raised her eyebrows, smiled, and her whole being calmed down. Here insight alone led to bodily relaxation.

At other times, nothing I said made much difference, and she remained agitated, angry, or dysregulated. It often felt impossible to find the correct calming psychological interpretation. Alvarez's (2012) innovative thinking has pushed us to carefully consider our therapeutic technique; in particular, whether we might work at too cognitive a level with certain patients. In therapy with overtly abused patients, I often find it necessary to work at a more psychophysiological level, such as down-regulating powerful emotions and managing over-arousal.

Asking questions with genuine curiosity about bodily experiences can unleash profound associations. In another session Paula was talking angrily about someone who had upset her. I was struck by the unusual way that she started to rub her cheeks, which had reddened. I asked what was happening, what she was feeling in her face. She falteringly told me how her father would slap her on her cheeks when she was getting upset. This brought up an extraordinary stream of material about childhood experiences with her father. These would never have come to light had I not enquired about how she was rubbing her cheeks which had reddened as if the medium for the expression of consciously forgotten but bodily remembered childhood experiences.

Sometimes we can actively guide patients to become more aware of bodily states. This can be relatively non-directive, such as wondering if it is okay to stop holding oneself tightly against tears, which is tantamount to giving someone permission to cry. For example, when Paula was near sadness but bracing against this, I suggested she might breathe more deeply, showing my trust that we could manage her feelings together.

A step further is actively encouraging awareness of body states by offering some instruction. For a few years I met with senior psychoanalytic psychotherapy colleagues who shared an interest in both brain science and mindfulness. We had all benefitted from our own mindfulness practices, including becoming more cognisant of bodily states, breathing, and arousal levels, and believed we needed to work more actively with bodily awareness with very dysregulated patients. In my own work, this has often meant guiding people through body scans as well as being consistently curious about what might be going on in their bodies, as I hope some cases below might reveal.

Learning experientially

As stated, my earlier integrative psychotherapy training included a substantial amount of body understanding, based in the theories of Reich (1945), Keleman (1975), Lowen (1975), and others. My training especially examined how defences get structured in the body. In recent years, I have been trying to bring these understandings into my psychotherapy practice and supervision of others. With Roz Read, I set up a workshop in the Tavistock for therapists and trainees to think about trauma, neuroscience, and the body, aiming to enhance awareness of embodiment, including of the embodied countertransference. I also, like others (Sletvold, 2014), ask supervisees to include their somatic counter-transference in session notes and I do more live supervision, including physically role playing patients. This was because I too often heard case descriptions which conveyed little sense of embodied states, voice tone, or gestural feel, without which I struggled to make sense of sessions. Increasing awareness of supervisees' body states and their clients' has had a powerful effect on supervisees' work.

For example, one trainee psychotherapist, Mark, had been seeing Bryn, an eight-year-old boy, three times weekly for over two years, and receiving weekly individual supervision on his work with the boy. Bryn was born a twin. Both were healthy at birth, although their mother suffered with post-natal depression. She always favoured Bryn's twin who at eighteen months died in a tragic incident. Mother then entered a deep depression, becoming unable to care for Bryn or his older sister.

I found it a challenge to work in therapy with Mark role playing Bryn who resorted constantly to manic, aggressive actions. He was very active, barely able to contact feelings. He constantly blocked attempts by Mark, his therapist, to think with him, generally presenting as omnipotent, defiant, self-critical, and destructive. Mark's account of presenting in the workshop now follows:

> When invited to get up and embody Bryn in front of the group I initially felt my body tense and heart race. Graham encouraged me to find a place in the middle of the group, where he had placed some chairs. I stood, hoping to settle. A shift occurred: I felt myself drawn to Graham's words, encouraging me to become Bryn and talk as him in the first person. An instinct told me I needed to be on the floor, I took a deep breath and once there, began to feel anxious again: where do I start?
>
> My attempts to recall a specific scene triggered anxious energy in my abdomen and chest. I felt that I couldn't move. I heard Graham ask me to describe what was going on inside.
>
> I struggled initially, and then a shift occurred. No longer occupied with thoughts, I began to feel heavy, as if weighted into the floor, even imagining that I would be pulled right into it. Graham asked what I was feeling. I said that I felt heavy and weighed down (in body and mind). Graham asked what was happening in the different areas of my body. Attention was drawn to my right leg and I noticed that it was shaking;

going into spasm. A powerful feeling of being stuck was prominent. I noticed myself leaning to the side as if I might topple over. Something was happening that I had little control over, but I stayed with this, sensing its significance.

I found it difficult to verbalise my experience. I heard Graham say that he felt a tremendous sadness. With Graham naming the sadness, I too felt a wash of grief and my eyes filled, tears falling down my right cheek, into my hair and ear. I cannot recall what happened next. I think Graham named depression. This resonated strongly. Without the usual defences of mania, grievances, or self-abasement, I could feel first-hand some of the strength of Bryn's powerful depression. Afterwards the group and myself processed the experience. The palpable sadness resonated and I continued to feel heavy, and later, very tired.

Mark saw Bryn five days later and the session was atypical. Mark reported looking forward to it rather than his normal tense bracing. Bryn seemed more contented, reporting receiving three smiley faces at school. He then talked about being at his dad's house, expressing anger and despair about his dad moving to a new house again, insisting that he really didn't want his dad to move because he was feeling settled now. Bryn then said that it was the second anniversary of his dad's dog's death. He was sitting on the sofa, and his head dropped and he began to sob. Without it yet being named, although this happened later, clearly both were in touch with the tragic loss of Bryn's twin. He continued to sob for much of the session, coming close to Mark. Between sobs, he asked Mark many questions, such as "Have you ever had to move from a house you don't want to?" "Have you ever lost a dog?" He desperately needed someone to understand his experience of loss and pain. When Mark talked about this Bryn showed clear relief. Both moved between relief, laughter, tears. Mark, more present to his own emotions than usual, said how connected they felt to each other, and he felt very paternal.

Previously Bryn had almost never been able to stay with any upset. Usually his despair and sadness shifted quickly to mania, attacking and omnipotent states. This sadness was a new experience for both, one which could now be built upon. It was triggered by Bryn's therapist having a new experience of being in touch with Bryn's deep emotional states via his own embodied awareness.

Matt: tiptoeing up to trauma

Ten-year-old Matt was in foster care, having been physically abused by his stepfather. He had been locked in his room without food or a toilet, and subjected to blistering verbal assaults. During the last year he had been settling well with a thoughtful foster carer. He was referred after hurting a child and threatening another at school.

In one early session he enacted a scene in which, being scared, he called the police. Holding a pretend phone, I said, "Hello. Police here, how can I help?" He replied, "My step-dad is hurting me." I said, "Oh dear, that sounds terrible, what is he doing?" Matt described being scared to leave his room in case he was hurt, but hating staying there as his mum was being hurt. I said, "Oh dear, that sounds so frightening, horrible, that should not happen to any boy of your age. What would you like me to do?" Matt looked uncertain. I asked whether I should come and arrest his step-dad, and he said yes. Then he said he must stop the call as his stepfather was outside the room.

Such work left me hopeful. He seemed able to communicate memories of traumatic experiences in symbolic form through play, allowing us to process them together. To an extent this was true, and he seemed calmer in the following weeks. The play then took a different turn. He enacted scenes of his stepfather being angry and violent. I joined in, assuming this also was a hopeful development; good therapeutic work helping to process his experiences. The scenes were physically and verbally aggressive.

Unbeknown to me, this play was having a bad effect. Matt became agitated at home, and there were incidents at school, the first for months. His sleep had worsened, and he was having nightmares. Most worryingly, he told his foster carer that he had been seeing his stepfather's face, and evidently he had been having flashbacks.

I realised belatedly that the dramatic re-enactments had re-evoked his trauma, leaving him fragile. I needed to review my approach. While traumatic experiences can also be avoided, here the timing and approach were unhelpful, and indeed re-traumatising. I changed tack, not encouraging memories, allowing more space for the ordinary play that boys indulge in at Matt's age. This seemed less like "real therapy" to me. We played emotionally neutral games, football, building towers, duller activities. He now could settle down, be like other boys, experience the safe uneventfulness of ordinary life, build up trust in the predictability of his new life, a needed contrast to the chaotic terror he grew up with.

Late middle childhood years are often marked by calmer, ordinary game-playing, and social learning. Psychoanalysis describes this as the latency period, when powerful urges, sexual and otherwise, dampen down, at least until adolescence. In my day, this was marked by collecting stamps or cards, or playing with toy cars or conkers. Latency is known for less emotional lability, although not for dysregulated children who have suffered maltreatment like Matt.

Matt needed an experience of safety, an absence of threat, even if this makes for uneventful therapy with too much football! Even football and ball-throwing help embed social skills, turn-taking, and trust, all vitally important for such children. Matt needed this before re-encountering his traumatic past. It is easier to face and process difficult experiences when one has developed some sense of calm and ease and deeper trust in the psychotherapist.

This case illustrated how newer understandings of trauma help us see why it can be vital to also build positive, safety-based feeling states before facing the worst. Highly traumatised patients like Matt need preparation before approaching the extreme suffering they have endured. Putting them in touch with the trauma too quickly can trigger re-traumatisation, redoubling defences and more worryingly, dissociative states.

Trauma, by definition, is overwhelming. Flashbacks feel as if terrifying past events are happening in the present, the sufferer lacking a vantage point from which to make sense of the experiences. Parts of the personality capable of providing a sense of safety, calm, and trust need to be built first, a secure vantage point from which to revisit and process difficult experiences.

Helping children develop a sense of safeness, that something in the world can be trusted, helps develop what psychoanalysis describes as a good internal object. Therapeutic technique often rightly focuses on taking up what we call the negative transference. Yet, many of the most disturbed children and adults need good experiences and reliable figures, inside or outside the self, including their therapist, to enable sufficient trust, before the negative can be successfully borne.

When danger, real or imaginary, looms, reflective, thoughtful, or empathic circuitry is tuned right down. After serious trauma, dissociative numbed states are also often triggered, particularly following ongoing multiple traumas. The dangers increase when there have been too few good experiences to provide emotional inoculation against the effects of bad experiences. Many children like Matt live in a world of danger, threat, or even terror, even in contexts such as classrooms where other children are interpreting the same environment as ordinarily benign. Such children need help building up a "window of tolerance" (Ogden, 2006; Siegel, 2012) which provides a safe place to return to, a vantage point from which to visit more difficult experiences.

Jess: a girl who has been abused

By the time I saw fourteen-year-old Jess, my understanding of trauma had thankfully increased. Jess had been sexually abused over years by her maternal uncle. Her mother too had been abused, an intergenerational pattern. Jess struggled with friendships, often felt rejected and a victim. She was placed with her aunt, her father's sister, by social services. The aunt and uncle had raised their own biological children, and while with them she had her first experience of a safe protective home.

I had learnt by now that Jess, like most trauma survivors, would not be able to address traumatic incidents too quickly. The complexity of my task was increased by being a male therapist. I learnt from school how she could frequently withdraw into dissociative "fugue-like" states and was easily triggered into flashbacks.

I immediately made it clear that we could go slowly, not talk about anything too difficult until she was ready. When I said this, she visibly relaxed. Much of the initial work concerned very ordinary issues, what happened in her friendships, how she was getting on in drama club, her struggles with adapting to a big new school. On the surface, this might not have looked like psychotherapy, but I had by now learnt that building up trust in ordinary good experiences is crucial. I made sure that we gave plenty of space for things she was beginning to feel good about, especially feelings of being cherished by her aunt. I would explore these positive feelings in detail, asking exactly how she felt, what was going on in her body, what the warm feelings were like.

One week she told me about having a birthday sleepover with close girlfriends. She had a smile on her face and was clearly unused to such happy feelings. I said, "How great it is that you have had such a good time, that you have people around who care about you and can look after you, who keep you safe." She smiled, looking almost tearful. I asked what it was like to have her friends over; what were the best things about the experience? A few years back I would have felt that asking about "the best things" was defensive, manically avoiding the painful ones, but by now I knew that Jess needed help in building such hopeful parts of herself. She told me about the fun, the giggling, the lack of worry. The best part, she said, was the look of love on her aunt's face. I asked, "What does it feel like when you imagine her face like that?" She smiled, her eyes moistening, saying, "I don't know how to describe it, sort of warm, soft, a bit dreamy." I asked her to really hold onto that feeling as one to go back to, checking where she felt it, what was happening in her chest, face, muscles. I was hoping that such good feelings would become a body memory.

Over time we built up a repertoire of such good feelings. We talked about her bedroom becoming a safe place where she could relax and feel at ease. She said, "And when I am there my breathing, it sort of, becomes soft, gentle. Sometimes, it sounds daft, but I almost purr, I just know nothing bad will happen there." We spent time getting to know this kind of breathing, comparing it to her breathing when anxious, becoming familiar with the journey backwards and forwards from her threat system to her soothing, calming affiliative systems (Gilbert, 2014). In trauma, we try to build up trust in safeness, places where we can feel love, compassion, self-care, and relaxed well-being. Jess was building trust in her own lovability, through her new family, therapy, and friends.

Sometimes, like at exam time, her anxiety skyrocketed. I said, "You sound like you feel like the hugest disaster is about to happen. What is happening now in your body, your breathing?" "Yes," she said, almost surprised, "I am tight, tense, hardly breathing." At this she relaxed, deliberately breathing more deeply, and in almost the next sentence said, "Actually, I know my aunt won't care how I do as long as I do my best, that's what counts."

Not surprisingly, when she was approached by a boy who liked her, and whom she also quite liked, her stress went through the roof.

She started having nightmares and a repetition of occasional flashbacks. She was scared by her feelings of attraction as memories of her abuse flashed back. Also not surprisingly, as she guiltily admitted to me, some of her experiences, including sexual ones, with her abusive uncle had been pleasurable.

"That is all so confusing," I said with feeling, trying to normalise that she felt some good things in the abuse, the specialness, even sexual pleasure. At the same time I also stressed how inappropriate and wrong it was. She was struggling to separate out feelings about her uncle and the boy and slowly some clear space between them emerged. Jess had never trusted that it was safe to be excited, have pleasure, and seek out good things. For Jess, excitement and anxiety were almost the same, and of course they use similar bodily systems. Slowly she learnt to separate out feelings like anxiety, excitement, and fear. Jess began to experience ordinary teenage sexual feelings with anxious pleasure rather than terror or dread.

For a long time, she was easily triggered into panic and sometimes even dissociated before knowing what was happening. In time, she got to know the triggers, the first signs, such as her heart beating faster, muscles tensing, breathing getting shallower. We could track this in sessions. "Hmm," I might say, looking at her arms and mimicking her, tensing myself, holding tight and breathing shallowly. She laughed and her body softened. We practised this in sessions, acting tense and seeing what happened, examining what happened in her body as she became fearful, both in role play and by thinking about her bodily responses to actual anxiety provoking situations. She learnt that she could take a deep breath and regulate herself. We returned often to the experiences of safeness that we had built up, that could now be more trusted.

As safeness developed we could begin to confront some of the trauma, a little at a time. If she edged towards dissociative states we would focus on basic body sensations, like feeling her feet on the ground, or the tingling in her fingers. My aim was re-embodying and staying present, bearing whatever arose, but from our newly developed viewing point, a constant to-ing and fro-ing from safety and out of it, learning that she could return to her window of tolerance, recognising when she was moving out of it.

When we are triggered into sympathetic nervous system reactivity, prefrontal parts of our brain turn off and survival is all that counts.

This is even more the case in numbed dissociative states in which the dorsal vagus system is dominant. As Van der Kolk (2014), showed, parts of the brain central to language, such as Broca's region, become inactive in such frozen states. By helping patients like Jess move into their window of tolerance, difficult experiences can be processed without re-triggering trauma.

Such work takes patience, many steps backwards as well as forwards. By the end Jess could talk about her trauma with me and others close to her. She started to feel that she was a whole person, with capacities and a future, not just a traumatised person, the "damaged goods" she had once felt herself to be. She now had robust hopeful aspects of her personality that were solidly there to rely on.

A healthy life depends on being able to embrace good experiences as well as managing difficult ones. In psychotherapy we can focus too soon on negative emotions. However, we also need to develop our two primary positive emotional systems. One is the CARE system (Panksepp & Biven, 2012), linked to affiliation, attachment, and feeling secure in relationships. This is where we experience safety and well-being, so badly needed by trauma survivors. The other main positive affect system is the appetitive or SEEKING system (ibid.) and leads to pleasure, hope, and excitement; it's linked with moving towards and not away from experiences, to increasing good feelings, not just avoiding negative ones. Jess by the end could inhabit both positive systems without feeling overwhelmed.

Digital worlds, new challenges

These days the internet and digital technology confront us with challenges unknown to previous generations of professionals and parents. Typical with regard to this is fourteen-year-old Mitchell. He was living with his father, his mother having tragically died of cancer three years earlier after a long illness. His father had then retreated, working long hours, unable to process the death. Mitchell's schoolwork deteriorated and he became increasingly withdrawn. He moved in with his paternal grandmother, his father visiting regularly. Mitchell withdrew into his bedroom immersed in computer games, and little could entice him away. He was increasingly unconfident anyway, and socialising had little allure. When he transitioned to secondary school he struggled to cope with the hurly-burly of a huge school, and feeling less held in mind as he no longer had a single teacher thinking about him.

It makes sense to think of Mitchell's gaming as addictive. Such games offer multiple rewards, hooking players with never-ending prospects of ascending levels and higher scores. We have known about the brain states involved for over sixty years. When rats found that pulling a lever stimulated the *nucleus accumbens*, a brain area central for dopamine release, they prioritised such pleasure-seeking over everything, including sex and food (Olds & Milner, 1954). Something similar can happen with games and other forms of technology overuse.

These can be used in part to fend off difficult feelings like loneliness, anxiety, poor confidence, or other emotional difficulties. Compared to the old-fashioned games of my generation, today's gaming environment has built-in tricks that hook users in extraordinarily sophisticated ways.

Video games and social media work on the powerful principle of variable rewards, keeping people hooked. If we know that putting X into a slot machine always results in receiving a Y, then we will do this when wanting a Y, but not constantly. If putting that same amount in might result in a huge range of potential rewards, but we never know quite what, then it keeps us coming back to check. This is what happens with Instagram, Twitter, Facebook, and other media. When life is difficult, as Mitchell's was, such potential rewards can trump real relationships and social connections, which ideally would be life's main reward.

In Mitchell's case, it was not targeting his addiction that made the difference, but rather taking seriously the emotional gulf in his life. In family sessions, with Mitchell's father alongside his grandmother, space was made for Mitchell's feelings. Early tentative sessions explored the illness, death, and the feelings they had all struggled to face. It was imperative to help the father bear his own sense of loss. He spent early sessions tense, sitting near the door, clutching his phone, ready to retreat, warding off overwhelming grief and sadness. Mitchell reminded dad of Mitchell's mum; in one session father said, "It is like, well I look at Mitch and I just see, just see …" (his eyes started to tear up and his voice choked), "Oh god, I just see Jan" (Mitchell's mum). The whole room was in tears, including me. Afterwards the feeling of relief was palpable; there was a new stillness and sense of closeness.

Dad began spending more time with Mitchell, who in turn seemed happier. Mitchell had felt rejected by his father but was now experiencing being thought about, liked, and indeed, loved. He spent less time on his computer. Dad made plans to move in, and to get a place together. Dad also had met a new partner with whom Mitchell seemed to get along. Positive change was unusually quick in this case. Mitchell began to feel more confident, started to socialise, and as we often see, his schoolwork improved.

Mitchell had had a reasonably good start, with several good years with a loving mother before losing her, retaining a deep sense of his lovability, and that life could be okay. This is often not true of more vulnerable children who succumb addictively to the lure of digital technology. Mitchell had been using gaming to ward off difficult feelings, but we caught Mitchell's situation in time, before the technology had got its claws completely into him.

Addictions don't fill the gap: Jeremy

Jeremy was an adolescent who moved to the UK with refugee parents at eight years old, was struggling in school, and spending hours watching pornography alone in his room, masturbating over ten times a day. The pornography that he watched was becoming increasingly violent, although still legal.

His background was chaotic and a bit frightening. His mother came from a tough family, suffering much verbal abuse in childhood. His father had been quite absent in Jeremy's early years and when present used excessive physical chastisement. Both parents came from backgrounds of migration and ethnic discrimination over generations. As a young boy Jeremy had ADHD-like symptoms, being fidgety, jumpy, unable to concentrate.

He was a vigilant young man. When hearing any noise outside, his mind left the therapy to attend to expected danger. He often had fantasies about the therapy room being broken into, once saying, as he looked up at a window that had rattled, "I know exactly what I would do if someone tried to climb through, I have planned how I would defend myself," explaining the martial arts moves he would enact.

Also, he was vigilant to the tiniest changes in the room, such as a book being moved or something new on my desk. He found relaxation almost impossible, needing to be constantly active, although paradoxically, at the cost of not doing anything well. Hence, despite a bright mind, he was failingly academically.

While such compulsive pornography use and masturbation is increasingly common in young men, some, like Jeremy, have more proclivity for addictive behaviours. He often gorged on unhealthy food, and overindulged in gaming, and also occasionally he stole on an impulsive whim.

Jeremy's issues can be understood from many angles, perhaps most obviously his lifelong struggle with emotional and bodily regulation. He was likeable but it was not restful to be with him. His leg would shake often as he spoke, his attention darting around, his mind as jumpy as his legs. I often wanted to do what a male therapist simply cannot do, put a hand on one of his to calm him down. I did sometimes suggest he take a deep breath alongside me. I felt what he needed, and had lacked, was a calming, caring parental presence.

His mother reported high levels of anxiety while pregnant and in his early months. Probably Jeremy was born predisposed to stress, given how maternal stress affects the developing foetus (Music, 2016). Mother had post-partum depression and reported that he was hard to soothe. She was not especially psychologically minded and unable to help him make sense of his experience in a soothing, calming way.

In such environments, infants have physiological signs of distress but are not consciously aware of their bodily responses or their meaning. Many children and adults with similar presentations are also extremely unaware of their body states. Jeremy too, with poor interoceptive capacities, had little ability to recognise emotions or body states.

With him I adopted a more psycho-educational approach than usual. I thought that Jeremy would benefit from making basic links between his behaviours, impulses, and their triggers. Initially his emotional vocabulary and range of known feeling states were minimal, mainly consisting of describing himself as "cool" or "good" (his positive affect states) or "pissed" or "shit" (his negative emotional range). There were few nuances to build on.

"What has been happening?" I asked several months into therapy. Jeremy looked uneasy and then, with something of a smirk, told me that yesterday he had "wanked" and eaten nearly all afternoon. "It's been bad," he said, but I felt that he was pleased, triumphant, the "fuck-it button" victorious (Nathanson, 2016). Often, I asked how he felt and he told me what he had been doing rather than describing a feeling. Trying to make sense of what had emotionally driven him to masturbatory acting out was difficult.

In one session, at a noise of someone coming down the nearby stairs, he jolted, looking around as if preparing for danger. I asked what was happening in his body in that moment, could he feel his heart beat, was it different to usual? He said, as often, "I don't know." I asked him to put his hand on his chest and feel his heart, which he did, almost to placate me, but he became a little interested. It was, of course, beating quite fast. I suggested he keep his hand there and see if he could feel what happened in the next few minutes. He did and was surprised to note that he felt his heart-rate slow with his breath.

As Damasio (1999) helped us understand, emotions are body states which can be "read", if we have the mental equipment with which to read them. With Jeremy, I spent time guiding him through some mindfulness based body awareness exercises. It was fascinating how, when there were noises elsewhere in the clinic, he noted a tensing of his body or his pulse quickening. This was the beginning of making links between external triggers like a door closing loudly, and a body state which might be called a feeling state, such as anxiety. I asked, "It might sound daft to you but when you reacted then, could we say you were anxious, or at least unsettled?" Jeremy almost looked interested, albeit still loath to ascribe emotional labels to himself.

Finding that he could actively ground himself by focusing on his body states was liberating and transformational. He could find a place outside the previously overwhelming thoughts, and when triggered into a panicky state or fantasy he could step back, watch the thoughts arise and disappear, become aware of his body sensations in response to these, such as fast heart rate or shallow breathing, and then find a way back to calmer breath. This was never about avoiding his feelings, but rather embracing and bearing them, something that mindfulness and psychoanalysis share.

We stayed a lot with the body sensations he experienced, both when anxious and when aroused. I became braver in my adventures into guided techniques. I had felt stumped by his insistence that he had no clue why he moved to his addictions, insisting he just "liked it". Those few moments of pleasure, that bite of junk food, that moment of ejaculation, he claimed, made life worthwhile. He craved such sensations like a junkie craved their next hit.

This makes sense in terms of what we know about addictive processes. In all addictions, whether drugs, gambling, shopping, alcohol, or pornography, the dopaminergic system is triggered. Key areas of such brain circuitry, such as the ventral striatum, are more activated at even the sight of a cue of their addiction, such as a laptop for a porn user (Brand et al., 2016), or the bottle for the alcoholic (Kraus et al., 2016).

Our dopaminergic system evolved for good reasons. It drives us towards what we need to survive and reproduce, such as sex and food. Yet this system can be hijacked by modern technology in a way for which that evolution has not prepared us. Most of what modern humans feel is as ancient as our species, including negative emotions such as sadness, anxiety, or grief. Alluringly, technology offers the false hope of taking such feelings away, promising respite from pain or difficulty with new exciting allurements.

In time Jeremy learnt to stay with his feelings and fantasies, getting to really know them in all their granularity. Interspersing psychodynamic work and mindfulness, he learnt to explore his feelings and fantasies in a titrated way, to move between explorations of his sexual thoughts and focusing on his immediate body sensations and his breath. Jeremy had been gloriously unaware of what triggered his addictions. It took a long time before he could become stiller, learn to link his bodily states and emotions, and then link such emotions to his drives towards pornography or overeating. Thankfully Jeremy was keen to learn about himself and curb habits that he knew were unhealthy.

We know clinically, and from research (Grubbs et al., 2015), that often people turn towards pornography, and indeed any addiction, when in distress. This leads to shortcutting the possibility of bearing and processing the triggering feelings. Instead in a flash we see enactments, such as turning towards an addictive habit. For Jeremy, change meant slowing down reactivity to witness and then stay with the initial experience that he was fleeing. For example, I would ask what happened just before he turned on pornography. He eventually started to notice triggers, such as when he felt slighted. Then, in time, he could start to stay with the feelings stirred up by such triggers.

Luckily Jeremy enrolled on an eight-week mindfulness training. He became increasingly interested in his body states, and even began to do yoga and other body-based practices. This though would have been insufficient without an experience of another, me, staying with his experiences, showing interest and empathy for his states of mind and emotion and not shirking how his mind could trick him. Jeremy in time started to relinquish the pornography as he entered an intimate and fulfilling sexual relationship. In this period, he developed other capacities. For example, he started to read novels voraciously, itself a helpful thing, enhancing concentration, self-regulation, and empathy (Kidd et al., 2016). He started to gravitate towards young people who were more emotionally literate, forming real friendships. In effect, he was developing the kind of capacities we see in secure attachment relationships. At the time of leaving therapy, he was in a stable relationship, had lost at least thirty pounds in weight, and had not masturbated for several months.

Figure 1.1 "Window of tolerance"

Conclusion

Many common clinical presentations feature difficulties in emotional regulation, something we see often in cases of trauma. Many traumatised hypervigilant children have less access to prefrontal brain areas central for empathy, emotional regulation, and self-reflection. In traditional Freudian language, such patients might be thought of as controlled by id impulses but having little ego functioning (Solms & Panksepp, 2012).

Much research shows the link between being able to defer gratification and multiple better later life outcomes (e.g. Mischel, 2014). Yet impulsivity is so linked to trauma, stress, and anxiety. When we feel safe and at ease, and have that sense that Winnicott (1954) called "going-on-being", we have an internal and bodily stillness, the kind we see when a baby, knowing he or she is loved and safe, moulds into the mother's body, and the breathing deepens and the body is relaxed. This is a rare experience for many of the more vulnerable children with whom we work.

This internal and bodily stillness is the kind of state that we hope to facilitate in our easily triggered clients. I have shown examples of such a movement in children I have described here. I know that the therapeutic progress these patients made would not have been possible without an understanding of the importance of a safe, mutually trusting relationship. With this as a baseline I use psychoanalytic understandings alongside those from neurobiology, attachment theory, trauma theory, and mindfulness, amongst others, to facilitate a move towards a healthier way of being. When we feel the world is safe and we can relax, a host of other possibilities arise, such as for loving, trusting relationships, for playfulness, curiosity, and for hope for the future. It is a privilege of our therapeutic work that we can see changes in these directions, in children reclaiming what Symington (1993) called the "life-giver", becoming open to and embracing life's potential.

References

Alvarez, A. (2012). *The Thinking Heart: Three Levels of Psychoanalytic Therapy with Disturbed Children*. Oxford: Routledge.

Aron, L. (2001). *A Meeting of Minds: Mutuality in Psychoanalysis*. New York: Analytic Press.

Brand, M., Snagowski, J., Laier, C., & Maderwald, S. (2016). Ventral striatum activity when watching preferred pornographic pictures is correlated
with symptoms of Internet pornography addiction. *NeuroImage, 129*:
224–232.

Damasio, A. R. (1999). *The Feeling of What Happens: Body, Emotion and the
Making of Consciousness*. London: Heinemann.

Gilbert, P. (2014). The origins and nature of compassion focused therapy. *British
Journal of Clinical Psychology, 53*(1): 6–41.

Grubbs, J. B., Stauner, N., Exline, J. J., Pargament, K. I., & Lindberg, M. J. (2015).
Perceived addiction to Internet pornography and psychological distress:
Examining relationships concurrently and over time. *Psychology of Addic-
tive Behaviors, 29*(4): 1056–1067.

Keleman, S. (1975). *Your Body Speaks Its Mind: The Bio-energetic Way to Greater
Emotional and Sexual Satisfaction*. New York: Simon & Schuster.

Kidd, D., Ongis, M., & Castano, E. (2016). On literary fiction and its effects on
theory of mind. *Scientific Study of Literature, 6*(1): 42–58.

Koole, S. L., & Tschacher, W. (2016). Synchrony in psychotherapy: A review
and an integrative framework for the therapeutic alliance. *Frontiers in
Psychology, 7*: 862.

Kraus, S. W., Voon, V., & Potenza, M. N. (2016). Neurobiology of compulsive sexual behavior: emerging science. *Neuropsychopharmacology, 41*(1):
385–386.

Lowen, A. (1975). *Bioenergetics*. New York: Coward, McCann & Geoghegan.

Mischel, W. (2014). *Marshmallow Test*. New York: Little, Brown.

Music, G. (2016). *Nurturing Natures: Attachment and Children's Emotional,
Social and Brain Development*. London: Psychology Press.

Nathanson, A. (2016). Embracing darkness: clinical work with adolescents and
young adults addicted to sexual enactments. *Journal of Child Psychotherapy,
43*(3): 272–284.

Ogden, P. (2006). *Trauma and the Body: A Sensorimotor Approach to Psychotherapy*. New York: W. W. Norton.

Olds, J., & Milner, P. (1954). Positive reinforcement produced by electrical stimulation of septal area and other regions of rat brain. *Journal of Comparative
and Physiological Psychology, 47*(6): 419–427.

Panksepp, J., & Biven, L. (2012). *The Archaeology of Mind: Neuroevolutionary
Origins of Human Emotions*. New York: W. W. Norton.

Reich, W. (1945). *Character Analysis*. New York: Farrar, Straus and Giroux.

Rizzolatti, G., Fogassi, L., & Gallese, V. (2006). Mirrors in the mind. Mirror neurons, a special class of cells in the brain, may mediate our ability to mimic, learn and understand the actions and intentions of others. *Scientific American*, 295(5): 54–61.

Siegel, D. J. (2012). *The Developing Mind: How Relationships and the Brain Interact to Shape Who We Are*. 2nd edn. London: Guilford.

Sletvold, J. (2014). *The Embodied Analyst: from Freud and Reich to Relationality*. Oxford: Routledge.

Solms, M., & Panksepp, J. (2012). The "Id" knows more than the "Ego" admits: Neuropsychoanalytic and primal consciousness perspectives on the interface between affective and cognitive neuroscience. *Brain Sciences*, 2(2): 147–175.

Symington, N. (1993). *Narcissism: A New Theory*. London: Karnac.

Van der Kolk, B. A. (2014), *The Body Keeps the Score*. London: Allen Lane.

Winnicott, D. W. (1954). Mind and its relation to the psyche–soma. *British Journal of Medical Psychology*, 27(4): 201–209.

CHAPTER 2

Experiences of being held: creating a space to think and play within a family

Neela Basu

Introduction

As part of my training in integrative child psychotherapy, the weekly infant observation brought fully and brilliantly alive the importance of attunement and parent–infant communication in early years development. I also developed skills that would enrich my work: the capacity to wonder deeply about another's inner experience, to notice sequences of non-verbal interactions, and to "sit with" my own and others' emotions. I felt privileged to watch and learn from this family.

Both parents have busy and established careers. Amy is their first child.

Amy was nine days old when I received a friendly email from the mother stating they would be happy to take part in an observation. Her email also described a "nightmare week" with a difficult forceps delivery. Amy had developed severe jaundice with suspected sepsis, and ended up in the special baby care unit. She had made a good recovery and they were able to return home again at the end of the week. I imagined that it would take the family time to settle in together and recover after such a difficult birth. When I explained the infant observation process their only query was around committing to two years. I inwardly wondered if the dramatic transformation of the couple into a family made a stable future hard to visualise. I visited the home a few days later, hoping my presence would not be disruptive after such a tumultuous time.

First meeting

When I arrived the health visitor was there, with the mother and father both asking questions and being given advice. Amy was barely visible, wrapped up in a blanket.

> **Amy: twelve days**
> The baby makes little leg raises but is generally still, lying flat in the mother's arms.

Amy seemed still part of her mother's body as if she had not fully arrived as an individual in my mind. The mother said that she recognised the baby's hiccups and movements; that the baby used to hiccup at the same time every day when in her womb and out. She hadn't imagined that it would be so clearly the same. This reinforced my experience of the baby as still part of the mother. I recalled Winnicott's description of the earliest stages of holding in which the baby and maternal care cannot be disentangled, and are a unit (1960, p. 587). I also considered the experience of nine months of pregnancy and baby's developing presence in mother's body and the parents' minds.

During the first visit the father changed Amy's nappy.

> **Amy: twelve days**
> With the cold air the baby makes a bleating cry, opening eyes … She cries open-mouthed cries, red-faced, eyes shut tightly. Father picks her up and rocks her until she quietens again, cheek snuggled against his chest.

The baby swiftly reacted to changes in her environment. When her body was laid flat, feeling the cold air, she appeared in a state that was excruciatingly vulnerable. I was reminded of Bick's (1968) thinking, about the experience of the newborn as an astronaut thrown into space feeling the intolerable anxiety of falling to pieces. Once held and apparently safe again the baby was quickly soothed. The father's rocking motion and the closeness of his skin seemed to gather her up, perhaps linking her back to the feeling of being inside her mother.

Amy: twelve days

The baby's head rests, with gently curled hands, against father's lower neck and chest, with her legs koala-like, splayed across his chest. After she falls asleep she begins to make snuffly snoring sounds. The mother gets up to check that the baby is breathing okay. The baby is totally asleep with her arms flopping backwards. The father raises the baby's hand and gently lets it flop down again. Once again the mother checks that the baby's grip is okay. She talks about the baby's breathing and grunting.

The mother seemed anxious about the baby's ability to survive outside her womb. I wondered whether complications during the birth had made these feelings more acute. It felt difficult for me to watch, perhaps because of the parents' level of anxiety regarding whether or not this baby was strong enough and going to survive.

The mother expressed some anxieties about being the primary carer, saying the father would be returning to work after some days of paternity leave. With them both at home they could take it in turns being on call for Amy's needs. The father had been first to hold the baby—for the first half hour after birth as mother was recovering. As the months progressed it felt important that the parental couple were together, acting as a cradle of emotional containment for the baby (Magagna, 2012, 2013). There appeared to be a strong acknowledgement that the father shared care for the baby and also supported the mother as her partner.

Holding and handling, enabling thinking and play: first six months

In my second visit, the mother held the baby very tenderly in her arms after breastfeeding her. Resting in this very safe, comfortable state, the baby explored her mother's body with her eyes and fingers.

Amy: fifteen days

The mother holds the baby cradled in her arms while they look into each other's faces. When the baby looks at the mother with wide eyes and open mouth, the mother raises her eyebrows in response. The baby is gripping the mother's thumb in one hand and with the other is gently expanding and contracting fingers with her rotating hand sometimes touching the mother's blouse. The baby makes whimpering guttural sounds from the back of her throat, more communicative than breathing. The baby looks intently at her mother—legs occasionally move up and down, both hands now gently rotating, fingers stretching and relaxing. The mother is gently rubbing the baby's back and then kisses the baby on the forehead.

Securely held, the baby was able to explore the surface of her mother's blouse, her touch, and her gaze. This seemed to be a continuation from breastfeeding, a drinking in of her mother's presence, amassed through sensorial experience. The mother and the baby appeared to be working at seeing and seeking each other.

Amy: four weeks

The mother told me that the family had gone to register Amy's birth, saying: "She officially exists now. And she's getting bigger, she's putting on 300g a week."

The mother seemed to be settling in to being with, and thinking about Amy. One week later Amy made her presence as a personality clear with smiles and the beginnings of conversation.

Amy: five weeks

The mother smiles at her and says "Hello". Amy's whole face engages with her mother now, just for a second: her mouth opens wide as she smiles delightedly at her mother. I smile to see her face as her mother smiles again. "Hello Amy," she says, "are you talking?" as Amy makes aah, aah sounds. Her lips push outward and open. Her hands and arms waft in and out as she makes sounds while very briefly her fingers on one hand catch hold of the fingers on the other and then they continue their large, conductor like gestures, each finger wiggling independently. The mother counts each finger and then each toe. As her mother touches her, Amy's movements seem more controlled and slower.

There was a wonderful reciprocity of touch, facial gesture, and vocal sounds. Using the word conductor in my write-up felt very appropriate to the observed call and response that Trevarthen (2002, p. 161) describes as "narrative musicality of the first protoconversations". It seemed the mother was helping to make sense of and verbalise their beautiful meeting. Her smiling reflecting face, and touch—counting each finger and toe—defined the edges of Amy's body, holding and outlining where their meeting took place. This brought to mind Winnicott's (1972) depictions of a mother holding and handling, encompassing both the baby's physical and emotional processes and fostering grounding the self within the body.

As an observer I could not help but smile at this scene. I tried to be sensitive and receptive to the communications and expressions I witnessed but at times the baby's experiences were difficult to bear. When, at sixteen weeks, Amy was waiting for a feed I felt identified with her, feeling impatient, desperate, and helpless.

Amy: sixteen weeks

Amy is crying loudly, face pinkish-red, lips quivering and downward. Lying on her back she kicks quickly while putting her arms out at right angles with tight fists in line with her ears. Her arms and fists are shaking now. The mother lifts Amy up and holds her against her body, head against her shoulder for a moment, while she still cries. The mother gives voice to Amy's cries, "Oh, oh, nasty mummy." She pulls at her dress to reveal her breast and says "There you are," and Amy latches onto the nipple immediately, sucking and letting out a few moans. As she feeds, I become aware of my own body and how I have been sitting very tensely on the very edge of the sofa, tightly holding an elbow in each hand, toes gripping the floor.

As Amy fed and gradually fell asleep I relaxed. Perhaps my own muscular tension reflected some of Amy's distress and her tight fists. I was reminded of Bick's (1968) second skin, a musculature defence against falling apart. Amy's kicking legs also seemed to be evacuating some painful feelings.

O'Shaughnessy's (1964) writing on the absent, withheld object helped me to think about the experience of the "nasty mummy". The mother was able to receive and make sense of the painful split-off "nasty mummy" projection while continuing with the everyday physical care of Amy, facilitating a return to a relaxed feeding state. The mother showed capacity to bear her baby's feelings, to think about them and give them a voice, to be curious and not destroyed. This experience is highlighted by Bion (1962) describing concepts of maternal reverie and containment, a receptive focusing in on the inner world of the infant, making the experience tolerable. This brief experience of the absent object, at a level of tolerable frustration, is linked by O'Shaughnessy and Winnicott (1971) to emotional growth.

Over the next weeks during moments of separation Amy looked towards the light of the window, sucked her thumb, or held her own hands and feet as ways of holding herself together. At other times, when her mother left her for a longer period, Amy seemed to draw on her surroundings but also found my face and eyes to hold herself together (Bick, 1968).

Amy: twenty-five weeks
Amy makes some babbling sounds for a while. Then the sounds become a little more whiney and protesting, although not loud … Her eyes hold mine. She doesn't smile but her frown lines disappear as she has somehow latched on to my gaze.

My use of the word "latched on" to describe eye contact recalls early experiences of breastfeeding and "nipple in mouth holding" (Symington, 2002, p. 101). Amy appeared to be able to use and remember my gaze and presence. She would turn to look at me, and seemed to have a sense of where I was throughout her play. Occasionally I wondered if she was combining her mother's voice and my gaze to anchor herself in her play, echoing Amy's experience of being with two parents.

Holding, seeking, and separating: six to twelve months

Over the next few months, while there was still plenty of physical holding, cuddling, and closeness, a seeking, curious Amy emerged;

exploring solid food and moving towards crawling and grasping objects. Breastfeeding was no longer mentioned or observed. Amy developed sounds that linked to the external world and had a keen interest in investigating objects and toys alongside her parents. Mahler's concept of hatching, with "tentative experimentation at separation–individuation" (Mahler et al., 2000, p. 54) came to mind.

I had not observed the father often, but the mother was now preparing to return to work so he became more present. When Amy was six months old her mother went to work for the first time since she had given birth. As her mother was preparing her notes and work clothes, Amy's father knelt beside her, chatting to her about a toy.

Amy: six months

Amy looks up at her father and places her five little fingers of her left hand on his knee and says "Da-da-da" very lightly and sweetly. The father says, "Oh yes, dada! Dada!" and smiles.

Their shared moment displayed a sense of connection, seeking, and togetherness. I felt very lit-up inside, and I imagined that the father did too. Amy's use of "Dada" seemed special and her father's warm response may well have helped link the sound to himself in a loop of positive feedback and affirmation.

I noticed that as the date of her return to work approached, the mother would encourage Amy's crawling, and her language was peppered with words such as "strong". Did this express the mother's need for Amy and herself to be prepared for coping with being apart? Waddell (2002, p. 70) sensitively noted the "complex mixture of loss and gain" that occurs as the dependency of the intense early experience is renegotiated within the maturing relationship.

A few weeks before returning to work, I observed the mother and Amy play "peekaboo". They were enthralled in this game together but I also felt a sense of poignancy, from their playing out of separation and exploration of object permanence. They delighted in each other's faces each time they found each other. Perhaps Amy was experiencing that she could hold her mother in mind and her mother could hold her in mind even when out of sight.

Amy: seven and a half months

The mother puts the cloth over Amy's face and says, "Where's Amy?" in an exaggerated, musical tone. Amy grabs the muslin cloth with two hands and slowly drags it downwards off her face. When her face is revealed, the mother, massively over the top with surprise, grins saying, "Oh, there you are!" This seems wonderful for Amy as she gives a little chuckle, her shoulders moving up and down a little. "Again?" she asks her mother. This time Amy swiftly removes the cloth and laughs even harder from her stomach, laughing with her whole body once mother gives her a "peekaboo".

At around eight months, Amy had a childminder, and her mother and father planned their work so that they could each have a day with Amy. To fit into the family's working week, I began visiting in the evenings. Over the next weeks Amy cried upon my arrival, which was new to me and felt uncomfortable.

Amy: seven and a half months

Amy's mother picks her up, bringing her into her torso where Amy nuzzles into her neck, wrapping her fingers around mother's neck and face—a tender sensual gesture. Her mother wonders, "Oh aren't you going to show her your crawling, Amy? Come on—it's just us … you know all of us." But Amy turns and looks at me while her eyes widen as she cries again. I feel like a threat, a stranger.

At this moment I found myself feeling "in the way". It was an unpleasant, difficult feeling. I noticed that I had to centre and calm myself to continue to be present. I sought the comfort and advice of my seminar group who contained my anxieties. They helped me to consider that Amy might be using me to express negative feelings about her change in her daily routine. Perhaps I had become a repository for the angry feelings she felt.

The mother was able to lovingly hold and support Amy during these fearful moments and after some time her intense reaction of feeling persecuted by my arrival diminished.

Amy: eleven months

Amy tries but fails to reach the television remote control and her mother is not helping her. Amy's face looks stern and straining as she rapidly shakes both hands and arms in front of her very quickly whirring them round. "Oh dear, Amy," says her mother. "It's just not fair is it?" Her voice catches some of the frustration Amy is feeling. Amy leans into her mother's body, half collapsing in and half happily burrowing her face into her mother's breasts.

Amy appeared comforted and soothed by the physical warmth and softness of her mother's breasts, bringing to mind her early experiences of breastfeeding. Her swiftly altering emotional states were kept tolerable for her by her mother. Amy used her hands to both communicate to her mother and physically vent frustration in a swirly fast movement. Stern's (1985, p. 138) writing on cross-modal vitality affects provided a useful frame for this observation. The mother's voice caught and attuned to Amy's frustrated hand gestures. Following her mother's attunement, Amy appeared able to come to her for comfort and to once again find delight in her company.

Amy: eleven months

Amy regains interest in her mother's face and using her fingers reaches out to grasp at it … poking at her mother's mouth and then squeezing her nose. "Ow, Amy!" says her mother. When Amy grips her mother's nose, her mother makes some funny comic voices—the sound altered by the nasal pressure … Amy now holds her own nose and makes some silly sounds herself. And now they are both squeezing their own noses—both making a funny voice and joking together.

Amy's ability to join in the game of squeezing noses, processing her aggression, appeared to me to show a thoughtful, playful space to work through the anxieties of ruptured moments with her mother and the ways to repair the relationship (Schore, 1994).

Holding, playing, thinking: Amy, two years

During her second year, Amy attended a nursery with a baby room four days a week. She was dressed more like a little girl, wearing clips in her blonde curls, walking sturdily and often carrying a toy or book in her hand. She played alongside another girl at nursery and seemed to take comfort in finding companionship there.

I was still visiting in the evenings, after Amy's long day at nursery and would often see her happily welcoming her father when he returned home. Frequently he would swing her into the air with a big physical greeting and smile. On one occasion I found myself shocked by a sequence of events: Amy was held in her mother's arms when her father entered the house:

Amy: one year, two months

Her father walks down the hallway towards Amy who greets him with, a sing-song "peekaboo" and a very large smile. He says, "Let me put the bag down," walking away for a second to put the bag in the hallway. Amy's face falls and while still in her mother's arms she hit her mother in the face.

After this, Amy was firmly told "No" by her father while still held in her mother's arms. I stood, still feeling shocked, while struggling to remain open and thoughtful. I was curious about the connection of these interactions to oedipal anxieties (Klein, 1945). Was a rivalrous Amy attacking her mother directly or retaliating against feeling rejected by her father? I sensed that she felt hurt and shocked by her father not completing the peekaboo, felt a hurtful slap in her heart, that she gave to her mother; a projective identification for the mother to process. Also, as her father and her mother were now united, I wondered if Amy was becoming more aware of a mother–father relationship outside her own understanding? It drew to my mind the otherness created by the triangle of the mother–father–infant relationship.

I began to think about her held sense of self through relationships within her family of three. The triangularity of the oedipal situation explored by Britton (1989) and later Fonagy (Fonagy et al., 2004) described this presence of a third figure as a bridge allowing separation from the intense mother–infant relationship as well as enabling a child to conceive of being observed and thought about. Amy's experience of two attentive and thoughtful parents may have created a space in which she could begin to think about herself. This brought to mind Winnicott's transitional, intermediate space, between the me and the not-me; a space of play and symbolic processing (1971).

Around this period, I noticed a huge increase in symbolic play, and as well as drawing, an increased interest in books and a swiftly expanding language.

Amy: one year, three months
"Cup o' tea?" she asks smiling delightedly and her mother smiles back, taking the cup and slurping out the tea with an "Mmm, thank you." They gaze into each other's eyes and smile … Amy feeds the doll pretend cake from a plastic plate then her mother who makes big eyes and noisy swallowing actions.

I sense that there was a developing familiarity and shared ritual of playing at tea parties with the toy objects. I wondered if Amy was also identifying with being a grown-up Mummy in this game. She appeared to be thriving on mother's attention and communication, internalising an attentive thoughtful way of being.

Amy: one year, six months
Amy puts the two bears down, laying them flat on the floor and saying, "Ah, sleeping" as she pats them lovingly on their backs. Her mother sits one up "Ah, I'm awake. I don't want to go to sleep … Oh no, what shall we do?" Amy scoops the bear up in her arms and cuddles it saying, "Ah" and kissing it with her mouth slightly open saying, "Mwah."

Their interplay was wonderful to watch and her mother looked very pleased. It seemed Amy had internalised a good mother and could use this to respond to herself and others, represented by the bear, in a caring manner (Klein, 1946).

Amy: one year, six months
When her father comes home, Amy, hearing the door, pauses and then rushes towards him squealing. Then, returning to her play space, Amy declares, "Den." Her father clearly wants to join in immediately. Now her father, her mother, and Amy play den and peekaboo, Amy flooding the room with infectious cascades of giggles. When the energy has lessened, her mother leaves for the kitchen to make a snack, saying

to her partner, "You are in charge of keeping the den game up." Amy responds, "More den."

Watching this family of three playing I was alert to the symbolism of the den as an expanded holding space, which appeared to be both safe and roomy enough to explore. As a privileged observer I was also sensitive that my position was outside the den, and outside the family unit.

A second pregnancy—making space for one more

In the next few observations the mother was absent and in moments spent with the father I began to notice Amy's play exploring inside and outside forms.

Amy: one year, eight months
Amy stuffs Donkey and Peter Rabbit into the seat of the pushchair so that they are precariously dangling off the front while being held lightly by the seatbelt. When the toys fall out, Amy continues pushing the pushchair. She kneels to turn the wheels and lift the pushchair on its side so she can investigate the wheels further.

Amy was very interested in the structure of the pushchair. What could it hold? Connected to the den, I wondered about the pushchair as a parent symbol, with the infant-toys carried inside. The toys were dropped and Amy became more interested in exploring the pushchair body itself, perhaps trying to make sense of how it works and how it holds.

When I observed the mother again, I noticed her body looked voluptuous and different. I remained with the feeling of "not knowing" while wondering with my seminar group if she were perhaps pregnant. I felt curious and anxious that the parents were keeping something from me. I had the impression that Amy might be trying to make sense of these feelings too. Similar to the mysteries of the mother–father relationship was the separateness and otherness of the mother's changing body.

Amy: one year, eight months
Her father helps Amy to put the baby doll down behind the straps of her dungarees at the back as if it is in a baby sling. She then picks up

George the Pig and he goes there too. Her father says, "Like Mummy did" as Amy walks proudly with the two toys in her baby sling. With a protruding chest she walks along with a certain swagger. He holds Amy up to the mirror so she can see and she smiles and says, "Woody too?" The father says, "No room." The father holds Woody on his back and as they walk around the room together, Amy lets out a peel of laughter.

Amy and her father seemed deeply involved in this game together. I had the impression that Amy was playing at being the mummy. Through play she could safely explore her role within the family.

In the end of the following observation of the mother and Amy alone, the mother confirmed my suspicions that she was expecting a baby in five months. Amy would be two years and two months when her sibling would be born.

Amy: one year, nine months

Her mother lies down on her side on the mat, as if it is a bed. Her rounded belly is visible. Amy lies down beside her and rolls around and then lies down herself on her back and kicks her legs in the air. Next she kicks towards her mother, looking at her. Her mother says to Amy, "Be careful," as she holds onto Amy's feet and waggles them back and forth.

The mother in her holding of Amy's feet managed to control the kicking movements, making them safe and manageable. Amy's aggression was pointedly towards her mother, or perhaps towards the baby in the bump that had shifted Amy's place from her mother's lap. Adamo and Magagna (2005, p. 102) suggest that, with the arrival of another baby in the mother's womb, the firstborn suffers a loss of the mother accompanied by losing her identity as "the baby in the mother's lap". I noticed that, with the mother's pregnancy and work, the father had become increasingly involved in the care of Amy. I felt in myself a sense of anxiety and loss of the mother's presence in the observations, and perhaps this was partially what Amy felt. I wondered about a shift of focus within the family to a new dynamic as they began to think about the presence of the new baby. I also connected my feelings of loss regarding approaching my ending of two years of being present with the family during the observations.

I reflected on Amy's anxiety regarding where her mother and "bump", the baby, were when they were not with Amy. In the following observation, Amy was waiting for her mother and asking for her to return home from work:

Amy: one year, ten months

Amy is looking at pictures of her mother and herself on the smartphone. Gripping the phone closer to both herself and her father, she adds, "And Amy" and leans back into father's torso. Amy is now sitting in her father's cross-legged lap, her bare calves resting on father's long hairy shins.

While looking at photographs of her family with her father, Amy was held physically, her legs cradled with skin contact with her father and her back supported against her father's chest. I wondered if Amy, pointing out her own image in her mother's arms was locating an Amy "held in mind" by her mother too.

Amy's developing language allowed her to question her father and attempt to make sense of the changing situation in the family. In one of my final observations I witnessed a "thinking, questioning Amy" asking for help in understanding from her father:

Amy: one year, eleven months

Amy lies down under the rug, pulling the cushions in a big heaving action up to her chest. Then she drums with her hands against the bulging mat. Looking up at her father Amy says, "Mummy got a baby," and pauses before slowly repeating, "Mummy got a baby." Kneeling right beside her, her father looks down at her and smiles while saying, "And we have you, our baby." "No, bigger ... bigger," Amy says, emphatically shaking her head so her curls move to and fro. Her father asks, "Where is mummy's baby?" Amy kicks the rug up with her legs and with both hands pats low down between her stomach and crotch and responds, "There." In a very slow, thoughtful way she questions, "Open it up?" "Not yet," replies her father, raising his eyebrows and smiling. She nods in an exaggerated and slow movement, "Keep it closed, keep it warm." Smiling, her father nods while looking thoughtful.

The calm sense-making father reminded and reassured Amy that she was still their baby too. Amy's "No, bigger … bigger" response suggested that she was exploring her own role as not-a-baby. Perhaps she was also referring to the growing of the mother's pregnancy bump too. Amy's curiosity about her mother's body, and her sense of self within the family, played out by the protective cushion tummy and the tapping of her own body, could be explored thoughtfully and entrusted to her father's thinking and empathic mind.

Conclusion

Observing her development within this family I was alive to Amy's sense of safety experienced through both parents holding her both physically and psychically. Their holding made plenty of space for Amy's exploration, frustration, aggression, love, and play while also facilitating her capacity to think and make sense of the world and the relationships around her. Experiences of being safely held built up to create a strong foundation in Amy, an internalised sense of being held, facilitating her capacity to exist separate from her parents and develop her own separate identity.

Amy was able to make use of her parents' emotional containment throughout the changes brought about by her mother's return to work and second pregnancy. Together, the parents as a couple provided a secure space for the firstborn through the experience of the birth of a new baby in the family. Amy had a strong sense of being held very lovingly in mind which alongside the continuing sensitive support of both her parents will stand her in good stead. The den Amy made with her parents, a symbol of safety and a place to play, is an image I hold in mind when thinking of this family.

Acknowledgement

My thanks to the late Ann Syz, seminar leader and tutor at IATE, who supervised this infant observation; for her generosity of spirit, brilliance, and unwavering curiosity.

References

Adamo, S. M., & Magagna, J. (2005). Oedipal anxieties, the birth of a second baby and the role of the observer. In: J. Magagna (Ed.), *Intimate Transformations: Babies with Their Families* (pp. 90–111). London: Karnac.

Bick, E. (1968). The experience of the skin in early object-relations. *International Journal of Psychoanalysis, 49*(2–3): 484–486.

Bion, W. R. (1962). *Learning from Experience.* London: Heinemann.

Britton, R. (1989). The missing link: parental sexuality. In: R. Britton, M. Feldman, & E. O'Shaughnessy (Eds.), *The Oedipus Complex Today: Clinical Implications* (pp. 83–101). London: Karnac.

Fonagy, P., Gergely, G., & Jurist, E. L. (Eds.) (2004). *Affect Regulation, Mentalization and the Development of the Self.* London: Karnac.

Klein, M. (1945). The Oedipus complex in the light of early anxieties. *International Journal of Psycho-Analysis, 26*: 11–33.

Klein, M. (1946). Notes on some schizoid mechanisms. *International Journal of Psycho-Analysis, 27*: 99–110.

Magagna, J. (Ed.) (2012). *The Silent Child: Communication without Words.* London: Karnac.

Magagna, J. (2013). The development of language in the early months of life. *International Journal of Infant Observation, 16*(2): 112–129.

Mahler, M. S., Pine, F., & Bergman, A. (2000). *The Psychological Birth of the Human Infant: Symbiosis and Individuation.* New York: Basic Books.

O'Shaughnessy, E. (1964). The absent object. *Journal of Child Psychotherapy, 2*: 13–23.

Schore, A. N. (1994). *Affect Regulation and the Origin of the Self.* Hillsdale, NJ: Lawrence Erlbaum.

Stern, D. N. (1985). *The Interpersonal World of the Infant.* New York: Basic Books.

Symington, J. (2002). Mrs Bick and infant observation. In: A. Briggs (Ed.), *Surviving Space: Papers on Infant Observation.* London: Karnac.

Trevarthen, C. (2002). Making sense of infants making sense. *Intellectica, 34*: 161–188.

Waddell, M. (2002). *Inside Lives: Psychoanalysis and the Growth of the Personality.* London: Karnac.

Winnicott, D. W. (1960). The theory of the parent–infant relationship. *International Journal of Psychoanalysis*, *41*: 585–595.
Winnicott, D. W. (1971). *Playing and Reality*. London: Psychology Press, 1991.
Winnicott, D. W. (1972). Basis for self in body. *International Journal of Child Psychotherapy*, *1*(1): 7–16.

CHAPTER 3

The effects of chronic trauma and neglect

Karlien Smith-Claassens

Introduction

In this chapter, I will discuss how chronic trauma and neglect affect a child's attachment security and development. First, I will explore what happens when things go well in a parent–child relationship. Using theory by Bowlby (1969, 1980), Fonagy et al. (2004), Howe (2005, 2011), Porges (2011), and Schore (2003a, 2016), I will examine how the delicate interplay between sensitive, attuned caregiving, emotional regulation, and mentalization leads to the development of a secure attachment.

When chronic trauma and neglect happen in the context of the attachment relationship, where the parent is the source of the distress, and in the context of a developing mind supremely susceptible to the quality of the caregiving experiences, the effects are pervasive and long-lasting. Van der Kolk (2005, p. 404) observed: "When trauma emanates from within the family, children experience a crisis of loyalty and organize their behavior to survive within their families." Using theory by Perry et al. (1995), Perry (2002), Main and Solomon (1986, 1990), and Main and Hesse (1990), I will illustrate how this survival comes at great cost to neurophysiological development and attachment security.

This developmental trauma (sometimes also referred to as relational or complex trauma), persistently inflicted on children by their attachment figure(s) during critical periods of neurophysiological development, will be the focus of this chapter.

Developing a secure attachment

Attachment is described as an affectional and long-lasting emotional bond from one person to another across time and space (Bowlby, 1980). This process of bonding starts in utero; from the second or third trimester of pregnancy, under the influence of oxytocin (a hormone associated with promoting attachment and bonding) mother and foetus start psychobiologically attuning to each other, meaning that their systems are increasingly "in tune" with each other (Lahousen et al., 2019). After birth, the baby—not yet knowing their external or internal world and unable to regulate their own arousal—needs the help of a parent to regulate and make sense of the baby's internal states and experiences. Schore (2016) described how a parent initially acts as an external psychobiological regulator, who amplifies the child's positive emotions and tries to understand the root of a child's distress by being responsive and able to contain the emotional distress so the child synchronises with the parent's regulated state.

Parents can communicate their understanding both verbally and non-verbally; the use of facial expressions, eye contact, tone of voice, and body language are all instrumental ways of conveying to a child that the child is understood and appreciated. Schore (2003a) considers these repeated relational experiences instrumental for the development of a child's nervous system, which—simply put—connects the body to the brain; it tells the body what to do—breathe, walk, talk. It also "stores" sensory experiences and memories, both cognitively and viscerally. By processing sensory information such as friendly, expressive faces and calm, prosodic voices, our nervous system allows us to assess whether situations and people are safe, using "neuroception": an unconscious threat detection system which lowers one's defences when situations and people are perceived as safe, promoting social engagement and attachment (Porges, 2011, p. 11).

The development of a child's brain and nervous system is experience-dependent; when a caregiver has provided a child with attuned and co-regulatory experiences, these become internalised gradually allowing the child to regulate their own body and mind. Perry et al. (1995) described how the human brain and nervous system develop sequentially and hierarchically. This means that the most primitive parts of the brain, such as the brainstem (responsible for storing arousal states, for example) develop first, and the more complex parts of the brain, such as the limbic system (responsible, for example, for processing emotional information and attachment) and the cortical areas (responsible for executive functioning, for example) are last to develop. Perry (2001) postulated that the majority of the brain's systems and structures responsible for emotional, behavioural, social, and physiological functioning develop during the first three years of a child's life. He explained that there are critical periods during which a certain brain area is particularly sensitive to experiences; for attachment this critical period is thought to be in the first year of life. Therefore, these sensitive, regulating experiences in early childhood are at the root of the development of attachment security as well as healthy neurophysiological development.

Children learn about themselves and the world around them through interpersonal experiences with their caregivers. An important part of the co-regulatory experience is the caregiver's capacity to understand, reflect on, and respond to her (or his) own and the child's emotional states. Fonagy et al. (2004) proposed that the capacity for mentalization (the capacity to understand and reflect on mental states in self and others) happened through experiencing our internal states being understood by another mind. Through purposeful, mentalizing interactions with caregivers, children begin to develop a sense of themselves as individuals with thoughts and feelings, the ability to reflect on their own and others' mental states, and to develop a coherent narrative of themselves, others, and the world around them.

Children's first relational experiences also provide them with an unconscious relational template, an "internal working model" (Bowlby, 1969). These internal working models allow children to predict how the world and relationships work based on past experiences. The models provide a lens through which children sees themselves, others, and the world around them. Although these relational templates are not set in stone, as a child grows older these templates become increasingly harder to change (Bowlby, 1969). Children who have had a caregiver who has been sensitive and responsive to their emotional needs and who has shown—repeatedly and consistently—that she is able and willing to respond thoughtfully to their distress, develop a secure attachment. "Secure" describes the child's confidence that the attachment figure will be available, able, and willing to respond in times of distress (Bowlby, 1979). For securely attached children, their internal working model will include mental representations of themselves as worthy of love and protection, beliefs of others as available and responsive, and expectations of relationships as a source of comfort, safety, and support (Howe, 2005).

Children with a secure attachment tend to develop the ability to organise their thoughts and process cognitive and sensory information. They have the ability to self-regulate and understand the intricacies of social relationships based on their sensitively attuned, co-regulating, and mentalizing experiences with their caregivers.

Chronic trauma and neglect

When children do not have such attuned, regulating, and mentalizing experiences with their caregivers, these deficits also become internalised and have a devastating impact on neurophysiological development and attachment security (Schore, 2003b). Studies into adverse childhood experiences (ACE) have linked early traumatic experiences to an increased risk in developing physical, emotional, and social problems later in life (Felitti et al., 1998; Hughes et al., 2017).

For a child who grows up in a caregiving environment with chronic trauma and/or neglect, dysregulation is at the core of the caregiving relationship. Like bonding and psychobiological attunement, dysregulation and child maltreatment can also start in utero. Maternal substance abuse during pregnancy can have a serious effect on foetal brain development and can be linked to problems in concentration, empathising, and communicating (Gerhardt, 2015). When a pregnant mother is in a volatile relationship, her fear and agitated state of mind can lead to a rise in the level of cortisol, a stress hormone, which has a detrimental effect on foetal brain development (Music, 2011). These dysregulating experiences in utero already seriously alter neurophysiological development before the child is even born.

Although neglect can also be seen as a form of chronic trauma, for the purpose of this chapter I will refer to chronic trauma to describe repeated interpersonal acts of commission over a long period of time, for example physical, emotional, or sexual abuse and witnessing domestic violence. The Department for Education described neglect as "the persistent failure to meet a child's basic physical and/or psychological needs, likely to result in the serious impairment of the child's health or development" (2018, p. 104), but it may also include the *absence* of attuned, co-regulating, and mentalizing experiences. Neglect is thought to have a more severe and adverse impact than abuse (Perry & Pollard, 1997). A complicating factor in neglect is that it is age-dependent as a child's developmental needs differ by age (Perry, 2002). For example, sensory experiences—such as touch—are essential in the first year of life for the process of sensory integration, but touch has a different importance during adolescence in terms of frequency and appropriateness.

Chronic trauma and neglect each have their distinct caregiving characteristics and where the impact on development and attachment security differ, I will make this explicit.

Emotional dysregulation and the impact on neurophysiological development

Children who grow up in an environment with chronic trauma and/or neglect will often find themselves in a state of emotional dysregulation. However, rather than providing regulation for the child or protecting the child from danger, the caregiver is the source of the dysregulation either by his or her presence in the case of chronic trauma or by his or her absence in the case of neglect. When a child's emotional arousal is not regulated and modulated with the help of an attuned, co-regulating caregiver, the nervous system becomes overstimulated and a child goes into a state of hyperarousal, which is characterised by "a breakdown in the capacity to regulate internal states" (Van der Kolk, 2005, p. 403). Because long-lasting periods of dysregulation can feel life-threatening to a young child, the child will unconsciously activate primitive adaptive responses in an attempt to survive in the face of unbearable fear as a result of the perceived threat. There is a continuum of adaptive responses which differ for each child. Age and gender are thought to play a role, with younger children and girls thought to favour the freeze/dissociation response over fight/flight (Perry et al., 1995).

The fight/flight response allows the child to feel in control by mobilisation of the sympathetic nervous system and is characterised by a set of physiological responses such as increase in heart rate and blood pressure and also hypervigilance, which is an enhanced state of sensory awareness. In the therapy room, a child's fight response may present as a need for constant movement, which can be seen as an attempt to attain emotional and/or physiological regulation by moving their body. I interpret this as a function of the child not feeling safe in their environment and I may share my observations. For example, I might say: "I think your body is showing me that it needs to be busy *all the time* ... I wonder if this busy body is helping you feel safer while being in the room with me ... how clever!" By sharing these observations in the present and accepting the child's need for movement as a function of past experiences, acknowledging their need to feel safe, I aim to start making links between the body and the mind. A child's fight response can also be seen in their play data, for example violent battles, characters attacking each other, and a sense that there is no respite, no safe space. A child's flight response can present subtly in therapy; for example, the child might change the subject every time feelings are mentioned or reflected upon by the therapist. It can also present more concretely with the child not wanting to attend therapy or by attempting to leave the session early. I have come to see these responses as the child's vital communications of their experience and state of mind. By accepting where a child is psychologically and helping them make sense of this in the present, it is my experience that—over time—these feelings and responses can be worked through thoughtfully in therapy.

For young children, the fight/flight response might physically not yet be available and the child may need to resort to another response for protection. The freeze response is characterised by lowering the heart rate and blood pressure. In the most extreme cases, if the experience is still too overwhelming, the child will ultimately disengage from all external stimuli and "flee inside" in an attempt to exclude the experience from conscious awareness (Schore, 2009). This response is known as dissociation. In my clinical experience, dissociation may often be accompanied by a blank staring into space; and in the countertransference, I feel as if I have "lost" the child despite their physical presence. In order to bring the child safely and sensitively back within the boundaries of their "window of tolerance" (Siegel, 2012), I might introduce some gentle movement to ensure the child returns to the present and an emotionally regulated state. Grounding exercises, such as asking the child to name five things they can see, four things they can hear, three things they can feel, two things they can smell, and one thing they can taste, can also be very effective. Focusing on the five senses (sight, sound, touch, smell, and taste) and encouraging the child to engage with the external environment in the present helps bring the child back into their body and mind (Pederson, 2012). If I feel the child is at a stage in the therapeutic process that they are able to "hear" and engage with observations, I might gently wonder (without expecting an answer): "I have the feeling you went somewhere else [*pause*]; where did you go?" in order to convey that I have noticed the protective response and make the child aware of it as well.

Perry et al. (1995) stated that the human brain develops in a use-dependent fashion; when a child is exposed to long-lasting states of dysregulation and persistently uses the fight/flight or freeze/dissociation responses to survive, these adaptive responses become ingrained in the child's neurobiological make-up and alter the child's baseline for emotional arousal (Perry, 2004). A child who favours the fight/flight response might end up with a nervous system that is *hyperaroused* and a child who favours the freeze/dissociation response might end up with a nervous system that is *hypoaroused* (i.e. shutting down). Perry also reminded us of another important principle when thinking of brain development, "use it or lose it" (2002, p. 84). Unused neural connections will not survive. Although critical periods in brain development make for wonderful windows of opportunity if all goes well, they also make the brain extremely vulnerable to adverse experiences during that time. For example, when children have suffered severe neglect that included sensory deprivation during a critical period of brain development, their brain will not have as many rich neural connections, impacting on its functionality, and the brain itself will—quite literally—be smaller in circumference (Perry, 2002). Due to the "use it or lose it" principle, as a result of these experiences, it might not be possible to reverse the damage done to the brain.

A child's nervous system "wired" in the context of persistent threat and fear will have a distorted sense of what situations and people are safe. The child's neuroception is faulty, resulting either in an inability to inhibit the defence system, severely impacting on the ability for social engagement and forming attachments, or they do not see danger when they should, resulting in an inability to activate the defence system, making the child extremely vulnerable to further traumatic experiences (Porges, 2011).

These adaptive responses, although appropriate to survival in the context of a traumatic or neglectful caregiving environment, are mal-adaptive in a different context. In therapy, we may see a hyperaroused child presenting with ADHD-like features such as hyperactivity and impulsivity, and the child can be prone to angry outbursts and hyper-vigilance (Van der Kolk, 2015). For these children, school can be a dif-ficult environment and their presentation impacts on learning and the ability to form and sustain peer relationships. A hypoaroused child can present with a very flat affect and may appear numb, depressed, or sleepy (Siegel, 2012). For these children, school is also a difficult envi-ronment. The tragedy is that due to their presentation these children are often overlooked, as they tend not to be as disruptive in the classroom as a hyperaroused child. It is important to support teachers to notice children with both presentations.

When working clinically with children who present as either hyper-aroused or hypoaroused it is crucial to establish safety first. Keeping the therapy room unchanged and keeping the therapist's appearance consistent by wearing the same or similar clothes, can support feelings of safety and consistency. It is also important in our clinical work with these children to work with the body in order to start working towards establishing a "new" emotional baseline. This means "down-regulating" the nervous system in the case of hyperaroused children, for instance by doing push–pull activities and squeezing clay, putty, or a stress ball. In my experience working with school-aged children who present as hyperaroused, I have also seen the positive impact of playful, dyadic breathing exercises, such as hissing like a snake and breathing fire like a dragon; and inviting the child to ground their feet, use their upper body (arms, hands) and facial expressions to embody the animal, while focusing on long exhales, thereby activating the parasympathetic nervous system and helping the child attain a more regulated state while remaining playful and creative. In the case of hypoaroused children, it means "up-regulating" the nervous system, for instance, by introducing free flowing movement in the session or the use of musical instruments.

Porges observed that voice and vocal prosody are powerful conduits through which safety can be conveyed and can therefore "promote calmer physiological states" (2011, p. 213). This resonates with my clinical experience. How I use my voice in sessions can have a considerable effect; for example, using a calm, sing-song voice with hyperaroused children helps them (and me!) feel more regulated.

Lack of mentalization and impact on internal working models

Chronic trauma and neglect also have an adverse effect on mentalization. In environments with chronic trauma, there is another mind present, however disturbed or dysfunctional, to provide feedback and explore mental states. The child may find an image of themselves as the source of the anger or distress in the mind of the caregiver, resulting in an internal working model of the self as bad, dangerous, and unworthy of love and protection (Fonagy et al., 2004). In the case of chronic trauma, the internal working model may also include mental representations of others as frightening, threatening, and unpredictable, and expectations of relationships as unsafe and a source of fear and discomfort (e.g. Howe, 2005). In the therapy room, these internal working models can show themselves in the narrative of a child's play, for example violent characters, catastrophic metaphors, good moments followed by cataclysmic events, and the absence of helpful or protective characters.

In cases of neglect, the absence of a caregiver may result in an inability to experience any form of mentalization. In such dire circumstances, children may be completely deprived of the opportunity to make sense of their experiences, or to understand their own mind and the mind of others. Left alone for long periods of time, these children may develop an internal working model of themselves as abandoned. Their internal working model may also include beliefs and expectations of others as unavailable and they may attribute limited value to relationships due to the lack of interpersonal experiences. Howe (2005) described how these children may see others as interchangeable as long as they are able to get some of their basic needs met. These internal working models make for an incoherent narrative of self and others and children end up with a flawed sense of how trustworthy relationships work, having missed out on predictable and consistent reciprocal experiences.

This lack of reciprocity can also be present in the therapy room, which can feel as an impediment to the work when therapist and child are working towards forging a therapeutic alliance. In this context, I find Alvarez's thoughts (1992, 2012) on "undrawn" children most helpful to support my clinical thinking: these children have an impoverished internal world as they have not yet had the pleasure to be enjoyed, to be known, and to come alive. In the countertransference, I experience a sense of not being able to grasp or read the child, as if there is nothing there. In response, I find myself on the edge of my seat in sessions, leaning in, adopting a more proactive therapist-led approach, and I am aware of my inclination to keep trying harder to reach the child. The therapeutic work may be slow, the perceived progress microscopic, and there are times when the work might feel near impossible, but I have learned that with patience, acceptance, and perseverance, there are moments when you can see the light go on in the child's eyes as they work towards an awakening and find out that they have a mind of their own and their mind is worth knowing.

A child's inability to form a coherent narrative also has a devastating effect on attachment security, as the child has been deprived of meaning-making experiences as a result of the absence of the caregiver. Without the opportunity of having another mind thoughtfully make sense of their internal and external world, these children miss the necessary building blocks for attachment security. Sensitively attuned, co-regulatory experiences by a responsive caregiver who is present alongside the child are vital to make sense of the caregiver's own and the child's mental states through purposeful, mentalizing interactions.

Impact on attachment security

When a caregiver is not consistently responsive to a child's emotional needs (*insecure-ambivalent*) or responds to a child's emotional needs by rejecting or dismissing those needs (*insecure-avoidant*), the child's confidence in the responsiveness of their caregiver is affected (Ainsworth et al., 1978). In order to feel safe and protected and feel their emotional needs are met, these children will have to adapt their own behaviour. Howe (2011) described how children who experience their caregiver as "unresponsive" or dismissive tend to minimise—and therefore sacrifice—their own attachment needs in order to maximise their chances for parental availability, proximity, and care. This adaptive strategy tends to lead to an overregulation of their emotions. Children with an inconsistently responsive caregiver tend to amplify their distress and therefore heighten their emotions to optimise their chances that the caregiver will respond to their needs (Howe, 2005).

Although children with either an insecure-avoidant or insecure-ambivalent attachment pattern have had to resort to adaptive strategies to have their emotional needs met, they have managed to organise their thoughts and behaviour enough to get some of their needs met by their caregiver, if not all of the time and perhaps not fully. The ability to organise thought and behaviour is an incredibly important mitigating factor combating the effects of trauma, providing a buffer so the day-to-day stresses can be faced in a more or less organised way (Cook et al., 2005).

Brisch proposed that there is a "strong propensity (up to 80%!)" in children who grow up in an environment with chronic trauma and neglect to develop a disorganised attachment (2014, p. 39). Children who have developed a disorganised attachment pattern have not been able to formulate a coherent response to their caregiving environment. Their attachment figure's behaviour may not only have lacked consistency, it will also have induced fear in the child (Main & Hesse, 1990). Main and Solomon (1986, 1990) described how in these circumstances two contradictory behavioural systems are activated, fear and attachment. As the attachment figure is the source of fear as well as potential comfort, children find themselves in an irreconcilable situation, therefore unable to organise a coherent behavioural response. Howe (2005) observed that in cases of severe neglect—in which there is an absence of caregivers or multiple ruptures in care in the early months and/or years of a child's life—children might not develop the capacity to be selective when making attachments, resulting in indiscriminate behaviour. These children appear unaware of "stranger danger" and do not differentiate when approaching adults as long as the adult is perceived as able to meet their basic needs.

Unlike securely attached children, whose confidence in their caregivers' responsiveness allows them time and space to play and explore, children with a disorganised attachment pattern, left to fend for themselves, use all their energy on survival. As they mature, these children may adopt controlling behaviours such as compulsive caregiving or more punitive control, in order to compensate for the disorganisation and the unpredictability of their frightening caregiving environments (Solomon & George, 1999). However, these behavioural strategies tend to break down when experiencing moments of higher stress, for instance when a child's attachment system is activated due to a perceived threat or frightening experience, as the child lacks the internal structure to hold the behavioural strategies together and will unconsciously revert to the internalised disorganised pattern of attachment.

For these children there is no energy left to thrive; their sense of safety, ability to make and sustain friendships, and their physical and mental health are all at great risk of being compromised. These children also have the highest vulnerability for developing psychopathology (Brisch, 2014).

Conclusion

Attachment security and neurophysiological development depend heavily on the child's experience. In the event that this experience has been predominantly attuned in the presence of a co-regulating and mentalizing caregiver, a child will develop a secure attachment and a nervous system primed for social engagement and exploration. If one or all of these factors are compromised, it has a devastating effect on a child's neurophysiological development and attachment security. As a result, these children have a higher risk of developing physical, emotional, and social difficulties as well as psychopathology.

For integrative child psychotherapists working with children who have suffered developmental trauma, it is essential to understand how a child's early life experience impacts on their attachment security and neurophysiological development. The ever-expanding body of neurophysiological evidence allows us to gain a deeper understanding of the effects of chronic trauma and neglect on young bodies and minds. With this knowledge, integrative child psychotherapists will be able to support children and their families through sensitive, trauma-informed work. It is also important for integrative child psychotherapists to advocate on children's behalf to help teachers and the wider network have a better understanding of developmental trauma and its far-reaching consequences on a child's neurophysiological, emotional, and cognitive development; and to work collaboratively to formulate a holistic approach with the child's well-being kept in mind.

References

Ainsworth, M. D. S., Blehar, M. C., Waters, E., & Wall, S. (1978). *Patterns of Attachment: A Psychological Study of the Strange Situation*. Hillsdale, NJ: Lawrence Erlbaum.

Alvarez, A. (1992). *Live Company: Psychoanalytic Psychotherapy with Autistic, Borderline, Deprived and Abused Children*. London: Routledge.

Alvarez, A. (2012). *The Thinking Heart: Three Levels of Psychoanalytic Therapy with Disturbed Children*. London: Routledge.

Bowlby, J. (1969). *Attachment and Loss, Volume 1: Attachment*. London: Pimlico, 1997.

Bowlby, J. (1979). The making and breaking of affectional bonds. In: *The Making and Breaking of Affectional Bonds* (pp. 150–188). London: Routledge 2005.

Bowlby, J. (1980). *Attachment and Loss, Volume 3: Loss*. London: Pimlico, 1998.

Brisch, K. H. (2014). *Treating Attachment Disorders: From Theory to Therapy*. 2nd edn. New York: Guilford Press.

Cook, A., Spinazzola, J., Ford, J., Lanktree, C., Blaustein, M., Cloitre, M., DeRosa, R., Hubbard, R., Kagan, R., Liautaud, R., Mallah, K., Olafson, E., & Van der Kolk, B. (2005). Complex trauma in children and adolescents. *Psychiatric Annals*, 35(5): 390–398.

Department for Education (2018). *Working Together to Safeguard Children. A guide to inter-agency working to safeguard and promote the welfare of children*. Available at: https://assets.publishing.service.gov.uk/government/ uploads/system/uploads/attachment_data/file/779401/Working_Together_ to_Safeguard-Children.pdf (last accessed June 28, 2020).

Felitti, V. J., Anda, R. F., Nordenberg, D., Williamson, D. F., Spitz, A. M., Edwards, V., Koss M. P., & Marks, J. S. (1998). Relationship of childhood abuse and household dysfunction to many of the leading causes of death in adults. The Adverse Childhood Experiences (ACE) Study. *American Journal of Preventive Medicine, 14*(4): 245–258. doi: 10.1016/s0749-3797(98)00017-8 (last accessed June 4, 2020).

Fonagy, P., Gergely, G., Jurist, E. L., & Target, M. (2004). *Affect Regulation, Mentalization and the Development of the Self.* London: Karnac.

Gerhardt, S. (2015). *Why Love Matters: How Affection Shapes a Baby's Brain.* 2nd edn. London: Routledge.

Howe, D. (2005). *Child Abuse and Neglect: Attachment, Development and Intervention.* Basingstoke, UK: Palgrave Macmillan.

Howe, D. (2011). *Attachment across the Lifecourse: A Brief Introduction.* Basingstoke, UK: Palgrave Macmillan.

Hughes, K., Bellis, M. A., Hardcastle, K. A., Sethi, D., Butchart, A., Mikton, C., Jones, L., & Dunne, M. P. (2017). The effect of multiple adverse childhood experiences on health; a systemic review and meta-analysis. *Lancet Public Health, 2*(8): 256–366. doi: 10.1016/S2468-2667(17)30118-4 (last accessed June 4, 2020).

Lahousen, T., Unterrainer, H. F., & Kapfhammer, H.-P. (2019). Psychobiology of attachment and trauma—some general remarks from a clinical perspective. *Frontiers in Psychiatry, 10*(914): 1–15. Available at: https://doi.org/10.3389/fpsyt.2019.00914 (last accessed July 5, 2021).

Main, M., & Hesse, E. (1990). Parents' unresolved traumatic experiences are related to infants' disorganized attachment status: Is frightening and/or frightened parental behaviour the linking mechanism? In: M. T. Greenberg, D. Cicchetti, & E. M. Cummings (Eds.), *Attachment in the Preschool Years: Theory, Research and Intervention* (pp. 161–182). London: University of Chicago Press.

Main, M., & Solomon, J. (1986). Discovery of an insecure-disorganized/disoriented attachment pattern. In: T. B. Brazelton & M. W. Yogman (Eds.), *Affective Development in Infancy* (pp. 95–124). Norwood, NJ: Ablex.

Main, M., & Solomon, J. (1990). Procedures for identifying infants as disorganised/disoriented during the Ainsworth Strange Situation. In: M. T. Greenberg, D. Cicchetti, & E. M. Cummings (Eds.), *Attachment in the Preschool Years: Theory, Research and Intervention* (pp. 121–160). London: University of Chicago Press.

Music, G. (2011). *Nurturing Natures: Attachment and Children's Emotional, Sociocultural, and Brain Development.* Hove, UK: Psychology Press.

Pederson, L. (2012). *The Expanded Dialectical Behavior Therapy Skills Training Manual: Practical DBT for Self-Help and Individual & Group Treatment Settings.* 2nd edn. Eau Claire, WI: PESI.

Perry, B. D. (2001). *Bonding and Attachment in Maltreatment Children: Consequences of Emotional Neglect in Childhood.* Available at: https://7079168e-705a-4dc7-be05-2218087aa989.filesusr.com/ugd/aa51c7_a9e562d294864796bdd5b3096a8d8c86.pdf (last accessed June 4, 2020).

Perry, B. D. (2002). Childhood experience and the expression of genetic potential: What childhood neglect tells us about nature and nurture. *Brain and Mind*, 3(1): 79–100.

Perry, B. D. (2004). Maltreatment and the developing child: How early childhood experience shapes child and culture. The inaugural Margaret McCain lecture, September 23. The Centre for Children and Families in the Justice System, London. Available at: https://7079168e-705a-4dc7-be05-2218087aa989.filesusr.com/ugd/aa51c7_1052a376f51b40219ac48304da3af5ed.pdf (last accessed June 28, 2020).

Perry, B. D., & Pollard, R. A. (1997). Altered brain development following global neglect in early childhood. Society for Neuroscience: Proceedings from Annual Meeting, New Orleans. Available at: https://7079168e-705a-4dc7-be05-2218087aa989.filesusr.com/ugd/aa51c7_c741590d634447e1b-dafb1d2ea1fef5c.pdf (last accessed June 4, 2020).

Perry, B. D., Pollard, R. A., Blakley, T. I., Baker, W. L., & Vigilante, D. (1995). Childhood trauma, the neurobiology of adaptation, and "use-dependent" development of the brain: How "states" become "traits". *Infant Mental Health Journal*, 16(4): 271–291.

Porges, S. W. (2011). *The Polyvagal Theory: Neurophysiological Foundations of Emotions, Attachment, Communication and Self-regulation.* New York: W. W. Norton.

Schore, A. N. (2003a). The effects of a secure attachment relationship on right brain development, affect regulation, and infant mental health. In: *Affect Dysregulation and Disorders of the Self* (pp. 128–177). London: W. W. Norton.

Schore, A. N. (2003b). The effects of relational trauma on right brain development, affect regulation, and infant mental health. In: *Affect Dysregulation and Disorders of the Self* (pp. 178–233). London: W. W. Norton.

Schore, A. N. (2009). Attachment trauma and the developing right brain: Origins of pathological dissociation. In: P. F. Dell & J. A. O'Neil (Eds.),

Dissociation and Dissociative Disorders: DSM V and Beyond (pp. 107–144). New York: Routledge.

Schore, A. N. (2016). *Affect Regulation and the Origin of the Self: The Neurobiology of Emotional Development*. New York: Routledge.

Siegel, D. J. (2012). *The Developing Mind: How Relationships and the Brain Interact to Shape Who We Are*. 2nd edn. London: Guilford.

Solomon, J., & George, C. (1999). The place of disorganization in attachment theory; linking classic observations with contemporary findings. In: J. Solomon & C. George (Eds.), *Attachment Disorganization* (pp. 3–32). New York: Guilford.

Van der Kolk, B. A. (2005). Developmental trauma disorder: Toward a rational diagnosis for children with complex trauma histories. *Psychiatric Annals*, *35*(5): 401–408.

Van der Kolk, B. A. (2015). *The Body Keeps the Score: Mind, Brain and Body in the Transformation of Trauma*. London: Penguin.

CHAPTER 4

Porges meets Winnicott

Irene Alberione

Introduction

This chapter aims to compare and integrate the works of paediatrician and child psychoanalyst Dr Donald W. Winnicott with neuroscientist and psychiatrist Professor Stephen Porges, taking inspiration from Graham Music's riveting paper "Bringing up the bodies: psyche–soma, body awareness and feeling at ease" (2015). I shall explore how Winnicott's theory of the individual (emerging, always incompletely, from a matrix of communality), and Porges's research (2003b), with its focus on understanding the underlying neural platform of social behaviour, permeate and complement each other. I shall also investigate how the work of Porges (2011), "with a newer understanding of the autonomic nervous system, has put exciting scientific flesh on the bones of some of Winnicott's flashes of clinical genius" (Music, 2015, p. 5), and illustrate how the polyvagal perspective has cast bright new light on the fundamental tenets of the Winnicottian vocabulary. In addition I shall conclude that Winnicott's insights, overcoming the Cartesian mind/body dichotomy and postulating that the Self is fundamentally shaped by embodied interactions, dovetails with Porges's theory of the social engagement system as the locus where our embodied-relational patterns are created and stored.

Environment

Porges (2005) began by studying a complex network of cranial nerves that maps what he termed "the social engagement system". In earlier species, this apparatus was devoted to absorbing oxygen and food. In humans, it merged with a system of facial, visual, and vocal interaction, further evolving to facilitate the absorption of relational nourishment from the social context. Thus, witnessing and reciprocity became the most powerful variable of co-regulation of physiological states in infants, laying the biological foundations of Winnicott's concept of the "facilitating environment" (1963a, p. 89).

The famous statement, "there is no such a thing as a baby" (Winnicott, 1952, pp. 99–100) vividly portrays how the emotional health of the infant depends on the psychic environment that either facilitates or damages the child's inherited potential (Winnicott, 1963c).

Identifying with her baby, the mother enters a state of "primary maternal preoccupation" (Winnicott, 1956a, p. 304), becoming highly sensitive to her infant's physical and emotional needs and meeting him by sufficiently holding, handling, and introducing him (or her of course) to the world by intervening at the right moment. The "good enough" mother's capacity to provide her offspring with a springboard for self-understanding means putting her own affective states and preoccupations to one side and making available an internal space into which the child's feelings can be projected, held, and represented (Holmes & Slade, 2018).

Winnicott (1965), following Darwin, posits that we do not need to work at human evolution as it simply unfolds as a matter of course, given a facilitating environment; this might be "polyvagally" defined as a context eliciting a neuroception of safety.

Neuroception (Porges, 2011) is a neural process that happens in primitive parts of the brain (without our conscious awareness) and is responsible for evaluating risks from inside and outside the body and between people. In other words, if the environment is perceived as safe, our nervous system disables the neural circuits regulating the defensive mechanisms of fight, flight, and freeze through the involvement of oxytocin (Porges, 2005) and triggers adaptive neural circuits that promote social interaction.

Safety could thus be considered an essential feature of Winnicott's facilitating environment, where not only the child trusts the mother but the mother also trusts the child (Winnicott, 1960b), relying on the baby to signal for help when needing "a supplementary brain for co-regulation" (Holmes & Slade, 2018, p. 137), bringing about the state that Winnicott calls "going-on-being" (1960b, p. 54). A sufficiency of "going-on-being" is only possible if the mother provides ego-coverage for the child: the infant experiences repeated recovery from the threats posed by the violence of his innate drives of annihilation (Winnicott, 1956a). In agreement with Winnicott, Porges (2015a) states that the ability to self-regulate one's own physiological states is built upon a platform of successful co-regulation in childhood. When there is a violation of trust from the cradle there is no memory of a safe relationship to help navigate the complexity of the world. In Winnicott's vocabulary, "impingement" (the privation of attuned holding, handling, and object-presenting) interrupts the infant's "continuity of being" (Winnicott, 1963c, p. 88). This state is needed for the psyche to come to "indwell in the soma" (Winnicott, 1949b, p. 244): the infant comes to existence by feeling that his sense of Self is centred inside the body—body and mind are integrated. The extraordinary relevance of Winnicott's intuition is that embodiment and relationships are inseparable: "If we explore embodiment, we encounter relationship; if we explore relationship, we encounter embodiment" (Totton, 2015, p. xvi). Porges would say that it is not a coincidence that suffering trauma, abuse, and neglect hinders the ability to be present in the body and building and maintaining safe and meaningful relationships.

Dependence

Winnicott's approach to human growth and development can be seen as an "exercise of dependence" (Kahr, 2016, p. 147). Initially the baby is in a stage of absolute dependence, being completely merged with the mother. By receiving what he needs when he needs it, the infant feels he has created the object: this is the illusion of omnipotence (Winnicott, 1960b).

This phase is followed by relative dependence, when the mother emerges from the state of primary maternal preoccupation: the infant requires the mother to de-adapt, to fail, in order to separate, introducing the reality principle as part of the disillusionment process (Winnicott, 1963c). This failure, which takes place from six months to two years, contributes to the development of the infant's sense of Self (me) separated from the mother (not-me).

Failures that are repaired allow the child to reach the "stage of concern" (Winnicott, 1962b, p. 74), where ambivalence is accepted, and to have the ability to use the transitional space, leading the infant to a stage of "towards independence" (Winnicott, 1960b, p. 46).

Echoing Winnicott, Porges (2015a) states that at the beginning of life co-regulation provides the internal resources for the child to move towards autonomy. In other words, co-regulation (the ability to mutually, synchronously, and reciprocally regulate the physiological and behavioural state of the other) is a biological imperative (Porges, 2011): the human quest, initiated at birth, to calm neural defence systems (by detecting features of safety), continues throughout the lifespan (Winnicott would suggest that we are never completely independent).

The need for trusting and loving relationships to effectively co-regulate each other is the base of social behaviour, and this is intertwined with the phylogenetic origin of the mammalian autonomic nervous system (Porges, 2003a). This incarnates the survival of the fittest in that the members of our species who could tell when someone was safe to approach, survived and thrived. Thus, social communication, mutual help, and cooperation are essential for our existence.

Traditionally, the autonomic nervous system is described as having two components: the sympathetic (fight/flight), and the parasympathetic (rest/digest), and these work to achieve equilibrium. The main constituent of the parasympathetic branch is the vagus nerve, a bilateral and bidirectional highway of motor and sensory fibres that provides information from the brain to the body and from the body's organs to the brain.

Polyvagal theory (Porges, 1995, 1998, 2003b, 2007, 2011) was born out of the "vagal paradox": how the vagus and its tone, measured in newborn and premature babies, could be both a marker of resilience and a risk factor. Porges solved the enigma by theorising that two vagal circuits differentiated through evolution: the ventral vagal ("smart", newest, uniquely mammalian, myelinated) and the dorsal vagal (ancient and unmyelinated). Hence polyvagal theory postulates that the autonomic nervous system is made of three subsystems that are not antagonistic but hierarchical: the sympathetic, and the dorsal and ventral vagal parasympathetic.

When we feel safe, our social engagement system, mediated by the ventral vagus, enables us to access both higher and lower brain structures: the former facilitates creativity and generativity; the latter regulates health, growth, and restoration (Porges, 2001). When we perceive danger or threat, we first turn to our social engagement system to re-establish safety (we call upon those to whom we are attached). In a sequence that is rigid and out of our control (Porges, 1995), if social behaviour is not conducive to the regulation of our physiological states, we firstly resort to our fight/flight response and, in case of further failure, we will recruit the most ancient survival mechanism of shutdown and collapse (mediated by the dorsal vagus).

The key to understanding polyvagal theory's contributions to Winnicott's intuitions is comprehending the centrality of the social engagement system, which explains how our physiological states influence our behaviour, feelings, and our ability to interact with others from the time when we were babies, when we were already eliciting care from our caregivers through our faces and voices. As a matter of fact, the mammalian vagus starts its maturation during the third trimester of gestation, enabling the full-term baby to coordinate sucking, swallowing, breathing, and vocalisations (Porges & Furman, 2011).

It might also be argued that Porges adds a new dimension to the Winnicottian concept of the antisocial tendency (Winnicott, 1956b, 1967c), seen as a sign of protest against the child's deprivation (when failures are not mended) and hope of a positive response from the world.

If the fighting/fleeing children are "alive" and mobile, those who have suffered inescapable abuse often feel that their bodies have failed them. Polyvagal theory eliminates the shame in not mobilising, fighting, or trying to escape a traumatic event. Freezing and collapsing are the expression of the heroic nature of our body protecting us (Porges, 2017a), thus giving trauma survivors feelings of validation.

Mirroring

Winnicott (1967a) suggests that the mother's face is the mirror for the baby: the embodied sense of Self emerges from an infant who has internalised the experience of seeing himself through being seen by the mother. Porges (2003a) defines mirroring as the features of safety being manifested in the face: the myelinated vagus in the brainstem unites the neural regulation of the face (in particular the orbicularis oculi), head, and voice with the heart and the visceral pathways, allowing us to attune to the voices, faces, and gestures of others and to convey our physiological states in our facial expressions and vocalisations. Wearing our heart on our face is essential in forming social bonds and surviving. Porges (2009) argues that when we feel unsafe, our faces become expressionless and still, the middle ear muscles lose their tone, we become very sensitive to low-frequency predator sounds, and struggle to extract the high-frequency harmonics of the human voice from background noises.

As our physiological state is influenced through neuroception by the other's physiological state, if the child's distress is met with the "good enough polyvagal informed mother" who intuitively conveys calmness through her vocalisations and facial expressions (the fight/flight or freeze of the infant met with the ventral vagal system of the caregiver), the child will calm down, developing and reinforcing strategies to stay out of those defensive states (Porges, 2018). Polyvagal theory thus explains, on a neurophysiological level, what we intuitively knew, that a kind face and a soothing voice move us from fear to safety. Winnicott (1968) says that when the aggression towards the mother is met without retaliation, the infant will experience the survival of the object, strengthening his ability to see how the rage that he feels to be true is not necessarily real. If this process is missed or thwarted, the child will develop a "false self" (Winnicott, 1962a, p. 102), a persona that is outwardly good but which suppresses his vitality and creativity, resulting in him feeling dead inside.

Hate

In his paper "Hate in the countertransference" (1949a), Winnicott normalises hateful feelings between therapist and client, stressing the developmental importance of the hatred that the mother experiences in response to the ruthless love of the infant during the stage of absolute dependence. As with the mother hating the baby, the therapist must be able to tolerate hating and being hated by the client: only by being aware of the hatred in the countertransference can the therapist, just like the early environment, "survive" and become an object the client could use. At times the mother's hatred is linked with her feeling persecuted by the infant's demands.

Arguing that the responsibility of the co-regulatory relationship is to keep our autonomic nervous system out of states of defence (Dana & Grant, 2018), polyvagal theory provides an understanding of the neural platform detecting when the therapist's defensive systems are being physiologically activated in the countertransference. This can help her to consciously move from a bottom-up defensive reaction to openness and engagement through top-down regulation (Howes, 2013). Relational safety is the precondition for co-regulation and meaning making in therapy, where the core of the work would be "enhancing the smart vagal system while dampening down sympathetic nervous activation" (Music, 2015, p. 15), with the goal for the client to open up to accessibility and therefore vulnerability (Eichhorn, 2012).

Winnicott, pioneering the role of play in psychotherapeutic work, "shifts therapy towards quieter and less verbal states in which "relaxation" (Porges's immobilisation without fear) and "being" can occur" (Music, 2015, p. 15), through the embodied communication of play. He famously stated that "psychotherapy has to do with two people playing together" (1967b, p. 38), where "the play space is more important than the interpretation because it allows for the client's creativity" (1968, pp. 86–87). As the infant's ability to play and symbolise precedes the use of language, Winnicott values the way in which meaning is conveyed in sessions. Porges (2015b) provides the neurophysiological explanation of the Winnicottian intuition: since the neurosystem that recognises the features of facial and vocal expressivity is linked to social communication to which our body responds, it is not the words that matter but how we say them. More than a talking cure, we can then champion a relating cure, where safety is the treatment (Porges, 2017a, p. 187) and trust is the work.

Play

In the journey from absolute to relative dependence, the infant will use a transitional object—the first not-me possession or non-material object of attachment, which is the child's first use of a symbol (Winnicott, 1951), representing the internal unity of baby and mother. The transitional space, the intermediate area that keeps inner and outer realities separated and yet interrelated, is the bedrock of relatedness and marks the beginning of play, fantasy, and thought, culminating in shared cultural experience (Winnicott, 1966). Play is crucial, because it is in playing that the individual is able to be creative, discovering the Self and feeling alive. Creativity is the retention through life of what belongs to the infant's experience: the ability to create the world, stored as the countless repetitions of the mother meeting the baby's needs (Winnicott, 1971). Enjoyment of play is therefore the hallmark of the growing child's health (Winnicott, 1946).

Echoing Winnicott, Porges (2017a) describes play as a mixed physiological state that activates the sympathetic nervous system to support movement without shifting into defensive fight/flight behaviours, by diffusing cues of threat with the social features of voice and face through the myelinated vagus. Both Winnicott and Porges notice how many of our clients never had the opportunity to play as children, due to a lack of safety, thus compromising their ability to regulate their fight/flight/collapse responses.

Porges (2017b), like Winnicott, recommends that we play: we live in a traumatised society, bombarded by cues of danger that keep us mobilised and more productive but do not foster compassion and creativity. Playfulness is a neural exercise which dampens defence behaviours and activates the social engagement system, allowing us to gain resilience to deal with the disruptions in our lives (Porges, 2015b) and to become alive, so that we can start to appreciate the true aspects of being human (Winnicott, 1971).

Stillness

In Winnicott's terms, the child who has experienced being held in the mind of the mother can happily play alone as he has internalised her presence, which becomes a resource to live creatively. However, if the world is not perceived as safe, if impingements interrupt the child's "continuity of being", the infant will find ways to protect himself, "but at great cost to his sense of Self, [resulting in] premature ego development" (Abram, 2018, p. 240). In polyvagal terms, there is a bias for all social interaction to be more negative, leading to faulty neuroception and psychopathology; this is defined by Porges (2004) as reading environmental cues that are not dangerous as if they were or vice versa.

Winnicott's (1960a, pp. 146–147) "false self" child complies with the demands and needs of the caregiver at the expense of his sense of reality, agency, and creativity (the "true self"). However, a degree of "false self" coexists and protects the "true self" in everybody: in health, the splitting of the Self is an achievement of personal growth; in pathological formation, due to gross impingements, the "false self" blocks any access to the "true self" (Dethiville, 2018). Winnicott's central statement is that the individual is an isolate for there is an *incommunicado*, a private, secret Self permanently unknown, but he also affirms that "it is a joy to be hidden and a disaster not to be found" (Winnicott, 1963b, pp. 186–187). This leaves us to bear the ambiguity of the existential paradox of loneliness, authenticity, and relating, on which Porges might shed some light. Being alone in the presence of the mother (Winnicott, 1957b), one of the most important signs of emotional maturity, and essential for us to feel real, can be "polyvagally" described as "immobilisation without fear" (Porges, 2011, p. 13), a quiet state of vigilant inactivity between mother and baby, when just being is enough. "Polyvagally" we can say that when my heart meets yours, words are not necessary (Porges, 1997): the internalised feeling of safety supported by the ventral vagal complex enables our richest intimate experiences, in which we feel the most alive.

Conclusion

I have argued that Winnicott's pioneering insights are consistently backed up by Porges's research which provides us with a more sophisticated understanding of the biology of safety, trust, and relatedness. In addition I have considered how neuroscientific findings and transdisciplinary research have progressively enriched the landscape of psychotherapy, with the concomitant abandonment of the outdated neo-Cartesian dichotomy of mind/body (Damasio, 1999): as there is no baby separated from the mother-and-baby system (Winnicott, 1957a, p. 88), there is no mind separated from the mind/body/environment context.

In conclusion, we could argue that if Descartes had been polyvagally and Winnicottian informed, instead of stating, "I think therefore I am", he would probably have said, "I truly feel myself, therefore I am" … and our society would be looking at health, well-being, and interpersonal connectedness with completely different eyes.

References

Abram, J. (2018). *The Language of Winnicott: A Dictionary of Winnicott's Use of Words*. 2nd edn. London: Routledge.

Damasio, A. (1999). *The Feeling of What Happens: Body and Emotion in the Making of Consciousness*. New York: Harcourt.

Dana, D., & Grant, D. (2018). The polyvagal playlab: helping therapists bring polyvagal theory to their clients. In: S. W. Porges & D. Dana (Eds.), *Clinical Applications of the Polyvagal Theory: The Emergence of Polyvagal-informed Therapies* (pp. 185–206). New York: W. W. Norton.

Dethiville, L. (2018). *Donald W. Winnicott: A New Approach*. S. Ganley Lévy (Trans.). London: Routledge.

Eichhorn, N. (2012). Safety: the preamble for social engagement: an interview with Stephen W. Porges, PhD. *Somatic Psychotherapy Today*, Spring: 52–54. Available at: http://static1.squarespace.com/static/5c1d025fb27e390a78569537/t/5cce0254eb3931597f8fe2a4/1557004884326/Preamble-Social-Engagement-Interview-Porges-1.pdf (last accessed May 28, 2020).

Holmes, J., & Slade, A. (2018). *Attachment in Therapeutic Practice*. London: Sage.

Howes, R. (2013). Wearing your heart on your face: the polyvagal circuit in the consulting room: an interview with Stephen W. Porges, PhD. Available at: https://pesi.com/blog/details/967/wearing-your-heart-on-your-face-the-polyvagal-circuit (last accessed May 27, 2020).

Kahr, B. (2016). *Tea with Winnicott*. London: Karnac.

Music, G. (2015). Bringing up the bodies: psyche–soma, body awareness and feeling at ease. *British Journal of Psychotherapy*, *31*(1): 4–19. doi: 10.1111/bjp.12122.

Porges, S. W. (1995). Orienting in a defensive world: mammalian modifications of our evolutionary heritage. A polyvagal theory. *Psychophysiology*, *32*(4): 301–318. doi: 10.1111/j.1469-8986.1995.tb01213.x.

Porges, S. W. (1997). Emotion: an evolutionary by-product of the neural regulation of the autonomic nervous system. *Annals of the New York Academy of Sciences*, *807*: 62–77.

Porges, S. W. (1998). Love: an emergent property of the mammalian autonomic nervous system. *Psychoneuroendocrinology*, *23*(8): 837–861. doi: 10.1016/s0306-4530(98)00057-2.

Porges, S. W. (2001). The polyvagal theory: phylogenetic substrates of a social nervous system. *International Journal of Psychophysiology*, *42*: 123–146. Available at: https://static1.squarespace.com/static/5c1d025fb27e390a78569537/t/5ccdfeab104c7b981c2f77c0/1557003948682/Polyvagal–Theory–substrates.pdf (last accessed June 3, 2020).

Porges, S. W. (2003a). Social engagement and attachment: a phylogenetic perspective. *Annals of the New York Academy of Sciences*, *1008*: 31–47. doi: 10.1196/annals.1301.004.

Porges, S. W. (2003b). The polyvagal theory: phylogenetic contributions to social behaviour. *Physiology and Behaviour*, *79*: 503–513. doi: 10.1016/S0031-9384(03)00156-2.

Porges, S. W. (2004). Neuroception: a subconscious system for detecting threats and safety. *Zero to Three*, May: 19–24. Available at: https://static1.squarespace.com/static/5c1d025fb27e390a78569537/t/5ccdff181905f41dbcb689e3/1557004058168/Neuroception.pdf (last accessed June 1, 2020).

Porges, S. W. (2005). The role of social engagement in attachment and bonding: a phylogenetic perspective. In: C. S. Carter, L. Ahnert, K. E. Grossman, S. B. Hrdy, M. E. Lamb, S. W. Porges, & N. Sachser (Eds.), *Attachment and Bonding: A New Synthesis* (pp. 33–54). Cambridge, MA: MIT Press.

Porges, S. W. (2007). The polyvagal perspective. *Biological Psychology*, *74*(2): 116–143. doi: 10.1016/j.biopsycho.2006.06.009.

Porges, S. W. (2009). The polyvagal hypothesis: common mechanisms mediating autonomic regulation, vocalizations, and listening. *Handbook of Behavioural Neuroscience*, January (*19*): 255–264. doi: 10.1016/B978-0-12-374593-4.00025-5.

Porges, S. W. (2011). *The Polyvagal Theory: Neurophysiological Foundations of Emotions, Attachment, Communication and Self-regulation*. New York: W. W. Norton.

Porges, S. W. (2015a). Making the world safe for our children: down-regulating defence and up-regulating social engagement to "optimise" the human experience. *Children Australia*, *40*(2): 114–123. doi: 10.1017/cha.2015.12.

Porges, S. W. (2015b). Play as a neural exercise: insights from the polyvagal theory. Available at: https://legeforeningen.no/contentassets/6df47feea036 43c5a878ee7b87a467d2/sissel-oritsland-vedlegg-til-presentasjon-porges-play-as-neural-exercise.pdf (last accessed June 5, 2020).

Porges, S. W. (2017a). *The Pocket Guide to the Polyvagal Theory: The Transformative Power of Feeling Safe*. New York: W. W. Norton.

Porges, S. W. (2017b). Vagal pathways: portals to compassion. In: E. M. Seppälä, E. Simon-Thomas, S. L. Brown, M. C. Worline, C. D. Cameron, & J. R. Doty (Eds.), *The Oxford Handbook of Compassion Science* (pp. 189–202). Oxford: Oxford University Press.

Porges, S. W. (2018). Polyvagal theory: a primer. In: S. W. Porges & D. Dana (Eds.), *Clinical Applications of The Polyvagal Theory: The Emergence of Polyvagal-Informed Therapies* (pp. 50–69). New York: W. W. Norton.

Porges, S. W., & Furman S. A. (2011). The early development of the autonomic nervous system provides a neural platform for social behaviour: a polyvagal perspective. *Infant and Child Development*, *20*(1): 106–118. doi: 10.1002/icd.688.

Totton, N. (2015). *Embodied Relating*. London: Karnac.

Winnicott, D. W. (1946). What do we mean by a normal child? In: *The Child, the Family and the Outside World* (pp. 124–130). London: Penguin.

Winnicott, D. W. (1949a). Hate in the countertransference. *International Journal of Psychoanalysis*, *30*: 69–74.

Winnicott, D. W. (1949b). Mind and its relation to the psycho–soma. In: *Collected Papers: Through Paediatrics to Psycho-Analysis* (pp. 243–254). 2nd edn. London: Hogarth.

Winnicott, D. W. (1951). Transitional objects and transitional phenomena. In: *Playing and Reality* (pp. 1–34). London: Routledge Classics.

Winnicott, D. W. (1952). Anxiety associated with insecurity. In: *Collected Papers: Through Paediatrics to Psycho-Analysis* (pp. 97–100). 2nd edn. London: Hogarth.

Winnicott, D. W. (1956a). Primary maternal preoccupation. In: *Collected Papers: Through Paediatrics to Psychoanalysis* (pp. 300–305). 2nd edn. London: Hogarth.

Winnicott, D. W. (1956b). The antisocial tendency. In: C. Winnicott, R. Shepherd, & M. Davis (Eds.), *Deprivation and Delinquency* (pp. 103–112). London: Routledge Classics.

Winnicott, D. W. (1957a). Further thoughts on babies as persons. In: *The Child, the Family and the Outside World* (pp. 85–92). London: Penguin, 1964.

Winnicott, D. W. (1957b). The capacity to be alone. In: *The Maturational Processes and the Facilitating Environment: Studies in the Theory of Emotional Development* (pp. 29–36). London: Routledge.

Winnicott, D. W. (1960a). Ego distortion in terms of true and false self. In: *The Maturational Processes and the Facilitating Environment: Studies in the Theory of Emotional Development* (pp. 140–152). London: Routledge.

Winnicott, D. W. (1960b). The theory of the parent–infant relationship. In: *The Maturational Processes and the Facilitating Environment: Studies in the Theory of Emotional Development* (pp. 37–55). London: Routledge.

Winnicott, D. W. (1962a). Morals and education. In: *The Maturational Processes and the Facilitating Environment: Studies in the Theory of Emotional Development* (pp. 93–105). London: Routledge.

Winnicott, D. W. (1962b). The development of the capacity for concern. In: *The Maturational Processes and the Facilitating Environment: Studies in the Theory of Emotional Development* (pp. 73–82). London: Routledge.

Winnicott, D. W. (1963a). Fear of breakdown. In: C. Winnicott, R. Shepherd, & M. Davis (Eds.), *Psycho-Analytic Explorations* (pp. 87–95). London: Karnac.

Winnicott, D. W. (1963b). Communicating and not communicating leading to a study of certain opposites. In: *The Maturational Processes and the Facilitating Environment: Studies in the Theory of Emotional Development* (pp. 179–192). London: Routledge.

Winnicott, D. W. (1963c). From dependence towards independence in the development of the individual. In: *The Maturational Processes and the Facilitating Environment: Studies in the Theory of Emotional Development* (pp. 83–92). London: Routledge.

Winnicott, D. W. (1965). *The Family and Individual Development*. London: Tavistock.

Winnicott, D. W. (1966). The location of cultural experience. In: *Playing and Reality* (pp. 128–139). London: Routledge Classics.

Winnicott, D. W. (1967a). Mirror-role of mother and family in child development. In: *Playing and Reality* (pp. 149–159). London: Routledge Classics.

Winnicott, D. W. (1967b). Playing: a theoretical statement. In: *Playing and Reality* (pp. 51–70). London: Routledge Classics.

Winnicott, D. W. (1967c). Delinquency as a sign of hope. In: L. Caldwell & H. Taylor Robinson (Eds.), *The Collected Works of D. W. Winnicott: Volume 8, 1967–1968*. Oxford: Oxford University Press. doi: 10.1093/med:ps ych/9780190271404.001.0001.

Winnicott, D. W. (1968). The use of an object and relating through identifications. In: *Playing and Reality* (pp. 115–127). London: Routledge Classics.

Winnicott, D. W. (1971). Playing: creative activity and the search for the self. In: *Playing and Reality* (pp. 71–86). London: Routledge Classics.

CHAPTER 5

Autism and sensory sensitivity

Jessica Olive

In this chapter I am looking behind the behaviour of the autistic child to consider his experience of the world, focusing specifically on how he may experience and respond to sensory information, by which I mean elements of the world that are encountered through the senses, for example lights, noise, or texture. I consider this to be relevant to children with classical autism as well as those with Asperger's syndrome or high functioning autism, and therefore will use the term "autism" throughout to encompass all of these areas. I shall refer to Joseph, a child with whom I worked for two years. At that time he had a diagnosis of high functioning autism. I shall also consider whether difficulties in processing sensory information are features that belong to the autism condition itself, or whether it may be the case that a co-morbid disorder such as ADHD or anxiety may be present. Finally, I shall consider how ideas applied to my work, based on findings from the above research, supported my client in achieving his potential both emotionally and academically.

Children with a diagnosis of autism often experience impairments in one or more of the following areas: (a) social interactions, (b) verbal and non-verbal communication, and (c) a restrictive and repetitive range of interests (Rutter et al., 2010 p. 759). Those with Asperger's syndrome (Asperger, 1944) or high functioning autism commonly show impairment in social interactions and a restricted range of interests but commonly can master language and communicate with others. A child diagnosed with autism spectrum disorder (ASD), will have many facets to his (or her) experience and behaviour, and it is important not to adopt a "one size fits all" approach when considering his experience or how he may be supported (Bromfield, 2010; Moat, 2013). The aetiology of autism is still not especially well understood, and the subject of some debate (Goodman & Scott, 2012, p. 52).

The study of sensory information processing is only one aspect of ASD, although in the case of Joseph it is an important consideration. For example, his weekly therapy sessions were originally organised to take place on a Friday morning, a time that clashed with the collection of the refuse bins outside in the street, which brought a cacophony of noise and unpleasant smells into our therapy room. Naturally, this would be distracting for most people; however, Joseph seemed particularly distressed in the moment. He would begin talking about the refuse collection on the way to the room; he would tell me that they may not come today, and when they invariably did, he would crawl under the table, his hood pulled right up over his face and ears, rocking backwards and forwards, squeezing his eyes shut and placing his hands over his ears and both thumbs in his mouth. I realised that it was necessary for me to move the time of his session, which resolved this particular issue. However, I wondered what it was that he had experienced at the time of the weekly passing of the refuse lorries. In his new time slot, other distractions became figural for him, such as a flickering light or the smell of the food arising from the dining hall below. Since it would not be possible to remove all distractions from our sessions, I resolved to better understand Joseph's experience in order to support him and his family.

Such hypersensitivity to sensory stimuli is considered a feature of autism (World Health Organization, 1992). Bromfield writes, "These children seem not to have the sensory equilibrium and censoring that protect and maintain the rest of us. The world literally pounds on their doors and ears, in their eyes, on their skin and through their noses" (2010, p. 6). As I observed with Joseph, these children's response to unwanted sensory information is often noticeably different to neurotypical children. Autistic children may rock backwards and forwards, repetitively roll an object, cover their eyes or ears, or carry out any number of other physical motions in an attempt to soothe themselves (WHO, 1992). Olga Bogdashina explores the reasons behind these "so-called bizarre responses" of autistic individuals, seeing these as "compensatory strategies to regulate their systems and to cope with information overload" (2011, p. 148). Rather than viewing behaviour such as rocking as something odd that the autistic child needs to learn to stop doing, this can be viewed as employment of a defensive or protective strategy, and if seen this way, it becomes as common as the need any human may have to cover their ears when a loud jet plane passes by overhead.

Frances Tustin identified how "sensation-dominated" autistic children are, which she connected to their need to feel safe in a world that was often highly unpredictable. Writing about the "protective shell" she believed autistic children created around them and inhabited (1990), Tustin observed, "By concentrating on certain of their bodily sensations to the exclusion of almost everything else autistic children have constructed their own 'asylum' and have encased themselves in their own sensation-dominated 'strait-jacket'" (pp. 31–32).

It is understandable that a child living in such a protective shell may well object violently to any outside stimulation that might impinge upon this protection. Relying as he is on his senses to keep this protective shell intact, if those senses are suddenly overloaded, the child is unable to maintain his shell, feeling suddenly vulnerable in an unsafe world and responding by doing what he can to limit this sensory assault and to restore the equilibrium of the shell. Tustin's theory can, in my opinion, be considered alongside later neurological research as a credible explanation for the experience of the autistic child in processing sensory information.

When Leo Kanner (1944) originally introduced the concept of autism he observed how autistic individuals give unusual attention to parts rather than wholes (p. 246). Following this concept, Uta Frith (1989) presented the "weak central coherence theory" which was later examined in studies by Frith and Happé (1994, 2005). Frith proposed that autistic individuals were unable to take in meaning from an overall mass of details, seeing only individual aspects and not the wider picture (for example seeing only individual trees when others may see a forest). This is illustrated by Joseph; it seems that he was unable to experience his therapy session as a number of parts making a whole, of which the passing of refuse lorries was just one transient part. For him, the lorries became his whole, leaving him utterly overwhelmed and unable to return to the activity he had been doing in therapy or the thoughts he had been thinking moments earlier.

We recognise that many autistic children have "an inability to filter out the information ... and distinguish the relevant from the irrelevant" (Bogdashina, 2011, p. 152). This distraction by external, irrelevant stimuli renders the child unable to process relevant information and may lead to difficulties making choices or decisions (Bogdashina, 2003). In turn, this is likely to have an impact upon social interactions when they find themselves in the company of other children who can easily and swiftly make choices in their daily lives (Bogdashina, 2003). Baron-Cohen (1995) describes how many autistic children have "mindblindness", meaning that they are unable to experience joint attention with other children, resulting in difficulties in imagining what others are thinking or feeling.

In this sense it seems that the inability to filter out irrelevant information could have a far-reaching impact upon the development of the child. Piaget (1983) presented the "sensorimotor" stage of development, taking place in the first two years of childhood; this being the time when infants learn about their environment through their senses. For an autistic child who may be receiving sensory messages that are confusing and at times overwhelming, it is likely that the sensorimotor stage would be negatively impacted in the sense that the child's ability to learn about the world through his environment would be compromised.

Jasmine Lee O'Neill (1999, p. 25) describes the autistic brain as one that "zeroes in rather than zeroes out", explaining that an autistic child may hear every element of an unfurling candy wrapper in enhanced detail yet be oblivious to a loud crash that startles other people in the room. She describes this as "selective deafness" (1999, p. 25). It is almost as though if the child did not hear it, the crash did not happen and no danger is present. Joseph's under-sensitivity to sensory information had a level of sophistication for he could simultaneously use his senses to observe the minutiae of sound and also to block such sensory information from his field of perception. Joseph's teacher had mentioned how Joseph sometimes seemed to drift away in class, unresponsive to the teacher's attempts to connect with him, and I wondered if perhaps this was a reaction to sensory information that had deeply impacted Joseph but gone unnoticed by others in the room. This does not appear to be a conscious decision, which would suggest a need to explore what processes might be taking place within the brain.

Neurobiological research into the autistic brain is not yet consistent or conclusive in explaining autistic features. A large field of research has concentrated on a link between autistic symptoms and injury to the cerebellum area of the brain (Pierce & Courchesne, 2001). Cozolino explains that in addition to its responsibility for social and emotional functioning, the cerebellum plays an important role in maintaining balance and equilibrium (2006, p. 356). When considering the specific area of interest for this project, if there is damage to this area of the brain the individual could experience difficulties in maintaining their sense of balance and equilibrium when faced with stress. This is supported by studies on mice using eyeblink conditioning, in which mice with cerebellar mutations receive multiple sensory information at once in the form of a flash of light and a puff of air, revealing that those with cerebellar mutations show an adverse reaction to the sensory information coming from multiple channels (Wang et al., 2014).

Furthermore, Cozolino hypothesises that "[T]he rhythmic self-stimulation and need for predictability seen in autism could provide an internal substitute for an absent or chaotic internal regulation of sensory input, timing and interpersonal navigation" (2006, pp. 357–358). This demonstrates that behavioural traits such as rocking are effective for the autistic child in replacing the regulation that the cerebellum would usually provide. Bick (1968) suggests that non-stop movement holds the body self together. Goodman and Scott claim that there is not yet a theory that accounts "satisfactorily for the repetitive and stereotypical behaviours seen in autism" (2012, p. 53). However, if these behaviours are seen as a protective strategy to maintain equilibrium in an unstable world, I consider that they are indeed satisfactorily explained by cerebellar studies.

Dr Temple Grandin has a different view regarding her own autistic condition, claiming, "I have always felt that my senses were more like those of an animal. Does my brain have deeper access to the ancient anti-predator circuits that humans share with animals?" (Grandin, 2000,

p. 12). Perhaps there is some connection to the original reptilian brain that has developed differently for those who have autism, but I have not yet found any scientific research to support this hypothesis. Because there is a lack of a conclusive framework for understanding autism it is sensible to keep abreast of neuroscientific and neurobiological research, to be open to new developments.

It is common for autism to be co-morbid with other mental health disorders; particularly anxiety (Moat, 2013, p. 101). For many autistic children experiencing anxiety their adverse reaction to sensory information may be connected to anxiety rather than the autistic condition. I have noted how Joseph displayed anxious thoughts about the approach of the refuse lorries and his reaction certainly shared some features with anxiety, such as high arousal. Alternatively, attention deficit hyperactivity disorder (ADHD) impacts an individual's ability to pay attention; this, as I have discussed in detail above, is displayed by autistic children when they find themselves overloaded by sensory information.

This is a difficult question, since many individuals with autism also share symptoms of anxiety or ADHD and it is not easy to separate out which symptoms may belong to which disorder. Perhaps it is not always necessary to separate symptoms this way, unless a course of medication is under consideration, which may be the case for a child whose symptoms of anxiety or ADHD are impairing his functioning or attention on a daily basis over a long period of time. However, for those who have a diagnosis of autism, I believe that difficulties with processing sensory information would be present, whether a co-morbid disorder was in existence or not. While there are a number of hypotheses about why or how the autistic child may at times experience sensory overload, the fact that it is present in many autistic children is not contested. I believe that in cases where a condition such as anxiety is co-morbid with the autism, the reaction could be exacerbated by the anxiety, rather than caused by it. It is extremely important to remember that if a child is simultaneously experiencing both autism and ADHD symptoms, each may be heightening the other causing the child to be acutely distressed.

As previously mentioned, the way in which the autistic child processes sensory information can impact early development and the forming of social relationships. It is therefore essential to consider how we support such children. Richard Bromfield describes the need to keep the therapeutic environment as similar as possible from week to week and to eliminate excess noise, smells, and bright lights, and the therapist could try to wear colours and clothing that are not too overstimulating to the child wherever possible, as "the definition of safety includes protection from sensory assault and discomfort" (Bromfield, 2010, p. 30).

For the therapist, it is important to keep in mind that the autistic child may be experiencing their dialogue differently from how she does. What may seem to the therapist a straightforward question may become tangled along with other information, multiplying as it arrives with a confusing mass of noise, light, sound. The child may not be deliberately avoiding a question; he may not be able to hear or process it. Patience, understanding, and tolerance are required for the child who may at first appear to be refusing to enter into dialogue, when the reality for him may be something altogether different.

Experiencing anxiety and panic attacks in adolescence, Temple Grandin values "deep touch pressure" and invented the "squeeze machine"[1] to give her the experience of a deep hug, recalling that "As a child, I craved to feel the comfort of being held, but would pull away when people hugged me" (Grandin, 1992).

I was inspired by Grandin's description of her need to feel safely held and the concept that some form of deep touch pressure may feel helpful to Joseph at times when he felt overwhelmed. Joseph had some challenges with proprioception; however, the distress that he communicated at times of being overwhelmed seemed to reach beyond this; it was as if his whole body were in pain. Whilst it was not practical for me to replicate a squeeze machine within the school environment, I needed to think carefully about how to calm Joseph at the times when he was experiencing a hypersensitive reaction, given that I understood that physical contact with another person may actually be more distressing for him. As an alternative, I brought a large weighted scarf to use in my therapy room, to allow Joseph to experience a feeling of being held

---

[1] Grandin's machine was designed in a long "V" shape, allowing an individual to lie down on their front, using hand-held controls to adjust the pressure of sensory pads that could deliver deep touch pressure stimulation along both sides of their body. Her intention was to allow the user to feel surrounded and embraced in an environment that felt safe, always retaining control of the level of pressure applied by the machine.

without actually being held. It seemed that lying with the scarf around his shoulders was in itself a sensory experience. I noticed how his speech became less rapid and he brought his hands to his face less frequently, seeming more relaxed under the pressure of the scarf.

I was interested in what may have been causing Joseph's mind and body to apparently settle under the weight of the scarf and found that there has been considerable research to support the benefits of weighted blankets and scarfs (Champagne et al., 2015). Researchers at Harvard University have noted the connection between affective touch and the limbic system, in which emotion is processed (Kuehn, 2016). They identify the importance of predictable, consistent touch, rather than a sudden gust of wind, for example, which may startle an autistic individual. Research into the effects of massage therapy reported an decrease in cortisol and an increase in levels of dopamine and serotonin (Field et al., 2005), and it has been suggested that deep touch pressure can dampen "fight or flight" messages arising from the sympathetic nervous system and to calm and increase activity in the parasympathetic nervous system (Edelson et al., 1999), encouraging the social engagement system online, allowing for greater capacity to communicate with others in an open and engaged manner (Porges, 2011). I believe that this research helped me to respond to Joseph with containment and attunement to his needs, rather than to exacerbate his distress by attempting any form of physical contact or adding my voice to the deafening noise that he was already experiencing.

It is possible that cognitive behavioural therapy (CBT), commonly used in treating anxiety, may be of benefit to autistic children who find that sensory overload is a common occurrence and a perpetual source of anxiety or distress (Moat, 2013). Similarly, eye movement desensitisation and reprocessing (EMDR) may be beneficial to autistic children who are "frequently traumatised by the daily living experiences" (Morris-Smith, 2007, p. 1). Whilst it may not be practical for one therapist to specialise in all areas, it would be beneficial to be aware of the principles behind each of these therapies to enhance the support that may be available to the client and to understand when it may be appropriate to refer the client for specialist treatment in this area.

I have found the writing of O'Neill (1999) illuminating in turning the experience of the autistic child on its head, allowing an appreciation for those who have the unique ability to use their senses so masterfully.

For every experience that may be overwhelming or distressing, there may be another that is beautifully vivid, allowing the child access to a world of deeply felt illumination. I felt it was important to recognise and nurture Joseph's capacity to feel in such glorious technicolour as well as to support him at times when the environment became too much for his senses to bear.

In summary, I have explored a number of theories about the experience of autistic children in relation to sensory information, considering research and ideas posed by theorists and neurologists over recent decades. From the psychoanalytic early ideas of Tustin through the fragmentation of Frith's "weak central coherence theory", I have shown how an inability to process sensory information may impact development and relationships, and I have explored neuroscientific research to consider how the autistic brain may function differently to the non-autistic brain in relation to sensory information.

I have found that the various theories that I have explored do not necessarily contradict one another; in fact I find it helpful to imagine that all may be true to some extent, and that I could see them as a variety of ideas that I have at my disposal when getting to know each individual autistic child that I work with. What may be true for one may not be so for another, and this allows for flexibility in my clinical work.

Returning to Joseph, I understood that he would likely live with sensory hypersensitivity for the foreseeable future. I felt it was important to support him to find a language to express his experience, for himself, to me and to his friends, family, and teachers. As I continued my efforts to establish a sense of felt safety within the room as outlined above, I noticed that over time, as our work together continued, he began to show more interest in exploring the art materials within my therapy room. Joseph frequently drew images of a boy within a cave, which felt reminiscent of my understanding of Tustin's protective shell (1990). Joseph's image allowed an opportunity for me to introduce a dialogue with him in the metaphor about the boy in the cave and what it was like to be him. Whilst I could not truly know how it felt to be Joseph, I believe that the effort and consideration I put into understanding what he may be experiencing was important for us both. We were able to develop a shared language for the difficult times when the world impinged upon his senses in the hope that Joseph felt understood, safe, and supported, able to bring his whole self to the therapy room. Through working with Joseph, I have learned of the value of remaining available and consistent in myself. Bromfield observes, "What they've let me know is that what they do want and expect is my constant effort to be there for them … it means therapeutically to never give up on getting to know them and to never give up on them" (2010, p. 174). I intend that to be a guiding principle for myself in the future.

References

Asperger, H. (1944). Autistic psychopathy in childhood. In: U. Frith (Ed.), *Autism and Asperger Syndrome* (pp. 37–92). Cambridge: Cambridge University Press, 1991. Originally published as "Die 'Autistischen Psychopathen' im Kindesalter", *Archiv für Psychiatrie und Nervenkrankenheiten, 117* (1944): 76–136.

Baron-Cohen, S. (1995). *Mindblindness*. Cambridge, MA: MIT Press.

Bick, E. (1968). The experience of skin in early object relations. *International Journal of Psychoanalysis, 49*(2–3): 484–486.

Bogdashina, O. (2003). *Sensory Perceptual Issues in Autism and Asperger Syndrome: Different Sensory Experiences—Different Perceptual Worlds*. London: Jessica Kingsley.

Bogdashina, O. (2011). Sensory perceptual issues in autism: why we should listen to those who experience them. *Annales Universitatis Paedagogicae Cracoviensis, Studia IV*: 146–157.

Bromfield, R. (2010). *Doing Therapy with Children and Adolescents with Asperger's Syndrome*. Hoboken, NJ: John Wiley & Sons.

Champagne, T., Mullen, B., Dickson, D., & Krishnamurty, S. (2015). Evaluating the safety and effectiveness of the weighted blanket with adults during an inpatient mental health hospitalization. *Occupational Therapy in Mental Health, 31*(3): 211–233.

Cozolino, L. (2006). *The Neuroscience of Human Relationships*. New York: W. W. Norton, 2014.

Edelson, S. M., Edelson, M. G., Kerr, D. C. R., & Grandin, T. (1999). Behavioral and physiological effects of deep pressure on children with autism: A pilot study evaluating the efficacy of Grandin's Hug Machine. *American Journal of Occupational Therapy, 53*(2): 145–152.

Field, T., Hernandez-Reif, M., Diego, M., Schanberg, S., & Kuhn, C. (2005). Cortisol decreases and serotonin and dopamine increase following massage therapy. *International Journal of Neuroscience*, *115*(10): 1397–1413.

Frith, U. (1989). *Autism: Explaining the Enigma*. Oxford: Blackwell.

Frith, U., & Happé, F. (1994). Autism: beyond "theory of mind". *Cognition*, *50*(1–3): 115–132.

Frith, U., & Happé, F. (2005). Autism spectrum disorder. *Current Biology*, *15*(19): R786–R790.

Goodman, R., & Scott, S. (2012). *Child and Adolescent Psychiatry*. Chichester, UK: Wiley-Blackwell.

Grandin, T. (1992). Calming effects of deep touch pressure in patients with autistic disorder, college students and animals. *Journal of Child and Adolescent Psychopharmacology*, *2*(1).

Grandin, T. (2000). My mind is a web browser: how people with autism think. *Cerebrum*, Winter, *2*(1): 14–22.

Kanner, L. (1944). Early infantile autism. *Journal of Pediatrics*, *25*: 211–217.

Knickmeyer, R., Baron-Cohen, S., Raggatt, P., & Taylor, K. (2005). Foetal testosterone, social relationships, and restricted interests in children. *Journal of Child Psychology and Psychiatry*, *46*(2): 198–210.

Kuehn, E. (2016). Research into our sense of touch leads to new treatments for autism. [Blog.] https://sitn.hms.harvard.edu/flash/2016/research-into-our-sense-of-touch-leads-to-new-treatments-for-autism/ (last accessed April 24, 2017).

Moat, D. (2013). *Integrative Psychotherapeutic Approaches to Autism Spectrum Conditions*. London: Jessica Kingsley.

Morris-Smith, J. (2007). What can we learn from using EMDR with children on the autistic spectrum? Presentation at the 8th EMDR Europe Association Conference, Paris, France.

O'Neill, J. L. (1999). *Through the Eyes of Aliens*. London: Jessica Kingsley.

Piaget, J. (1983). *Piaget's Theory*. In: P. Mussen (Ed), *Handbook of Child Psychology. Vol. 1*. 4th edn. New York: John Wiley.

Pierce, K., & Courchesne, E. (2001). Evidence for a cerebellar role in reduced exploration and stereotyped behavior in autism. *Biological Psychiatry*, *49*(8): 655–664.

Porges, S. W. (2011). *The Polyvagal Theory: Neurophysiological Foundations of Emotions, Attachment, Communication, and Self-regulation*. New York: W. W. Norton.

Rutter, M., Bishop, D., Pine, D., & Scott, S. (2010). *Rutter's Child and Adolescent Psychiatry, 5th Edition*. Hoboken, NJ: John Wiley.

Tustin, F. (1990). *The Protective Shell in Children and Adults*. London: Karnac.

Wang, S. S. H., Kloth, A. D., & Badura, A. (2014). The cerebellum, sensitive periods, and autism. *Neuron*, *83*(3): 518–532.

World Health Organization (1992). *The ICD-10 Classification of Mental and Behavioural Disorders*. Geneva: WHO.

CHAPTER 6

"Finding Dory": a story of an eight-year-old's journey from loss to hope and strength

Celine Allder

This chapter was originally a "live" case presentation delivered to a group of trainee child psychotherapists. The figures are the slides from the presentation which served to illustrate and accompany it.

Exploration

- The client & initial thoughts
- Part one—early phase

    "Windows"—Skin, Defences, Boundaries, Containing
- Part two—developing

    "Windows and Doors"—False Self and Fears
- Part three—communicating
- Part four—the wider circle
- Reflections, conclusion and framework

Figure 6.1 Exploration

The client

The Client

Referral
Parent meeting
Observation
Length of work

Figure 6.2 The client

Dee, an eight-year-old girl, was referred to me for weekly psychotherapy by her school in London. Her mother had approached the school for help as Dee could become anxious about her mother, who was disabled with ongoing health challenges which resulted in her being hospitalised at times. In addition, the school raised a query in the referral around Dee and the possibility of her somatising her anxieties as she had regular time off from school for health reasons. I sensed, however, that the school was somewhat ambivalent around this and not overly concerned.

In my initial meeting with Dee's mother, I gained a fuller picture of the history. Throughout her pregnancy, Dee's mother was taking care of her partner who had a terminal illness. Dee was then born prematurely and needed incubation for the first few days. Her father died when she was just a few months old.

I began to get a sense of Dee as I heard from her mother that Dee preferred structure and liked to conform at school, for example, she must wear the right school uniform. She did not like upsetting people and could be very sensitive. Dee would try to be in charge at home and she could get very "wound up", often taking herself off on her own to calm down. She once kicked a big hole in a wall at home. She sometimes got "really stroppy" with her mother but could also be clingy and want to be in the same room as her, especially at night. Dee had eczema, mild asthma, and hypermobility in her joints, although this was improving as she had injuries less often. She also wet the bed at night but had been prescribed tablets that were helping to prevent this from happening as much.

Dee's mother was disabled, and described Dee as her "young carer" although she was not officially recognised as such. Dee, I was told, worried about her mother and liked to take care of her. In this initial parent meeting, my countertransference was that of wanting to take care of mother and to nurture her.

When I observed Dee in class she was quiet, softly spoken, very compliant, and was described as "such a lovely girl" by her teacher. I held all these perceptions, from both mother and school, as well as my own thoughts from what had been shared and what I had observed, as I began the work with her.

Initial thoughts

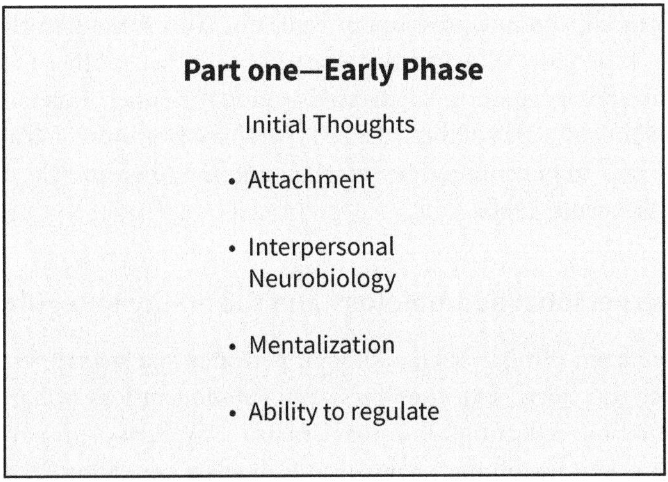

Part one—Early Phase

Initial Thoughts

- Attachment

- Interpersonal
  Neurobiology

- Mentalization

- Ability to regulate

Figure 6.3 Early phase, slide 1

Thinking about somatisation, I found a paper on fabricated or induced illness before starting the work. This paper stood out for me as it cited a mother's sense of abandonment alongside her need for a relationship (with a doctor) that provides care and support as a major factor in the aetiology (Schreier, 1992). It resonated with the history and I found myself wondering about the abandonment through the partner dying, and if Dee sometimes felt a need to identify with her mother's grief, and that Dee had a need to be cared for and supported herself.

Attachment

From what her mother shared about her being clingy, but also being angry with her and fluctuating between the two, I held in mind that Dee might have an insecure anxious/ambivalent attachment. I found during the initial sessions in the room that she would draw me in but then would keep me at a distance, which made me curious about what her attachment style might have been.

I wondered about how Dee might take care of her mother at home. The idea of compulsive caregiving and/or compliant attachment behaviours, as described by Crittenden (2016, p. 40), stood out, where a child might inhibit negative affect, use "false-positive affect", or employ caregiving tactics in order to bring a parent closer, particularly if the parent has a preoccupation, depression, or is distant. This seemed to ring true with the experiences she had had in early life, as her mother may have been quite preoccupied and distressed around the father. This reminded me of Winnicott's idea of the "false self": perhaps Dee presented a happy, positive face to her mother, her teacher, and me to ensure she kept us close (Winnicott, 1960).

Interpersonal neurobiology and the ability to regulate

They had been through such a difficult period in the last trimester and after Dee was born, with the illness and subsequent loss of her father, that it had me reflecting upon that crucial early period. In particular, how important the mother–baby dyad is in affect regulation, in attuned interactions using the voice, face, touch, to soothe or to share joy, and the intersubjectivity needed to grow and develop (Fonagy et al., 2002; Stern, 1985).

Furthermore, I thought about how Dee's developing mentalization might have been impacted via these shared experiences. Had Dee had help to grow a sense of agency and subjective self? Had she had help through affect mirroring and regulation to understand the *meaning* of her feelings, as reflected back by her mother (Fonagy, 2002)?

I was curious around her mother's capacity to be present during these much-needed early developmental stages with baby Dee, while preoccupied with nursing Dee's father and then facing the loss of him when Dee was so small. How much time would she have had, to just be with her daughter, to make lovely eye contact, to share affect, and in particular, joy? I doubt whether she was feeling anything near joyful. Perhaps she might have felt unable to soothe Dee if she felt overwhelmed herself. Dee's early birth may also have been linked to the mother's higher levels of stress which in addition may have impacted the mother's ability to interact with her (Music, 2011, p. 37).

I held all this in mind as we began our sessions and reflected on how integrated Dee might be; how much her prefrontal cortex could help her regulate and soothe, and whether her brain had integrated enough to create a "balanced and coordinated nervous system" (Siegel, 2012, p. 3-3).

Part one—the early phase

"Windows"—skin, defences, boundaries, containing

Early Phase

"Windows"—Skin, Defences, Boundaries, Containing

- "Finding Dory"
- Crab, turtle, leopard— the drawer
- Skin. Stickers. Boundary.

The mother *"as containing object is experienced concretely as skin" (Bick, 1968)*

Figure 6.4 Early phase, slide 2

The early sessions were marked by "objects". We made a contract for our work together in the sand tray and she chose a "Finding Dory" character for herself and a crab, turtle, and leopard for her mother, me, and the teacher. The characters used in this initial sand tray weaved in and out of the sessions to come. These characters had to be "protected" each week before leaving the session and she would put them in her drawer (a secure place just for her, where her artworks and objects could be kept in a locked cupboard in the therapy room). It became part of our closing ritual at the end of each session for her to choose what to place there.

In these sessions I began to notice how the characters would either have hard shells (the crab and the turtle) or if not (the leopard and "Finding Dory") would be covered with stickers. Knowing that she could suffer from eczema I began to wonder about the significance of the skin, and with my supervisor's guidance I explored more around the skin as a boundary, containing the self or acting as/representing her defences.

From reading Esther Bick's 1968 paper on skin, and how an infant has "The need for a containing object … in the infantile unintegrated state … a light, a voice, a smell, or other sensual object", I began reflecting on whether there might be a connection between her early infancy experiences and her eczema and hypermobility. Bick (1968) proposes the containment a mother provides as being felt concretely as skin by the infant; providing an experience of boundary, or being held together by this live layer that separates one from the world. Any mishaps in this developmental phase of being contained can create a sense of feeling unintegrated, which can manifest as needing to develop one's own "partial" or "muscular shell", often seen as a rigid posture, like a holding of the body together, or skin problems. I wondered if her eczema reflected this. I also wondered if the looseness of her joints was connected to the difficulty of holding herself together as an unintegrated infant (Bick, 1968). If the early phase of her life may not have been the experience of a mother able to properly contain Dee's infantile feelings, projections, and aggressions due to the circumstances and events in their lives, had she developed her own shell and adaptations to help her contain them?

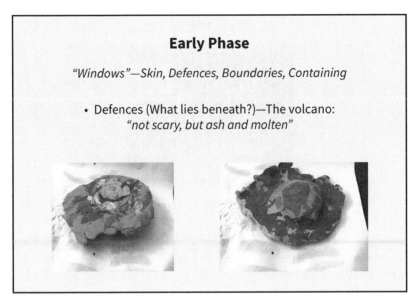

Figure 6.5 Early phase, slide 3

We used playdough and clay and Dee made a volcano over two weeks, spending much time on the inside and filling it with paint. It was not a "scary volcano but is just ash and molten", she told me. This gave me more glimpses into what may be happening in her inner world, although at this stage she was not ready, despite some attempts, to explore this further. In Greek the word eczema means "to boil" and Maguire (2004, p. 58) describes eczema as "an increase in psychic tension", which really did reflect what I was starting to feel in the room. The following quote from Winnicott (1958, p. 265) also resonated with me about the possible lack of early experiences with the mother, "[L]ove is … impulse, gesture, contact, relationship and it affords the infant the satisfaction of self-expression and release from instinct tension."

In the room Dee was braced and sometimes I found myself tensing my body. She often treated the room and me as if she had to take care of us, partly by knowing what she wanted to do and taking charge. Perhaps she was treating me as she did her mother, and I did my best to let her be in charge in these early sessions as we began to build a relationship; beginning I hoped, to move into transferential work, and treating me as she might treat her mother.

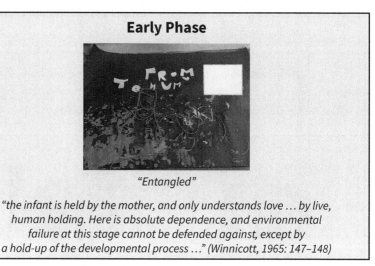

Figure 6.6 Early phase, slide 4

When Dee made this picture (in Figure 6.6) during session seven, which I came to think of as an entanglement, it seemed to be a moment of insight. It really connected me with Winnicott (1965) and the early period of "primary maternal preoccupation", and the importance of the "holding environment".

"The infant is held by the mother, and only understands love ... by live, human holding. Here is absolute dependence, and environmental failure at this stage cannot be defended against, except by a hold-up of the developmental process" (Winnicott, 1965, pp. 147–148).

There was something of this appearing in the use of the wires that Dee painstakingly took time to entwine and to stand up three-dimensionally before covering in paint. She also spent much time looking in all the corners of the cupboards and despite there being many other crafting materials in the drawers, she took a sponge from the very bottom of the cupboard where the cleaning materials were kept and wanted to make the letters from this. I reflected on how a sponge soaks up all that it comes into contact with, how what is around it becomes a part of it. As she made this she described how they were "joined together", and it really made me curious about her boundaries with her mother. I wondered whether Dee and her mother were bound together, not separated into "me and not me" or "I am" which Winnicott (1965) describes as a necessary part of the maturational process into becoming separate from the mother.

I found myself wondering whether Dee had the experience of moving into her own individual self, developing her ego strength via a good containing early experience, one where her mother has survived the attacks made on her. I further wondered if Dee had developed a "capacity to use an object … something that depends on a facilitating environment" (Winnicott, 1971, pp. 119–120). Or had there been difficulties due to the early birth, traumatic events, and difficult experiences?

Dee often found it hard to leave at the end of sessions and even with a routine of letting her know we were getting nearer the end, it frequently took some effort for her to go as she would want to do something else, or "just finish this off". Perhaps a reflection of her ambivalent attachment, a clinginess, but reminding me also of the idea of "adhesion", a need to "stick" to something (Bick, 1968) in lieu of having a sense of being contained internally.

Part two—developing phase

"Windows and doors"—false self and fears

Part two—Developing Phase

"Windows and Doors"—False Self and Fears

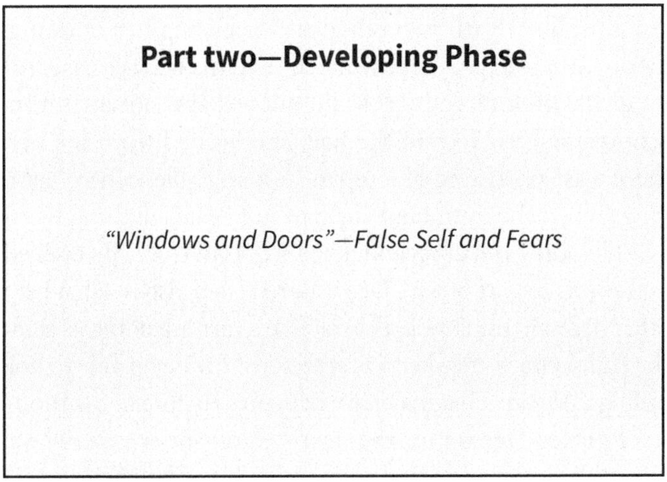

Figure 6.7 Developing phase, slide 1

One of Dee's favourite games in the room was "Guess Who?" She would often select who she wanted to be from the cards available, rather than shuffle and choose at random. Often the same two or three women were chosen who might have resembled her mother. I was reminded of the object she sometimes used for herself in the sand tray, "Finding Dory", and I held in mind how perhaps she might have needed to be found. This may not have happened if the mother's mind was preoccupied during those early years, a holding environment that perhaps was not quite "good enough" in Winnicottian terms.

In the seventh session I found I needed to repair something that I had done. I had been told at the initial parent meeting of a surprise upcoming holiday and was asked by Dee's mother to keep it secret from her. It was not an ideal situation. When Dee came to the session after the holiday, she said, "You knew, didn't you?" and even though she said it was "fine", when I explored it more with her I felt there had been a rupture in the trust we were hopefully starting to build in the room. When at the end of this session she had been setting up the dolls' house, she made everything crash down onto the floor and shut the house up, before leaving. I knew repair was needed and that perhaps she was starting to treat me transferentially and I really needed to survive this.

That same day, after this session, we saw each other in the hall at lunchtime and she was visibly wobbly. I stopped to ask why, not feeling I could walk past and ignore her distress, and she started to cry. There had been a problem with two other girls accusing her of doing something "wrong" and she was very worried that this was the case. Although I did not deal with it directly, as it did not feel appropriate for me to do so, I accompanied her to find the help she needed from the person on duty. There was something of a repair in being able to help her contain her feelings when she found out she had not done anything wrong.

The visible worry and upset about not being good or right opened a door for me to see this as part of who Dee was, reflected also in what her teacher and mother had said initially. It also felt like a turning point, as standing by her in the hall perhaps gave her a first sense of my being able to hold some of her feelings, despite what may have happened before in the room.

When I picked Dee up for the next session she was really quiet and pale, and I felt a real sadness as we walked up the corridor. This was not unusual for me to feel when I collected her, but this week she didn't mask it with a smile on her face. I was beginning to see and feel what was hiding underneath the "false self" smile. As we entered the therapy room she started to say how she had a painful tooth, and we started to explore, using dolls, about doctors and dentists and how much her mother had to go to the doctor. She then told me her mother had a really important hospital appointment that day.

I felt a little sick and was quiet. I explored what might be going on as she was so quiet and she said she had been feeling sick. She then vomited twice. Following school policy on sickness, I let her teacher know, who arranged for her mother to be called to collect her. While we waited for her mother to arrive, I suggested Dee could curl up on the little sofa in the therapy room and I helped her get settled comfortably with a cushion and blanket. I found myself feeling like a mother tucking a baby up for a sleep and I felt Dee's defences soften much more in the room than they had before. It felt such an important part of the developmental process for her, despite her having been sick, to feel held and contained in the room, on this little sofa with me nearby, much like a little baby might be held and contained in a mother's arms. Although we didn't get around to thinking directly about what had happened in the hall the previous week, I wondered if the experience had helped her feel that I was an advocate. I suggested I read her a story while we waited and she chose a Mog book, all about Mog dying. It was really quite sad and we sat there together with the sadness, quietly.

When her mother arrived at school I walked Dee to reception to meet her. As we approached her, her mother collapsed into me for a hug, taking me off guard as I was not expecting this physical contact. It was as if her mother needed propping up. I felt an overwhelming "Oh poor mother, I need to support her, to take care of her." Yet, here was Dee feeling sick and her mother was the one who needed holding. As they left I wondered if this was often how it was for Dee, with her mother getting the hugs and holding, when Dee was the one who also really needed it in that moment. As I explored this with my supervisor, I was reminded of how Dee's needs were eclipsed by those of her mother, but I was also helped to understand that Dee might have been supported through the support I gave her mother.

"If, however, the environmental pressure is greater or less than the pressure within the bubble, then it is not the bubble that is important but the environment. The bubble adapts to the outside pressure" (Winnicott, 1949, pp. 174–193).

Looking back, I may have got caught up in a projective identification as in the moment it happened it was really quite powerful. I also wondered if Dee being sick was too much for her mother to manage: perhaps it was difficult for the mother to feel someone else might be sick, after caring for her dying partner.

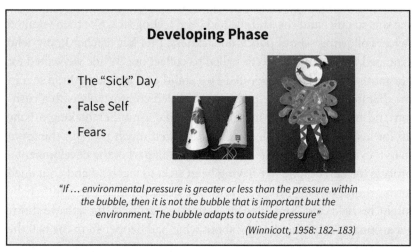

Figure 6.8 Developing phase, slide 2

After the "sick day" there was a shift in the work. I found some little card-people to paint, and invited Dee to paint them herself. The dots and spots on her body were still there, and the smile that seemed to be false, as she began to reveal how worried she was about her mother and her health. She did not seem upset, but I found myself sad, wobbly, and scared, and reflected this back to her. Again, my countertransference was really helpful.

In a later session, Dee came in feeling very low and sad and she began to talk of her fear about her mother getting a new nebuliser that day and how these devices really scared her: "They are really noisy and she can't talk when she uses it." It felt that she was starting to be able to name some of what might be going on inside her, so I suggested we make our own nebulisers and see what we could do in the room with them. We had some fun seeing if we could speak and testing out what we could do with them.

Over the next few weeks, this session opened the door a little more to her fears about her mother and her health challenges. Dee then asked, "What will happen to me if Mummy is not here? I have no one." It helped to bring the death of her father into the room, and we imagined "what a daddy might do". I asked her how she imagined what a day with Daddy might be like. As she began her story, she said it would be like "someone to cuddle you at the beginning of the day, and someone who will be really interested in you and what you are doing. Someone who chats to you and listens." We spent the rest of the session practising what it was like to chat, to listen, and to be interested. I reflected how sad it was that she didn't have a father to do all these things with her. I felt really quite sad after this session.

As Dee began to access some of her "core feelings" (Sunderland, 2015, p. 168) around feeling anxious or afraid, it was hard, and she often needed to have a break to do something else before I then tried to come back to it. Her "window of tolerance" (Siegal, 1999) was clear to me and we played with other things in the room during the much-needed breaks from the deeper work. These breaks would often be to play on the keyboard, where we would make tunes and silly songs, sometimes loudly and joyfully. There was one session where, using the sand tray, she opened a door to a time when she was bullied. This had the feel of something dark, angry, and powerful, but then she shut the door tightly again and I needed to respect her window of tolerance, with her not wanting to explore more at this time. I held it in mind should an opportunity arise to return to it in later sessions.

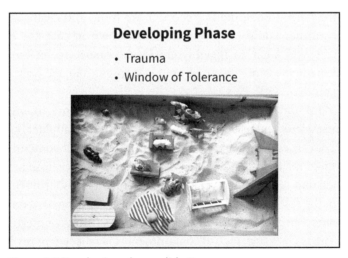

Figure 6.9 Developing phase, slide 3

Part three—communicating

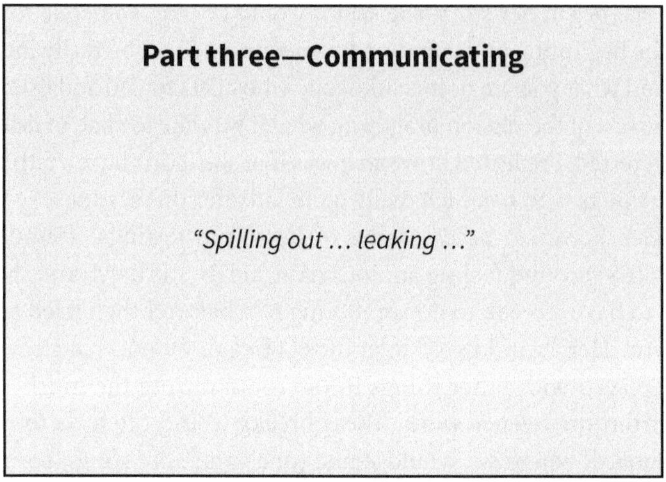

Figure 6.10 Communicating, slide 1

Dee's mother came to meet me for the termly check-in. She brought a letter that Dee wrote for the tribunal her mother was attending later in the week, disputing her disability payments. In it, Dee had listed all the things she did for her mother, from washing her hair when she was in the bath, to helping her shop, make food, and clean, and also that her mother could never go out on her own in case she did not feel well. It was such an insight into Dee's perspective of her home life, and made me more aware of how Dee might manage both herself and her mother.

The same day, the deputy head unexpectedly came to my room between sessions and asked about both mother and daughter, and said she felt concerned for them. I found myself leaking out something that Dee had told me in her session that day. After the deputy head left, I was concerned that I had not maintained confidentiality by sharing information from the session. My supervisor helped me to not be hard on myself for this and I began to connect more deeply with my countertransference. Perhaps Dee's own lack of containment was reflected in my leaking out information from our session. It may even have been related to her bed-wetting at night.

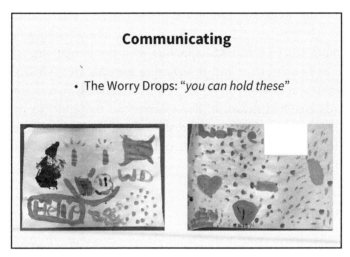

Figure 6.11 Communicating, slide 2

A breakthrough session followed this when I began to share with Dee how much I knew she did at home, and that her mother had shown me the letter (she had asked her mother to bring it in) and we explored painting something around this. She painted "The Worry Drops" and said, "You can hold these." The next week she made the "help" picture and I noticed there was still a smiling face on it, possibly masking her fear and anxiety. I felt she was also letting me know the value of the therapy and how it was supporting her.

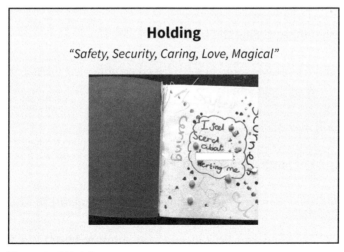

Figure 6.12 Holding

The following week she brought her journal and was able to show me, through drawing, what had happened in the week and how she felt. A quite scary event had happened with her neighbour, who had been verbally aggressive and threatening towards Dee when she was in her garden at home. The police had been called by her mother and afterwards Dee had drawn in her journal and brought this in to the session to show me. The picture really helped the feelings to be contained, in the drawing, in the room, opening a door to talk about keeping feelings inside.

Session eighteen

Therapist: I think you were really brave to come in today and say how you were feeling, because I know sometimes you keep it in.

Dee: I do.

Therapist: And I know it's sometimes hard to say you are worried.

Dee: I like keeping stuff in.

Therapist: You do, don't you.

Dee: But I cannot lie, I get really bad stomach aches!

Therapist: Do you?

[Dee pours glitter in her hair from the little tubes she is using in the picture]

Therapist: Oh wow! Sparkles in your hair.

Dee: Do you want some?

Therapist: Yes please, some blue! [Dee pours glitter on therapist's head] Shall I put some on you?

[Dee hands over the pink]

Therapist: I'm putting magic sparkles on you.

[Pause for some moments as Dee draws in her diary again]

Therapist: So when you lie you said your tummy hurts ... I wonder when you hold all those feelings in, does it sit somewhere in your body?

[*Dee points to head, tummy, heart*]

Therapist: In your head, tummy, heart. That kind of area?

   C: [*quietly*] Yeah.

Therapist: And what is it like when you share those feelings and not keep them in?

  Dee: Happy! [*Dee goes back to the picture and blows glitter by accident and gets it in her face and she really laughs*]

Then began a phase where we used more of the room, using more space with our bodies taking up much more space. She had more agency, and felt more confident to move, "to run, even up the stairs!" she said, whereas before her hypermobility prevented her from any strenuous physical activity. Through drama and role play, we enacted her beginning and end of day, her waking up and sleep routines, as if giving a solid structure to herself and her day.

Part four—the wider circle

Part four—The Wider Circle

Parent, school, systems

- school and parent
- police—housing
- bereavement counselling

Figure 6.13 The wider circle

Communicating with Dee's mother was as crucially important as it was to communicate with her teachers and other school staff. We held "team around the family" meetings at regular intervals. During these meetings at school, I discussed how I felt Dee's mother could benefit from some therapeutic support herself and suggested we contact a local bereavement counselling charity to see if they could offer her sessions. We also explored the support Dee might be able to receive as a carer for her mother and referred the family for support from a local family organisation.

I worked with Dee to identify other adults in the school she felt able to go to if she was worried or needed to talk to someone, when I was not there. When there had been the difficult situation around home with the neighbour, the police were involved and Dee had found this reassuring.

It felt important to engage the wider community in supporting this family to become part of the containment. This allowed for Dee to feel more supported and enabled her to feel freer in expressing herself and more able to seek support.

Reflections and conclusion

Reflections and Conclusion

- in hindsight—"the sick day"

- missed moments—anger?

- positive transference/internal object—idealised?
  "this is my happy space"

- supervision—did not appear often

- just beginning—containing, integrating

- boundaries

Figure 6.14 Reflections and conclusion

At the beginning of therapy it was quite easy to work with Dee; she was in charge of what she wanted to do, led the sessions, and took care of me, the room, and even the work itself. Creating a holding environment was a key part of the work but I was also aware, as we developed a containing space, that I had to make sure I didn't collude with her defences. At the same time I needed to be very sensitive as to how much she could manage, making sure we had fun and joy in between the deeper explorations of the work.

Themes around anger were mostly explored in the sand tray, but sometimes I felt I missed moments to explore her anger further. There were also glimpses of the negative transference in the room, but she did like to keep sessions as her "happy space" as she described recently. Was I an idealised object I wonder? It felt important to be able to work in the negative transference, but perhaps giving Dee an experience of a joyful, playful relationship was equally important as her day-to-day experiences were so often burdensome.

In hindsight, the sick day really was an interesting day, with many layers. In supervision we explored what I could have done differently to manage both mother and daughter. What might I have been able to say in the moment to Dee or to her mother? Also, what might it be showing psychologically, that she couldn't digest too much? Or perhaps this needed containing? Yet, as Dee came to trust the space, to trust that I could hold and contain her feelings, even her "sick" perhaps, she began to explore, with me alongside her, her inner world of feelings and her sense of self and place in the world.

The artworks used in the room, the early characters needing an extra skin of spots, stickers, or a hard shell reflected her need for containment, her need to develop her own boundary and sense of self. The later parts of our work, the colourful scattering of "Worry Drops" in the sky that Dee felt could be expressed and then held by me, her journal drawings and writing to express her inner world, showed her progress as she developed a stronger sense of self, her trust in the world around her to manage her feelings, without feeling overwhelmed by her inner world. As she became stronger in her joints, more robust, and able to run, it felt this also reflected the way she felt held together—previously her joints were hypermobile, and it was difficult for her to feel she had a strong bodily structure that supported her development.

I was aware that I did not bring Dee, "the quiet one" to supervision as often as I brought other children. I also wondered whether in my countertransference she became a little forgotten about, as perhaps reflected in her being a "caregiver" child, rather than perhaps a "cared for" child. I was also aware how her mother still takes up quite a lot of space in the work. So when deciding on which client to bring for this presentation, I reflected how important it was to use this opportunity to explore my work with Dee within the containment of the assessment group.

In the latest two sessions, I had to remind Dee of boundaries as she wanted to take things out from the room. Bick (1968) talks about firmness and the importance of boundaries in the therapy and I am reminded how Dee left things in the room to start with and now wanted to take them out, reflecting perhaps her boundaries and contained self, no longer needing her objects to be protected or kept hidden in a drawer. Perhaps she also wanted to take something from our relationship to enable her to get out and explore the wider world.

Framework

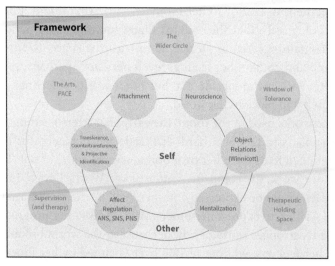

Figure 6.15 Framework

I created this diagram as a way to understand the parts of my integrative practice that, together, give a cohesive structure that holds and contains me in my work with clients. Although I've not referred to the PACE model—playfulness, acceptance, curiosity, and empathy (Hughes et al., 2019)—the model underpins my approach as a therapist and so I have also included it here.

Reflections on the case presentation

Despite this coming at the end of what I felt was the most arduous year of the training, I found I really enjoyed the live aspect of this assessment. Moving away from the constraints of previous written assessments, which I found wholly stressful and seemed to give my critical inner voice a loudspeaker, this live presentation opened up an inner space of movement, of curiosity, that quieted my doubts and instead, opened up the possibility of enjoyable exploration. It was a true privilege to hear of my colleagues' creative work with their clients, their stories of triumph and defeat, and to be able to share my journey with them.

With any client there seems to be a myriad of inner world pathways to explore and sometimes we don't have the time or opportunity to explore as many as we would wish, but rather focus on the ones that seem to rise quickly to the surface and need the most attention. Preparing this case presentation of my work with Dee was a reflection of this process, choosing which pathways to journey along within the setting of the assessment, and what to bring to life from the work. The depth of this reflective process was not unwelcome. It gave me further insights into developing my framework and what it is that sustains me, so that I am able to help clients explore fully their sense of themselves in the world. It really was the beginning of building a strong foundation of who I am in my work as a child psychotherapist. It is not lost on me that Dee's need to find her sense of self was perhaps exactly what was needed for me to grow and integrate as a therapist.

References

Bick, E. (1968). The experience of the skin in early object-relations. *International Journal of Psychoanalysis*, 49: 484–486.

Crittenden, P. M. (2016). *Raising Parents: Attachment, Representation and Treatment*. Abingdon, UK: Routledge.

Fonagy, P., Gergely, G., Jurist, E. J., & Target, M. (2002). *Affect Regulation, Mentalization and the Development of the Self*. New York: Other Press.

Hughes, D. A., Golding, K. S., & Hudson, J. (2019). *Healing Relational Trauma with Attachment-Focused Interventions: Dyadic Developmental Psychotherapy with Children and Families*. New York: W. W. Norton.

Maguire, A. (2004). *Skin Disease: A Message from the Soul: A Treatise from a Jungian Perspective of Psychosomatic Dermatology*. London: Free Association.

Music, G. (2011) *Nurturing Natures: Attachment and Children's Emotional, Sociocultural and Brain Development*. Hove, UK: Psychology Press.

Schreier, H. A. (1992). The perversion of mothering: Munchausen syndrome by proxy. *Bulletin of the Menninger Clinic, 56*(4): 421.

Siegel, D. (1999). *The Developing Mind: Toward a Neurobiology of Interpersonal Experience*. New York: Guilford.

Siegel, D. (2012). *Pocket Guide to Interpersonal Neurobiology: An Integrative Handbook of the Mind*. London: W. W. Norton.

Stern, D. N. (1985). *The Interpersonal World of the Infant: A View from Psychoanalysis and Developmental Psychology*. New York: Basic Books.

Sunderland, M. (2015). *Conversations that Matter: Talking with Children and Teenagers in Ways that Help*. Broadway, UK: Worth.

Winnicott, D. W. (1949). Birth memories, birth trauma, and anxiety. In: *Collected Papers: Through Paediatrics to Psycho-analysis*. London: Tavistock, 1958.

Winnicott, D. W. (1960). Ego distortion in terms of true and false self. In: D. W. Winnicott (Ed.), *The Maturational Processes and the Facilitating Environment: Studies in the Theory of Emotional Development* (pp. 140–152). London: Karnac. 140–152.

Winnicott, D. W. (1965). *The Maturational Processes and the Facilitating Environment: Studies in the Theory of Emotional Development*. Oxford: International Universities Press.

Winnicott, D. W. (1971). *Playing and Reality*. Abingdon, UK: Routledge.

CHAPTER 7

Making sense of the pieces

Adina Belloli

Introduction

My therapeutic framework is flexible and integrative, allowing me to meet my clients' needs creatively and adaptively. The power of such an approach lies in the fact that it combines various psychodynamic theories and views them through an interpersonal lens. Within this I see the therapeutic relationship—one based on the therapist's attuned presence and commitment to open communication—to be key. I aim to find the right therapeutic rhythm for each client; a co-created ebbing and flowing between non-directive and directive, phenomenological and interpretative, which also makes use of the arts, metaphor, and the body.

Several theories are fundamental to informing my theoretical approach. Attachment theory and Bowlby's "internal working model" (IWM) (1969) have given me a greater understanding of the shape of my client's interpersonal and intrapsychic landscape. In the therapy room, I use Hughes's (2006) PACE model (playfulness, acceptance, curiosity, and empathy), which uses right-brain attunement to enable the development of a secure attachment, or the repair of a ruptured one (Hughes, 2011). Object relations theory, including Bion's (1962) concept of "containment" makes me aware of creating an environment where

105

detoxifying hostile projections from the child/client within the mother/therapist's psyche can take place. Klein's (1946) concepts of splitting, denial, and projection also inform my thinking around a child's defences.

I use the arts, image, and metaphor to help facilitate the expression of feelings for which, often, there are no words. I see myself not only as a therapist but also an advocate for the child as I work collaboratively with parents, teachers, and other professionals to address the systemic stresses impacting the client and their family. The Code of Ethics and Professional Conduct of the Institute for Arts in Therapy and Education provides the moral framework for my clinical practice. This is supported by personal therapy and both a psychoanalytic and an integrative supervisor.

Context of referral and presenting issues

Seven-year-old Azra is a British Muslim born to wealthy parents of different Middle Eastern heritages. She has two siblings, Mohammed, aged thirteen, and Parvin, aged eleven. All three children are predominately cared for by a governess. Azra was referred for therapy by her school during a period when her parents were engaged in a difficult divorce. Her teacher was concerned about her aggressive behaviour towards other children, reporting that her writing contained images of blood, violence, and aggression.

At our initial meeting, Azra's mother Nedda disclosed there had been ongoing domestic violence between herself and Azra's father, much of which had been witnessed by the children. Seven months previously she filed for divorce after a particularly violent episode and now lived with the children and a full-time nanny-housekeeper. I found Nedda warm and engaging but noticed her tendency to focus on herself and found myself having to continually bring Azra to her attention. I considered how Azra might feel if there was no space for her in her mother's mind. After this meeting with mother, it was difficult to make any further contact with Azra's parents. Under the guidance of my supervisor, therefore, most of the familial systemic work was conducted with Azra's governess as a substitute attachment figure. I also met weekly with Azra's class teacher.

First impressions

My initial contract with Azra was for weekly sessions of fifty minutes for a minimum of one academic year. In our first session together, I was struck by Azra's dishevelled appearance. Her hair was messy and her uniform was dotted with holes and food stains. I felt a strong maternal transference, leading me to consider Azra's unmet need for a nurturing mother. She immediately sat down at the table. As we spoke, she continuously wriggled her foot under the table. Countertransferentially, I had a feeling of unease; I considered if she was wondering what I already knew about her. Sunderland (2015) describes the importance of informing a child of one's prior knowledge in order to foster trust. I asked Azra if she would like me to share what I knew about her life, and she nodded. As I shared the basic details of her life experiences, I noticed a softening in her body and an increase in eye contact.

I asked if perhaps she felt nervous about coming to see me and again she nodded. I offered my curiosity regarding her experience, simultaneously letting her know that I understood that meeting new people could evoke nervous feelings. She smiled and followed with:

Azra: I didn't go to clubs today because I'm being punished for being naughty to my governess … My mum doesn't even know that I'm sad—angry.

Therapist: I wonder if what I'm hearing is that underneath the anger is sadness and perhaps you feel both of these feelings?

Azra: [*nods*] I'm sad about my parents getting a divorce. I don't even know if it really is a divorce or if they are just separated. It's confusing.

Drawing from Clarkson's (1992) "conflict, confusion, and deficit model" (CCDM), I considered how Azra's confusion might link with not having a reliable adult with whom to check the validity of her beliefs. This potentially led her to use "magical thinking", causing even more confusion and inner conflict (Clarkson, 1992). Perhaps Azra's behaviour indicated an experience of lived deprivation in a home without structure or boundaries. It seemed likely that her mother's distress diverted attention away from Azra's needs.

Initial assessment

Azra came from a wealthy, privileged family, however, developmental trauma can occur in any family as shown by the original and multiply replicated ACE study, the CDC-Kaiser Permanente Adverse Childhood

Experiences (Felitti et al, 1998) which was based on a middle class cohort. Of the ten questions and at the time of the assessment, Azra would have scored for at least two ACEs: her parents' divorce and witnessing violence.

In considering Azra's difficulties through a psychiatric lens, I initially explored whether she might meet the diagnostic criteria for post-traumatic stress disorder (PTSD) (*DSM-V*, 2013, p. 143) and oppositional defiant disorder. However, although many of her symptoms met the criteria for these diagnoses, they did not capture the developmental effects of complex trauma exposure.

This led me to consider Van der Kolk's (2005) white paper on developmental trauma disorder (DTD). I felt Azra's presentation might best be understood as an affective and behavioural response to profound adverse life experiences (Martinez-Torteya et al., 2015). Based on the information provided by Nedda and the governess, it seemed that Azra's first few years of life had been marked by a lack of predictable care, safety, and access to a consistent, loving caregiver. This might have impacted her brain during a critical period of neurosensitivity (Stern, 1985). "Complex trauma" describes the chronic nature of traumatic events within a caregiving context and impacts attachment, cognitive function, affective regulation, and physical and emotional development (Van der Kolk, 2005). This seemed to encapsulate the breadth of Azra's symptoms and developmental impairments.

Anticipated direction of therapy

I considered that Azra's trauma seemed highly relational, and that therefore my biggest challenge was to help her form a secure base. I planned to do this by providing a secure holding environment where her feelings of rage, shame, and disgust could be held through intersubjective ways of relating, using mind-mindedness (Meins, 1997), mirroring (Stern, 1985), attunement, and reflection. Given that extreme mental stress can cause an attack on the linking of different thoughts (Bion, 1967), Azra would likely need help to create the "thinking" and feeling links between the experiential fragments she brought to therapy. This process of containment was described by Bion (1970, p. 15) as "container–contained". In consideration of the aims of the work from a neurological perspective, I anticipated that repeated interactions of "co-regulation" and "attunement" (Hughes, 2006) would aid Azra in developing new neuronal pathways in her frontal lobe (Rempel-Clower, 2007). Once she had a sense of internal and environmental safety, opportunities for exploration could be reinstated, enhancing "biological integrity" shifting from right-hemisphere dominance to "primary reliance on the left-hemisphere", to neural integration and communication between both hemispheres of the brain (Van der Kolk, 2005).

I planned to use the arts and the PACE model of playfulness, acceptance, curiosity, and empathy (Hughes, 2006) to help Azra process her trauma, enabling her to think, integrate, regulate, and ultimately develop better vagal tone (Porges, 2011; Stern, 1985). Perry (2007) writes that traumatised children need repetitive experiences appropriate to their developmental needs. Thus I planned to use activities selected to address and bridge developmental gaps. It was also very important to develop her sense of safety. I hoped to achieve this by providing a nurturing, reliable, predictable, and safe environment where she could develop a sense of trust (Bowlby, 1969) through the consistency of timing, boundaries, and the use of materials.

I also considered Azra's wider systemic network. I remained aware that the referral came from the school, which might inadvertently prioritise external conformity over inner transformation. It remained important that I was vigilant about safeguarding and mindful of the historic and potentially ongoing trauma. I was hyper-aware of Azra's safety given her high economic status. My concern was Bion's (1962) "unthinkable thought": that social services and the school could not think about a neglected child living in a "palace". Working systemically with clear and consistent communication would therefore be a vital element in the intervention.

Beginning the treatment

It felt important to establish a strong therapeutic alliance and boundaries early on. Azra already struggled with the latter, and I considered whether this might be linked to difficulties in executive functioning, particularly regarding self-monitoring and self-control. I also needed to enhance Azra's capacity to modulate arousal before I could help her to restore equilibrium following dysregulation. She seemed unable to manage "co-regulation", possibly because she had an internal working model of adults as engendering fear rather than safety.

I also had to earn Azra's trust. During the early sessions, she seemed to lack an organised internal pattern of relationship. I considered my initial thoughts about her disorganised attachment style and whether the mess she made was a defence, a way to retreat from being with me (O'Brien, 2004). In session four, Azra initiated a game of hiding toys in the sand tray for me to find. This progressed to asking me to find her buried hands. I sensed she was testing to see if I could find her—both literally and metaphorically. I responded by tracking her, aiming to attune accurately with her internal states and external manifestations, and hoping to foster a sense in her of being known. Whilst using a puppet, for example, I gently fed back what I noticed: "Did you notice Mr Frog, when I talked about daddy, Azra turned away a little, maybe she was thinking: 'Don't like that!'"

Sea urchin

During session six, Azra made something out of pipe cleaners (Figure 7.1). She asked me to guess what it was. After numerous unsuccessful attempts I responded, "So hard when I don't know—wanting me to know you, and what you made, so much." I wondered if she was showing me how she was feeling at home, not knowing what was going on. Once the sea urchin was identified Azra refused to engage with my curiosity about her creation, replying: "I'm done with it now! I want to jump in the sand tray and put my face in the sand!"

Figure 7.1 "Sea urchin"

Perhaps Azra used the metaphor of the sea urchin to describe her internal world. It had spikes to keep itself safe and to keep others away. Reflecting on this self-protective, avoidant mechanism I thought of her "false self" (Winnicott, 1971) blocking feeling states and pushing others away (Howe, 2005). I wondered if she questioned if I was interested in finding her. Once she felt I was, perhaps she wanted to disappear and hide in the sand. She was not yet comfortable with showing me her internal world.

The dump

During our seventh session I began to understand the depth of pain and destruction this internal world held. Azra used a baby-like voice to ask if she could break some toys or cut the doll's hair off. I offered an alternative and suggested she drew a doll on a piece of paper and cut that up so she could "show me" what she needed to do to the doll. I considered if this desire might represent a form of identification with a doll cut into bits. Winnicott (1960) describes children as needing to be "held together" in order to have a clear sense of self and other. Alvarez (1992) further suggests that traumatic experience needs to be "absorbed in tiny pieces", as children might have a fragmented sense of self. At the same time, I was aware that Azra could not bear to hear me say "no". I wondered if perhaps she also wanted to break the toys because she wanted to attack me; by breaking my things perhaps she was attempting to hurt me by proxy.

Azra seemed to be showing differing developmental ages as she played. I began to address the separate parts of her as suggested (Rustin, 1977), talking to the "sane" part of the child about the more vulnerable "baby self". I subsequently began to ask the seven-year-old Azra and I to work together to help the "little baby Azra". Holding in mind Stern's (2004) "affective magic", I addressed how hurt "little Azra" was. For much of this phase of our work together I used this technique to address her overwhelming feelings by helping to bolster the more robust, resilient, and developmentally mature parts.

The use of the arts and play enabled a conscious reflective dialogue between Azra and me. In our ninth session, she buried a doll in the sand tray. I noticed a countertransferential feeling of loneliness and commented on how lonely it might feel to be hidden and not found.

Azra responded by removing the doll from the sand, seemingly rejecting my intervention. I had wanted to test her capacity for an "explanatory level" of intervention and see whether she could hold both feelings and thoughts (Alvarez, 2012). However, it seemed too much "loud empathy" (Hughes, 2006) was experienced as persecutory, evident in her immediate removal of the doll. Had I been more sensitive to the level of intervention she could tolerate, perhaps I could have allowed the image to evolve further. I tried to repair the relationship by carefully using my voice and tone to bring Azra back into contact. She tipped the entire container of toys into the sand tray (Figure 7.2).

Figure 7.2 Sand tray

      Azra: [*throwing the baby dolls into the sand tray*] They're thrown in the dump.

Therapist: They're just thrown around. What's that like?

      Azra: [*laughing*] Goodbye babies! Everything is in the dump. Everything. Everything. Everything. Even the box.

Therapist: Even the box has to go to the dump. There's nothing saved from the dump.

I tried to sensitively attune to Azra's position in the "window of toler-ance" (Seigel, 2012). It seemed as if her laughter was hollow, affectively disconnected from the material shown. I wondered what this might indicate; perhaps that nothing could be saved and everything was swal-lowed up in the "dump". Or perhaps that she felt she herself had been dumped. I recalled my initial hypothesis of insecure disorganised attach-ment. Howe (2005, p. 49) suggests that in the internal working model of children classified as disorganised, the self feels "unloved, alone and frightened" whilst other people are represented as "frightening, reject-ing and unavailable". We briefly sat together in silence before Azra took out a small glass stone (Figure 7.3) and told me it was "safe". I wondered if she was salvaging something, perhaps a "good" or "safe" object. I had a countertransferential feeling of hope as I contemplated her capacity to "find" this safe experience and take it into herself during our time together. I considered whether the imagery worked towards facilitating the process of integrating her trauma into a cohesive narrative, support-ing the attachment repair and affect regulation in right-brain-to-right-brain connection (Stern, 2004).

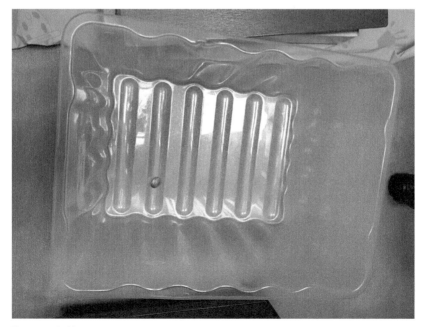

Figure 7.3 Glass stone

As the work progressed, I felt it was important that we acknowledged the different parts of the images she presented, and therefore also the requisite parts of her. Being the one who got to "dump" seemed to bring her pleasure (Alvarez, 2012). I thought about the domestic violence she had witnessed and Balbernie's (1999, p. 216) belief that a "small child can only find the answer to rejection or ill-treatment in fantasy, identifying with the very person who poses the threat in an effort to acquire closeness through sameness". I also wondered if she wanted to know if I could tolerate the little girl who wanted to make mess and hit and hurt. At the end of the session, she left her image and "the mess" as it was. It felt as if she was offloading all of her "rubbish" and leaving it with me.

I felt deep empathy for what I imagined was the disregarded baby-self inside Azra. She had left things in the sand tray for me, perhaps leaving her baby-self with me to hold. I used supervision to think about how I could challenge myself to hold all of Azra—the good, the loving, the hateful, the destructive, and the angry parts.

Role-play

Following the break (sessions eleven to fifteen) I became aware of a change in Azra's behaviour. She began to engage in a reciprocal and collaborative way, with a growing capacity to adhere to boundaries. I wondered whether my providing a different experience in not reacting or retaliating towards her behaviour had defused her hyper-vigilance, and lessened her self-protective strategy. I considered how stressful it might have been for Azra not to be in control of the rules and boundaries of our sessions as this had likely been her maladaptive strategy for ensuring safety and survival. I also hypothesised that the break may have promoted growth. Alvarez (1992, p. 64) illustrates the value and importance of "absence and separateness" in the therapeutic relationship; perhaps the absence allowed for a development of her capacity to think (Bion, 1962).

In session eleven Azra instigated a role play about a dog being mistreated. I was to be the dog while she took the role of the dog owner.

She described wanting to punish and treat "the dog" (me) badly. As with the dumping of the babies in the sand "dump", it seemed she was exploring the embodiment of more powerful, persecutory, or aggressive self-states. Identifying with the aggressor is linked with a dissociative defence, having two enacted relational parts: that of the victim and that of the aggressor (Frankel, 2002). I wondered if Azra's role play was perhaps a re-enactment of how aggressor and victim self-states interrelated in her internal world.

An externalisation of the different roles of persecutor and persecuted was evident in the role play. I speculated this was her way of splitting off and separating her identification with each of these states (victim and persecutor). I utilised tone, prosody, and pace to empathically capture the central affect of this projection with statements like "Gosh, it feels like I am just so unwanted and unloved … It feels really sad and lonely." It seemed important for Azra that I described and imagined into this disturbing experience. Through consistent modelling and reflection, I hoped that the capacity for mentalization (thinking and feeling together) (Fonagy et al., 2004, p. 480) could develop over time. My intention was that this would promote Azra's forming of a core sense of self. I did not return the projection or make any links or interpretations, instead I provided "descriptive lending of meaning of containment of projective identification" (Alvarez, 2012, p. 4).

Needing a frame

Around the time of our fifteenth session I was informed that Azra's governess was leaving. The live-in housekeeper had been taking primary responsibility for her day-to-day life and well-being. This sudden loss became a prominent theme during sessions fifteen to twenty-two.

In our twenty-third session Azra cut up pieces of paper into tiny bits and put them onto another piece of paper. She said the tiny bits "needed a frame" (Figure 7.4). I wondered if just as the paper provided a frame for the disparate parts, I provided a frame for Azra by accepting and holding all the different parts of her. Perhaps the metaphor was her way of trying to make sense of this intersubjective stance (Trevarthen, 1995).

Figure 7.4 Frame

After her governess had been away for over a month and by the twenty-fifth session, Azra's behaviour and grades were deteriorating in the class-room. Drawing on attachment-based strategies from Bomber (2007), I supported Azra's teacher with practical strategies, such as suggesting the teaching assistant become a "key attachment figure" for her. In this role she would provide emotional holding and containment for Azra, letting her know she was being held in mind. Children with attachment difficulties may also have developmental vulnerabilities (Geddes, 2006). I therefore felt Azra needed opportunities in school that were directly linked to her developmental needs, matching the task to her level of development (Palmer & Dolya, 2004).

An independent robot

In the following session, Azra struggled to make an ice cream cone out of playdough and promptly gave up. I wondered out loud why she felt that she could not ask for help. I considered that perhaps she had created a compulsive self-reliant and avoidant strategy having learnt she could not count on anyone (Crittenden & Ainsworth, 1989). I also wondered if she had not experienced many opportunities to struggle and learn mastery (Oaklander, 2007).

Therapist: Perhaps little Azra thinks she has to do everything all on her own. Gosh that seems like a lot for a little girl to think and feel, that she has to do everything all on her own.

Azra: Yes it is and I want to do everything on my own. I'm an independent robot.

Therapist: I wonder if little Azra has felt like that for a very long time.

Azra: Yes, even when I was a baby I did ... but I like it that way and I don't feel anything. [*pause*] I wish I never told you about that.

Given her response, I wondered if Azra now had some capacity to tolerate anxiety and pain. I responded:

Therapist: I understand that. Because it might feel like when you finally open up and share one little thing Adina just goes on and on about it and it's just so annoying!

Azra: [*laughing*] Exactly!

Therapist: [*smiling*] I know what you mean and maybe Azra is feeling angry at me for doing that too.

Azra suddenly opened her mouth to put the playdough in. I said firmly that she was not to eat it. She laughed and put it in her mouth. I told her she needed to take the playdough out of her mouth immediately as it was not safe to ingest. She took it out of her mouth, said it was disgusting, and told me I could have it before handing me her wet playdough. I felt a strong countertransferential feeling of disgust and said, "Adina can take all of the disgusting bits." I thought about the contradicting forces of eating (taking in) and spitting out the playdough, and Bion's (1967) "alpha function" required to psychologically digest experiences. I wondered whether her inability to take in the "good" that I was giving her was because it was experienced as a threat to her pseudo-autonomous self and thus felt as "indigestible" and "disgusting" to her. I knew her emotional nourishment up until this point had largely been "toxic".

Shortly after this, Azra picked up a pen and drew on her face while looking directly at me. I felt her desire to provoke me. I told her I needed to take the pen away. While handing her a wet wipe to clean her face, I said:

Therapist: It seems like it's really hard to be here with me. Maybe there's an Azra that feels like she has to be independent. I make sure you are safe in here. Maybe that feels uncomfortable because it's something different. Something little Azra isn't used to.

Azra: [*wipes her face and then takes her finger and cleans her ear*] I'm cleaning my ear to hear what you've said.

Therapist: I wonder if you are working out whether Adina has angry feelings too, and if so, what they might look like. Is Adina a grown-up who shouts? A grown-up who hurts?

At the time, I wondered if Azra cleaning her ears was her way of telling me that she was not listening to what I said, a way of attempting to hurt me. Maybe she wanted to see not only whether I was strong enough to contain her, but also what kind of grown-up I might be, and whether I might hit or shout at her like an abusive parent. I went on to acknowledge these possible fears and explain that I would never shout or hit. I told Azra that when I felt upset or angry I wrote angry words, took a long drink of water, or talked to someone about my feelings.

Azra followed along as I showed her how I might use my breath or focus on sensations in my body to regulate myself (Grossman, 2008).

In supervision, we discussed an alternative perspective: that Azra cleaning her ears was an expression of her effort to listen because what had been said was important to her. The governess's leaving could have been a trigger that reaffirmed an internally held belief that everyone leaves and no one can be trusted—that "robot-Azra" is safest. She struggled to receive nurture, and a part of my role as her therapist was therefore to give her repeated positive experiences so that she could build up an internal sense of value. We considered whether Azra was "doubly deprived" (Henry, 1974); depriving herself of good care when it was offered to her. I was mindful of her defences and worked with them gently, aware that they were established as a form of protection from unbearable experiences and that behind the strong facade was a little girl in pain (Music, 2011).

Heartbroken

I was experienced as both an object of love and of hate for Azra. She began to dare to show her fury, anger, and disgust to me, perhaps as a preliminary step towards being able to tolerate these feelings in herself. She needed to see that I could survive the attacks and not retaliate; that I was a solid repository for her aggressive and sometimes persecutory feelings. At the same time there were glimpses of her being able to get in touch with her more scared and vulnerable feelings. In this phase of our work I felt I was helping to provide "emotional scaffolding" (Lieberman, 2004); supporting her to express, recognise, and attune to her own feeling states by initially doing some of this for, or with, her.

A parent drop-in for Azra's classroom was scheduled on the morning of the day we had our twenty-eighth session. Parents were invited to come and look at their child's work. Azra's teacher sent reminders to Azra's mother but she did not attend. An hour later, during our session, Azra began to play music with the instruments and banged really hard on the drum. I wondered out loud what Azra's beats might be saying. She replied, "I feel sad that nobody came to see my work today." I told her that I was really sorry that no one had come, and how sad I could see she was. She picked up some pipe cleaners and started to make a candy cane. I told Azra that I was really proud of her for telling me how she felt. As her facial expression changed to what seemed like a look of deflation she said, "I can't do it. Can you help me?" This asking for help felt like an important moment in our relationship; we were now able to facilitate a mastery experience together (Oaklander, 2007). We finished making the candy cane together. She then connected two to make a heart. After a brief pause Azra broke the heart in half.

Therapist: I wonder if that might be how your heart feels today. Broken in half.
Azra: [*tries to mend the heart*]
Therapist: Trying to mend the heart ... stitching the heart back together. [*pause*] Perhaps this heart is feeling broken because mummy did not come today.

In hindsight I should not have named her mother here; she became defensive. Perhaps she could not bear to hear me name her mother's absence. I wondered if, by Azra taking the blame, she needed to keep her mother "good" in her mind (Freud, 1936). We moved away from the feeling of sadness and the moment of processing her experience was lost. In supervision we explored the possibility that I had experienced a projective identification of Azra's primitive anxieties of frustration and despair developed from repeated experiences of maternal deficit (Winnicott, 1971). She needed me to help her by bearing the pain of her "broken heart".

I noticed an increase in Azra's dysregulation. I attempted to repair the rupture by attuning to her non-verbal communication. I used PACE (Hughes, 2006) to attempt to reconnect with her present emotional experience and bring us back into a place of regulated attunement.

The crying girl

Following a three-week break for school holidays, I picked Azra up from the classroom for our thirty-fifth session. I noticed she had something in her hand which she quickly put in her pocket. Once we were in the therapy room, taking a letter out, she said she had something for me, but she could not be near me when I read it. She hid under the desk whilst

I silently read her letter (Figure 7.5). I felt shock and then tremendous sadness for Azra. Perhaps I was shocked that she had managed to hold the "good therapist" in mind by acknowledging her feelings and putting them in a letter. Through the consistency and boundaries provided by therapy, Azra had come to feel held and safe, leading to the internalisation of a "good enough" object that she could draw on even in my absence (Bowlby, 1976, p. 111).

Figure 7.5 Letter

Azra sat under the desk on the opposite side of the room. I noticed her peering to look at my face as I read the letter. When I finished, I asked if I could move a little closer to her. Once I was about a foot away, she asked me to "scoot back" a little, which I did. She spoke about her family turmoil. Mohammed wanted to stay with their mother, Parvin wanted to move in with their father; she felt torn and unsure what to do. She did not want her family to split apart. Slowly she began to come out from under the desk and made eye contact. I noticed she was flustered and was reminded of her ongoing trauma from her parents' divorce. I suggested taking a few long deep breaths together in order to increase body awareness and groundedness (Ogden, 1986). By using the inter-subjective relationship, I hoped we could mitigate Azra's breach in her "window of tolerance" through mindful awareness. Furthermore, using directed mindfulness could teach her to selectively attend to stimuli and begin to regulate and calm herself while simultaneously stimulating neuroplasticity in her brain (Siegel, 2007, p. 32).

With guidance from my supervisor, I worked with Azra over the follow-ing weeks (sessions thirty-six to forty) to remain present with her feelings of uncertainty and fear. I also wanted to communicate how brave I consid-ered her to be. Together we explored her turmoil at not wanting to choose between her parents. I used a "big empathy drawing" (Sunderland, 2015) drawing out an image that visually represented the internal split in her feelings and used it to articulate empathy for her felt experience. Together we reflected on the meaning of her feelings and she was able to digest this "explanatory" level of communication (Alvarez, 2012, p. 14).

Ending phase of therapy

I had been working with Azra for a year and a half when I was informed that she would be finishing therapy at the end of the school year, leav-ing us with eight more sessions. I realised I needed to prepare for and manage this transition period carefully. I made a calendar with all our remaining sessions highlighted (Oaklander, 2007), but when I showed it to her she ripped it up, upset by the visual reminder that we would not be seeing each other anymore. Countertransferentially, I was aware of deep feelings of loss and sadness encapsulated in this response. I was also aware of an acute maternal transference—a desire to wrap her up and keep her close to me—and the importance of the relationship we had developed.

As we worked towards our ending, I considered the metaphor of a planted seed to represent our work together, as well as the hope I held for her (Treisman, 2017). I used the metaphor of the plant to facilitate a space for the negative feelings by referring to the weather the little plant might experience: sometimes sun, sometimes rain, or possibly a storm. As Azra spoke of her future goals, I made a link to this seed of hope we had planted together. I hoped this metaphor might convey the message that the ending of our therapy together was not the ending of the work, or of her growth.

Later in the session, Azra said she wanted to take everything from the therapy room home with her. I empathised with her desire to take all of our time with her, wanting to hold on to all of the Adina–Azra moments. I reminded her of our capacity to hold onto one another inside. I asked her how she would like to spend our time in our last session. She said she did not know or care. I was mindful of how an ending could provoke a need in her to dissociate or regress, aware that this loss may trigger other losses. I acknowledged that perhaps she might be experiencing mixed feelings towards the ending and that was expected. In supervision, I decided it would be most helpful to have a celebratory last session as a way of marking all that we had accomplished.

This was an ending and loss that encompassed the others that surrounded it, for example, the ending of her parents' marriage. I was therefore aware that I was holding a space for this ending to be experienced with presence and mindfulness. I became aware of my own feelings of shock, sadness, and loss towards the abrupt ending in addition to a desire to get the therapeutic ending "right". Perhaps I felt a need to offer a reparative ending because Azra had experienced so many ruptures and losses. I wondered whether she also wanted to get something right, possibly as a means of leaving me with an image of "good Azra".

The last session

I knew our ending would be important for Azra. Rather than trying to get it right, I went into it with a feeling of trust and hope. I brought a cupcake for both of us. It felt like a celebration. I noticed myself feeling proud of her and of us, perhaps for what we had survived, the dance towards connection and attunement we had taken together.

As soon as Azra came into the room and saw the cupcake she burst into tears. I sat next to her, gently offering words for her tears and naming the loss. Azra said she did not want to stop seeing me and asked why I could not come and see her at her home. As I held on to feelings of sadness, loss, and her desire to hold on to me, I simultaneously reminded her of how far she had come. I marvelled at her bravery and the hard work she had put into therapy. I noticed her becoming dysregulated as she began to stamp her feet. This led me to suggest doing a mindful breathing exercise together. We sat facing each other so that our breathing was in sync and I could regulate the pace. The ritual of this familiar routine seemed to provide the interpersonal containment she needed to return to a more regulated state.

Once Azra settled I attempted to connect with her by recalling the image of the stone from our seventh session. I felt this stone represented safety to her. As I showed it to her, I reminded her that the stone had overcome so many obstacles and barriers after having found itself in the "dump". I used this as an opportunity to try to magnify Azra's strengths and resilience (Treisman, 2017). I told her she could keep the stone. I felt it would be a symbolic gift that she could hold onto as a reminder of her therapeutic journey. Azra smiled as she held the stone tightly in her hands.

Outcomes of the therapeutic work

In my initial assessment I felt Azra did not have an internal working model of positive human relationships, resulting in a catastrophic aloneness as she tried to manage the unmanageable on her own. The aim of my work was therefore to create experiences of regulating, empathic and attuned relating, within which developmental deficits were seen and met (Stern, 1985). My role as Azra's therapist was to provide her with a secure base from which she could explore the various unhappy and painful aspects of her life (Bowlby, 1969). Through the use of empathic connection, reciprocity, and trust, the therapeutic relationship became a container, providing context for Azra to understand relationships in a new way. I believe we developed a secure attachment, which helped her to internalise a message that she deserved love (Bowlby, 1969).

My work was to help Azra to develop a psychological structure which would enable her to hold feelings and think about them, so that she could then move towards a position of psychic integration. As the therapy progressed and our therapeutic relationship developed, she became less defended as her "window of tolerance" widened, enabling a greater capacity for the processing of emotional pain (Meltzer, 1967). Throughout the course of our therapeutic journey together, Azra was able to move from "descriptive levels" of communication to "explanatory" and begin to reflect on why she felt a certain way (Alvarez, 2012, p. 14). I believe she became more whole, connected, and integrated as she began to experience herself and others differently, evident in her less controlling behaviour.

Conclusion

My journey with Azra has been a rich and rewarding one, leading to a greater and embedded understanding of the role of integrative child psychotherapy as a vehicle for working with the emotional and psychological complexity of complex trauma. Highlighted throughout this therapeutic journey was the importance of personal therapy and supervision as a containing frame. The role of supervision in providing an experience of the "container–contained" (Bion, 1962), allowed me to feel confident when faced with complex and unpredictable situations. Moments of misattunement in my work with Azra provided opportunities to grow my capacity for working with negative transference and repair. In addition to therapy and supervision, I learnt how vital self-care was in my work as a trainee therapist.

The end of our journey together did not have an "endpoint" with everything "resolved" (Lanyado, 2004, p. 122). Instead, it was filled with uncertainty. However, I am hopeful that Azra now knows what it is like to have someone believe in her. I hold onto the hope that she now knows what it feels like to be held and to hold others in mind, as evidenced in our final session:

Azra: I know that I am in your heart.
Therapist: How do you know?
Azra: Because I can feel it. Sometimes at home I think of you and I think that you might be thinking of me too.

References

Alvarez, A. (1992). *Live Company: Psychoanalytic Psychotherapy with Autistic, Borderline, Deprived and Abused Children.* 5th edn. London: Routledge.

Alvarez, A. (2012). *The Thinking Heart: Three Levels of Psychoanalytic Therapy with Disturbed Children.* London: Routledge.

Balbernie, R. (1999). Inadmissible evidence: An example of projective identification. *Clinical Child Psychology and Psychiatry,* 4(2): 215–223.

Bion, W. R. (1962). *Learning from Experience.* London: Heinemann.

Bion, W. R. (1967). Attacks on Linking: *International Journal of Psychoanalysis,* 40: 308–315.

Bion, W. R. (1970). *Attention and Interpretation.* London: Tavistock. Reprinted in: *Seven Servants: Four Works by Wilfred R. Bion.* New York: Jason Aronson, 1977.

Bomber, L. M. (2007). *Inside I'm Hurting.* London: Worth.

Bowlby, J. (1969). *Attachment and Loss: Attachment.* London: Hogarth.

Bowlby, J. (1976). *The Making and Breaking of Affectional Bonds.* London: Routledge.

Clarkson, P. (1992). *Transactional Analysis Psychotherapy.* London: Routledge.

Crittenden, P., & Ainsworth, M. (1989). Child maltreatment and attachment theory. In: D. Cicchetti & V. Carlson (Eds.), *Child Maltreatment: Theory and Research on the Causes and Consequences of Child Abuse and Neglect* (pp. 432–463). New York: Cambridge University Press.

DSM-V (2013). American Psychiatric Association *Diagnostic and Statistical Manual of Mental Disorders* (5th edn.). Arlington, VA: American Psychiatric Publishing.

Felitti, J., Anda, R., Nordenburg, D., Williamson, D., Spitz, A., Edwards, V., Koss, M., & Marks, J. (1998). Relationship of childhood abuse and household dysfunction to many of the leading causes of death in adults: The Adverse Childhood Experiences (ACE) study. *American Journal of Preventive Medicine,* 14(4): 245–258.

Fonagy, P., Gergely, G., Jurist, E. L., & Target, M. (2004). *Affect Regulation, Mentalization and the Development of the Self.* London: Karnac.

Frankel, J. (2002). Exploring Ferenczi's concept of identification with the aggressor: Its role in trauma, everyday life, and the therapeutic relationship. *Psychoanalytic Dialogues,* 12(1): 101–139.

Freud, A. (1936). *The Ego and the Mechanisms of Defence.* London: Karnac.

Geddes, H. (2006). *Attachment in the Classroom: The Links between Children's Early Experience, Emotional Well-being and Performance in School.* London: Worth.

Grossman, P. (2008). On measuring mindfulness in psychosomatic and psychological research. *Journal of Psychosomatic Research, 64*(4): 405–408.

Henry, G. (1974). Doubly deprived. *Journal of Child Psychotherapy, 4*(2): 29–43 [reprinted as Double deprivation. In: G. Williams (1997). *Internal Landscapes and Foreign Bodies. Eating Disorders and Other Pathologies* (pp. 33–49). London: Duckworth].

Howe, D. (2005). *Child Abuse and Neglect: Attachment, Development and Intervention.* London: Palgrave MacMillan.

Hughes, D. (2006). *Building the Bonds of Attachment: Awakening Love in Deeply Troubled Children.* Lanham, MD: Jason Aronson.

Hughes, D. (2011). *Attachment-focused Parenting.* New York: W. W. Norton.

Klein, M. (1946). Notes on some schizoid mechanisms. In: *Envy and Gratitude and Other Works 1946–1963* (pp. 1–24). London: Hogarth, 1975.

Lanyado, M. (2004). *The Presence of the Therapist: Treating Childhood Trauma.* New York: Routledge.

Lieberman, A. F. (2004). Child–parent psychotherapy: A relationship-based approach to the treatment of mental health disorders in infancy and early childhood. In: A. J. Sameroff, S. C. McDonough, & K. L. Rosenblum (Eds.), *Treating Parent–Infant Relationship Problems: Strategies for Intervention* (pp. 97–122). New York: Guilford.

Martinez-Torteya, C., Bogat, G., Levendosky, A., & von Eye, A. (2015). The influence of prenatal intimate partner violence exposure on hypothalamic–pituitary–adrenal axis reactivity and childhood internalizing and externalizing symptoms. *Development and Psychopathology, 28*(1): 55–72.

Meins, E. (1997). *Security of Attachment and the Social Development of Cognition.* Hove, UK: Psychology Press.

Meltzer, D. (1967). *The Psycho-Analytical Process.* Perth, UK: Clunie, 1990.

Music, G. (2011). *Nurturing Natures.* Hove, UK: Psychology Press.

Oaklander, V. (2007). *Hidden Treasure: A Map to the Child's Inner Self.* London: Karnac.

O'Brien, F. (2004). The making of mess in art therapy: Attachment, trauma and the brain. *Inscape, 9*(1): 2–13.

Ogden, T. (1986). *The Matrix of the Mind.* Northvale, NJ: Jason Aronson.

Palmer, S., & Dolya, G. (2004, July 7). Freedom of thought. *Times Educational Supplement*, London.

Perry, B. (2007). *The Boy Who Was Raised as a Dog: And Other Stories from a Child Psychiatrist's Notebook: What Traumatized Children Can Teach Us About Loss, Love and Healing*. New York: Basic Books.

Porges, S. (2011). *The Polyvagal Theory*. New York: W. W. Norton.

Rempel-Clower, N. L. (2007). Role of orbitofrontal cortex connections in emotion. *Annals of the New York Academy of Sciences, 1121*: 72–86.

Rustin, M. (1997). *Psychotic States in Children*. London: Duckworth.

Siegel, D. (2007). T*he Mindful Brain: Reflection and Attunement in the Cultivation of Well-being*. New York: W. W. Norton.

Siegel, D. (2012). *The Developing Mind*. 2nd edn. New York: Guilford.

Stern, D. N. (1985). *The Interpersonal World of the Infant: A View from Psychoanalysis and Developmental Psychology*. New York: Basic Books.

Stern, D. N. (2004). *The Present Moment in Psychotherapy and Everyday Life* (Norton Series on Interpersonal Neurobiology). New York: W. W. Norton.

Sunderland, M. (2015). *Conversations that Matter*. Broadway, UK: Worth.

Treisman, K. (2017). *A Therapeutic Treasure Box for Working with Children and Adolescents with Developmental Trauma*. London: Jessica Kingsley.

Trevarthen, C. (1995). Mother and baby—seeing artfully eye to eye. In: R. Gregory, J. Harris, P. Heard, & D. Rose (Eds.), *The Artful Eye*. Oxford: Oxford University Press.

Van der Kolk, B. (2005). Developmental trauma disorder. *Psychiatric Annals, 35*(5): Psychology Module, p. 401.

Winnicott, D. W. (1960). The theory of the parent–infant relationship. *International Journal of Psychoanalysis, 41*: 585–595.

Winnicott, D. W. (1971). *Playing and Reality*. London: Karnac.

CHAPTER 8

Space rockets and mobile homes: reaching the place of hope by traversing the landscape of trauma and loss

Sarah Marx

Introduction

Molly came into therapy with a history of relational trauma, neglect, unresolved loss, and attachment difficulties. These experiences began in utero where Molly was exposed to both maternal stress and a range of toxins including heroin, cocaine, and alcohol. Following an incident of domestic violence Molly was removed from her parents at the age of fourteen months and placed in foster care in another county. Molly had no further contact with either of her parents. When Molly was six her mother died of a drug overdose and this seemed to evoke Molly's longing and rage as well as feelings of guilt as she believed she could have saved her mummy had she been there.

Following the death of her mother, Molly was referred for therapy and saw another therapist before me for almost a year. Because this therapy ended prematurely, I suspected that Molly may not have had time to fully experience her feelings or phantasies around separation and loss, either in external reality or in the transference–countertransference relationship with her previous therapist. It was possible that the impact of another sudden loss for Molly could have resulted in her avoiding emotional involvement with me for fear that I too would abandon her.

The first meetings with Molly

Molly, aged nine, arrived, tall and long-limbed. She seemed awkward in her gait, as though she were almost tripping over herself. She sat on the floor with somewhat collapsed shoulders and I noticed that both her fine and gross motor skills appeared clumsy. Her speech was at times hesitant and flat, at other times hurried and slurred, making it hard for me to understand her. She would often dribble or have a runny nose which she would wipe on the inside of her jumper.

It had been suggested by her school that Molly might have mild learning disabilities or possibly foetal alcohol spectrum disorder, although neither had been formally assessed. I also understood that childhood trauma can have a profound impact on the emotional, behavioural, cognitive, social, and physical functioning of children (Perry et al., 1995).

Working with deficit

Early experiences of trauma, neglect, and abuse can impact dramatically on an infant's developing brain, and in particular the development of the right hemisphere, responsible for establishing the basic structures of attachment and emotional regulation (Schore, 1994, 2003, 2012). Given the intergenerational nature of trauma, Molly's mother may have experienced trauma and attachment difficulties of her own and this combined with her known violent behaviour, drug and alcohol dependency, and poor mental health suggests she lacked the capacity to regulate her own level of arousal and affective states. As a result, it would have been likely that Molly experienced her mother as oscillating between being withdrawn and unavailable, to being intrusive and frightening; a pattern shown to lead to the development of disorganised attachment behaviour (Van IJzendoorn et al., 1999).

My early observations seemed to suggest that under less stressful conditions Molly's attachment had become more organised into an insecure-avoidant pattern. For example, she seemed to need to control me while showing little motivation to connect with me. She found it incredibly difficult to tolerate my attempts to offer understanding or empathy and instead would reject, deflect, or interrupt me if I tried to engage her with anything that might bring her closer to her feelings. If Molly herself introduced feelings into a conversation they would be either minimised or quickly dismissed.

Talking about her previous therapist, Molly offered me an insight into how she managed her expectation of loss in relationships by employing a strategy of "don't think, don't feel". "When I got to know her, I kinda started to ignore her a little bit because I didn't want to really think about her, just in case she left, like she has." Over the coming weeks Molly recreated the basic artwork she had made in her previous therapy while interacting with me very little other than to ask for more glitter, glue, or Sellotape. Her using a lot of these materials seemed to be another indication of the depth of deprivation and emptiness she felt in her inner world. Klein (1959) wrote that greed is increased by the anxiety of being deprived, robbed, and experienced as not being good enough to be loved.

In the early sessions I found it hard to be with Molly and felt an irritation towards her greed, and frustration at the mess she made. Her dismissive, rubbishing manner, to herself and her artwork, extended to me and I felt in the shadow of her previous therapist. In my early countertransference I felt myself to be both unappealing and uninteresting and this contributed to a growing sense of apathy. I was struck by the parallel of how taking into therapy a child from another therapist I had, like her grandparents, taken on someone else's child. I wondered then if in Molly's transference to me I had become a substitute object, lacking in vitality.

After several weeks, Molly's engagement with the art materials stopped and she began to wander aimlessly about the room. She occasionally picked something up but nothing seemed to hold her attention long enough for her to either explore it or create something symbolic from it. According to Bick (1968) children who have not been able to internalise a containing presence lack the internal space needed to develop the capacity to elaborate emotional experiences through play. Occasionally Molly would stop moving and without much emotional interest, share a little of the pain and fear she carried inside her. In these moments I felt an overwhelming sadness for her but my attempts to be empathic or curious were shut down with a shrug or a dismissive "I dunno". Alvarez (2012) questions whether feelings and meanings actually matter to patients in affectless states whose sense of self and internal objects are experienced as dead and empty, uninteresting, or unvalued. This certainly resonated with my early countertransference experiences when with Molly.

Breaks, ruptures, and repair

Working in a school setting meant that Molly's therapy was often interrupted by holidays. In the first spring term of therapy we had to contend with Easter, bank holidays, and INSET days. Molly became unsettled by this lack of containment, demonstrated by her growing preoccupation with the physical container, or the skin of therapy. For example, she became persecuted if the membrane of the physically containing setting was punctured by noise outside, although she would often want to break it herself by opening the door or asking to get something. I realised that through these breaks in the setting I had inadvertently become another unreliable person to Molly, someone who drifted in and out of her life, providing little hope. Prior to yet another break, I watched as Molly tried to work out the school calendar. She became muddled and seeing a link between what she felt in the present with me and what she had experienced in past relationships I decided to share my thinking.

Therapist: I think it's really hard for you, Molly, when people come and go in and out of your life. It seems you're really showing me, by putting the dates on the board, that you are thinking about when I will go away, because that's what's happened before, people go away and that really hurts.
Molly: Er, goodbye.

Molly's "goodbye" told me in no uncertain terms that I had mis-attuned to the confusion and fear of loss that she was experiencing in her inner world. I had moved too quickly into trying to add meaning to her experience and through my impatience had imposed my theoretical understanding on her which had been too much for Molly. Reflecting on this intervention it would have been helpful if I had added, "You know though that we shall be meeting again when school begins."

Around this time Molly also found a small red ball and began to throw it at the door. I wondered if the back and forth movement might again represent her anxieties experienced though my going away and a reassuring action signifying that I returned. Bick (1968) wrote that in infantile unintegrated states there is a frantic search for a containing object.

Over the coming weeks her use of the ball became all-consuming and I found it increasingly difficult to stay emotionally in touch with her. I now wondered if Molly might be using the ball as an autistic object (Tustin, 1990) and that by keeping in physical contact with it as a sensation object, she was protected from experiencing loss. During this time my words had to compete with the constant thudding of the ball against the door and this resulted in staccato exchanges between Molly and me which seemed to agitate and dysregulate us both even further. Her words still seemed flat and her stock responses of "nah" or "dunno" to anything I said made me feel that anything I offered was irrelevant and unwelcome. At times I experienced her projections as so violent, frightening, and intolerable that I would push them back into Molly through patient-centred inter-pretations which began with "you". Even if accurate these interpretations contained too much feeling for her to bear and they were immediately defended against. At other times I felt so deadened by Molly that I spoke simply to keep myself alive. I was certain that in the transference, Molly had now come to experience me as frightening and intrusive for my countertransference had become disturbingly reactive and defensive.

Increasingly Molly attempted to avoid hearing my thoughts alto-gether by interrupting, grunting, cursing, or laughing hysterically when-ever I spoke, all of which felt dissociative and dysregulated. Bion's (1959) work on destructive attacks on verbal thought helped me to understand how Molly was not only attacking the linking that she perceived in me, but also attacking her own capacity for both thinking and understand-ing. Without these secondary processes Molly's ego had become threat-ened by the intensity of feeling she felt in my presence.

Supervision was vital in helping me maintain a therapeutic stance in the midst of these intense, uncomfortable feelings both in me and Molly.

My supervisor provided me with a desperately needed "thinking breast" (Bion, 1962) and her containment enabled me to feel understood and emotionally regulated. In supervisory sessions I was thus able to process some of what was happening in the room between Molly and me; however, as soon as I was again with Molly my capacity to think diminished and we would quickly find ourselves re-enacting Molly's early trauma within the transference–countertransference relationship.

Tustin (1990) writes that in order to provide a situation in which the child can begin to forge mental links with the therapist, the child's use of autistic objects and shapes has to be moderated. Molly's use of the ball had become an effective means for her to avoid engaging with me, and so after much consideration and consultation with my supervisor, I made the difficult decision to remove the ball. I carefully explained to Molly that whilst I understood the ball was important to her, her use of it meant that I could not really get to know her, or her me, and that it was for this reason that I had decided to take it away. Her initial reaction was one of panic at losing her protective ritual, and rage, and I was left in no doubt of her desire to annihilate me. Molly refused to talk to me, other than to tell me how angry she was with me. Knowing that I had to survive Molly's attacks before we could process what this and other losses meant to her, I held the boundary. I timed my interventions carefully, sometimes talking for her to show my understanding of her sense of loss, and acceptance of her angry and destructive feelings. At other times I offered little more than empathic sounds in order to keep a sense of rhythm and holding.

A space rocket to nowhere land

Over the coming weeks, Molly's rage softened and seemed to give way to a sense of sadness. She began to slowly explore the room, hesitating near the sand tray. She then created her first sand tray image which conveyed something of Molly's bleak inner world. The scene was one of emptiness, unpopulated apart from a few glass beads hidden in the sand below a small rubbish bin. She paused and with her head hanging, quietly told me that she wanted to go in a space rocket to "nowhere land". She added that I could go with her, but immediately retracted this, saying she would have to kick me out. The image of being kicked out of a space rocket brought to mind Bick's (1968) description of the newborn baby as being like an astronaut, shot into space without a space suit. I thought about Molly's infancy and imagined times when she might not have been gathered up and held together in the way she had needed. Kicking me out of the space rocket was Molly's way then of projecting into me her primitive agony of "falling to pieces" (Winnicott, 1963).

Glimpsing her infant self, I felt renewed compassion and a deeper understanding of Molly's primitive protections to psychologically survive her early relational experiences. I reflected on how so often my words were of little comfort to her but instead were experienced as overwhelming and dysregulating. It was clear to me now that Molly's trauma was not reachable through language alone, but was woven into the very fibres of her being. Through advancements in neuroscience and interpersonal neurobiology it is now understood that attachment experiences influence the maturation of both the central nervous system (CNS), which processes and regulates social-emotional stimuli, and the autonomic nervous system (ANS), which generates the somatic aspects of emotion. Optimal arousal maintains autonomic balance between sympathetic and parasympathetic arousal, something that Molly had little experience of. Instead, Molly's early experiences of a frightening caregiver most likely resulted in the simultaneous activation of both the sympathetic and parasympathetic components of her autonomic nervous system, leaving her in a state of chronic arousal and dysregulation. This had then been replicated with me when too much feeling was aroused partly through my interpretations in our sessions.

Moving to a different tune

I now understood that I had moved too quickly into trying to work with Molly's trauma and needed to slow down and help her establish a sense of safety in our relationship. I became more mindful of my use of language and began to say far less. I also began to pay less attention to Molly's words and more to her vitality affects (Stern, 1985, 2010). Observing and tracking the minutiae of her facial expressions, her prosody, as well as the movement, intensity, and duration of her expressed affects felt akin to listening to a piece of music and allowed me to gain a better sense of the parameters of her extremely narrow window of tolerance (Siegel, 2012).

I also became more aware of how I could use my body as an instrument in this delicate duet. For example, when I took my lead from Molly and synchronised my movements with hers she seemed to rely less heavily on her second skin defence (Bick, 1968) of physical movement to hold herself together. This was particularly noticeable at the beginning of sessions. Rather than taking a seat as I had previously done I remained standing with Molly. As she moved, I gently followed, ensuring that at all times my body language remained open and non-threatening. In this dance of co-regulation, I held the image of a swinging pendulum gently coming to rest, and as it did Molly was able to settle into an activity.

The space rocket lands

Molly resumed her theme of the space rocket through her using Lego pieces to build it. I joined her on the floor, watching quietly, while experiencing a sense of ease between us. She asked me to find pieces for her, marking a significant shift in our relationship from one in which I must be kept out, to one in which I could be supportive and of help to her. A couple of weeks later, she returned to the Lego and transformed the rocket into a house. While this house looked unsteady I felt it symbolised how Molly was starting to move away from a therapeutic relationship based on isolation and towards one of greater relational thinking, intersubjectivity, and psychic intimacy. Molly then produced a small, plastic peg from her pocket and began to embellish it with patterned paper and glitter. Naturally, I wondered if this plain, rather nondescript object represented Molly and the decorating of it was a way to show me that colour was beginning to seep into her internal world and internal objects. Perhaps the house was a metaphor for therapy and how we were now co-creating something that was meaningful and valuable, but as Molly placed the peg in the house I wondered if she was showing how the building of walls occurred as a protection of her Self. I suspended my thoughts about the house representing the therapeutic relationship and instead acknowledged the protection that Molly had needed to employ:

Therapist: I think you've built something really strong here, to keep this safe, [*pointing to the peg*] maybe a bit like what you've done for yourself. I wonder, Molly, if maybe you built a house, not so different from this, to put around your feelings?

Molly shifted slightly and went back to looking for Lego. In response I too shifted back and followed her deflection. Molly was finding this hard to acknowledge and needed to take her time. When I sensed she was feeling calmer and safer I picked up the thread again, this time talking for her.

Therapist: You know, Molly, I think what you might be saying is something like "I have to keep you out Sarah, I have to keep everyone out."

Molly: Technically yes.

Therapist: Because what, when people get in, they break?

Molly: To be honest this is what I think, if they get in then they, erm, they basically break me.

Therapist: Oh Molly, you would get broken! How painful to imagine you could be broken.

In this brief exchange Molly has been able to both keep her thinking connected to the play and my interpretation and share with me her core fear of being broken. Molly remained motionless, her gaze focused on the ground. I moved towards her and in little more than a whisper continued:

Therapist: You know, Molly, I think you got broken by Mummy. Then maybe broken a little bit more when [*previous therapist's name*] left. Then I came along and you thought, "I'm not going to let her get close to me," and I think you know that you've just been trying to keep yourself safe. All closed up inside a little house, just like the one you've been building here.

By bringing in Molly's life experience I was able to cut across the transference and help her begin to make sense of who I was for her. By my lessening her omnipotent control, Molly and I were able to sit together with her sadness and grief. This offered her a chance to begin to mourn her lost objects in the presence of another, thus creating a new intersubjective experience for her.

Paying such close attention to the intricacies of Molly's psychobiological experience meant that I found it much easier to sensitively attune to her and as a result she began to feel more comfortable with the ebb and flow of her emotional experience. Her new way of being remained fragile and tentative though, and it never took much for Molly to be spooked back into a state of dysregulation. When this happened, she would return to physical activities such as kicking the cushions, which felt reminiscent of her use of the ball. However, unlike before she was now able to let me join her in a back and forth game. To begin with this game would be littered with complicated rules, made up by Molly, which conveyed how difficult and confusing she found relationships. Over time though these rules lessened and I felt a growing sense of trust between us as we learnt about the proximity range in which Molly felt safe both emotionally and physically. My involvement also meant I could more easily co-regulate Molly, so when I felt her begin to tip into hyperarousal or dissociation, I slowed the pace of the game, adding in pauses and talking about my own embodied experience. Through these experiences of affective resonance, I began to model for Molly a way to self-regulate, and on a subtle level how to manage engagement, separation, and reunion (Schore, 2003).

From avoidance to ambivalence

Over the coming weeks I experienced Molly as far less avoidant and this led me to think again about her attachment. Whilst in the past I had considered her to have a disorganised attachment, with behaviours typical of an insecure-avoidant style, I now began to recognise more ambivalent behaviours. I was reminded of the adaptive component of Crittenden's Dynamic-Maturational Model of Attachment and Adaptation (1999) which emphasises how self-protective organisation occurs in response to fear, making it possible to understand attachment behaviours as safety promoting adaptations to circumstances. Understood through this lens Molly clearly felt less threatened by me which allowed her to relinquish some of her avoidant strategies. However, this undoubtedly gave rise to anxiety and confusion as it brought Molly into contact with her pain and longing. Perhaps then her ambivalence was another adaptation born out of her need to protect herself from intimacy and the pain of further losses.

Molly brought this ambivalence to me, explaining that:

Molly: Sometimes one part of my brain says one thing, and another part says something else.
Therapist: And does that happen here sometimes too?
Molly: Yeah, sometimes.
Therapist: It does, it happens here too. That's so good you can notice that, Molly.
Molly: I dunno why though.
Therapist: Yeah, sounds confusing … Well, maybe a part of you wants to come and see me but another part thinks I don't really want to feel close to Sarah.
Molly: Yeah, every now and then.
Therapist: Yeah, every now and then … and I wonder, Molly, if that's because you've been let down so many times. So, when someone else comes along maybe you think, "I better not get close because this person will just leave as well."
Molly: Firstly, that is exactly what I thought but now I know you, literally my brain is completely muddled up.

In this exchange Molly demonstrated her growing capacity for emotional two-track thinking (Bruner, 1968) as she starts to hold two fairly opposing thoughts about me, that I could both be there for her and abandon her. According to Segal (1957), the capacity to register two different versions of the object plays a part in the development of symbol formation and may be a precursor to experiencing depressive anxieties. Klein also advocated that managing ambivalent, mixed feelings is one of the most sophisticated psychological achievements (1946) which permit depressive anxieties to become more prominent.

Symbol formation and the exploration of our relationship

Molly also began to use the art materials to symbolically demonstrate developments in our relationship. For example, when Molly made glitter jars by taking two empty pots, making a paper spout and pouring a mixture of different glitters into them, I took this to be a representation of Bion's container–contained relationship (1962). Molly was now able to explore how she could pour into me and how I could contain her. The freedom of movement from one pot to another seemed to capture the easier flow between us, and her growing capacity to take in and receive. I was also aware that glitter was something of value to Molly and so this flow of colourful and appealing particles suggested that Molly was beginning to internalise me as a good and sustaining object (Klein, 1948, 1955). I sensed a shift in Molly's transference and I noticed how she would enthusiastically tell me about her day-to-day experiences, like reaching her reading target. In response I experienced a loving maternal countertransference and these positive experiences between us added to Molly's growing expectation that I could delight in her and that she could feel delighted by this.

Molly also began to show signs of being interested in the theme of misattunement, rupture, and repair, arriving at one session carrying a plastic pencil case from home which was slightly broken.

Therapist: So, you thought, "I know, I can take it to Sarah and I can show her it's broken."
Molly: And I can fix it … and also, I'll have the help if I need it … and I might need some help.
Therapist: You know, Molly, that's really good that you know you can come here and get some help when you need it.

Molly moved closer to me and together we worked quietly on fixing the pencil case. This co-operative, sharing of focus with mutual encouragement and affirmation seemed to represent Molly's growing capacity for secondary intersubjectivity (Trevarthen & Hubley, 1978). I thought about the significance of a pencil case as a container, something that holds the potential for creativity, and something that might represent our relationship which could be broken and repaired.

Working towards ending

When she brought the broken pencil case I was aware that Molly was probably communicating something about her own broken parts and fears around ending. As Molly would be moving on to secondary school at the end of the academic year there was no possibility of therapy continuing in her new school. For this reason, at the beginning of the spring term, we started thinking more about the expected ending of therapy. I felt concerned that Molly might experience our ending as premature and yet another loss. I therefore needed to be incredibly sensitive to the process of our ending and utilise it as a primary intervention (Many, 2009). If Molly could experience our ending as a non-traumatic loss and one which she knew she could survive, she might be able to develop more of a sense of trust in future relationships, as well as internalise a new model in which loss could be experienced as a natural albeit painful part of healthy growth and change.

Whilst I knew that I had to provide Molly with a carefully planned, predictable, and appropriately paced ending, I suspected that Molly's traumas would become triggered in this process. As I remained vigilant to smaller losses such as the end of each session and approached these as an opportunity to make an intervention, my suspicions were confirmed as Molly once again employed her avoidant strategies of "don't think, don't feel". In the session that proceeded our Easter break, I reminded Molly of the number of sessions we had left and talked about our ending therapy in the summer. My own anxiety about the ending meant I slipped back into my own familiar pattern of being over-reliant on language and this seemed to reactivate Molly's original transference.

Molly became extremely disorganised, anxious, and dysregulated and ran between kicking the door and jumping on the chair, yelling "I just need to run!"—indicating that she had moved into a fight/flight response. Molly was once again unreachable through words. Her rapid, jerky movements reminded me of the ball-throwing against the door and how she came to rely on it as a way of avoiding loss. I felt waves of panic at how quickly my thinking could be disrupted even though Molly's responses were familiar to me from the beginning of therapy. I said nothing to Molly but instead sat for a few moments in order to regulate myself so that I could remain open to and hold her projections. I then stood up and as Molly bounced from door to chair, I walked alongside her. I made my breathing audible, lengthening my out-breaths, and using my own body and rhythmic movement to offer Molly another experience of co-regulation. Molly responded and her movements slowly became more organised. She stopped crashing into the door and together we synchronised our pace until Molly stopped and stood quietly on the chair. Before I could speak she jumped down and moved to her glitter jars. She picked up the spout, told me it was broken and frantically set about mending it by attaching lots of stickers.

Having previously understood the glitter jars and connecting spout as a metaphor for our relationship I could see that Molly was indirectly trying to express her feelings about the rupture that had just occurred. Sunderland (2015) talks about how the use of metaphor allows even the most defended of children to explore their experiences, which might be too frightening, painful, or shaming to speak about directly. Coming out of metaphor too quickly and linking to the child's life story therefore risks evoking these strong feelings in the child and may result in further rupture to the therapeutic relationship.

However, when Molly stopped and with a look of confusion asked me, "Why have I used so many stickers?" I felt that she was demonstrating her capacity to tolerate a more direct response. I tentatively replied:

Therapist: Maybe to fix us … it seemed like everything kinda went really wrong just then and you had to keep me out … and now maybe you are trying to make it all good again … to make sure we hold together through the break.
[*Molly visibly relaxed. She added one more sticker*]
Molly: There, that should hold it.
Therapist: Yes, that should hold us together.

Working the theme of rupture and repair through this metaphor allowed Molly to experience it safely and make sense of what had occurred. Her initiating the repair to our relationship and attachment demonstrated both the strength of our relationship and how she did not want to lose me on a bad note. Knowing that she could make me, and us, good again made me feel more hopeful that she would be able to call me to mind and experience me as a sustaining internal object (Bion, 1962) both in the break and beyond therapy.

Mobile homes

As Molly and I approached our ending she once again returned to her Lego house and asked me to help her find certain pieces. These pieces she then placed inside the house, to accompany the embellished peg. She filled the house up to the top and then built a Lego roof. I thought how symbolic this was and how her internal world had become more populated with meaningful objects. Molly then attached three sets of wheels. I thought how this house, this co-created container, served as a metaphor for the progress Molly had made in therapy. It represented what she had been able to internalise through our relationship. In the time we had left together Molly and I explored how this house was in fact a little like what we had built together, and while the structure was still a little wobbly on its wheels, it could nonetheless move and therefore be taken with her. I asked Molly:

Therapist: I wonder, Molly, if you could have a name, what you would call this house?
   Molly: Erm, I'm not sure … maybe the safe house.

Ending with Molly brought mixed feelings. The work had been incredibly challenging, so for me, and perhaps Molly too, there was a sense of both relief and sadness at having to say goodbye. Despite the progress she had made, I was aware of how much still remained unresolved and as a result our ending still felt somewhat premature. Certainly, at the start of therapy I had not fully understood the extent of her relational deficit or anticipated just how slowly and carefully I would need to go with her. It has to be said that as a trainee, working with Molly often felt like a baptism of fire, plunging me into the dark realms of developmental and relational trauma. However, it was in these challenging places that I learnt a great deal, not only about Molly but also about myself and about the work.

Working from an integrative model provided me with solid theoretical foundations both from the fields of psychoanalytical theory and attachment theory. As my self-awareness grew and I became more trauma informed I was also able to integrate much more from the areas of neuroscience and interpersonal neurobiology. This enabled me to become far more attuned to Molly's affective communication and sensory needs and work in a much more embodied way. It was this I believe that helped me to grasp in a much deeper sense both the complexities and subtleties of Molly's trauma.

Conclusion

My work with Molly clearly demonstrates the need to follow a trauma protocol of establishing a sense of safety before moving into addressing trauma. Molly's avoidance and need to control me at the start of therapy coupled with her hesitancy around working with the arts often left me feeling impatient or disabled and as a result I pushed to deepen the work before Molly was ready. My mis-attuning in this way served to recreate Molly's early trauma and led to some extremely powerful, negative transference and countertransference feelings as well as what at times felt like unbearable projections from Molly.

There were times in my work with Molly that felt so challenging and futile that I quite literally felt as though we had been launched into space, to "nowhere land", and I would find myself searching for some thread of therapeutic faith to hang on to. Thankfully, Molly and I found a way of connecting, out there in the darkness, and we slowly came back to land. Together we crafted our wobbly mobile home and in it we shared moments in which Molly allowed me to glimpse more of her and experience a sense of being both heard and understood. By the end of our time together Molly and I had begun to explore new territories and had arrived at a place of greater hope.

References

Alvarez, A. (2012). *The Thinking Heart: Three Levels of Psychoanalytic Therapy with Disturbed Children*. Oxford: Routledge.

Bick, E. (1968). The experience of the skin in early object relations. *International Journal of Psychoanalysis*, 49: 484–486.

Bion, W. R. (1959). Attacks on linking. In: C. Bronstein, C. & E. O'Shaughnessy (Eds.), *Attacks on Linking Revisited: A New Look at Bion's Classical Work*. London: Karnac, 2017.

Bion, W. R. (1962). *Learning from Experience*. London. Heinemann.

Bruner, J. (1968). *Processes of Cognitive Growth: Infancy*. Worcester, MA: Clark University Press.

Crittenden, P. (1999). Danger and development: The organisation of self-protective strategies. In: J. I. Vondra & D. Barnett (Eds.), *Atypical Attachment in Infancy and Early Childhood Among Children at Developmental Risk* (pp. 145–171). Oxford: Blackwell.

Klein, M. (1946). Notes on some schizoid mechanisms. In: *Envy and Gratitude and Other Works 1946–1963*. London: Random House, 1997.

Klein, M. (1948). On the theory of anxiety and guilt. In: *Envy and Gratitude and Other Works 1946–1963*. London: Random House, 1997.

Klein, M. (1955). On identification. In: *Envy and Gratitude and Other Works 1946–1963*. London: Hogarth, 1975.

Klein, M. (1959). Our adult roots in infancy. In: *Envy and Gratitude and Other Works 1946–1963*. London: Hogarth, 1975.

Many, M. (2009). Termination as a therapeutic intervention when treating children who have experienced multiple losses. *Infant Mental Health Journal, 30*(1): 23–39.

Perry, B. D., Pollard, R. A., Blakley, T. L., Baker, W. L., & Vigilante, D. (1995). Childhood trauma, the neurobiology of adaptation and "use-dependent" development of the brain: How "states" become "traits". *Infant Mental Health Journal, 16*(4): 271–291.

Schore, A. (1994). *Affect Regulation and the Origin of the Self*. New York: Routledge, 2016.

Schore, A. (2003). *Affect Dysregulation and Disorders of the Self*. New York: W. W. Norton.

Schore, A. (2012). *The Science and the Art of Psychotherapy*. New York: W. W. Norton.

Segal, H. (1957). Notes on symbol formation. *International Journal of Psychoanalysis, 38*: 391–397.

Siegel, D. J. (2012). *The Developing Mind: How Relationships and the Brain Interact and Shape Who We Are*. New York: Guilford.

Stern, D. (1985). *The Interpersonal World of the Infant: A View from Psychoanalysis and Development*. London: Karnac.

Stern, D. (2010). *Forms of Vitality*. Oxford: Oxford University Press.

Sunderland, M. (2015). *Conversations that Matter: Talking with Children and Teenagers in Ways that Help*. Broadway, UK: Worth.

Trevarthen, C., & Hubley, P. (1978). Secondary intersubjectivity: Confidence, confiding and acts of meaning in the first year of life. In: A. Lock (Ed.), *Action, Gesture and Symbol*. New York: Academic Press.

Tustin, F. (1990). *The Protective Shell in Children and Adults*. London: Karnac.

Van IJzendoorn, M. H., Schuengel, C., & Bakermans-Kranenburg, M. (1999). Disorganised attachment in early childhood: Meta-analysis of precursors, concomitants, and sequalae. *Development and Psychotherapy, 11*(2): 225–249.

Winnicott, D. W. (1963). Fear of breakdown. In: C. Winnicott, R. Shepherd, & M. Davis (Eds.), *Winnicott: Psycho-Analytic Explorations*. London: Karnac.

CHAPTER 9

All in bits: trauma, fragmentation, and the journey of piecing back together

Megan Holland

An integrative model of practice

As operating in a relatively "young" modality, integrative child psychotherapists are faced with the task of constructing a theoretical schema that both draws on the analytic strength of its psychodynamic foundations, and adopts an increasingly relational, intersubjective stance. Outside the context of a single-school approach, the challenge is thus one of holding an informed and dynamic theoretical rapprochement, rather than a more hodgepodge eclecticism. In my own attempts at this endeavour, I have found the image of a spiral a useful one, beginning internally with an examination of intrapsychic structures before curving outwards towards an interpersonal and subsequently wider systemic focus. In this way I aim to maintain a narrative between what Hycner (1991) outlines as the parallel influence of the dialectical-intrapsychic and the dialogical-interpersonal. It is, of course, important to highlight that psychotherapy is at its core a dialogue, not a one-sided relationship in which "one party 'does' to the other" (Evans & Gilbert, 2005, p. 65). In the context of a constantly evolving, coconstructed relationship, the integration of theory might therefore be seen as the coming together of many past and present dialogues in a way that supports and shapes the "how" of therapy.

Beginning with an internal focus, I draw heavily on the work of early object relations theorists (Bion, 1959; Klein, 1946; Mahler et al., 1973) to gain a greater understanding of the structures and dynamics at play in the developing psyche. In particular, the way in which primitive anxieties are managed via intrapsychic splitting and projection (Klein, 1975), also how such mechanisms may reflect systemically, across both familial and professional systems. When considering projection, I further draw on Bion's (1962) concept of "containment", the mother/therapist who catches, processes, and finally returns the "contained" raw projections. Winnicott's (1975) "holding environment", in many ways akin to Bion's "container", provides a link for me between the intrapsychic leaning of Klein and later theorists who emphasised more dominantly the role of the environment.

Turning to an interpersonal focus, Bowlby's (1969) evolutionary based work on attachment introduced a framework for understanding and classifying the nature of psychological connectedness and the subsequent impact on internal relational schemata. Through the identification of observable behaviours, Ainsworth et al.'s subsequent empirical classifications (1978) enabled insight into the nature of a child's often adapted ways of seeking and maintaining contact. In considering the role and function of attachment behaviours, however, I find Crittenden's (1999) identification of a range of identifiable self-protective strategies a very useful template for thinking about differing experiences of trauma and loss. Her preference for Damasio's (1994) "dispositional representations" over Bowlby's (1969) "internal working model" of relationship perhaps helpfully reflects the complexity of internal attachment encodings where mutual and at times conflicting neural representations of relationship may be the norm for maltreated children.

In more closely addressing early failures in socioemotional development, I draw on the work of intersubjective thinkers such as Fonagy (1989), Stern (1998, 2003), and Meins et al. (2002). Stern (2003, p. 66) describes how "categories of affect" in the infant need to be matched by the mother's "vitality of affect" for empathic attunement and co-regulation of feeling to take place. This in turn enables the development of a capacity to self-regulate. In clinically applying such principles, I am influenced by

Hughes's (2006) PACE (playfulness, acceptance, curiosity, and empathy) approach in facilitating attuned and regulating interactions. Grounding my practice in relational neurobiology embeds such interrelational processes in current findings on whole-brain integration (Siegel, 2011), trauma and regulation (Schore, 2001a, 2001b; Siegel, 1999; Van der Kolk, 2014), and affective neuroscience (Panksepp, 1998). For instance, while the importance of image and metaphor may be understood psychoanalytically as a form of unconscious symbolism, it may equally be viewed as a vital tool for enabling the expression of unspoken or preverbal trauma encoded in the right brain. In time, underpinned by the psychobiological attunement of right brain to right brain relating (Schore, 1999), the child may be supported to find words to accompany their pain, perhaps only previously expressed through image. This provision of right brain experience with language, located in Broca's area in the left hemisphere, offers the possibility of cross-hemispheric linking (O'Brien, 2008) or to circle back to a psychoanalytic perspective, to allow for the reparation, or initial formation, of previously attacked thought links (Bion, 1959).

Finally, and perhaps most importantly, a systemic consideration of context is paramount, not only regarding the referred child, but also of the therapy setting and the therapist. Whilst in the current climate there is perhaps some long overdue consideration of questions of race, privilege, and supremacy, against a backdrop of Eurocentric psychanalytic psychotherapy, there is an increasing urgency for clinicians to consider difference both systemically and dynamically. While the dominant theoretical models may at times serve an exploration of difference, for instance Thomas's (2013) application of Winnicott's (1965) "false self" dichotomy, there may be other times when quite simply, "the master's tools" (Lorde, 2018) can't be applied without risking compound trauma and systemic silencing.

Referral and presenting issues

Mia was referred to me in March 2017 by the special educational needs coordinator (SENCo) of the British city primary school she attended; she was six years old at the time. Her class teacher reported that she was prone to extended periods of crying and screaming, often accompanied by lashing out and kicking over classroom furniture. Her "falling apart" usually culminated in her crawling under a table and refusing to come out. Most of Mia's classmates were wary of her, finding it hard to predict her behaviour; her teacher could not name one close friendship. She also noted a pattern of behaviour in Mia of attempting to elicit physical closeness from both staff and peers, but that her attempts appeared confused and were often accompanied by sudden aggression. Academically, Mia was below average in all core subjects, and paired with her lack of self-regulation, learning was a serious struggle.

Background

Mia was the second child to a white British mother and Ethiopian father. Along with her older sister Zala, she lived with her parents until she was five-years-old. Mia's mother Zoey described her as having been "a very good baby", who sat silently in her rocker for hours. Zoey described a history of domestic violence between herself and Mia's father, Yonas, occurring since Mia's infancy. The relationship between Mia's parents had ended after a particularly violent episode, resulting in a neighbour removing the children from the house. At the commencement of therapy, Mia lived with her mother and sister, as well as her maternal aunt, in a single bedroom, high-rise, local authority flat close to the school. Along with her sister, she visited her father at the weekend but these visits were characterised by regular last-minute cancellations. The SENCo informed me that social services had been involved with the family in the past but that after several months of support at "child in need" (CIN) level, the case had been closed. Although with Zoey's permission I attempted to contact Yonas before the start of the work, he politely declined meeting, expressing that he felt his daughter did not need therapy.

Assessment

Before agreeing to work with Mia, I carried out a three-session assessment, structured in accordance with Mees's (2017) "state of mind" framework. This began and ended with a parent meeting and included a brief report that was made available to the SENCo, as the point of referral. These sessions were explained to Mia as a brief period for us to get to know each other, for her to find out what happened in the therapy room, and for us together to decide if she would like to continue seeing me. Regarding the parent sessions, in addition to gathering a more detailed developmental history, a primary goal was to establish if Zoey could reliably support the therapy.

Whilst I lean towards a more psychoanalytically structured assessment, focusing on the child's internal conflicts, defences, and deficits, as an integrative practitioner I simultaneously hold in mind a number of other models. In particular, the overlapping spheres of a biopsychosocial model (Engel, 1977) and Perry's (2006) neurosequential model of therapeutics. In this way an investigation of the mind can be held in tandem with a consideration of the brain–body connection within a neurodevelopmentally and trauma-informed schema.

First impressions

Zoey

Zoey came to our first meeting dressed entirely in black. She was a large woman, her height nearing six foot. I noticed myself feeling physically insubstantial sitting opposite her and wondered if I might be getting a glimpse of how comparatively small Mia might feel. Zoey described her daughter as a "girly girl" who liked everything pink and glittery, the opposite of how she herself had been as a child. "I don't do girly," she told me. I wondered about her acceptance of, and ability to meet a child she saw as so very different from her. I was curious that while Zoey seemed to struggle to identify with the glitterfilled world Mia gravitated towards, she nonetheless described herself as unable to tolerate the difficult emotions in her daughter, a feature that she seemed to have made a part of her own identity, expressed through the slogans on her clothing. I considered how the emotional range seemed to have become split within the family; Zoey described anger and sadness as a key facet of her identity while simultaneously describing her desire for Mia to "only have good feelings". With tears in her eyes she told me that she "would do anything to get [her] little girl back". I noticed, however, that the Mia she described before the family breakdown seemed lacking in substance or detail. I wondered how much space Zoey had had to hold her daughter in mind while struggling with depression, sickness, and an often violent relationship.

Mia

Mia stood silently in the corridor outside her classroom as I introduced myself, her eyes wide, her lips firmly pressed together. She was
a tiny, thin child, appearing much younger than her chronological age.
I was aware that I had imagined her to be much bigger prior to meeting, perhaps to match the bigness of the rage described by Zoey and her
class teacher. I observed later that she had appeared almost fairylike.
I wondered to what extent the world of fairies had become an almost
physical manifestation and potential psychic defence against all that was
not pretty in her life.

In our first assessment session, Mia arrived with a backpack of Disney
princesses. My sense was that she had literally brought her "false self"
with her in physical form. I wondered at the resourcefulness of arriving
with attractive dolls she could present to me and place between us, perhaps unconsciously aiming to cover a sense of internal lack. I noted that
for the most part, these dolls had white skin. I considered the possibility
that she may have brought the child she felt I would want. On gently ver-
balising my interest in their skin colour, Mia told me that the princesses
were "like that in the film"; she turned away, seemingly closing down.
I noticed a sense of discomfort in myself, aware of my location racially as
part of the dominant ethnicity. On reflection, I realised that my discomfort may well have been a projective identification (Klein, 1946) with
discomfort or shame in Mia. I did not yet know how Mia understood
her own ethnicity, nor what ethnicity she perceived in me. I felt it highly
likely that Mia's racial identity would be comprised of many different
projections and experiences, not all positive. At this early stage I knew I
would need to remain aware and curious about how difference operated
within the relationship. I considered the need to maintain "an atmosphere of open enquiry" (Lapworth et al., 2001, p. 69), aware that racial
and cultural meanings may be fluid.

Throughout the session I was acutely aware of the strength of Mia's
defence systems. Where I expressed curiosity regarding the thoughts
or feelings of characters in her play, Mia remained silent, on one
occasion physically turning her back to me and presenting me with a
faceless wall. Her play was filled with themes of spoiling, deprivation,
and powerlessness. The princess got mud on her dress, Superman's

cape stopped working and in the midst of chaos and sometimes brutal violence, the baby doll was "happier when asleep". Countertransferentially, I found myself feeling overwhelmed by a sense of disorganisation, an unconscious communication perhaps of the nature of an internal world with no available "containing object" to help her process her feelings (Bion, 1962).

An integrative perspective on Mia's presenting issues

As a result of Mia's early experiences of domestic violence, maternal depression, and parental separation, she seemed to be acting out unregulated feelings of betrayal, fear, and shame. In addition, she appeared to be re-enacting her experiences of chaos, violence, and abandonment through episodes of dysregulated rage (falling apart) and grief. From an object relations perspective, Mia's relationship to her internal "objects" appeared predominantly characterised by processes of splitting and projection (Klein, 1946), particularly in relation to vulnerability and rage. An image that I held in mind at this time was one of a puzzle where each piece was separated; I felt that this was a little girl whose internal states were "all in bits" (Segal, 1998, p. 213).

Holding together Mia's experience of early relational trauma, descriptions of her behaviour both at home and school, and her presentation in therapy, her experiences appeared to have resulted in an insecure attachment style (Main & Solomon, 1990). Moreover, her frequent episodes of disintegration, paired with the presence of approach–withdrawal behaviours, indicated a lack of organised attachment behaviour when either under stress or seeking to navigate interpersonal contact. While from the referring data it appeared that Mia's behaviour lacked an organisational strategy, often characterised by behavioural disintegration and dissociation, certain interactions in our assessment sessions appeared to indicate her management of stress via avoidant responses. These differed from what Main and Hesse (1992) described as disorganised behaviours marked by "fear without solution", a description that fitted the scenarios at referral of screaming, throwing objects, and hiding under the table.

I considered at this point, therefore, that Mia may have different internal attachment schemas stemming from the variably available and containing caregivers she had experienced thus far. Whilst a more disorganised pattern appeared to have predominated, when offered a one-to-one, sensitive, and attuned focus, a more organised, albeit avoidant behavioural attachment strategy appeared available to her. This was tempered, however, by the dominating play themes that continued to characterise her small-world play; characters vacillated between "good" and "bad", fantastical themes tended towards repetitive, catastrophic endings, and interpersonal conflicts could only be solved via magical omnipotence or total annihilation. Such themes suggested a dominating disorganised internal attachment schema, as categorised within the "disorganisation" construct formulated in the "story stem assessment profile" (Hodges & Steele, 2000).

In addition, although usually present to a degree in all insecure styles, a high need to control is a trait identified by Hughes (1997) as key to children with disorganised attachments; high control behaviours were described by both Mia's mother and teacher and characterised the assessment sessions. Crittenden and Claussen (2002) attribute this trait to a felt sense that it is unsafe to let a helpless or hostile caregiver remain in charge, leading to strategies of either compulsive self-reliance or punitive aggressive control.

From information Zoey provided in our first parent meeting, I understood Mia's early experiences of her mother as likely to have involved long periods of daytime sleep, depressed episodes, and at times, hostile and violent behaviour. Zoey described Mia's father as prone to unpredictable rage while simultaneously struggling with bouts of low mood, all factors that would likely have created a "wired-in" (Balbernie, 2001, p. 245) hypervigilant response in Mia. Here the brainstem and midbrain, the areas controlling reactions to perceived danger, become undermodulated, resulting in increased unconscious risk scanning. Her potential neurochemistry and stress reactivity, in conjunction with a possible genetic vulnerability, represented part of my consideration of biological factors for Mia. Given their own struggles with mental ill health and poor attachment histories, both parents were likely to have struggled to attune to Mia's early emotional and psychological needs. As well as indicating potential interruptions or "gaps" from a neurosequential perspective, regarding attachment theory, this would have left Mia in uncontained states of anxiety, resulting in a chronically activated attachment system (Ainsworth et al., 1978). As Schore (2001b, p. 16) notes, "[S]everely compromised attachment histories are … associated with brain organisations that are inefficient in regulating affective states … engender[ing] maladaptive infant mental health."

I hypothesised that Mia had internalised a psychological construct of herself as bad, unloveable, and deserving of abandonment, of others as either weak and vulnerable or cruel and frightening, and of relationships as unpredictable and unsafe. In exploring Mia's attachment to her key caregivers, I considered whether her relationship to her aunt might be considered as a potential protective factor. On meeting with me during a later family session, she described a deep love for Mia, although she found both her sister's and niece's behaviour hard to think about and understand.

Whilst I was aware that Mia fulfilled the *DSM-5*—"Axis I" (American Psychiatric Association, 2013) criteria for both reactive attachment disorder (RAD) and post-traumatic stress disorder (PTSD), like many children who have experienced abuse and neglect during critical developmental periods, Mia did not fit easily into the *DSM-5* framework. Both diagnoses appeared limited in encapsulating the breadth of symptoms and developmental impairments arising from "complex trauma" (Cook et al., 2005), or trauma that has impaired multiple domains such as attachment, cognitive function, affective regulation, and physical and emotional development. This temporal view of trauma across key developmental periods was further elaborated in Van der Kolk's (2005) proposed diagnosis of developmental trauma disorder. Although not published at the time of assessment, I subsequently feel that the "Power Threat Meaning Framework" (Johnstone & Boyle, 2018) offers a helpful alternative to a more medicalised model by linking wider social factors to subsequent patterns of meaning-based responses to threat, through a culturally specific lens.

Anticipated direction of psychotherapy

From my assessment sessions I formulated a number of central goals. From a physiological perspective, my aim was to reduce Mia's episodes of disintegration and rage by attuning to, and co-regulating, her somatic and affective experience, particularly bringing the left brain's capacity for language to bear on her right brain's "felt but not fully understood mental states" (Howe, 2005, p. 234). I hoped that by containing Mia's split-off and projected parts, a process of psychic integration could occur, resulting in a more "depressive" (Klein, 1946) way of being. From an attachment perspective, I balanced my hopes that Mia would internalise more secure ways of being with Crittenden's (2006, p. 112) acknowledgement that where the original dynamics of insecurity perpetuate, "the goal of the treatment is psychological balance and not security". I subsequently aimed to expand the available attachment strategies accessible to Mia through repeated intersubjective interactions that would mirror those of secure parent–child relationships. Once sufficient physiological and affective regulation had been established, my ultimate aim was to support Mia towards a greater reflective capacity and the development of a coherent and congruent understanding of her lived experience.

Mindful of the complexities of this case and aware that Mia had needs that could not be met by therapy alone, I arranged to meet with Mia's teacher and the SENCo fortnightly. I suggested a programme of attachment-based strategies to support Mia in class, drawn from Bomber's (2011) practical approach to fostering secure attachments in school. I held in mind the need for team cohesion, aware of the risks of psychic splits within Mia becoming mirrored in the surrounding adults. I arranged to meet with Zoey twice termly. In accordance with the school's therapy framework, sessions with Mia were limited to one academic year.

Establishing the working alliance

"The therapeutic alliance is the powerful joining of forces which energises and supports the long, difficult and frequently painful work of life-changing psychotherapy" (Bugental, 1987, p. 49).

As part of our first session, I offered Mia a simple explanation of the boundaries of the therapy, including the frequency, confidentiality, and "contained" nature of the space; nothing could be taken from the room but instead would be kept safe in her box. Mia listened without making eye contact; I noticed her running her hand up the table leg and resting it flat against the wall above her head. I considered whether she might be physically exploring the spatial boundary as an unconscious response to my description of the therapeutic one, checking the safety of the space I offered. Given her history of multiple and often sudden shifts, I aimed to create a consistent and predictable structure. With these objectives in mind, I employed Hughes's (2006) PACE model as a means of fostering attunement, aware of research suggesting a correlation between the quality of the working alliance in early therapy and the final outcome (Horvath & Symonds, 1991).

While Mia responded to her box with expressed excitement, bouncing on her heels and reaching forward, almost immediately her affect flattened and she turned to tell me that she had an identical box at home, "only much bigger". Mollon (1996, p. 65) describes a key characteristic of disorganised attachment as the presence of an "internal controller" within the child. This part aims to guard against the danger of being devastated again as a result of dependence on another.

I felt that Mia's "internal controller" was here communicating a need to hold me, and what I offered, at a distance in order to feel safe. In this instance I felt her "bigger" box revealed a fragile grandiosity, a defence against believing that I might have anything good to offer. Within my own countertransference, I noticed that her words evoked a feeling of smallness and insufficiency. Winnicott described such emotional reactions as holding "valuable internal clues about what is going on in the patient" (1975, p. 195). This led me to consider Taransaud's (2011) concept of the "omnipotent self", an elaboration of Winnicott's (1965) "false self". For Taransaud, the omnipotent self performs the defensive function of protecting the split-off wounded self from further harm. This "illusion of control and omnipotence" (2011, p. 33) is maintained by displacing vulnerability and internal conflict onto others through projection. First explored by Klein (1946), this "schizoid mechanism" allows an individual to manage the split-off and projected part through controlling the other.

I felt that even in this small and seemingly insignificant interaction with Mia, she had presented me with the rigid defensiveness of her omnipotent self whilst I was left holding the projected impotency of her wounded self. It was thus clear from the beginning of therapy that I would need to allow the transference to "reverberate" (Wallin, 2007, p. 129) internally as a guide to understanding the meaning of her defences.

The process of a sudden flattening of affect following peaked excitement was later mirrored physically in the sand tray; Mia built up sand peaks then abruptly flattened them with her hand. On wondering out loud what it might be like for the sand to be built higher and then suddenly find itself squashed, Mia responded that the sand felt "nothing. It feels like nothing." I considered the "nothing" in conjunction with the toy baby who was described as "happier when asleep" from our assessment, viewing both as possible evidence of a dissociative cut-off from feeling. This aligned with what I had been told about her behaviour in class, moving from escalated screaming to sudden apparent calm, albeit often in a "zombie-like" manner. I imagined how Mia's "fear-terror" (Perry, 1995) was likely mediated by sympathetic hyperarousal before numbing into a parasympathetic dominant state of metabolic shutdown (Schore, 2009). I also considered whether the sand feeling, "*like* nothing" might reflect the depleted sense of self I imagined lay hidden beneath the omnipotent defence, perhaps an indicator of underlying shame.

Early in our work together I felt it important to let Mia know a basic version of the information I had been given about her. Using sand tray figures she had picked out to represent her family, I showed her the key information her mother had shared with me. After exploring basic family configurations together, I let her know that I had been told that when she was younger, she had seen and heard her parents fighting. I showed her with the characters how I knew that her family was now split between two houses. Finally, I told her gently that I imagined this might have created muddles, confusion, and hurt, feelings that I wanted to help her with. As I spoke, Mia slowly turned her back towards me and I saw her muscles stiffen; she started to play with the figures on the floor, literally hiding her family from my view. Aware that she was demonstrating a "defensive withdrawal" (Casement, 1985, p. 54), I made the decision to acknowledge her defence and the purpose it had served, while simultaneously suggesting alternative ways of being. I did this by speaking to the only part of her I felt she was showing me.

Therapist: Oh Mia's back, thank you for showing me that my words felt too much, you are doing such a great job of looking after her right now. The thing is, if I never mention the hard things, I leave her all on her own with hurting memories and tricky thoughts: what a lot for a six-year-old.

As I spoke, I noticed Mia's body softening. She wiggled her back in a way that seemed to suggest response. Finally, she turned towards me and put the family figures back between us on the floor. "Can we do playdough now?" she said. I felt that contact had been re-established, also that she had reached the upper limit of her narrow "window of tolerance" (Siegel, 1999). Although no doubt difficult for Mia, I felt this was a key moment in demonstrating that we could survive ruptures in connection and that these could be repaired (Beebe & Stern, 1977).

Winning and losing: bearing the projective identification

In considering Mia's behaviour within a framework of insecure attachment, her desire to control represented an "adaptive strategy for reducing danger" (Crittenden, 1999). Within our sessions this trait was characterised by her frequent initiation of competitive games. During this time, I came to understand a good deal of how Mia perceived failure. If she perceived herself to have "failed", she would fling a toy angrily towards the rubbish bin. I empathised with the feeling of being thrown away or being made to feel like rubbish; however, it seemed that only the relief of winning could temporarily dissipate the shame surrounding her fragile core self. This became apparent when she began to alter the rules, inventing clauses that allowed her to win based on arbitrary and constantly shifting factors. Schaefer and Reid (2001) describe the "working through" of a set of rules as often the first area of conflictual interaction within the therapy.

I wondered whether Mia was perhaps unconsciously setting up such interactions to bring the conflict she experienced within herself into the relationship. From a Kleinian perspective, I felt I was again being asked to hold her split-off feelings of disgust, insufficiency, and anger as she embodied the sole position of winner. With these positions held polarised in the room, I responded to what I perceived to be the communication held within the projection: "You are really letting me know what it feels like to be a loser, just how yucky it feels." By voicing the projective identification, also described by Klein as the "aggressive object relation" (1946, p. 8), my aim was to bring the expelled feelings into awareness. My thinking here was also influenced by Bion's (1962) theory of containment, my interpretation aiming to catch Mia's projected raw material and sit with the unprocessed pain of feeling rubbished. Simultaneously, it seemed Mia was identifying with the position of the aggressor (Ferenczi, 1933) described by Anna Freud as identifying with the "dreaded external object" (1937, p. 118). By taking on the role of persecutor and casting me in the role of victim, Mia was likely mirroring a dynamic she had experienced, perhaps even casting me in the role of her white-skinned mother.

I gently tested her awareness of parental transferences by asking if I reminded her, in that moment, of anybody she knew. "No," she answered. I subsequently proceeded to work with the submission/dominance dynamic purely within our relationship, employing a technique used by Hughes (1998) of playful protest when faced with controlling behaviour. Using enhanced prosody, I communicated my experience of the sudden shifts and changes in the game and my consequent feelings of disorientation and indignation, feelings I was aware were mirrored in her life: "I thought I understood what was happening and then, bam, shock, I'm back to being at the bottom again! How horrible!" This response seemed to do little to alter the relational dynamic, however, likely indicating Mia's insufficient prior experiences of intersubjective mentalization (Howe, 2005). Winnicott (1967) explores this developmental deficit, locating relational withdrawal as a consequence of inadequate maternal mirroring. This aligned with Zoey's description of Mia as a baby, sitting "silently in her rocker for hours".

After several sessions in this vein I began to notice feelings of boredom and annoyance emerge countertransferentially. I realised that I had in part become an avoidant, neglectful mother in the transference, struggling to look at and feel the weight of pain she was giving me. In response, I decided to bring in another character to the transaction as a voice for what Mia's unconscious might be asking me to bear. In the next session, during such a moment I brought in a puppet to say: "Megan, Mia's only showing you a tiny bit of what it feels like to be a loser, this isn't nearly as bad as it felt for her. You are talking so as not to have to feel it. Shut up and feel it."

I was influenced here by Sunderland's (2015) description of projective identification as the client's request of the therapist to "feel my feelings". In answer to my intervention, Mia responded by making eye contact. "Yeah, be the loser," she said. I responded by showing Mia what it felt like in my body to feel like a loser. She watched as I hunched my shoulders and knotted my stomach, joining in by telling me that I "wouldn't want to eat lunch". I noticed her take a step closer to me as I expressed how horrible it felt to be so knotted up with "loser feelings" that I could not even eat. I held in mind the relationship between trauma and the body, particularly the digestive system (Van der Kolk, 2014), indicative of acute emotional and physical dysregulation.

At the same time as competitive games became a prevalent part of our sessions, role play based on themes of domination also featured highly. The bossing and belittling was not confined to role play however. While this offered useful insight into the nature of Mia's object relations, I also felt the impact physically, at times experiencing an extreme fatigue. Holding in mind her need for me to feel, and survive, her lived experience, I additionally considered how I might best connect with Mia's process in a way that worked towards the linking together of thoughts (Bion, 1959) rather than risking re-enacting patterns of (potentially thoughtless) abuse.

After many weeks of feeling like my words fell into the space between us, I decided to restrict the "bossing" to role play, hypothesising that this boundary would provide an edge up against which Mia's absolute rage at not being truly omnipotent could be met. I explained this restriction to Mia using a game with puppets, knowing that this message would need to be sensitively communicated to navigate her potential shame. Together we explored the ways people were similar and different to puppets. I gently explained that unlike the puppets, I could not make her do things and she could not make me do things. Mia nodded, indicating that she had understood.

Winnicott (1969) described how attacks in the transference must be survived by the therapist without defensive retaliation if the client is to see the therapist as outside his omnipotent control. This facilitates the client beginning to use the therapist as a "real object" rather than as a projected part of himself. As Mia's desire for omnipotence met the boundary I had placed outside fantasy, I was then able to work with her fury by drawing it into the relationship. At my invitation, Mia wrote: "Megan is so rood tday and I dont lick [like] it" (Figure 9.1a), and "Megan is not doing what I am saying" (Figure 9.1b).

I celebrated her bravery in telling me how she felt while simultaneously empathising with just how upsetting it felt when I didn't obey her, expressed by her as "rudeness". At moments when I felt her move towards me and make eye contact, I tentatively referenced some of the reasons why this dynamic may have come into play in her life.

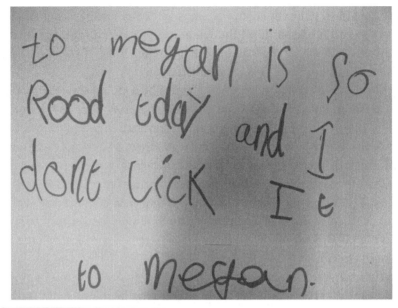

Figure 9.1a Note from Mia to Megan

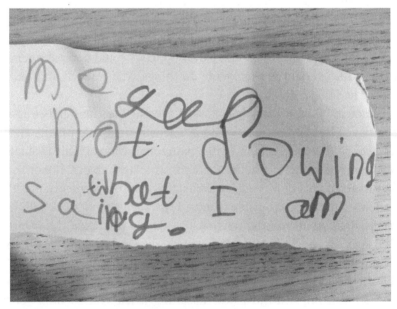

Figure 9.1b Note 2 from Mia to Megan

Therapist: You know, Mia, I wonder if maybe you really know what it feels like to not be in charge over big people … and for those big people to do things that made you feel small and not safe. [*long pause*] Maybe you decided to always, always be in charge because your heart kept getting hurt.

Mia listened, pulling out a new piece of paper and turned to face the wall. It was clear that she didn't want me to see what she had written. I discovered later that she had written, "My hart is brocan [broken]."

Making a way for care

In our second term of therapy, I saw a shift in Mia's play as she moved away from using me as an object to compete with, bringing instead a narrative replete with life data. Asking me to "be Mr Giraffe", a regular thinking character in our sessions, Mia directed me to hold the puppet over the sand tray while she fed it. Her inclusion of me in non-competitive play marked a development in our relationship, signalling an increase in trust. Mia told the story of a zookeeper who went away and left her in charge. The zookeeper had not looked after the giraffe, starving it for many days. I gently observed how hungry the giraffe must be, how alone he must have felt without any care. Mia continued to feed the giraffe with sand, asking me to join her. After a short time, however, she told me that she wanted to feed the giraffe alone. She took the puppet and cradled it in her lap, continuing to pour sand into its mouth. I felt at this point that she was taking and caring for a starved, neglected part of herself. This aligned with a switch in gender, the giraffe becoming female.

Mia: She is always hungry.
Therapist: Girl giraffe, kept hungry for such a long time. I wonder if she wishes she came from a family with a mummy and daddy giraffe who could give her all the food that she needs …
Mia: She does wish that. She has a family but they couldn't feed her.
Therapist: So painful to have a family and still not get what you need.

Figure 9.2 Mr Giraffe with plasters applied after being "beaten"

As the narrative progressed, Mia told me that before his departure the zookeeper had beaten the giraffe, punching her mouth. "There was a lot of blood," she said. I tracked her gently, empathising with the giraffe's experience, giving voice to some of the core feelings I felt might be present: shock, betrayal, fear, sadness. Internally, I balanced both the possibility of the giraffe as a maternal figure and as a part of Mia, who had identified so significantly and age appropriately with her mother and had perhaps herself felt beaten, bloodied, and abandoned.

Continuing to hold the giraffe, Mia took out the toy doctor's kit and began to unwrap multiple plasters, applying them to the puppet (Figure 9.2). She covered its mouth telling me that this was where it had been beaten. "She can't speak," she said. This image, reminiscent of Van der Kolk's (2014, p. 43) exploration of the "speechless horror" that occurs neurologically during trauma, simultaneously seemed to demonstrate the confusion familiar to familial violence; the plasters, usually an image of care, here seemed complicit in an act of violation. I was conscious of not wanting to mirror their role by taking away Mia's words with my own. I responded with little language, therefore, reflecting the weight of impact through my tone, prosody, and body stance: "And Giraffe couldn't even speak … all shut up … all alone."

Parent support sessions at this time involved an exploration of mirrored themes regarding deprivation and silencing, Zoey sharing in greater depth the different ways she had felt "shut up" by Yonas during their relationship, particularly after episodes of violence. Together we were able to think about what had happened to her voice, to the protest she had tried to mount, and how a sense of futility had led to its embodiment in a physical shutting down in bed-bound fatigue. In parallel, as she experienced empathic containment in relation to her own trauma, Zoey was incrementally able to consider what internal experiences her "good" baby may have had in infancy. In particular, the way in which witnessed abuse preverbally may be being voiced behaviourally in the present.

Confusion, mess, and shame: searching in the murky water

In the following sessions I began to witness a spilling out and overflowing quality to Mia's play, a quality that seemed to convey pure feelings of invasion, confusion, and overwhelm. Exploring the links between creativity and trauma, O'Brien (2008, p. 3) notes that it is possible that "[T]hrough the creation of mess, children may be reconnecting neural pathways by activating nearby parts of the brain through a visual process that retrieves emotional experience." I wondered if through her use of the materials, Mia was showing me what her internal space looked like, perhaps drawing into focus emotional experience inaccessible through language alone. In the early part of the work, Mia's artwork had predominantly focused on meticulously sketched princesses, often ripped symbolically into pieces if felt to not meet an impossibly high internal standard. In this later phase, falling towards the end of our second term of therapy, her images had transformed into floor sized creations of poured paint, sand, and flour (Figure 9.3). Holding little symbolism, I felt these images were an exposing and evacuating of her unintegrated somatic and affective experience of trauma, as well as an unconscious testing of what the therapy room, and by extension me as the therapist, could contain.

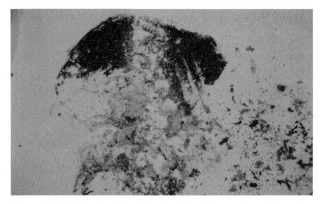

Figure 9.3 Mia's artwork of poured paint, sand, and flour

After a number of weeks of remaining alongside her "mess making", a process that at times included our standing barefoot together within her images and physically "feeling her feelings" (Sunderland, 2015), Mia asked why she came for therapy. I felt that her experience of the created mess had provided a mirror, bringing to consciousness her muddled feelings regarding both her story and how it might relate to what therapy offered. Her curiosity, however, emerged in tandem with a part of her that would attempt to attack any direct thinking about her lived experience at every turn. I opted, therefore, to employ metaphor as a less threatening avenue for communicating her life story.

Figure 9.4 Mia's painting of the frogs in the storm

I told Mia a story of a family of frogs who experienced an awful storm. The storm bashed and battered their lily pad home before finally lifting the father away, carrying him to the other side of the pond. Shortly into my telling of the story, Mia took over, urgently describing how the storm had not only lifted the father frog away from the daughter, but the mother frog as well. She painted the mother frog high in the sky where the clouds bashed together and rained blood (Figure 9.4). I felt here that Mia was communicating that she had not only been separated from her father, but through the violence, and perhaps subsequent depression, she had also lost her mother. In the image both parents were out of reach as the little girl frog sat alone on her lily pad.

> Mia: She's sitting here [*points to the girl frog*] … it's all smashed.
> Therapist: All smashed up … so, so alone … pieces everywhere.

In the following sessions, as Mia returned to her images of poured paint, sand, and water, symbolism began to develop. A recurrent theme emerged of animals losing their babies in the murky pots of paint water. Again, there was a strong sense of loneliness, abandonment, and confusion. I remained gently alongside Mia, tracking the experience of each lost baby, gently linking together narrative threads. In the transference I often felt cast in the role of the depriving maternal object (Klein, 1946), neglecting and abandoning the baby toys in my absence between sessions. This offered opportunities to reflect on what Mia might be telling me about her baby self not only in the past but also in relation to me in the present:

> Therapist: It really feels like I did not look after your baby, like I left her all alone. How frightened she must have been.
> Mia: So frightening … and crossing!
> Therapist: So crossing! Maybe this baby would like to say, "How dare you not be here for me every day! Not enough, I need so much."
> Mia: Yeah, how dare you!
> Therapist: Tell me.
> Mia: You didn't look after her all the days. And forever and forever for you to come back.

Therapist: Oh baby, so, so alone. Like the time between sessions stretches forever.

In meeting and containing Mia's expressions of abandonment and neglect through her "lost babies", a trust sufficient to hold a deeper exploration of the frog story emerged. Painting the mother, father, and little girl now trapped underneath the surface (Figure 9.5), Mia placed the girl frog underneath "the lovely silver part", while the mother and father were placed underneath the red of the blood rain. In the picture, Mia drew the girl frog now with long silver hair and outstretched hands:

Therapist: Little girl, what are you doing with your hands?
      Mia: I'm trying to see if I can find my dad.
Therapist: Ah, you're searching for your dad? Where did he go?
      Mia: He's gone now.
Therapist: He's gone.
      Mia: I said she's gone.
Therapist: It seems like when Daddy goes it feels like she goes too?

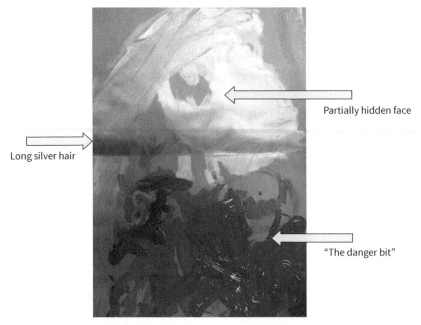

Partially hidden face

Long silver hair

"The danger bit"

Figure 9.5 Mia's painting of the trapped frog family

I felt here that she was showing me the unconscious expression of her own lost self when her father left. The splitting of good and bad felt central to the separation of father and daughter and with it the creation of a pseudo false self that needed to present as perfect in order to defend against suffocating shame. Jacoby (1994) observes how the presence of shame can lead to the development of a grandiose self that demands perfection. This was observable a few minutes later:

Therapist: [*talking to the image*] Dad, I was just talking to your little girl a minute ago. I wondered what happened that meant you weren't together anymore.

Mia: I'm in the danger bit.

Therapist: You're in the danger bit. What's it like there?

Mia: Not safe. Ah, I need to do the hair again. I messed it up a bit.

Therapist: I'm noticing that when we are talking about some of the difficult feelings of daddy frog in the picture, the little girl felt like she'd messed it up. When she feels messy she might need to do her hair again.

Mia showed here through the metaphor the intrapsychic process of being sucked down and hidden beneath the surface of her trauma, perhaps also protectively hidden behind the long, silvery, princess-like hair. On reflection I feel that in asking her what the "danger place" was like I reached her upper level of tolerance (Siegel, 1999), leading to an uncomfortable, messy feeling that she needed to tidy. While her proffered narrative regarding her image was that of the frog family, I was also aware that her picture simultaneously held qualities of a self-portrait: the projected silver "face", potentially replete with cultural whiteness, sitting atop an obscured body of slashed blood red.

This is my story

Falling at the beginning of our final term of therapy, Mia's exploration of her life story through the metaphor of the frog family, marked a significant development in her ability to tolerate an exploration of the wounded self that lay behind her omnipotent defences (Taransaud, 2011). This paved the way in the following session for a shift away from metaphor. Shortly after arriving, Mia picked up a puppet, telling me that as "teacher", she was going to tell me a "scary story". I understood this hierarchical reversal of the teacher/child role acting as a form of self-empowerment to stave off feelings of vulnerability. Within the role of teacher, Mia narrated the story of her early years from a third person perspective before lifting her voice dramatically and telling me that "The dad ... broke up ... with the mum." Mia went on to describe the night of violence that led to her removal from her parents' house two years prior.

> Mia: The police wanted to just sort out the argument. They just talked to them and then everything was fine until they broke up again. Then they broke up again. Then they broke up again. Then Kelly [*the neighbour*] just came.
>
> Therapist: Arguing and breaking up again and again and again ... so much for little Mia to hear and see.
>
> Mia: And Kelly took Mia and Zala. Well, Mia had to quickly put a dress on upstairs, and it was really cold.
>
> Therapist: So cold. I wonder if Mia could hear her mum and dad fighting when she had to dress so fast?
>
> Mia: I did. I did, because I'm Mia.
>
> Therapist: You're Mia. You are. And I think right now you are telling me something really important that happened to you.
>
> Mia: Yes. I am.

As Mia continued to tell her story, she interspersed snippets of fictional horror alongside a more literal telling, seemingly aiming to communicate the level of terror held within her own "scary story": "And then a zombie jumped out. And a ghost; a skeleton!" These fictional interruptions broke up and confused her own narrative, mirroring the jagged disorientation of trauma. They were simultaneously reminiscent of the disowned parts of herself that perhaps felt replete with evil and darkness, parts that she might have feared would shock me.

I wondered if she was showing me how her internal "ghosts" interrupted her sense of "going on being" (Winnicott, 1956) in daily life. When she revealed later that she understood her parents to have been fighting about her and her sister, I subsequently considered whether these phantoms were internal representations of self, neither fully alive nor dead, holding all the split-off badness of self-blame (Klein, 1946). I held in mind the potent imagery of Fraiberg et al.'s (1975) conceptualisation of "ghosts in the nursery", traumatic family phantoms echoing inter-generationally. On reflection, I feel it would have been additionally helpful to have expressed Mia's possible desire to scare me, just as she had been scared. Simultaneously to acknowledge, even internally, that her parents may have appeared to her as terrifying, similar to the fictional horrors.

Towards an ending

In the final weeks of therapy, Mia continued to examine her lived experience of relational trauma both in and out of metaphor, increasingly using me as a "safe holder" (O'Brien, 2008) for the reflective processing and integration of her often chaotic and fragmented memories. In exploring the violence she had witnessed between her parents, a gentle unravelling began of Mia's conflation of skin colour with "aggressive blackness", both as a socially driven racist trope but also as part of a systemic linking within her family of violence with race. From aligning, in Mia's words, "bad and black, black and bad", together we were able to explore her experience of cultural whiteness, particularly within the world of fairy tales, and her desire for me to feel as a white woman her experience of blackness within her world, her family, and her school.

In the final sessions Mia vacillated between an energetic avoidance of our impending ending, again leaning into the initiation of competitive games, and a more reflective reviewing of all the art objects she had made. Within the context of a life punctuated by repeated and sudden "thoughtless" losses, I held onto the importance of facilitating an ending where loss could be thought about and separation navigated in a way that was experienced as neither punitive nor persecutory.

Reflection on the therapeutic journey

In the ongoing presence of significant maternal depression and parental hostility, therapy provided Mia with a much-needed experience of continuity in a life marked by "too often repeated disruptions" (Kenrick, 2006, p. 71). Whilst at the end of our work Mia still leaned towards avoidant and controlling behaviours when faced with overwhelming affect, on the whole these defensive strategies appeared organised rather than tipping her into hyperarousal and behavioural disorganisation. There was also evidence of our relationship having been internalised by Mia as secure enough to travel through rupture to repair, and of herself as deserving of commitment, rather than the abandonment and neglect she had both experienced and come to expect. This was demonstrated poignantly in our penultimate session:

> Mia: I know you love me.
> Therapist: [*smiling*] How did you come to see that?
> Mia: Because you come back and back and back! Even when I wrote mean things about you, you still came back!

Regarding my own experience of working therapeutically with Mia, the unprocessed nature of her material at times triggered intense feelings of powerlessness, hopelessness, and frustration. On reflection, I realise there were moments when my feelings of impotency led to a misattunement with Mia's defence mechanisms, creating periods of impasse that could only be circumnavigated through working directly with the negative transference. I discovered, however, that where these misattunements mirrored early failures, an opportunity was created to facilitate a new experience of understanding and repair.

Menakem (2017, p. 8) describes trauma as "a wordless story our body tells itself about what is safe and what is a threat". In the context of a therapeutic journey that moved from wordless re-enactment towards a claimed narrative, I feel it fitting to end with Mia's words, taken from our final session. Mia held a stethoscope to her chest, listening carefully.

> Therapist: What can you hear?
> Mia: My heart.
> Therapist: Heart, I wonder what you might be saying to Mia today?
> Mia: [*pauses*] I'm healing now.

Conclusion

This chapter has explored the therapeutic journey of a multiply traumatised latency child, from a state of intrapsychic fragmentation, expressed via attachment disorganisation, towards the formation of more secure ways of being. Focus was paid to the necessity of bearing the projected hostility within the relationship as a means of creating a "containing" space in which the trauma narrative could later be told. A need to work concurrently with the embodied experience of trauma was held alongside the importance of internal psychological processing.

References

Ainsworth, M. D. S., Blehar, M. C., Waters, E., & Wall, S. (1978). *Patterns of Attachment: A Psychological Study of the Strange Situation.* Hillsdale, NJ: Lawrence Erlbaum.

American Psychiatric Association (2013). *Desk Reference to the Diagnostic Criteria from DSM5.* Arlington, VA: American Psychiatric Association.

Balbernie, R. (2001). Circuits and circumstances: The neurobiological consequences of early relationship experiences and how they shape later behaviour. *Journal of Child Psychotherapy, 27*(3): 237–255.

Beebe, B., & Stern, D. (1977). Engagement–disengagement and early object experiences. In: N. Freedman & S. Grand (Eds.), *Communicative Structures and Psychic Structures* (pp. 35–55). New York: Plenum.

Bion, W. R. (1959). Attacks on linking. *International Journal of Psychoanalysis, 40*: 308–315.

Bion, W. R. (1962). *Learning from Experience.* London: Karnac, 1984.

Bomber, L. M. (2011). *What About Me? Inclusive Strategies to Support Pupils with Attachment Difficulties Make It Through the School Day.* London: Worth.

Bowlby, J. (1969). *Attachment and Loss: Vol. 1 Attachment.* New York: Basic Books.

Bugental, J. (1987). *Art of the Psychotherapist.* New York: W. W. Norton.

Casement, P. (1985). *On Learning from the Patient.* Hove, UK: Routledge.

Cook, A., Spinazzola, J., Ford, J., Lanktree, C., Blaustein, M., Cloitre, M., De Rosa, R., Hubbard, R., Kagan, R., Liautaud, J., Mallah, K., Olafson, E., & Van der Kolk, B. (2005). Complex trauma in children and adolescents. *Psychiatric Annals, 35*(5): 390–398.

Crittenden, P. M. (1999). Danger and development: The organization of selfprotective strategies. In: J. I. Vondra & D. Barnett, (Eds.), *Atypical Attachment in Infancy and Early Childhood among Children at Developmental Risk* (pp. 145–171). Monographs of the Society for Research on Child Development. Hoboken, NJ: Wiley-Blackwell.

Crittenden, P. M. (2006). Attachment theory, psychopathology, and psychotherapy: The dynamic-maturational approach. *Psicoterapia, 30*: 171–182.

Crittenden, P. M., & Claussen, A. H. (2002). Developmental psychopathology perspectives on substance abuse and relationship violence. In: C. Wekerle & A. M. Wall (Eds.), *The Violence and Addiction Equation: Theoretical and Clinical Issues in Substance Abuse and Relationship Violence* (pp. 44–63). Philadelphia, PA: BrunnerMazel.

Damasio, A. (1994). *Descartes' Error: Emotion, Reason, and the Human Brain.* New York: Avon.

Engel, G. (1977). The need for a new medical model: A challenge for biomedicine. *Science, 196*: 129–136.

Evans, K., & Gilbert, M. (2005). *An Introduction to Integrative Psychotherapy.* Basingstoke, UK: Palgrave Macmillan.

Ferenczi, S. (1933). Confusion of tongues between adults and the child – the language of tenderness and of passion. In: *Final Contributions to the Problems and Methods of PsychoAnalysis* (pp. 156–167). London: Karnac, 1980.

Fonagy, P. (1989). On tolerating mental states: Theory of mind in borderline personality. *Bulletin of the Anna Freud Centre, 12*: 91–115.

Fraiberg, S., Adelson, E., & Shapiro, V. (1975). Ghosts in the nursery: A psychoanalytic approach to the problems of impaired infantmother relationships. *Journal of American Academy of Child Psychiatry, 14*(3): 387–421.

Freud, A. (1937). *The Ego and the Mechanisms of Defense.* London: Hogarth.

Hodges J., & Steele, M. (2000). Effects of abuse on attachment representations: Narrative assessments of abused children. *Journal of Child Psychotherapy, 26*: 433–455.

Horvath, A. O., & Symonds, B. D. (1991). Relation between working alliance and outcome in psychotherapy: A metaanalysis. *Journal of Counselling Psychology, 38*: 139–149.

Howe, D. (2005). *Child Abuse and Neglect: Attachment, Development and Intervention.* Basingstoke, UK: Palgrave Macmillan.

Hughes, D. (1997). *Facilitating Developmental Attachment: The Road to Emotional Recovery and Behavioral Change in Foster and Adopted Children.* Lanham, MD: Jason Aronson.

Hughes, D. (1998). *Building the Bonds of Attachment: Awakening Love in Deeply Troubled Children.* Lanham, MD: Jason Aronson.

Hughes, D. (2006). *Building the Bonds of Attachment: Awakening Love in Deeply Troubled Children. 2nd revised edition*. Lanhan, MD: Jason Aronson.

Hycner, R. (1991). *Between Person and Person: Towards a Dialogical Psychotherapy*. Gouldsboro, ME: Gestalt Journal Press.

Jacoby, M. (1994). *Shame and the Origins of Selfesteem*. London: Routledge.

Johnstone, L., & Boyle, M., with Cromby, J., Dillon, J., Harper, D., Kinderman, P., Longden, E., Pilgrim, D., & Read, J. (2018). *The Power Threat Meaning Framework: Towards the Identification of Patterns in Emotional Distress, Unusual Experiences and Troubled or Troubling Behaviour, as an Alternative to Functional Psychiatric Diagnosis*. Leicester, UK: British Psychological Society.

Kenrick, J. (2006). Work with children in transition. In: J. Kenrick, C. Lindsey, & L. Tollemache (Eds.), *Creating New Families: Therapeutic Approaches to Fostering, Adoption & Kinship Care* (pp. 67–83). Tavistock Clinic Series. London: Karnac.

Klein, M. (1946). Notes on some schizoid mechanisms. In: *Envy and Gratitude and Other Works, 1946–1963* (pp. 1–24). London: Vintage, 1997.

Klein, M. (1975). *Love, Guilt and Reparation and Other Works, 1921–1945*. New York: Free Press.

Lapworth, P., Sills, C., & Fish, S. (2001). *Integration in Counselling & Psychotherapy: Developing a Personal Approach*. London: Sage.

Lorde, A. (2018). *The Master's Tools Will Never Dismantle the Master's House*. London: Penguin Classics.

Mahler, M. S., Pine, F., & Bergman, A. (1973). *The Psychological Birth of the Human Infant*. New York: Basic Books.

Main, M., & Hesse, E. (1992). Disorganized/disoriented infant behavior in the Strange Situation, lapses in the monitoring of reasoning and discourse during the parent's Adult Attachment Interview, and dissociative states. In: M. Ammaniti & D. Stern (Eds.), *Attachment and Psycho-Analysis*. Rome: Gius, Laterza & Figli.

Main, M., & Solomon, J. (1990). Procedures for identifying infants as disorganised/disorientated during the Ainsworth Strange Situation. In: M. T. Greenberg, D. Cicchetti, & E. M. Cummings (Eds.), *Attachment in the Preschool Years* (pp. 121–160). Chicago, IL: University of Chicago Press.

Mees, P. (2017). State of mind assessments. *Journal of Child Psychotherapy, 43*(10): 1–15.

Meins, E., Fernyhough, C., Wainright, R., Gupta, M., Fradley, E., & Tuckey, M. (2002). Maternal mindmindedness & attachment security as predictors of Theory of Mind understanding. *Child Development*, 73(6): 1715–1726.

Menakem, R. (2017). *My Grandmother's Hands*. Las Vegas, NV: Central Recovery.

Mollon, P. (1996). *Multiple Selves, Multiple Voices. Working with Trauma, Violation, and Dissociation*. Chichester, UK. Wiley.

O'Brien, F. (2008). The making of mess in art therapy: Attachment, trauma and the brain. *International Journal of Art Therapy (formerly Inscape)*, 9(1): 2–13.

Panksepp, J. (1998). *Affective Neuroscience: The Foundations of Human and Animal Emotions*. New York: Oxford University Press.

Perry, B. (1995). Evolution of symptoms following traumatic events in children. [Abstract.] Proceedings of the 148th Annual Meeting of the American Psychiatric Association, Miami, FL.

Perry, B. D. (2006). The neurosequential model of therapeutics: Applying principles of neuroscience to clinical work with traumatized and maltreated children. In: N. Boyd Webb (Ed.), *Working with Traumatized Youth in Child Welfare* (pp. 27–52). New York: Guilford.

Schaefer, C., & Reid, S. (2001). *Game Play: Therapeutic Use of Childhood Games*. 2nd edn. Chichester, UK: Wiley.

Schore, A. (1999). Commentary on emotions: Neuropsychoanalytic views. *NeuroPsychoanalysis*, 1: 49–55.

Schore, A. (2001a). Regulation of the right brain: A fundamental mechanism of attachment development and trauma psychotherapy. Paper presented at the conference, Attachment, Trauma and Dissociation: Developmental, Neuropsychological, Clinical and Forensic Considerations, University College London.

Schore, A. (2001b). Early relational trauma: Effects on right brain development and the etiology of pathological dissociation. Paper presented at the conference, Attachment, the Developing Brain and Psychotherapy: Minds in the Making, University College London.

Schore, A. (2009). Relational trauma and the developing right brain: An interface of psychoanalytic self psychology and neuroscience. *Annals of the New York Academy of Sciences*, 1159: 189–203.

Segal, J. C. (1998). The role of a parent's illness in the emotional experience of a child: Evidence from Klein's *Narrative of a Child Analysis*. *Psychodynamic Counselling*, 4: 487–504.

Siegel, D. J. (1999). *The Developing Mind: How Relationships and the I act to Shape Who We Are*. New York: Guilford.

Siegel, D. J. (2011). The proven benefits of mindfulness. In: B. Boyce & the *Shambhala Sun* (Eds.), *The Mindfulness Revolution: Leading Psychologists, Scientists, Artists, and Meditation Teachers on the Power of Mindfulness in Daily Life* (pp. 136–139). New York: Random House.

Stern, D. N. (1998). *The Interpersonal World of the Infant: A View from Psychoanalysis and Developmental Psychology*. London: Karnac.

Stern, D. N. (2003). *The Interpersonal World of the Infant*. 2nd edn. New York: Basic Books.

Sunderland, M. (2015). *Conversations that Matter: Talking with Children and Teenagers in Ways that Help*. Broadway, UK: Worth.

Taransaud, D. (2011). *You Think I'm Evil: Practical Strategies for Working with Rebellious and Aggressive Adolescents*. Broadway, UK: Worth.

Thomas, L. (2013). Empires of mind: Colonial history and its implications for counselling and psychotherapy. *Psychodynamic Practice*, *19*(2): 117–128.

Van der Kolk, B. (2005). Developmental trauma disorder: Towards a rational diagnosis for children with complex trauma histories. *Psychiatric Annals*, *35*(5): 401–408.

Van der Kolk, B. (2014). *The Body Keeps the Score*. New York: Penguin Random House.

Wallin, D. J. (2007). *Attachment in Psychotherapy*. London: Guilford.

Winnicott, D. W. (1956). Psychoanalysis and the sense of guilt. In: *Psycho-analysis and Contemporary Thought*. London: Hogarth, 1958.

Winnicott, D. W. (1965). *The Maturational Processes and the Facilitating Environment*. London: Hogarth.

Winnicott, D. W. (1967). The location of cultural experience. *International Journal of Psychoanalysis*, *48*: 368–372.

Winnicott, D. W. (1969). The use of an object. *International Journal of Psychoanalysis*, *50*: 711–716.

Winnicott, D. W. (1975). *Through Paediatrics to Psycho-analysis*. The International Psycho-analytical Library, 100. London: Hogarth.

CHAPTER 10

Safety, trust, and maternal deprivation

Maria Furlong

Introduction

This chapter, a twenty-minute excerpt from a psychotherapy session with a young girl, Jade, aged ten, illustrates the way I have worked as an integrative child psychotherapist. This session was presented as an audio recording for my IATE qualifying viva. The viva is the final assessment after four years of training. The examiners listen to the recording while following the written transcript shown here and then cross-examine the candidate for forty minutes. They explore the trainee psychotherapist's in-depth thinking behind the therapeutic interventions made during the twenty-minute excerpt from a session. The trainee is required to show an ability to use creative interventions, transference and countertransference to inform their work with the child. In addition, the trainee must demonstrate an understanding of relevant underlying theories and the capacity to reflect on any mistakes or misattunements. In order to assist with my thinking during the exam, I made notes in the margin of the transcript. For the purposes of this chapter, I will embed my reflections within the transcript.

I chose this particular case as my viva recording because it illustrated creative interventions, for example, symbolic story making and songs, and their link with the child's internal and external worlds. It shows how evaluating symbolic content in order to link with defences can enable a child to reflect upon her own underlying vulnerability. The psychotherapy excerpt illustrates the child's internal and external conflicts and the interventions used to explore the child's created characters' feelings. Throughout the session, attention is paid to the child's arousal states and the use of PACE (playfulness, acceptance, curiosity, and empathy) (Hughes et al., 2019) to regulate the child's senses, hold painful feelings, and allow space to slow the child's mental processes as she experiences the need to flee from vulnerable feelings.

Referral

Jade was an eight-year-old girl when she was referred for therapy. Jade was tall, with curly blonde hair and a mischievous smile. The family consisted of mother, stepfather, and two younger siblings, a biological brother and a stepsister born during the first weeks of therapy. When Jade was ten months old, her mother was absent for four weeks due to complications in giving birth to her brother, who was later diagnosed with global developmental delay. During her first three years, Jade experienced violent rows between her mother and father, who subsequently left. Her mother found a new partner when Jade was seven years old. At eight, Jade showed great curiosity about her mother and stepfather's sexual relationship and witnessed them having sex. She also was discovered to be watching pornographic material via the internet.

Case history

The school referred Jade for therapy due to difficulty in her relationships with her peer group; she was regularly physically and verbally aggressive. They were concerned she had a precocious interest in sexual relationships and described her peer relationships as being full of drama and volatility. The school was concerned that she had become her mother's "confidante". Jade's mother also described having had a series of relationships since separating from Jade's father, prior to settling with her current partner.

I needed to consider the impact on Jade of exposure to the "primal scene". Freud (1905d) believed a child would perceive the sexual act as sadistic and would thus be traumatised by witnessing this. Given the volatile nature of the parental relationship, Jade may have been confused or scared her stepfather was hurting her mother. Britton (1989) talks about the arrival of the notion of a third, murdering the dyadic relationship, whether that be the nursing couple or the parental couple. For Jade, it seemed her relationship with her mother had been repeatedly intruded upon by the arrival of "a third"—her brother born when Jade was eleven months old, her stepfather, and the subsequent birth of a stepsister. There was a sense that Jade felt deprived of the parenting she required and thus created a hard, pseudo-mature persona to defend against her feelings of vulnerability.

Schore (2016, p. 115) describes "… a critical period for the maturation of the orbitofrontal cortex", occurring between ten and fourteen months, during which time the infant is most sensitive to the mother's "… emotionally expressive face" (p. 134). It was at this time in her life that Jade, between the ages of eleven and fourteen months, was deprived of her mother who was spending long periods with Jade's ill sibling in hospital. This stressful period may have left Jade's mother with little capacity to regulate Jade's internal affective state, which in turn would impact on Jade's subsequent ability to self-regulate in her interactions with her peers (Schore, 2016). In addition to this, the volatility of the parental relationship could have further impacted on Jade's sense of safety and danger. Porges (2011) discusses how "… neural circuits distinguish whether situations or people are safe, dangerous or life-threatening" (p. 11). During this viva extract, Jade's reaction to a bicycle bell ringing in the playground felt more like a response to a thunderclap. It seemed as if the relational stresses of her childhood made Jade hypervigilant.

I needed to view Jade's communications through a variety of theoretical lenses, in order to increase my understanding of her past and present way of relating to the world around her. I initially thought about attachment theory (Bowlby, 2005), and how Jade's early experiences with her mother and father may have impacted her attachment style and internal working model. Duschinsky (2018) shows how partner violence, marital conflict, and fear can lead to a child's disorganised attachment relationship with the mother. Crittenden's (2016) Dynamic-Maturational Model of Attachment and Adaptation (DMM) describes how children adapt their attachment behaviours to attract attention, bring their parent to them, and elicit a response from those around them. Jade's curiosity in pornographic material and the "primal scene" could be linked to her need for excitement to obliterate the need for comfort. "When comfort is pervasively lacking, sexuality may replace it" (Crittenden, 2016, p. 68). Perhaps Jade had developed a pseudo-mature "false self" (Winnicott, 1965) as a way of connecting with mother as well as defending against an unsafe environment and/or misattuned caregiver. "This is a defence whose success may provide a new threat to the core of the self though it is designed to hide and protect this core of the self" (Winnicott, 1965, p. 58).

Therapeutic journey

Jade initially presented with sexualised and manic behaviours in the therapy room. These seemed to obscure her emotional deprivation and sadness. During our early sessions she seemed to need to provoke and titillate me. In the countertransference I was sometimes overwhelmed and intruded on by her dramatisations involving puppets swapping sexual partners. It seemed she had developed a white noise of sexual excitement to obliterate thinking and feeling, particularly feelings of loss and abandonment. I also considered the possibility of her feeling very disturbed by her mother's frequent change of sexual partners and perhaps historical sexual abuse.

At the beginning of our therapeutic journey, Jade used three puppets to portray adults' sexual betrayal and revenge. I often felt recruited into a voyeuristic position. My early countertransferential feelings of suffocation and helplessness seemed to be projected into me in order that Jade could experience me as feeling, processing, and containing that which she could not hold inside herself (Bion, 1962). Jade's "window of tolerance" (Ogden, 2006; Siegel, 2012) was narrow; she was alert to sudden noises and initially hypervigilant when in the room with me. Any tender moments of closeness between us led Jade to quickly confuse them with adult passion (Ferenczi, 1949). This is further illustrated in the transcript which follows.

Chaotic periods in Jade's home life were also reflected in the themes of her play. She created a story of a separated couple, a murderous stepmother, children being abandoned to her care. There was little sense of nurturing, of protective, predictable parents, and Jade initially demonstrated little empathy as she showed babies being pushed away by their mother and cut to pieces. Her internal world seemed full of abandoning, shaming, attacking, persecutory objects.

Over the course of therapy, Jade's aggression towards her peers decreased. Her significant intellectual, verbal, and creative developments were noted by her teachers. In time, her mother separated from Jade's stepfather, after he became involved with criminal gangs. Subsequently I noticed in our review meetings, she was increasingly able to experience compassion for Jade and her difficulties. Over time, Jade began to allow me to stand alongside and process feelings with her, rather than subject me to them.

In the sessions prior to the following transcript, Jade had been working with material she brought from the musical *Heathers*, based on a dark 1980s movie about a clique of three popular but feared girls all called Heather. Another girl, Veronica leaves her friends and joined their clique in order to be popular. However, she disapproved of the Heathers' cruel behaviour and became friends with an outsider, Jason. They accidentally poisoned one of the Heathers and when Jason kills off two bullies, Veronica realises he is a psychotic murderer and she races to stop him blowing up the school. Veronica then returns to her old group of friends. In my work with Jade, I understood the Heathers and Veronica as enabling Jade to play out aspects of her internal and external world, her friendship difficulties, her home life, and her internal fragmented parts of herself (Fisher, 2017) and internal persecuting objects (Kalsched, 1996). We had also worked with Russian dolls, which she decorated, creating an external part that everyone sees, a Heathers part, a mother part, and a baby part. Giving voice to all these different fragmented aspects of Jade in order to integrate them formed the theme of the therapy sessions.

In the previous month of therapy, Jade's symbolic play had begun to reveal the presence of a more nurturing mother who made pillows for Veronica and Martha's hammock bed. This hammock bed was made from a small knitted string scarf which Jade, early in her therapy, had asked me to knit with two pencils and string (Figure 10.1).

Figure 10:1 Martha and Veronica on their hammock

The following extract provides examples of Jade's developing sense of safety and trust. Also illustrated is my difficulty in maintaining a "thinking mind" when faced with the teenage dramas she played out between her characters. Joseph (1985) discusses the way in which therapists can be unconsciously induced to act in a way consistent with the client's internal world. I felt sometimes like a mother distracted by such dramatic relationships that it was difficult to remain aware of and protect the vulnerable "little Jade". Throughout the session, I found the work of Hughes (2006; Hughes et al., 2019) invaluable in informing the way in which I nurtured the therapeutic relationship with Jade, creating an environment where I could attune to Jade through eye contact, voice tone, and facial expression to co-regulate emotional affect. In addition, working with playfulness, acceptance, curiosity, and empathy (PACE, Hughes et al., 2019) enabled me to offer affect regulation and attunement, as Jade navigated her way through the following complex and emotionally rich story.

Session seventy-one

Context of this twenty minute excerpt of a session

Jade was working with lollipop stick characters she had created to represent the characters in the *Heathers* musical (Figure 10.2). Just before this section, I had pressed pause, asking Jade to clarify elements of the *Heathers* story. I could sense a slight irritation, and she responded by singing a song *Welcome to my Candy Store* from the *Heathers* musical.

> [*Jade finished the song and threw Veronica aside*]
>
> Therapist: So Veronica has been thrown across the room now?
> [*I wondered whether Jade was discarding herself or me, as she threw Veronica aside*]
>
> Jade: I'm good. [*Jade looked at me and hesitantly leaned out of her seat*]

Figure 10:2 Starting from top left: Ram and Kurt, Heather 3's mother and Jason D, Heathers 1, 2, 3

Therapist: You feel like you want to go and get her? Okay.

Jade: She's the main character.

Therapist: Oh, right, she is the main character, so let's just have a think about this, just for a second.

[Jade picked Veronica up and sat back down while holding Veronica. I noticed Jade looking at the clock]

Therapist: You are looking at the time. What are you thinking?

Jade: It's almost time to finish.

I wondered if Jade was feeling uneasy and had begun to use a defensive strategy by mentioning the end of the session. I wanted to slow Jade down and keep her in the moment at this point, in order to gently explore her unease. At times, the connection to Jade felt fragile as if she was never quite sure about safety. I thought of Porges (2011) who devised the term "neuroception" to describe how our nervous system and neural circuits are unconsciously distinguishing whether situations or people are safe and can thus inhibit social engagement if there is any perceived threat. At this moment, I felt the least threatening intervention for Jade would be to remain in the moment and use PACE (Hughes, 2019). I wanted to convey my understanding that her story remained significant, and that I continued to be curious and accepting of what she was trying to communicate. At that point, I wasn't sure about exactly what that was, hence it was important that she knew I empathised with her need to repeatedly show me this story. Sunderland (2015, pp. 272–273) discusses the need some children have to repeat the same play story and how it can be a defence against painful feelings. It also can mean that the anxieties connected with the story have not been fully understood and contained by the therapist.

Therapist: It feels like, we've got time, but it feels like you've got such a lot to show me. You like to show me this story over and over and over, because it seems like it is just so important what you are showing me.

Jade: Mmm. [nodding her head and looking at me]

Therapist: There's something about this.

Jade: Hiccups now. [hiccupping as she looked at me]

Therapist: You've got hiccups. There's something about this that you can
        really feel inside you when you think about this story. Am I
        getting that right or? [*Jade reached for a pen*]

I wanted to connect Jade to her body and tentatively link her feelings
to her somatic response. Van der Kolk (2014) discusses the need, particularly where there is a history of trauma, to begin to link the inner
sensations in our bodies with what we feel. At this moment I wanted to
offer attunement to Jade by noticing her hiccups and their context and
connecting them to the meaning of her story. She responded with irritation as she tried to ruin Heather's eye by adding an Egyptian style wing
to her eyelid. Jade's tone of voice changed, and it seemed as if she was
regaining control by talking to me in a way I imagined she might talk to
her own friends. I found myself momentarily discarded and distracted
but decided to remain curious about what was happening between us.

Jade: Yeah, this can ruin Heather. [*she begins to put a wing shape on
        Heather's eyelid*]
Therapist: What, the pen can ruin Heather?
Jade: There we go, yes I did a wing in her eye.
Therapist: She's got a wing in her eye?
Jade: You know, like you do that wing?
Therapist: Yeah, yes, like that.
Jade: So all the Heathers have the wings.
Therapist: They all have wings here where their eyeliner is.
Jade: She looks like a flipping Egyptian, what the hell? [*holding the
        Heather doll out to me*]
Therapist: So now, when I stop you, what happens? When I stop you to
        ask about it, how do you feel?
Jade: Fine. [*looks away and down at the table*]
Therapist: I wonder if a little bit of you gets frustrated?
Jade: No.
Therapist: Or just wants to get on with the story?
Jade: Kind of. [*looks back at me*]
Therapist: Kind of, I thought. But I think because, the reason I stop you,
        do you want to know why I do?

Jade: [*looking at me*] To get into the story to make sure you know what's going on.

Therapist: Yeah, to make sure I know what's going on and to make sure I know what each person's feeling in this. Mmm? [*Jade lined up her characters and returned to the story characters*]

I wanted to give Jade space to explore the negative transference towards me and my interruptions to her story, to tiptoe up to her negative feelings (Meltzer, 2008) without shaming her. I used a soft voice, and gently enquired if she was feeling frustrated. Her following words were a clear message she wanted me to stop talking. And I wondered if she was concerned about how together we could manage that irritation.

Jade: [*as Heather 1*] Veronica. Now get in line.

Jade: [*as Veronica*] Sure.

Jade: [*as Heather 1*] If you want people to think we tolerate you, get the fuck near me.

Therapist: Okay, so they have basically got control of Veronica. Is that right?

Jade: Mmm.

Therapist: And the voices they use and the way they talk to her are very angry, controlling voices. I wonder if you hear those voices sometimes? [*Jade is staring at Veronica and Heather held out in front of her on the table*]

I was wondering if Jade had identified with the character of Veronica and I hoped to link what she was showing me with her internal and/or external world. I felt a tension in Jade as she stared in front of her. I wondered if we were getting in touch with some difficult feelings.

Jade: I didn't know there was weed, that's a fact.
[*a bicycle bell rang outside, Jade jumped and fixed her eyes on me suddenly, she seemed on edge*]

Therapist: You heard a bell. It gave you a shock? I'm thinking about the angry voices, whether thinking about that for you, Jade, has made you feel a bit nervous.

I sensed Jade was hypervigilant, and I needed to pay attention to her narrow "window of tolerance" (Ogden, 2006; Siegel, 2012), knowing that, due to her history, she could easily be triggered into arousal or dissociation. My aim was to gently bring her awareness to her arousal state in order to link what she was feeling in her body with her emotions.

> [*Jade nodded, opening the playdough pot and taking it out*]
> Therapist: A little bit? Because do you know what sometimes I think about? [*Jade was squashing up the playdough*] You're squashing that playdough up now.
> Jade: Mmm. [*looking at me again*]
> Therapist: The times you've heard angry voices in your house and in your life. [*Jade looks down to the playdough and forms a bed shape with it*]

I was speaking gently and hesitantly as I watched Jade squashing up the playdough. In supervision, we discussed how Jade may be expressing her aggressive and assertive self by squashing it up. Her following reference to the bed not being the best was perhaps a confirmation of my interpretation that at times home and family is not the best. There was a sadness in her tone as she told me, "It's not the best."

> Jade: That's not the best bed ever.
> Therapist: You're trying to make a bed.
> Jade: It's not the best.
> Therapist: It's not the best. So there's a bed there for Veronica, yeah?
> [*Jade continues her play with the stick characters of Jason and Heather*]
> Jade: [*as Heather 1*] Have you seen that new kid? He's like so flippin hot. You know what, I'm going to try and use my trick with him: Hey Jason!
> Jade: [*as Jason*] Hi Heather.
> Jade: [*as Heather 1*] Mmm—I've heard that you were kind of lonely today.
> Jade: [*as Jason*] Kind of, I'm always lonely.
> Jade: [*as Heather 1*] You're so hot aren't you.
> Jade: [*as Jason*] Thanks.

Jade: [*as Heather 1*] Maybe you could take me out for brunch?

Jade: [*as Jason*] If you bring money?

Jade: [*as Heather 2*] Oh, I knew it. Hi Jason.
[*Heather 2 is approaching feeling jealous of Heather 1*]

Jade: [*as Jason*] Hi Heather.

Jade: [*as Heather 2*] You look so hot. [*H2 tries to kiss Jason*]

Jade: [*as Jason*] Oh yeah, yeah, no, no, no, no, I've eyes for another girl, thank you very much.

Jade: [*as Heather 3*] Hi Jason.

Jade: [*as Jason*] Hi Heather.

Jade: [*as Heather 3*] Why you leaving so soon?

Jade: [*as Jason*] I've got to go and see someone. [*looking at me*] Now Heather's tricks always work.

I noticed Jade moved from the vulnerability of her bed not being the best, to the "new kid", the boy, sexual curiosity, and excitement. It was as if she wanted to cover the sense of loneliness by sexualising it; going from lonely to hot excitement. I linked her experience to Glasser's core complex (1979), which is about the use of sexualisation as a defence; intimacy is simultaneously a longed-for state which provides comfort, and a terrifying minefield which could prove annihilating. The theme continued in the next section as Jade talked about love tricks. It seemed Jade wanted to grab onto love, perhaps the mother love in me, but there was a lack of trust in love and a fear of being tricked. Upon reflection I felt that it may have been helpful to have added an interpretation about how hard it was for Jade to stay with the feeling of loneliness. Perhaps I had also been disorientated by her "tricks"?

Therapist: They always work do they? What sorts of tricks does she use?

Jade: Like love tricks.

Therapist: Love tricks. What are love tricks?

Jade: Like she makes a boy fall for her straight away. [*smiling shyly*]

Therapist: Oh, I wonder how she does that?

Jade: That's how she got them two in her group. [*meaning Kurt and Ram*]

Therapist: Ahh. So I wonder what she does to make boys fall for her?

Jade: She just flutters her eyes and flicks her hair around.

[Jade shows me how by fluttering her eyes at me and tossing her hair around her shoulders]

There was something seductive about Jade's movements now and I was aware that there were times Jade wished to seduce. I understood this as an attachment-seeking behaviour (Crittenden, 2016). I was aware of Jade's pseudo-precocious defence and her yearning for the attention of boys and so I acknowledged that yearning for love in the next intervention.

Therapist: Oh right. So it's important to her to get boys to fall for her?
    Jade: *[as Jason]* Okay, okay, I can't believe I just fell for that trick. Hi Veronica.
    Jade: *[as Veronica]* Hi Jason.
    Jade: *[as Jason]* Do you want to go out for brunch or something?
    Jade: *[as Veronica]* I dunno. Maybe.
    Jade: *[as Jason]* Tomorrow?
    Jade: *[as Veronica]* Today.
    Jade: *[as Jason]* Cool. Okay.
    [the characters move to another part of the table]
    Jade: *[as Veronica]* Jason, stop. *[the Jason stick character is trying to kiss Veronica]* This is really fancy.
    Jade: *[as Jason]* I know.
    Jade: *[as Veronica]* My gosh! The bowls are real gold. I wish I'd brought a bag.
Therapist: Wow, so they've gone somewhere really, really fancy doodle dandy.
    Jade: His dad has the company. *[the two characters begin kissing]*
Therapist: Oh right.

There remained the theme of yearning. The restaurant having a fairy tale quality about it, with the gold bowls, and the father owning such a company, was perhaps Jade communicating something of her longing for a rich dad. At this point in her life, Jade had no contact with her biological father, and nine months earlier her stepfather had left the home. Also, she had experienced her mother having many boyfriends before she lived with the stepfather.

Jade: Okay, now he's feeling a spark. [*looking at me and referring to the Jason character*]

As Jade looked at me, I sensed an emotional shift; I wondered if she was seeking maternal reverie (Bion, 1962, p. 36). I remained curious and accepting, being aware in the following interactions that Jade's surviving parental deprivation occurred through developing a pseudo-mature persona. Also she often confused tender maternal moments with adult passion (Ferenczi, 1949) and her maladaptive attempts at self-soothing often led to sexualised behaviour. Van der Kolk et al. (2009) also refer to this in their description of developmental trauma disorder.

Therapist: A spark! What's a spark?
Jade: Like someone in a relationship, if you have a relationship with, like a spark.
Therapist: Right I see, and I wonder whether you feel you'd like that somewhere, Jade?
Jade: Mmm. [*brief eye contact*]
Therapist: Or whether you wonder what that feels like.

By my remaining curious, and using the words "I wonder", it allows Jade to experience me as following her without intruding upon her, and to perhaps, with reference to the brief eye contact, begin to experience something of a "maternal spark" in her therapeutic relationship with me. I was conscious of her maternal deprivation and how it meant she had grappled with relationships in her life, often being out of step with her peers.

Jade: When I'm older.
Therapist: When you're older, but I wonder whether you want to know what it feels like to have that spark when somebody has that spark for you? [*Jade is nodding*] Relationships are difficult to figure out aren't they?

And just at the moment of connection, Jade took flight to drama. In my countertransference there was a sense of being discarded again, which had happened earlier at the beginning of the segment when Jade had become irritated with me. I tracked her as she then returned to the characters kissing; this was intense and I sensed my own discomfort and Jade's excitement as we explored briefly the meaning of friendship, love, and kissing for these characters. In the end it was all doomed, as there was no trust.

Jade: Mmm. [*looking at me and then away to the characters*] This girl always hits this girl. Look at the flippin size comparison. [*Jade has now picked up a small and large version of Veronica that she has*] Jesus, she could literally just knock her out. Bum dead. Two hours later.

Jade: [*as Veronica*] I'm so, I've kind of got to make up to Heather for what I did with the letter. [*Veronica had intercepted a forged letter to a fat unpopular girl, Martha, which was playing a trick on her, telling her Ram fancied her*]

Jade: [*as Jason*] Are you kidding? She's literally going to kick that friend's arse.

Jade: [*as Veronica*] Well, … [*now addressing me directly*] Wait, pretend they didn't know each other's names but they've just kissed.

Therapist: Oh right, Okay, so they've just kissed even though they didn't know each other's names.

Jade: [*as Jason*] Well, did you even know that they're going to kick your friend's arse?

Jade: [*as Veronica*] You can't just comment when I didn't even know your name. Well I didn't really catch your name.

Jade: [*as Jason*] Well I didn't throw it. Did I? Oh my gosh! [*Jade seems excited*]

Therapist: So this is quite an exciting part of the story where they are kissing?

[*Jason and Veronica are kissing again*]

Jade: Well they do kind of love each other.

Therapist: They do love each other? Okay.

[*Veronica is now talking to the Martha character who used to be her friend*]

Jade: [*as Veronica*] Martha, oh my gosh, I am so sorry.

Therapist: And Heather's made up, no Veronica's made up with Martha.

Jade: [*as Martha*] Are you sure? Because I don't really trust you, the Heathers have been talking to me.

Therapist: Oh No!

Jade: [*as Heather 1*] [*approaching Martha and Veronica*] Oh, has your pity friend been talking to you again?

Jade: [*as Martha*] Yeah, I can't believe she called me a nerd.

Jade: [*as Heather 1*] Mmm. Bitch!

Therapist: They're all sneaking around behind each other's backs and saying, "You've said this and you've said that," and trying to split up friendships. [*Jade is nodding vehemently*] Is that? Yeah.

Jade: [*as Heather 2*] Heather, one question. Why we hanging around with this piglet?

Jade: [*as Martha*] What, wait, I thought Heather was my friend.

Jade: [*as Heather 2*] Oh.

I sensed the pace of Jade's symbolic play was increasing and I was aware we had touched on themes of toxic love, doomed relationships, people only being kind out of pity, no one can be trusted. I decided to use the arts to deepen my understanding of the feelings behind Jade's symbolic play; I did this by interviewing the character/image of Martha, the kind character vulnerable to trickery. This also externalised the emotional pain of being vulnerable and betrayed, thus creating safety for Jade while further exploring these themes (Sunderland, 2015).

Therapist: So can I just ask you, Martha, you thought they were being kind to you and now they've just called you a piglet. Can I ask how you're feeling now, Martha?

Jade: [*as Martha*] Well, I think they were just throwing a plan on me.

Jade: [*as Heather 1*] Yeah, they were. I'm sorry Veronica's not your friend anymore. We've got her under our control. If you push a step one more further [sic], we can probably make her jump off a bridge or stab herself.

Jade: [*as Martha*] Stop, please, I'm going to tell her right now.

Therapist: So, Martha, you're trying to help.

Jade: She just jumped off a bridge. [*throws the stick figure Martha off the edge of the table*]

Therapist: And she's jumped off a bridge. And what's happened to her? [*Jade picks her up and lays her on the small blanket*]

Jade: She's in hospital.

Therapist: She's in hospital, but she was trying to help Veronica.

Jade: [*as Jason*] Listen, I think something's going on with the Heathers, get on my back.

Jade: [*as Veronica*] Wait, I need to go and make up with Heather if she wants to be my friend. [*they are heading to Heather 1's house—she is lying on the playdough bed*]

Jade: [*as Jason*] Shh, trust me, I know Heather is here. She even skips a late night at her grandma's even when she doesn't have a hangover. Here …

Jade: [*as Heather 1*] Oh finally you're here. Hey Jason, thank you. [*Heather 1 to Veronica*] Make me a hangover drink, and Jason you can stay here.

Jade: [*as Jason*] No thank you, I'm busy with a hangover myself. [*Jason and Veronica then make a drink for Heather 1*] Mix like a juice and puts chemical in it.

Jade: [*as Heather 1, pretending to choke*]

Therapist: So let me just press pause again here …

Jade: Yeah.

Therapist: Because. This tale is about people who are a good bit older than you, aren't they? [*Jade nodding*] Who are trying to get together, like older teenagers, yeah? But it's showing you something about friendships and the way in which people sometimes can't be trusted and can be very mean, which maybe feels like some of the friendships in your life.

It was important that I pressed pause again to help Jade digest and process such complex material. I began to sum up some of the themes of trust and friendship and offer a link to what Jade may have experienced in real life. I also wanted to touch on her internal world, accepting her internal defences and conflicts.

[*Jade begins to colour another lollipop stick, looking down*]

Jade: Oh my gosh!

Therapist: And maybe some of the parts of you that maybe you know can be tough and bullying, and then some of the other parts of you that can be really hurt by people.

What followed initially reminded me of my infant observation studies. At first, I sensed a challenge and defence in Jade's tone when she announced, "Staring contest!" I met her look with warmth in my gaze and Jade softened, and as she softened my countertransference feeling became more maternal. I was reminded of Bick (1986) and her concept of the eyes being "suction pads for adhesion" (p. 68) to allow the infant to hold her sense of self together and stop her from disintegrating. This also links to Porges (2011) who describes the use of intonation and facial engagement to get the social engagement system working in order to promote attachment. As I spoke softly and quietly to her I felt she was drinking in the look in my eyes and affection in my calming voice. Winnicott (1971) also asks the question, "What do I see reflected in my mother's face? Myself."

Jade: Staring contest! [*looks up quickly and stares straight at me*]
Therapist: What? Staring contest. Okay.
Jade: Three, two. You blinked.
Therapist: Is this a stare at each other?
Jade: Okay. Three, two, one.
Therapist: You want me to really see you. I did blink first. You want me to see you, all of you.
[*Jade now looks away*]

The tender moment was quite quickly sabotaged by Jade cutting herself off and losing herself in the ensuing drama. A vulnerable part of herself needed to be killed off in order for Jade to survive. As we moved from deep connection to references to *Moby Dick*, I became aware of a feeling of confusion. Through supervision, I realised I had unconsciously become caught in the drama and had lost track of Jade's vulnerable part (Joseph, 1985).

Jade: So he puts poison in her drink, he gives it to her, she drinks, he smashes her head on the table, dead. RIP Heather.

Jade: [*as Veronica*] Well, we didn't kill her right, this is more of a suicide thing. Look. [*Jade makes a small paper book*]

Therapist: So she's taken a drink.

Jade: [*as Veronica*] Look, she was reading *Moby Dick*.

Jade: [*as Jason*] Are you kidding me? Just coz she was reading *Moby Dick* doesn't mean we are going to call the cops.

Therapist: What does that mean, she was reading *Moby Dick*? I don't understand.

Jade: Because it's like a poem book of murder and stuff like that, and suicide.

Therapist: Okay. Oh I see.

Jade: [*as Veronica*] Are you joking, are the cops just going to get the detail thing that she killed herself?

Jade: [*as Jason*] Listen we have got to work together. I'm sorry [*Jason tries to kiss Veronica*]

Jade: [*as Veronica*] Get off me.

Jade: [*as Jason*] Fine. Write a note.

Jade: [*as Veronica*] Deh deh deh dhe dhe. Bye world. Scribble scribble scribble, bye world.

Therapist: Okay, so that's a note about a suicide.

Jade: [*as Jason*] Listen, we are not going to jail.

Jade: [*as Veronica*] Our fingerprints all over the cup. [*Jason kissing Veronica*]

Jade: [*as Jason*] So, they probably think we were going to have a day over or maybe earlier we've come over.

Therapist: So they've done something really bad and now they need to hide it. Is that right?

Jade: Mmm. [*looking at me*] But they can say earlier they come over and they were visiting Heather and she was perfect and fine but then they left and they heard her bump off the table.

I wondered if at this moment Jade was looking for help in figuring out how to protect herself from bad feelings. Wanting to deepen this through imagining into the images again, I addressed Veronica and Jason directly about how they were now feeling. There was a change in her tone, it became dull as she listed: disgusted, lovely, sick, depressed. This was a real turning point for Jade for now she was able to let me know about her painful feelings.

Therapist: Right, I see, so they've got a plan, a story because that's what people do sometimes when they do bad things. [*Addressing Veronica and Jason*] You've made up a story you two, can I just check how you are feeling now you've done that bad thing, and you've made up a story to cover it up. How are you both feeling I wonder?

Jade: [*now facing me then turning back to the figures*] Disgusted, lovely, sick, depressed.

Therapist: Disgusted, lovely, sick, and depressed, okay, I hear you.

Jade: [*as Jason*] So, since Heather's dead, it's our house. [*Jason lies on Veronica and she pushes him off*]

Jade: [*as Veronica*] Get off me, Jason.

Therapist: [*addressing Veronica*] So you don't want Jason on top of you?

Jade: Two weeks later.

Jade: [*as Ram*] Hi Veronica.

Jade: [*as Veronica*] Uurr, you have a right hand, use it.

Jade: [*as Ram*] Don't talk to me like that, you are going to hurt our feelings.

Jade: [*as Veronica*]Whose?

Jade: [*as Ram and Kurt*] You make my, they hang inside me. What did you …

Therapist: So this song the boys are now singing to Veronica—what's made you sing that song, lads?

Jade: [*smiling mischievously*] They're in love with her.

Therapist: [*addressing Ram and Kurt*] You really like her. You're in love with Veronica, I see. So is this what you do when you're in love with someone?

I remained curious and accepting here about the song. Perhaps though it may have been more helpful to ask Ram and Kurt what the song meant. Jade continued singing and seemed cut off from any vulnerability as she turned to teasing and excitement.

Jade: [*as Ram and Kurt*] No, this is our first time.

Therapist: No, aah I see.

Jade: [*as Ram and Kurt*] You make my balls so blue, they're hanging sadly, what did they do to you? [*singing to Veronica*] Look at them grow, they're beggin' you, don't make my balls so blue. Oooooo.

Jade: [*as Veronica*] Heather what are you doing here? Oh sshhhhhh oooooo. [*Heather 3 appears*]

Therapist: Oh! Heather, what are you doing here?

Jade: [*as Ram and Kurt*] Oh shhhhhhoooo you make my balls so blueee.

Jade: [*as Veronica*] Get me in the car [*trying to get away from Kurt and Ram who continue singing*]

Jade: [*as Ram and Kurt*] Oh no oh no oh no oooo. Oh no oh non you make my balls so blueeee. Just look at them growwww they're beggin' you, don't make my balls so blue. Ooooo oh no oh nononono. Yeah.

Jade: [*as Veronica*] Heather, what the hell?

Jade: [*as Heather 3*] You know what, actually, Heather's dead, so who's going to take over? Put her scrunchie on. [*Jade is making Heather 3's hair longer and adding Heather 1's red scrunchie*]

Therapist: Ahhh so you're getting a few adjustments to your hair, Heather number three? And you're getting a different colour on your top I see.

Jade: It's her hair like a ponytail.

Therapist: It's a ponytail, right I see, that's come around the front of you. You've got a long ponytail.

Jade then seemed lost in a symbolic power struggle between the characters. It seemed there was always someone to replace Heather and the characters were struggling to discover where they fit in and understand who had the power. Present were persecutory voices saying, "Shut up, Heather. I've been hearing that enough from the other Heather" (Kalsched, 1996). I understood this next section as reflecting Jade's constant shifting of internal and external states to appeal, attract, or adapt accordingly. I linked this to Fisher's (2017) work stating that all the internal fragmented selves of trauma survivors need to be heard and understood in order to be integrated.

Jade: So she hears Heather in her head.

Jade: [*as Veronica*] Come on, get the red scrunchy off her, get the red scrunchy off her, get the … Shut up Heather. Seriously, I've been hearing that enough from the other Heather.

Therapist: Veronica, you can hear Heather in your head talking at you.

Jade: [*as Heather 2*], I'm done. I'm boss. Can you see this. I'm boss. Do you really think this twat's [*Heather 3*] going to take over? Look at her! Miserable! I'm the queen. Adjustment, adjustment, adjustment.

Therapist: So there's another adjustment to Heather 2. She's getting long hair as well. Yeah?

Jade: Mmm.

Therapist: So what does the long hair mean on the Heathers?

Jade: Nothing really. It's just like a little detail.

Therapist: I see, so Heather 2 you've got long hair.

At this point in the session, Jade began to sing in an achingly moving voice, as if she were in touch with another part of herself where she was able to acknowledge a truth about her experience. I understood the raging black ocean as representing the manic stuff that intruded on her thoughts internally, and the external chaotic events at home that affected her. Are the "weakest" her vulnerable internal parts of herself? Once again the theme seemed to be "Who is in charge, internally and externally?" I wondered if Jade associated feeling vulnerable as being weak, helpless, and unable to survive.

Jade: [*as Veronica singing*] I'm so scared.
I'm riding a lifeboat in a raging black ocean with people so desperate.
For the weakest must go.
The tiniest lifeboat full of people I know.
Everyone's pushing, everyone's fighting, they'll throw me right over the side.
I'm hugging my knees but the captain is pointing. Who made her captain?
For the weakest must go, the tiniest lifeboat, full of people I know.

Therapist: Let's have a think about that song. That sounds like some-body's feeling helpless, watching weak people being left to drown. Is that right, have I got that right?

I realised my response hadn't quite articulated Jade's deepest emo-tions. A more helpful response may have been to say, "I think when you are here, you feel held, and we get to know the parts of you that feel weak and helpless. We are able to understand Jade's scared and vulnerable Self."

Jade: Mmm.

Therapist: And it sounds like there's real regret in that. Does that make sense? [*Jade nodding and noisily pulling out more pens*] Do you know what regret means? Something happens that you wish hadn't happened. [*Jade continues humming softly*] So she feels like all the weak people are getting destroyed. Is that right? [*Jade nodding, quite moved, blinking and concentrating on her colouring*] Because maybe in this world you need to be tough to survive, but maybe …

Jade: Time to go …

Therapist: I know, I'm conscious we've only got a few minutes left so shall we just do a sum up before we finish? Because we've done a lot today.

Jade: Next week's trailer.

Therapist: Well, shall we sum up before we do the trailer?

Jade: Yeah.

Again, Jade moved away from the acknowledgement of how tough it is to survive in her world. She wanted to entice me with next week's trailer and move on from the painful feeling of being weak and helpless. This is the point at which my twenty minute transcript ended. In the actual session I did go on to draw all the parts of the story and themes together. It was important to offer a few minutes at the end of therapy sessions with Jade to bring the session to a close and prepare her for returning to the classroom; we would often do this by going over what the main themes had been, when perhaps she would point out what I had missed or forgotten. Creating a closure to the session meant Jade was able to feel safely held, not too abandoned, in order that all her emotions intensified in therapy would not spill over into her school life.

This viva presentation was chosen to demonstrate to the assessors my skills in empathy and attunement towards an eight-year-old girl who had a turbulent, emotionally painful life both at home and in school. Music (2019, p. 187) talks about "… being sufficiently emotionally resonant to know deeply what the other is feeling (one foot in the ditch) to feel 'with' them, whilst simultaneously planting the other foot firmly outside the ditch, where we can reflect on, metabolise and process the experience". Through her rich, creative dramatisations, Jade certainly evoked a sense of her wanting to entice and pull me into the ditch with her, while simultaneously pushing me away. I understood this as a communication of her own experience of relationships. My first and primary task was to remain a holding and containing presence, able to offer safety and affect regulation (Porges, 2011; Schore, 2016). Malchiodi (2020) describes this sense of safety as an essential foundation for working with trauma. While being curious and empathic, I also needed to provide "alpha" function (Bion, 1962), and to imagine myself into her world filled with symbolic play and music.

I needed to maintain this thoughtful presence as I processed the viva examiners' questions and enquiries; I wanted to do Jade's story justice. During the viva, I also needed to be emotionally present and containing as I discussed Jade's story. I also felt protective towards Jade and her story involving her bravery in surviving repeated maternal deprivation, loss of paternal figures, and a turbulent and traumatic home life. In our therapeutic relationship, Jade needed to know that I could "hold" her and stay alongside her often chaotic presentation. In parallel, during the viva, I needed to "hold" her again in order to formulate and present her story, my integration of theory and practice in her case.

I was supported in my preparation for the viva through individual and group supervision with colleagues. Thinking about mis-attunements or times where I felt overwhelmed and lost for words provided further possibilities for understanding what Jade may be communicating through projections of her states of mind. It was important to understand my countertransference and the possible reasons for my mis-attunements. It was challenging to have my psychotherapy experience analysed in order that I might qualify as an integrative child psychotherapist. My work was laid out bare, with all of its flaws, flaws which have become my teachers.

Casement (1985) discusses the importance of sharing learning through clinical examples to illustrate what helps and hinders the therapeutic process. Jade and I both grew through our therapeutic encounter. As a trainee, I developed my own internal supervisor, becoming more adept at following her process and responding to the immediacy of the present moment in each therapy session, tentatively linking it to what her life experience may have been, and allowing her to alter, add to, or dismiss these links (Casement, 1992). In turn, Jade's belief in the safety of our relationship grew, allowing her to explore the more vulnerable parts of herself. This was expressed through Jade's later work with Russian dolls, symbolising aspects of herself that included a nurturing mother feeding a hungry infant.

References

Bick, E. (1986). Further considerations on the function of the skin in early object relations. In: A. Briggs (Ed.), *Surviving Space: Papers on Infant Observation*. London: Karnac.

Bion, W. R. (1962). *Learning from Experience*. London: Heinemann.

Bowlby, J. (2005). *The Making and Breaking of Affectional Bonds*. Abingdon, UK: Routledge.

Britton, R. (1989). The missing link: Parental sexuality in the Oedipus complex. In: J. Steiner (Ed.), *The Oedipus Complex Today: Clinical Implications*. London: Karnac.

Casement, P. (1985). *On Learning from the Patient*. London: Routledge.

Crittenden, P. (2016). *Raising Parents: Attachment, Representation and Treatment*. Abingdon, UK: Routledge.

Duschinsky, R. (2018). Disorganization, fear and attachment: Working towards clarification. *Infant Mental Health Journal*, 39(1): 17–29.

Ferenczi, S. (1949). Confusion of the tongues between the adults and the child—the language of tenderness and of passion. *International Journal of Psychoanalysis*, 30: 225–230.

Fisher, J. (2017). *Healing the Fragmented Selves of Trauma Survivors*. Abingdon, UK: Routledge.

Freud, S. (1905d). *Three Essays on the Theory of Sexuality: The 1905 Edition*. London: Verso, 2017.

Glasser, M. (1979). Some aspects of the role of aggression in the perversions. In: I. Rosen (Ed.), *Sexual Deviations* (pp. 278–305). 2nd edn. Oxford: Oxford University Press.

Hughes, D. A. (2006). *Building the Bonds of Attachment. Awakening Love in Deeply Troubled Children*. Lanham, MD: Jason Aronson.

Hughes, D. A., Golding, K. S., & Hudson, J. (2019). *Healing Relational Trauma with Attachment-Focused Interventions*. New York: W. W. Norton.

Joseph, B. (1985). Transference: The whole situation. *International Journal of Psychoanalysis, 66*: 447–454.

Kalsched, D. (1996). *The Inner World of Trauma: Archetypal Defenses of the Personal Spirit*. New York: Routledge.

Malchiodi, C. A. (2020). *Trauma and Expressive Arts Therapy: Brain, Body and Imagination in the Healing Process*. New York: Guilford.

Meltzer, D. (2008). *The Psychoanalytical Process*. London: Karnac.

Music, G. (2019). *Nurturing Children*. Abingdon, UK: Routledge.

Ogden, P. (2006). *Trauma and the Body: A Sensorimotor Approach to Psychotherapy*. New York: W. W. Norton.

Porges, S. W. (2011). *The Polyvagal Theory: Neurophysiological Foundations of Emotions, Attachment, Communication and Self-Regulation*. New York: W. W. Norton.

Schore, A. N. (2016). *Affect Regulation and the Origin of Self*. New York: Routledge.

Siegel, D. J. (2012). *The Developing Mind: How Relationships and the Brain Interact to Shape Who We Are*. 2nd edn. New York: Guilford.

Sunderland, M. (2015). *Conversations that Matter: Talking with Children and Teenagers in Ways that Help*. Broadway, UK: Worth.

Van der Kolk, B. (2014). *The Body Keeps the Score. Brain, Mind and Body in the Healing of Trauma*. New York: Penguin.

Van der Kolk, B., Pynoos, R., Cicchetti, D., Cloitre, M., D'Andrea, W., Ford, J., & Teicher, M. (2009). Proposal to include a developmental trauma disorder diagnosis for children and adolescents in *DSM-V*. Submitted February.

Winnicott, D. W. (1965). *The Maturational Processes and the Facilitating Environment: Studies in the Theory of Emotional Development*. 3rd edn. Abingdon, UK: Routledge.

Winnicott, D. W. (1971). *Playing and Reality*. London: Tavistock.

CHAPTER 11

The transformer and the measuring tape: using the relationship to process the trauma of an eight-year-old boy

Kate Clark

Background

Conor was an eight-year-old Irish boy referred to me because he was struggling to concentrate and stay on task in school. His levels of attainment were exceptionally low, and he was described as sometimes defiant. The school was concerned about his unpredictable home life. Conor's father was involved in a fight and died from being stabbed the previous year. Conor did not witness it but had been told the story of what happened. He lived with his mother who suffered from depression.

At the start of the work, Conor had a limited emotional range, and tended to disconnect from his experience. He was ambivalently attached and given the chance he would disappear off down a lone track of vivid but very disorganised imaginative play. In the countertransference, I felt cut off from him, abandoned and frustrated, which helped give me an insight into his inner world and his experience of relationships. As the work progressed, he began to use the therapeutic relationship as a safe base to explore his anxieties about separation and fears of abandonment. In the beginning, I used ideas taken from Theraplay® (Boothe & Jernberg, 2009) as well as Daniel Hughes's techniques, for example, using

PACE, the acronym for playfulness, acceptance, curiosity and empathy (Hughes, 2011). This, along with working with his body, fostered a more intersubjective experience that helped calm his over-active stress response system.

The context of this recording in relation to the whole session

This session took place after a year of work. Conor has just come into the therapy room and, as was our ritual, we started the session on the cushions. The recording was spliced, with the first and then the last ten minutes presented.

C1: I gotta tell you something.
T1: Okay.
C2: Kate?
T2: Yes Conor?
C3: You know to … You know what, umm, Sunday?
T3: Hmm, what happened on Sunday?
C4: It's too sad, I can't tell you.
T4: Oh.
C5: Okay, fine, I'll tell you.
T5: Okay.
C6: This lady died.
T6: A lady died.
C7: Yeah, and we had to go to a funeral.
T7: Oh. Was it a lady that you knew?
C8: Yeah … Umm, yeah, and my grandma. I didn't know, but my grandma did.
T8: Your grandma knew the lady?
C9: Yeah.
T9: And you went to the funeral.
C10: She was a good person. Umm, the children talked too much for, umm, the, umm, the lady. They talk, then after the lady keeps on talking too much because of the children. They won't, um, they keep on saying, when they keep being naughty, their mum says, "Stop, stop," they still do it, and then after, when they keep on

doing that, she died. Because of her children … they keep on doing that.

T10: Oh. So explain how that works? So there was a lady like this. And she had some children. [*I find a female figure and set up a little scene in the sand tray*]

C11: Yeah.

T11: Like this one and this one. [*I find two more figures and act them playing*] And were they talking?

C12: Yeah. [*Conor takes the children from me and uses them to act the imagined scene*] "Hey that's mine! No, that's mine! Oh no, no, no!" Then after, "Stop it, stop it, stop it!" [*sound of a punch*]

T12: Ahhh!

C13: Then she had a heart attack and died!

T13: And you think it was because the children were talking a lot?

C14: Yeah, that's what my mum and grandma said, that's because she heard it.

T14: That's because she heard it. And I guess that you're worried, that if you talk too much, that maybe you—

C15: [*interrupting*] Yep, my children … when I grow up.

T15: But maybe you're worried that if you do lots of talking and you do lots of fighting that maybe your mummy or your grandma might die as well?

C16: Yep.

T16: Is that something that you're worried about?

C17: Yep! Hey, look, I got a fact. If I stick this here, to here, guess what? Look what I'm going to do with it. [*Conor tries to put a little jacket on one of the characters*] Nope it's too small. [*he then goes back into roleplaying the children fighting*] And this is what they say, "Umm that's not fair, I wanna play, no, that's not fair!" They keep on fighting and talk, "It's mine, it's mine, no, no, no, no, no!"

T17: And then suddenly …

C18: She dies, uh! [*Conor acts out the lady dying*] And Kate?

T18: Yeah?

C19: You've forgotten something. About the toy. [*Conor holds up the transformer toy*] You know this?

T19: Mmm.

C20: You put it the wrong way. This is supposed to face in here. [*Conor shows me that the transformer toy has been put together wrongly*]

T20: Oh, okay.

C21: Yep. So when are you going to fix the hand?

T21: Okay, we can fix the hand, we can fix it.

C22: When?

T22: Kate can fix this. Do you want me to do it now?

C23: Mmm.

T23: [*I take the toy and start to fix it, turning its head back the right way*] And while I'm doing this, you know, I think that what you've told me this morning, I think there sounds like there's a bit of worry in here. [*pointing to his heart*] A BIG bit of worry! That maybe you think that if you're the sort of person who talks a lot, or has fighting, or says things that aren't always the right thing, then maybe the people around you are going to die! [*Conor looks down*]

C24: Yep.

T24: And maybe you think that because your daddy died, that maybe you're really scared that maybe your mummy will die too.

C25: And my grandma.

T25: And your grandma will die. Are you scared your grandma will die?

C26: Yep.

T26: And I bet you think, if she dies, just like daddy died, then who's going to look after Conor?

C27: My mum.

T27: Your mum.

C28: And then after, we'll talk too much, my mum will die, and who will we have to look after us?

T28: Oh! And you're scared that you're going to be all alone!

C29: Yep, and someone might knock on the door and we say, "Hello." Bam! We die. It might be a bad person, and we'll have to go to school by ourselves and WE CAN'T EVEN COOK!! And how are we supposed to dry our clothes?

T29: Oh! There sounds like there's a BIG bit of worry in there Conor!

C30: How can we buy food for us? We don't have that much money!

T30: Oh, it sounds like you have the whole world on your shoulders! Like so much, like this and this [*I gesture building on his shoulders*] and it just sounds like it's just never ending and soon it's just going to go topple, topple, topple, topple, topple. [*I gesture all his worries falling to the ground*] And I bet you've been worried about this for a long time.

C31: Yep. And my grandma says that if we keep on doing that, she'll die.

T31: Oh, you poor thing! What a hard thing to have to think, that maybe, maybe you're going to make your grandma die!

C32: And Kate?

T32: Yeah?

C33: And now you need to put this one here. How do you do it? [*Conor carefully instructs me how to fix the transformer toy*]

T33: Okay, let's try it like this, like that.

C34: Yeah.

T34: Here we go, it's fixed.

C35: It's not like that.

T35: Yeah.

C36: No, I don't mean like this, you, the hand, you know the hand is supposed, this hand, umm, this has to, has to take this off, and this hand off, and put this in the front. That's what I mean.

T36: Okay, okay. [*continues to fix the transformer*] But while I'm doing this, I'm thinking that you've just told me something that you're really, really worried about.

C37: Yep.

T37: And I think you need to remember that the most important thing for you to do is to be a child and to be looked after by other people and it's just too much for someone your age to think that you have to look after yourself … Too much! … so you need to make sure that you just are able to play, and that you can be looked after by all the grown-ups in your life.

C38: Mmm.

T38: Okay. [*still fixing the transformer*] Now Conor, you want me to turn this round and I'm going to do it for you, but it's a bit tricky, okay?

C39: I know sometimes it is a little bit tricky. I saw this boy once, had one of these transformers and he said, "Humm, can you take it off for me," and I said, "but I can't, it's too hard."

T39:   It *is* too hard. We don't want it to break.

C40:   Oh yeah. Kate?

T40:   Mmm?

C41:   I've put it the wrong way around.

T41:   Mmm. So it was right the first time, no?

C42:   Yeah, it was.

T42:   It was. But you know, we test these things out, don't we.

C43:   Yep.

T43:   Do you want me to help you again?

C44:   Yep. This one is easy, this one is hard.

T44:   Uh huh.

C45:   You do this part, I'll do this part.

T45:   Let me take that off you. [*at first we are working together but then Conor takes the transformer from me and tries to fix it, but he seems to be getting more into a muddle and the toy seems more broken*]

C46:   Ah, you take it and I do this part. It's so easy, let's put it here, put this one back.

T46:   You know what, let me take care of that for you, let's put him back together, because he's a bit alone at the moment, he's got all these different parts and he needs some help. And you know, I'm the grown up, so I'm going to help him to be put back together, but I need you to help me think about it. [*I continue to fix the transformer and try to put it back the right way*]

C47:   Okay.

T47:   Oh, that looks sore. You look a bit funny. [*Conor has tied a balloon around his head and puts it in his mouth*]

C48:   [*pretending he has plastic in his mouth*] You put it that way—this way. You forgot.

T48:   Oh! That looks a bit sore.

C49:   Kate?

T49:   Mmm?

C50:   You know what? I once, once—you know what?

T50:   Tell me.

C51:   Sometimes … Oh yeah, oh yeah, it was nothing. I've forgotten.

T51:   Do you wanna tell me?

C52:   Oh, my sticker. [*Conor finds the sticker in his box*]

T52:   Yeah, you forgot it last week.

C53:   Oh. I wonder …?

T53: What were you going to say just then?

C54: Oh yeah. I was forgotten.

T54: Sounded like it was maybe a hard thing to talk about.

C55: Oh man! You did it the wrong way!

T55: Mmm. Maybe you're right.

This is the last 10 minutes of the session. After some play, I prepare Conor for the ending as usual by sitting on the cushions. I use this time to process anything left over from the session, which helps to regulate him and prepare him for going back to class. We have just played the sticker game, a weekly ritual which helps him to cope with his separation anxiety and manage the ending, the stick acts as a 'transitional object', an adhesive agent so that I 'stick' in his mind until our next session.

C56: You know dis? Where's my transformer?

T56: There's your transformer.

C57: I've got my sticker.

T57: There it is, there it is.

C58: I'll put my sticker in my pocket. Do you remember what I told you about Conor and Kate? [*Conor takes out two toys, the transformer and a small measuring tape that have come to represent Conor and me*]

T58: Ahh huh.

C59: When we had—I brought you a Conor.[1] What was this? [*He shows me the measuring tape*]

T59: Uh huh.

C60: And this was my cyberzorg? [*Conor shows me his cyberzorg—the transformer*]

T60: That's right!

C61: [*Conor starts playing with the two toys; the transformer and the measuring tape*] And you said, "I love my cyberzorg Conor." "And I love mine too." "Okay, let's try and fly our cyberzorgs!" Okay they're inside their cyberzorgs. TRANSFORRRRM!! [*sound of flying around*]

---

[1] "cyberzorg" was a made-up word that Conor used for a special vehicle that the transformer and measuring tape could travel around in. It had a protective force field around it keeping them both safe.

T61:   So it sounds like you've been thinking about this a lot, is that true?

C62:   Yep.

T62:   And when did you decide that this was how it was?

C63:   [*Conor begins to play with the figures*] They done this, then after— this! Transfoooooorm! (da da da ah) and this was, this was my gripping thing for grip baddie. "I am a Queen, Evil Queen! Ha ha!" [*fighting noises*] Ayyy ya!! Ahhhhh! They kicked me and her. "You did a death, you kicked Kate. If you kicked Kate. This what I'm gonna teach you! [*fighting noises*]

T63:   [*gasp*]

C64:   I said if you hit Kate.

T64:   You know what it sounds like to me? It sounds like you were protecting me just then, is that right?

C65:   Yes it was.

T65:   Who were you protecting me from?

C66:   The evil baddies.

T66:   And who are the evil baddies?

C67:   They wanted to—when you were sleeping, they were evil, they wanted to take your power.

T67:   They wanted to take my power away! You know what? It sounds like you were worried that maybe someone might take *my* power away, or maybe they might take *me* away!

C68:   They take you *and* your power, and then after, when they take your power away—guess what will happen?

T68:   What will happen?

C69:   And when this goes off, [*Conor shows me a switch on the transformer and pretends to click a switch*] my power goes off, and then after, it will be the end of the world!

T69:   So, if they take all my power away then your power gets lost?

C70:   Yep.

T70:   Ah! That must be really scary!

C71:   And that's why I have to protect you. You have to protect yourself as well. "Come on!" [*Conor re-starts the play-fighting noises*]

T71:   So you—you feel like you've got to look after me? [*Conor makes the toys fly, half absorbed in the play*] Hey, you know what that sounds like to me Conor?

C72:   Yep.

T72: That sounds like a *big* bit of responsibility. That you have to look after me. All the time, so that, so that you're okay?

C73: [*Conor pretends to be a baddie*] Who are you? "I am the Prince and I'm going to take you far away! Muhahahahaaa! You and Kate." This is you. "I'm going to take your power away! Muhahaha!" "You are so dumb!" "Awh! Ahh! Oh nah! Now you made me!" [*fighting noises*] Transfoooorm! "Woah! How did you change to that?" [*fighting noises*] "I AM OPTIMUS PRIME!" [*fighting noises*] "Kate I need you ... ayyy ya!" [*several minutes of superheroes in action*] And then you flip.

T73: Uh huh.

C74: And you turn into power. And, and, umm, and someone who is invincible, they put on your power ranger clothes and you become a power ranger and you get your sword and pow! And you get to be a baddie.

T74: It sounds like a big new story that you're gonna have to tell me about next week.

C75: Yep.

T75: Can you come and sit down here while we end? [*ending the session on the carpet*]

C76: Where's Kate and Conor? [*referring to the transformer and measuring tape*] Oh there they are.

T76: So, Conor, today you told me some things. You told me that sometimes, sometimes it's a bit worrying because you think that if you and your cousins are always fighting and being loud and playing, that it's going to hurt your grandma. And that sounds like a big bit of worry. It sounds like you feel you have to protect her.

C77: Uh humm.

T77: So you feel like you have to look after her, and you know that I think that's a lot of responsibility. Do you know what that means?

C78: No.

T78: It's a big word, isn't it? I think it's a lot of hard work for you to always have to worry about everybody else, because, you know what? You need people to *just* look after you, because you're just a little boy.

C79: Yep.

T79:   And I think sometimes you're worrying that maybe when you come and see me, you're gonna have to protect me as well, because maybe you think something bad will happen to me as well.

C80:   Uh hum

T80:   And that everybody, *all* the big grown-ups in your life, you have to protect them, just in case something bad happens to them. Does it sometimes feel like that?

C81:   Umm. I'm thinking what you're saying. Let's see what the transformer's saying when he's spinning around. "I think that—that—that—dat da da daaaaa."

T81:   What does the transformer think?

C82:   Let the voice come.

T82:   Shall we ask him what he thinks? "Hey, transformer. Maybe you could help Conor out here. Could you speak for Conor?"

C83:   Of course! [*Conor speaks as the transformer*]

T83:   What can you say? Sometimes, does Conor worry that he has to protect everybody and save everybody? Because he thinks that everyone is going to leave him just like his daddy left him?

C84:   Yeah, I know. Once, you don't know about Conor, you know, when his dad died, I was there too! But you didn't see me. Conor didn't want me to tell you, because we keep it, I didn't want to tell you, Conor didn't want to tell you, because it was our secret.

T84:   It was your secret.

C85:   Yes.

T85:   And what did you see?

C86:   I seed, bad man. My sis, my gran, my dad was trying to save a good lady. The bad boys, they said to him, they were saying rude things to the girls. And said, and my dad said, "Hey, fuck off!" and then after, and then after my dad, then after they stab my dad.

T86:   And the transformer saw all of this?

C87:   Yep, and me and him keep it a *secret*!

T87:   Kept it a secret. And I guess when you think about that, it makes you feel really sad. [*Conor is fiddling and wrapping the long measuring tape around the transformer*] And you know what I've seen you do now?

C88:   Uh huh.

T88:   I think what you've done is "Kate" and "Conor" have been mixed together so that they are part of the same thing. Is that right?

[Conor has pulled out the tape part of the measuring tape and coiled it around the transformer]

C89: Yep.

T89: Do you think today you could let Kate look after Conor?

C90: Yeahhh.

T90: You know what? You see this? *[I point at the wrapped-up transformer]*

C91: Yep. *[Conor starts to lie down]*

T91: You see that Kate's *[still referring to the metaphor]* wrapped Conor up, so he's all protected, and so that he's safe.

C92: Kate?

T92: And you know what Kate's going to do now? Real Kate. Kate's going to wrap Conor up, so that he feels nice and safe. And she's going to do it like this, so she is going to put this under his head like this. *[Conor starts snoring, pretending to sleep]* and she is gonna lie him down, like that, and then she's going to get her friend *[big squishy pillow]* and she's going to wrap him up, so that you feel safe. *[more snoring]* She's going to get this under his head, and then she is going to get this nice heart *[big, heart-shaped pillow with long hugging arms]* and she's going to wrap this around him as well, so that on every side he feels nice and safe, just like the transformer is wrapped up, wrapped up, just like that. Do you see, do you see how it's the same? Do you see how it's the same? *[Conor is relaxed lying next to me, now covered in blankets and pillows, pretending to snore. I then gently put a pillow under Conor's head and arrange the hugging heart so it's covering him, and he pretends to sleep for a few moments. It is the end of the session and slowly we gather ourselves to leave]*

Reflections

Conor was my first long-term client. I worked with him for over two years and began our journey at the beginning of my training. Now, more than a decade later, and with the benefit of life experience and having grown as a therapist, it is interesting to reflect on this transcript.

I remember preparing for the viva, desperately trying to find the right bit of tape that would honour the body of work, demonstrate my skills as a therapist, and not contain too many blunders. It was certainly an exposing process, yet the viva itself allowed me to discuss the tape in the context of the work, look closely at my blind spots, and gave me an opportunity to explore my pitfalls and clumsy interventions. Looking back, it was certainly a rich opportunity for growth.

When I look back at this session, I am struck by the tenderness of our relationship, the fragility of a little boy, lost in a terrifying grown-up world, and me, an inexperienced therapist, and how innocently we were figuring it out and learning together. At times in the countertransference, I obviously feel helpless, and give very left-brain interventions instead of staying with his immense feeling of loss and fear. I put all the responsibility back on Conor's shoulders, "You just need to be looked after!"—perhaps drawing on my own fears of not being able to help. However, beneath the slip-ups and clunky interventions, there is a genuine sense of being alongside Conor and, at times, I can almost hear myself taking a deep breath and regulating myself.

There will always be things that you wish you had said or not said in a session, but holding in mind Winnicott's idea of being 'good enough', the experience has taught me that this lies in the quality of the therapeutic relationship. Building a strong working alliance, and attuning to the other continues to be at the heart of my work with clients. It is in the moment-to-moment intersubjective space between client and therapist, where the client feels truly "felt" by the therapist, that genuine repair takes place.

Conor would now be a young man in his early twenties, and, of course, as with nearly all my clients, I carry a sadness about not knowing how his life has unfolded. I wonder what he remembers of those sessions, and I imagine he may have a distant memory of playing with a "kind lady" in a playroom in his primary school. My hope is that I offered some containment to Conor at a time when life felt frightening and confusing, and, beyond this, that he may have internalised some of the goodness of our relationship and continues to carry it with him today.

References

Boothe, P. B., & Jernberg, A. M. (2009). *Theraplay: Helping Parents and Children Build Better Relationships Through Attachment-Based Play*. 3rd edn. San Francisco: Jossey-Bass.

Hughes, D. A. (2011). *Attachment-Focused Family Therapy Workbook*. New York: W. W. Norton.

CHAPTER 12

Working in schools: parents and the system around the child

Liz Murray-Bligh

Introduction

In this chapter I will discuss the main areas of environmental influence on the child, drawing on my extensive experience of working in primary school settings, and I shall consider our own place as therapists along with some of the struggles that arise in the holding of professional boundaries when working in a non-clinical setting. I will focus mainly on parents and schools, and then touch on collaborating with external agencies before taking a brief look at the impact of digital media usage on young children as we grapple with the powerful influences of this often unfamiliar and ever-shifting world in which the majority of children are so immersed. For the sake of economy I will use the term "parents" to include carers, and the term "therapist" to include counsellors. I have given pseudonyms to clients referred to in the case studies, and some of the information has been altered in order to protect their identities.

I have used mind maps to support my own thinking around the numerous children with whom I have worked and will use these to illustrate the complex web of interconnected external systems that impact on children's physical and mental well-being (see Figure 12.1).

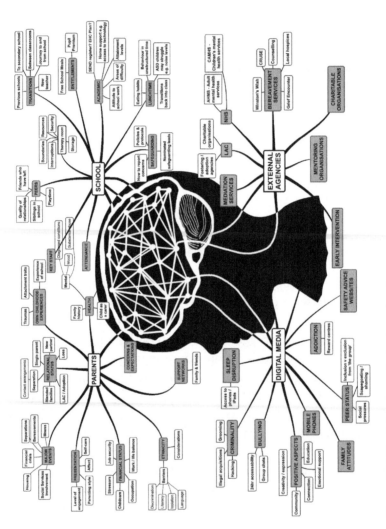

Figure 12.1 The interconnected external systems

However, they are by no means exhaustive and represent a fairly generic viewpoint. The non-linear presentation of this environmental data is reminiscent of graphic depictions of the neural connections within the brain itself. They are two separate and yet interrelated systems that are constantly shifting and evolving; the internal milieu impacting on the external world, and vice versa.

Parents

Perry (2008, p. 83) notes that "a good 'brain' history begins with a history of the caregivers' childhood and early experience". Meeting, developing a relationship, and working with parents provides a huge amount of contextual information about our clients (bearing in mind that every parent has their own subjective view on feelings and events shared within the family experience). This also provides us with an opportunity to identify ruptures and enhance the attachment between child and parent and, where appropriate, provide parents with alternative strategies to support their children.

Sensitivity and empathy are key and where family trauma is indicated, such as the sudden death of a loved one, a terminal illness, or a difficult family break-up, it is important to understand what the parent has shared with the child concerning the surrounding circumstances. This helps to maintain consistency, or it may alert therapists to the need to work with the parents to provide more clarity for the child. Sometimes such events are outlined in written referrals but are not broached either in the parent meetings or with the client for fear of causing upset, and can remain the proverbial elephant in the room. They can easily fall into the category of a no-go area which can create an impasse in the work and inexperienced trainees often need extra support around this from their supervisors.

It is crucial to approach parents with the understanding that they want the best for their children, but that sometimes their ability to parent well is negatively impacted by their own experiences of trauma, which can be transmitted intergenerationally (Bowlby; 1988; Schore, 2003; Van der Kolk, 2005; Wallin, 2007). Having been deprived of the opportunity to internalise a healthy maternal object, many struggle to provide the balanced model of parenting that we see in securely attached children.

The adult attachment interview

Just as we view children through the lens of attachment as a way of understanding particular behavioural traits, it can sometimes be helpful to think of parents in terms of George et al.'s (1985) adult attachment interview (AAI). Following the "strange situation" (Ainsworth et al., 1978) and the classification of attachment styles in children, the AAI focuses on the correlating parenting styles. These are clearly outlined by Siegel (1999, pp. 74–83), although he includes the caveat that "… some of the measures of personality found in behavioural genetics to have a large degree of heritability are not associated with AAI findings" (ibid., p. 78). This can provide us with a starting point in understanding the coping strategies of those whose parenting skills fall at the more extreme ends of the spectrum between emotional abandonment and neglect, and overwhelming preoccupation and impingement.

The autonomous parent

Whereas most of our clients present with adaptive and defensive behaviours in response to their specific attachment traits, at times children will be referred to therapy who present as securely attached. The reasons behind these referrals often relate to single-event traumas, such as parental separation, family illness, or bereavement. The supportive cooperation of reflective parents who are able to prioritise their child's needs often means that the work can be more focused and completed in a shorter time frame.

This pattern of cooperation can also be seen where parents have addressed their own traumas through personal therapy. Occasionally I am taken aback by the resilience and capacity of individuals to build better and healthier lives, both for themselves and for their children, having endured significant levels of trauma and adversity throughout their own childhood.

Case study

Timmy was referred to me shortly after he joined the school in Year 2. He was an energetic and likeable little boy but struggled to regulate himself whenever conflict arose with his peers, often resulting in a physical attack by him. I met with his mother, who presented as warm, open, and reflective and this belied the multiple experiences of trauma that she had experienced in her own childhood. Her own family life was regularly punctuated with incidences of domestic violence, and Timmy's grandfather was repeatedly in and out of prison due to his criminal activities, culminating in the mother witnessing Timmy's grandfather being repeatedly stabbed and almost killed by a criminal associate. She and her four siblings were all taken into care and the mother moved in with her grandmother. This pattern was repeated in her relationship with Timmy's father, with whom she became pregnant when she was sixteen. She had endured high levels of physical and emotional abuse in the relationship, which Timmy had witnessed, but was now settled with a supportive partner with whom she had had a second child. In our meetings she spoke with clarity about her experiences and Timmy was consistently at the centre of the conversation. The mother demonstrated a healthy capacity for self-reflection and ability to think about her son's subjective experiences.

The preoccupied/ambivalent parent

Parents come laden with their own experiences of school and I am always curious to know more about this. An overly anxious parent's concern for their child may be tainted by their own negative school experiences, which can be consciously or unconsciously passed down to their offspring. An exploration of their own journey through the education system can often mirror worries and fears that are fuelled by this. At times, meetings can easily drift into addressing the needs of the parent and it is important to be mindful of this and steer the focus back to the client. Such meetings focusing more on the parents' feelings may be a pointer to how the child's needs have not been prioritised, and indicate that preoccupation around the parents' well-being interrupts a healthier attachment.

Case study

Jonas, aged ten, was referred to me because he was struggling with some of his peers and presenting with anxiety. He was a delightful boy, who spoke warmly about both his parents and his older brother and he ticked all the boxes for secure attachment. However, I could see how some of his more pedantic, overly enthusiastic behaviours may have caused friction among his classmates. My initial meeting with his mother revealed her own struggles with anxiety, for which she had been prescribed medication in the past. I asked how school had been for her and she broke down as she recalled ongoing experiences of being bullied, both in primary and secondary school, and she spoke of her fears that this was being repeated in Jonas's peer relationships. When I enquired about his father's perspective, she told me that he did not share her concerns, so I arranged to meet with both parents together. During the meeting they began to adjust their positions, with Jonas's father acknowledging that there had indeed been challenges for Jonas while his mother recognised how her anxieties were closely related to her own experiences and may have been somewhat misplaced. With both parents modifying their views and sharing a more cohesive understanding about Jonas's presenting issues the family found a more unified and containing way forward, and this was reflected in an improvement in Jonas's feelings about school and his ability to focus on his work.

The dismissive/avoidant parent

These parents will often be supportive of therapy for their children in terms of "fixing" something as opposed to providing a safe and reflective space for them to explore thoughts and feelings, and they tend to discuss concerns around their children in practical rather than emotional terms. There is often an assumption that their children are either oblivious to, or not impacted by upsetting circumstances or events; for example, one parent said of his children, "They were upstairs when my partner and I were having rows and they couldn't hear it." Another parent, who had separated from his wife following high levels of domestic violence told me that, with regards to his children, "The arguing wasn't their business." His concerns were solely focused on their low levels of academic achievement, which he wanted me to address. He could not make the link between the children's poor academic achievement and the trauma that they had experienced, and which had culminated in the implementation of a child protection plan by social services.

Case study

Emma had just turned ten when she started seeing me. She was under the special guardianship of her maternal grandmother, Kim, having been removed from her mother's care due to her alcohol and substance abuse. This had resulted in high levels of neglect of Emma until, at the age of six, she moved to her grandmother's. Her biological father had been absent since her birth. The grandmother was open and cooperative, and happy to share the distressing details of her own family history, including witnessing chronic domestic violence perpetrated by Emma's great-grandfather. This was replicated in the grandmother's twelve-year relationship with her husband, whom she had left several years previously. Her relationship with Emma's mother was fractious and often resulted in the grandmother's angry rants about Emma's mother's behaviour. The grandmother spoke quickly, without pause, and left very little room for me to interject, and would deflect whenever I invited her to imagine into Emma's subjective experiences. The grandmother was fiercely protective of Emma, and fully supportive of the therapy, but her concerns were focused on Emma's behaviours, such as her reluctance to go out of the family home unaccompanied and her lack of engagement with her schoolwork.

The unresolved/disorganised parent

Parents often bring their own experiences of childhood trauma. The material shared can be challenging and at times triggering, and here careful supervision is imperative to support the therapist around the potential for secondary trauma, particularly with trainees. With an internalised model a far cry from Winnicott's "good enough mother" (Winnicott, 1987), they often struggle even with the basics and can present as fiercely overprotective of their children while simultaneously being dismissive of their emotional needs and oblivious to safeguarding issues. The parents' narratives can be inconsistent; they present as easily dysregulated; and there is often a sense that the child is providing the emotional comfort that was so lacking in the parents' own lives. The offer of therapy can be enthusiastically embraced but easily sabotaged if at any point the parents feel that their integrity as parents is threatened. Also, the management of disclosures can result in the parents terminating the child's therapy. For these parents, referrals to CAMHS for support with parenting can help to alleviate some of the pressures on the therapist, parents, and child thus creating more of a supportive team approach.

The absent parent

At times parents consent to therapy but are not willing to come in to meet with the therapist. This can feel contradictory and often the school's concerns understandably lean towards providing additional support for the child regardless of the parents' engagement. These parents present enormous challenges in that the therapist is, to a great extent, working in the dark and is deprived of insights that only a parent can provide, both with regard to the family history and in the parents' own presentation. "It is less important to determine what the parents do than what they are" (Kohut, 1984, p. 14). Feelings of inadequacy, marginalisation, shame, or disempowerment may impact on their willingness to voluntarily engage with professionals who may, in the past, have been seen as posing a threat to the family unit and in some cases, may have had involvement with social services. Considerations around the possibility of the work being sabotaged need to be explored, alongside the potential for the child to feel conflicted in their allegiances between the school and the parents. Poor school attendance can sometimes be an issue and result in the child having an unstable commitment to therapy. It can also be indicative of a more significant absence that the child experiences in the parental dyad, summarised in André Green's essay, "The Dead Mother":

> … loss of love is followed by loss of meaning; for the child, nothing makes sense anymore. Since "more often than not" a distant mother is accompanied by an absent father (who refuses or does not know how to respond to the child), the infant cannot turn to anybody and is caught in "a unique movement with two aspects".
>
> (Greene, 1986, pp. 150–151)

Parents who have separated

This can be delicate work where the therapist is at risk of being pulled into the split, particularly where a separation is recent, and feelings are still raw. At worst the therapist's advice can be used as ammunition against one or other parent, who may then sabotage the therapy or demand that it is terminated. Where contact is shared it is important to acknowledge this and, where possible, meet with both the mother and the father from the start and clarify the therapist's neutral position. The risk of slipping into the complex dynamics of a drama triangle (Stewart & Joines, 1987, p. 236) is significant, and where a therapist's own material is triggered, collusion can occur. Fathers are too often overlooked and have much to contribute to the emotional well-being of their children. Whereas separated couples will undoubtedly air their grievances during meetings it is important to keep the client at the centre of the discussion and to draw both parents towards a better understanding of their child's subjective experience of the breakdown of the family unit and the current parental conflicts.

In most cases, where children share their time between parents, they experience a contradictory cocktail of emotions. The heady excitement around the reunion with the other parent is often offset by feelings of guilt and concern around the one who has just been left, resulting in children becoming dysregulated and acting out. Once parents understand a child's complicated and confused feelings, they are in a much better position to relate to their child's anxieties and emotional outbursts.

Culture/difference

Issues of culture and difference often lie silently and invisibly at the heart of parent meetings and are more generally present in the form of socio-economic and ethnic variances between the parents and the therapist. In today's climate I notice a growing sensitivity on my part, as a white British, educated, middle-class woman, around my curiosity about ethnicity for fear of triggering a parent's concerns around their legal or social status or sense of being different. The experiences of first-generation parents will differ from those who were born in the UK. Conflict and political upheaval in their countries of origin may have impacted them either directly, for example those with refugee status, or indirectly, where family and loved ones remain in situ. The category "Black African", commonly listed on school data systems, feels overly generic and lacking in consideration of the multitude of cultural and historical differences between one country and another. It is helpful to do a little research around parents' own specific culture but more importantly it is essential for the therapist to be respectfully curious and learn from the parents themselves so as to avoid falling into the trap of forming stereotyped assumptions.

Aims

When meeting with parents a therapist's initial aims are to:

- Listen empathically to the parents' concerns around their child.
- Build a trusting but boundaried relationship with them.
- Where possible, provide them with a school email address and be clear around the days that the therapist will be available to respond. Avoid giving out personal contact details as this can lead to complications.
- Be mindful not to fall into the parents' transference onto the therapist as an idealised or persecutory figure.
- Encourage parents to think about the child's subjective experiences and to hold the child at the centre of the discussion. The parents' inability to do so may be an indication of unresolved trauma or a tendency to prioritise their own unmet needs over those of their children.
- Provide some psycho-education to support their understanding and thus raise their level of empathy towards their child's more challenging behaviours.
- Reflect on what the parents are doing well; Winnicott's concept of the "good enough mother" (1987) is an often forgotten but powerful message to share with them.
- Work towards strengthening attachments between parent and child and removing obstacles whereby the child finds it difficult to talk openly with the parent about their feelings, worries, and concerns. This work can often be done in parent/child sessions which the therapist may introduce once the therapeutic alliances with the child and the parent are firmly in place. It is important to bear in mind that

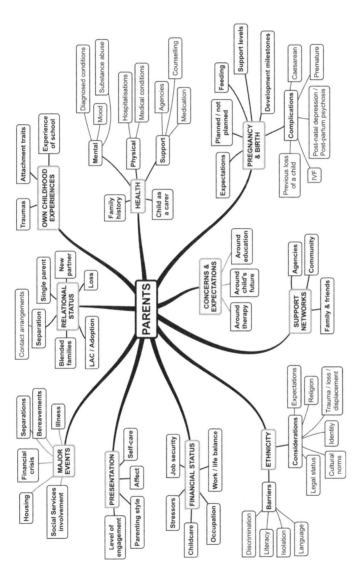

Figure 12.2 Parents: making sense of intergenerational transmissions

the child is the main client; with parents whose own needs have not been met it is sometimes easy to fall into prioritising the parent while sidelining the child.

• Assist parents in utilising local agencies that may be able to support their needs, for example, the general practitioner (GP); IAPT (Improving Access to Psychological Therapies) services, bereavement services, family support workers, parenting programmes, adult counselling services.

• Ask parents for permission to share basic information with relevant staff, on a need to know basis, bearing in mind GDPR (General Data Protection Regulation) directives. This provides teachers with some context and understanding regarding the child's presentation. It also promotes the teachers' more empathic and containing response when children become disruptive in class.

Figure 12.2 explores some of the environmental influences that can impact on an individual's ability to parent well and may highlight areas worth further exploration in the context of the child's presenting behaviours. The environmental influences are particularly relevant during the initial meeting with the parents when information is gathered in order to formulate a treatment plan, but often they are more forthcoming once a trusting relationship has been built. It is important to prioritise the client in the work; however, parental input adds depth and dimension to our understanding and provides opportunities to enhance their abilities to parent well.

Schools

Schools are a significant safety factor for vulnerable children, providing warmth, security, structure, food, and, for the most part, positive peer and adult interactions. Teachers and support staff play a vital role in shaping the societies of the future and ensuring the potential for social mobility and, as such, play a pivotal role in the community. They are dynamic and lively places to work in and it can take time to develop an understanding of the complex systems that evolve in individual settings and how these impact on clients (see Figure 12.3).

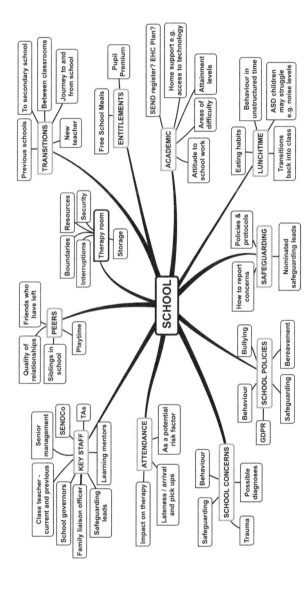

Figure 12.3 Schools: understanding how they function

Peer relationships

In my experience, for most children the negotiation of friendships and acceptance by their peers is paramount. When things go wrong it can lead to a preoccupation that can impact on their capacity for academic learning where a child's main focus is not on the lesson content but on their interactions with the adults and children around them. Where trauma has occurred a child's ability to self-regulate will most likely be impaired (Schore, 2003). Expectations of relationships with others can carry either an imagined or disproportionate level of rejection or attack, resulting in hypervigilance, often due to impairments in a child's abilities to read social cues (Schore, 2003; Siegel, 1999). This regularly plays out in the classroom setting, often creating disruption at varying levels. How their peer relations are experienced is intricately linked with their own personal development and well-being. "Our sense of 'I' is profoundly influenced by how we belong to a 'we'" (Siegel & Hartzell, 2003, p. 89) and this can often be traced back to a client's early experiences within the mother–infant dyad.

Their difficulties with peers are rooted in their attachment behaviours and it is important to spend time carefully exploring this with clients. These children can be beset by relational conflict or shunned by the group, and often experience high levels of shame. The therapeutic task involves elevated levels of sensitivity and empathy, often involving metaphor and projection to contain the trauma, and only embarked on once a strong therapeutic alliance has been formed. The establishment of the therapeutic space as a secure base provides an environment where mentalization skills (Fonagy & Target, 1997) can be encouraged and thus foster the development of a more resilient core self.

The words "playground" and "playtime" do not always accurately reflect the unsupervised chaos that some children experience outside the tightly structured world of the classroom. For some children it can present with limitless triggers, resulting in defensive attachment behaviours becoming activated so that play quickly spills over into verbal or physical conflict.

> Many children who have missed this early dance of attunement lack two essential ingredients for getting along with peers: they are unable to understand how their peers are feeling and therefore

are unable to take their feelings into account; and they are unable to play interactive games in an appropriate give-and-take manner.
(Jernberg & Booth, 2001, p. 43)

As the end of therapy draws near, for clients who continue to struggle with specific peer relationships and where reconciliation is sought, I may invite them to take part in a restorative session with the individual concerned. This can serve several purposes:

- Opportunities for self-reflection and ownership of behaviours are brought to the surface in a safe setting and addressed in real time.
- Conflict resolution can be modelled and, in most cases, problems explored and resolved.
- The transferential material between the child and therapist can begin to be gently dismantled.
- The outside world can come into the inside world of the therapy room creating a safe, transitional practising space.

This intervention can often be transformative, but preparation is key and I would recommend some training in Restorative Practices, which have been adapted for use in educational settings and adopted by schools and organisations both in the United Kingdom and internationally. The focus in the session is not on allocating blame, but on listening to each party and allowing them to acknowledge responsibility for their part played, and to offer an opportunity to repair any damage done. This resonates with therapeutic techniques and offers opportunities for clients to self-reflect, resolve conflicts, and repair relationships.

> The fundamental unifying hypothesis of Restorative Practices is disarmingly simple: that human beings are happier, more productive and more likely to make positive changes to their behavior when those in positions of authority do things with them, rather than to them and for them. This hypothesis maintains that the punitive and authoritarian "to" mode and the permissive and paternalistic "for" mode are not as effective as the restorative, participatory, engaging "with" mode. If this restorative hypothesis is valid, then it has significant implications for many disciplines.
> (Wachtel & McCold, 2004)

A surprising number of children who are trapped in long-term stand-offs will sometimes describe an incident that occurred several years earlier, which had never been acknowledged or repaired. The closer the friendship, the deeper the hurt can be, and it is important to explore this first. In these cases where close friendships have broken down, aggression comes from a place of deep hurt and loss and retaliation can be powerfully expressed. In the absence of a backstory this aggression is often perceived by adults as bullying.

Teachers

It is not surprising that the class teacher, often unknowingly cast in the role of mother or father by their thirty or so charges, is on the receiving end of so much transferential material (both positive and negative) and is, at times, easily pulled into conflict. "Teachers … can often find themselves feeling angry towards [these children] with no real sense of why" (Geddes, 2006, p. 70). Good working alliances between therapists and teachers, as well as the often-forgotten classroom assistants, are key to gaining further insights into the child's day-to-day experiences and monitoring difficulties and improvements. This involves working with staff to mitigate children's more challenging interactions within the classroom by providing strategies, insights, and understanding around a child's particular defence mechanisms. To this end, parents are often willing for therapists to provide basic information about the family situation with staff, but it is important to gain the parents' consent beforehand and be clear about what can be shared. Often, understanding the child's family context results in increased levels of empathy and helps staff to step back and experience negative behaviours from a more developed, less personal perspective.

In my own practice, I offer a confidential weekly drop-in session for staff. When school pressures are combined with challenging home circumstances, the drop-in session represents a neutral thinking space for them. Where there is a suggestion of more complex issues, I may recommend a visit to their GP as a way of accessing counselling. Alternatively, if they are in a position to pay privately, I may point them in the direction of the website of a licensing body such as the British Association of

Counselling and Psychotherapy (BACP) or the UK Council of Psycho-therapy (UKCP).

As a therapist in the school I choose not to spend time in the informal staffroom setting nor do I attend social school gatherings. This maintains the element of containment in the therapy room and avoids any anxieties around breaches in confidentiality where a staff member may not feel safe having shared with me details of personal or professional struggles.

External agencies

Signposting is an important element in therapeutic work in schools and it is important for therapists to familiarise themselves with the services available in their local area (see Figure 12.4 for some examples of these).

Social services

Many parents experience dread and foreboding when faced with the prospect of a social worker assessing their ability to parent effectively. Their ultimate fear, of course, is that their children will be removed from their care and the reality is that, under certain circumstances when interventions of support and education have been exhausted, legal processes are initiated that may result in this happening.

Children who have had a lot of contact with social services are often extremely wary, particularly where family members may have told them not to speak about their "private business". The child's hypervigilance towards social workers can be transferred onto the therapist, where the dynamics can often activate memories of meetings with friendly but curious professionals. For the most part, children are extremely protective around maintaining the integrity of their family lives, and it is important to name and respect this whilst also being clear around the limits of confidentiality in the therapeutic work.

In my own work I welcome the involvement of social workers and have often received direct requests from them to work with children who are under their care. Social workers are particularly exposed to being on the receiving end of frustration and, at times, anger from concerned parties

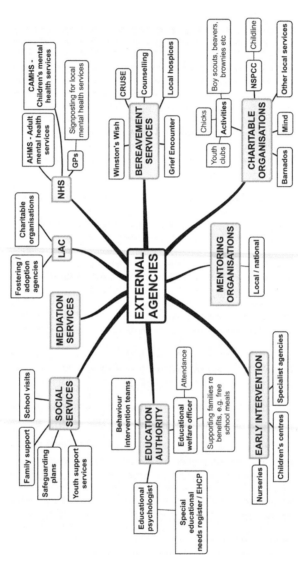

Figure 12.4 External agencies: awareness of local provision

who attribute their perceived failures to "fix" things as incompetence. The nature of their work means that successes are rarely acknowledged in contrast to incidents where services have been judged as failing, and where grievances are aired in the public arena. As with mental health services, limitations around funding and increasing need for support mean that thresholds are becoming increasingly higher leaving schools to carry greater responsibility for children who are vulnerable and may potentially be at risk.

Where social services are involved with a client, care needs to be taken around the sharing of information with regards to confidentiality, particularly if the therapist is invited to a CIN (child in need) meeting or CP (child protection) conference.

Child and Adolescent Mental Health Services (CAMHS)

Referrals to more specialist NHS services are imperative when a client's difficulties go beyond the therapist's clinical capacity and where the support of a multidisciplinary team may be more appropriate. Procedures can be found on the website of the borough's local CAMHS provider and often involve submitting a referral form. Common requests by the referrer may range from a general mental health review to a more focused assessment, such as for ASD, ADHD, or PTSD. It is normal practice in schools for the SENCo to lead on such referrals and here transparency and collaboration are vital. They are often happy to delegate the work to the school therapist who is well placed in terms of the ongoing relationship with the client and a more in-depth understanding of the presenting issues, but this depends on the individual.

Where parents are in agreement that an assessment may be beneficial, it is helpful to involve them in the referral from the start. Collaboration with the parents around this is always good practice, in terms of transparency. In this way they may feel more invested in the process and a sense of involvement can reduce anxiety. An additional, more detailed report by the therapist can provide extra information to assist the CAMHS clinician's decision to accept the referral for assessment. If the referral is accepted it can be reassuring for parents if the therapist, where possible, accompanies them to their initial meeting. However, constraints on the therapist's availability can often be an issue here. Where it is possible, CAMHS workers appreciate the insights that a school therapist can offer and making face-to-face links are important, as often the therapist will continue to support the child in school alongside any work that CAMHS may undertake themselves, particularly with the parents. Co-working can be very rewarding, and it is important for the school therapist to maintain close communications with the allocated CAMHS professional.

Case study

> Amelia, aged seven, had witnessed high levels of sustained domestic violence perpetrated by her father on her mother. The mother, Kathy, had been rehoused and social services had closed the case. In class, Amelia's behaviour was erratic and she regularly hit out at other children and, at times, adults, and she was soon referred to me. In sessions she presented as hypervigilant, fragmented, and unable to internalise good objects, and the quality of the relationship between us was erratic, suggesting disorganised traits. Her paintings were disconcerting, often depicting angry, distorted faces, and finished off with a flurry of red paint. Kathy was open to meetings with me, and spoke in detail about her own childhood, which was overshadowed by her own father's violent behaviour towards her, and about her struggles to "control" Amelia. She regularly expressed to me how Amelia was the centre of her world, but also came across as dismissive of Amelia's needs; and she told me that she used Amelia's father as a threat if Amelia misbehaved. With a sense of little or no progress being made, we both agreed that a referral to CAMHS would be appropriate in order to support her with parenting Amelia, and this was accepted. Following the assessment, it was agreed for me to co-work with a CAMHS clinician who would focus on supporting Kathy. Later, Amelia made a disclosure resulting in an assessment by a social worker. Kathy immediately terminated the therapy and soon after moved Amelia to a different school. Although the rupture in the work was challenging, particularly in terms of my concerns around Amelia's mental well-being, the involvement with the CAMHS clinician continued and she was able to give

support and guidance around providing the best outcomes for both Amelia and her mother.

Other signposting, which can often be accessed via GPs, may involve:

- IAPT services
- Local/national bereavement services
- Couples' counselling/mediation
- Local counselling services for parents
- Privately funded therapy (e.g. from directories found in the websites of licensing bodies such as BACP or UKCP).

Digital media

The impact of social media on children is hard to ignore. Undoubtedly there are positive influences but the darker, more abusive elements can have a devastating effect on children's mental health, particularly where insecure attachment or trauma is evident. The Education Policy Institute has identified the main concerns around children's mental health as being:

- The impact of excessive time spent online
- Sharing too much information
- Being cyber-bullied
- Social media influencing body image
- Sourcing of harmful content or advice, such as websites or social networks enabling the promotion of self-harm.

(Frith, 2017, p. 17)

We seem to be in a constant game of catch-up as we trail behind in the wake of ever-changing and advancing technologies and trends, with children often way ahead of us (see Figure 12.5).

If you are waiting for a definitive study telling us whether social media are "good" or "bad" for teens' mental health, you are going to wait for a long time. Instead, we are likely to start fleshing out

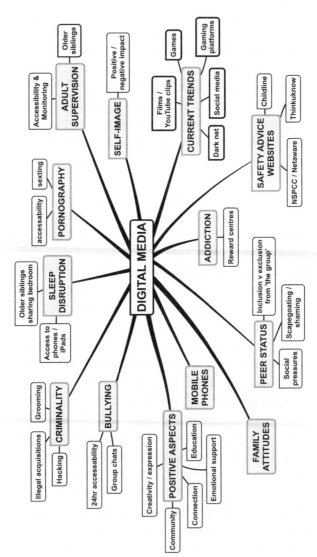

Figure 12.5 Digital media: keeping on top of an ever-changing phenomena

the very picture that young people themselves report when you ask them. "It's complicated."

(Walsh & Walsh, 2017)

I have had discussions with a nine-year-old who was able to hack into his classmates' Minecraft accounts, a skill that requires a degree of sophistication clearly learned from someone older and which skirted around the edges of legality. A seven-year-old client of mine was given a smartphone for Christmas by her mother. She was under the long-term care of her grandmother, who was drawn into a battle to limit the excessive time she spent on the phone, which represented not only a high-value item but a link with her idealised mother, who struggled with alcohol and substance abuse. There was a need to protect her from unsupervised contact, and the grandmother's limitation and supervision over her use of the phone was perceived by my client as persecutory and withholding, and caused a painful rupture in their relationship.

Children who share bedrooms with older children (siblings, half-siblings, cousins, etc.) often complain of disturbed sleep and are more likely to be exposed to inappropriate content. Characters such as Slenderman, Pennywise, and Chucky take on viral notoriety and become buzzwords around the school. In the past, children learned to familiarise themselves with their fight/flight systems by listening to tales such as Little Red Riding Hood, Jack and the Beanstalk, or The Three Little Pigs, in the presence of a regulating parent. Now, many youngsters face these highly charged and visually loaded experiences alone. The ability for parents to supervise their children's use of technology is increasingly challenged. More recent developments of 3D technologies, such as Oculus Rift, offer an even deeper immersion into a 360° digital experience where the enhanced audio and visual input is embedded in a VR headset leaving individuals completely cut off from any anchors to the real world.

It is easy to adopt a dystopian view of where this will lead. As a child, I clearly remember the warnings about watching too much television impacting on our eyesight along with our cognitive abilities. We also need to be mindful of the more positive aspects of the digital revolution such as increased communication, collaborative game play, and access to imaginative worlds. As the generational gap between users closes, children who grew up on a diet of Xbox and PlayStation games are now becoming parents themselves and may have a better understanding of the potential pitfalls in the digital environment.

Conclusion

This chapter looked at working therapeutically in a primary school setting and discussed the benefits, along with some of the challenges, of practising outside a clinical setting. It also considered the multiple environmental factors that impact on children's mental states, either positively or negatively, and examples of mind maps focusing on parents, schools, and external agencies; and digital experiences were used to throw light on the interrelated complexity of these systems.

Parents are a key element in the work, and while our main focus remains firmly on our clients, opportunities to modify and build on parenting skills can have a positive impact on outcomes. Various styles of parenting were considered, using the categories defined in the adult attachment interview as a baseline to support our understanding and enhance our empathic responses around some of the more challenging moments that may arise when meeting parents, or when their parenting skills present as insensitive or overly anxious.

The school environment itself was considered, particularly in terms of how attachment traits impact on the relational capacity of our clients, either among their peers or with teaching staff, and how insecurely attached children can become overly preoccupied with this resulting in disruptive behaviours in the classroom or playground.

Working in schools brings therapists into direct contact with an environment in which their clients spend a large proportion of their time, and as such has the potential to provide broader insights into their lived experiences and a richer understanding of this. Having an embedded therapy service can provide a bespoke model built on the specific needs of a school where relationships between the therapists and staff can be nurtured and developed, providing psycho-education, a deeper understanding of developmental issues, support with the management of challenging behaviours, and a safe and reflective space for children, parents, and staff alike.

References

Ainsworth, M. D. S., Blehar, M. C., Waters, E., & Wall, S. (1978). *Patterns of Attachment: A Psychological Study of the Strange Situation*. Hillsdale, NJ: Lawrence Erlbaum.

Bowlby, J. (1988). *A Secure Base*. Oxford: Routledge.

Fonagy, P., & Target, M. (1997). Attachment and reflective function: Their role in self-organization. *Development and Psychopathology*, *9*(4): 679–700. doi: 10.1017/S0954579497001399

Frith, E. (2017). *Social Media and Children's Mental Health: A Review of the Evidence*. London: Educational Policy Institute. Available at: https://epi. org.uk/wp-content/uploads/2018/01/Social-Media_Mental-Health_EPI-Report.pdf (last accessed September 26, 2020).

Geddes, H. (2006). *Attachment in the Classroom*. London: Worth.

George, C., Kaplan, N., & Main, M. (1985). Adult Attachment Interview. Unpublished manuscript, University of California, Berkeley, California.

Green, A. (1986). *On Private Madness*. London: Karnac.

Holmes, J. (2001). *The Search for the Secure Base*. Hove, UK: Routledge.

Jernberg, A. M., & Booth, P. B. (2001). *Theraplay*. San Fransisco: Jossey-Bass.

Kohut, F. (1984). *How Does Analysis Cure?* London: University of Chicago Press.

Perry, B. (2008). *The Boy Who Was Raised as a Dog*. New York: Basic Books.

Schore, A. N. (2003). *Affect Regulation and the Repair of the Self*. New York: W. W. Norton.

Siegel, D. J. (1999). *The Developing Mind*. New York: Guilford.

Siegel, D. J., & Hartzell, M. (2003). *Parenting from the Inside Out*. New York: Tarcher.

Stewart, I., & Joines, V. (1987). *T A Today: A New Introduction to Transactional Analysis*. Nottingham, NC: Lifespace.

Van der Kolk, B. A. (2005). Developmental trauma disorder: Toward a rational diagnosis for children with complex trauma histories. *Psychiatric Annals*, *35*(5): 401–408.

Wachtel, T., & McCold, P. (2004). *From Restorative Justice to Restorative Practices: Expanding the Paradigm.* Available at: https://iirp.edu/pdf/bc04_wachtel.pdf (last accessed September 26, 2020).

Wallin, D. J. (2007). *Attachment in Psychotherapy.* New York: Guilford.

Walsh, E., & Walsh D. (2017). It's complicated: Teens, social media, and mental health. *Psychology Today.* Available at: https://psychologytoday.com/us/blog/smart-parenting-smarter-kids/201709/its-complicated-teens-social-media-and-mental-health (last accessed September 26, 2020).

Winnicott, D. W. (1987). *Babies and Their Mothers.* C. Winnicott, R. Shepherd, & M. Davis (Eds.). Reading, MA: Addison-Wesley.

CHAPTER 13

Building a therapeutic service in schools—the role of an integrative child psychotherapist

Jane Brinson

Introduction

This chapter explores how integrative child psychotherapists' relational skills and theoretical approach can support a therapeutic service to thrive in schools. It argues for the important role that school-based services can have in supporting the emotional well-being of children and uses the example of a North London primary school to demonstrate how integrative child psychotherapists contributed to the growth of an award-winning service.

An integrative child psychotherapist puts relationships at the centre of their work with children. Within the context of a trusted relationship and a clear therapeutic frame, the child and therapist co-create a space in which change can occur. The child's thoughts and feelings are explored through words, art, story, and play. In doing so, the therapist conveys empathy and understanding of all aspects of the child's experience: the joyous and delightful, as well as the painful, terrifying, or overwhelming aspects. Through the therapist's deep empathy and curious, accepting attitude, the child is helped to understand and reflect upon their internal and external worlds. In the session, through repeated experiences of feeling "felt" (Porges, 2017) and contained (Bion, 1962), the child can develop a secure attachment to the therapist and in doing so develop a more regulated, integrated way of being in themselves and in relationships. This can be transferred to relationships outside therapy enabling the child to make changes to their challenging behaviours, thoughts, or feelings and enable them to thrive and grow in their lives at home and at school.

This chapter charts the development of the therapeutic service at Highgate Primary School and runs alongside the story of my development as a therapist. Highgate Primary was my first clinical placement and upon arriving at the school, hand in hand with a fellow trainee, I set about the process of seeing children for weekly psychotherapy.

Four years and many clinical hours later, the school's pastoral and therapeutic service was given an award for public service by *The Guardian* newspaper. The awards ceremony and accompanying press coverage gave everyone involved a chance to celebrate their hard work. It was a great compliment to the communal effort it had taken to create a service that was making a real difference to children in the school. Reporting on the award, David Brindle of *The Guardian* commented:

> Swansea Council and Highgate Primary School in North London have similarly swum upstream of developing family and behavioural problems that can require costly interventions by multiple agencies. More importantly, they are transforming children's lives.
>
> (2017)

In this chapter I will argue for the pressing need to provide therapeutic support in schools, and will chart the journey of how this service developed. Sessions with children are the central aspect of a therapist's work, along with the careful, thoughtful support for parents and families. This chapter will consider other aspects of the therapist's role. In particular, I will focus on how a relational approach applied throughout the wider school, similar to the one that the therapist applies in sessions, can support the development and increase the impact of an in-school service.

Psychotherapy in schools

Integrative child psychotherapists training at the Institute for Arts in Therapy and Education undertake clinical placements in education settings, with their initial training placements embedded in primary schools.

The clinical experience gained in these settings is fundamental to the developing therapist and the therapy they provide is an invaluable source of support for children. Providing therapy for children in schools is a growing model and there is increasing evidence to support the efficacy of this type of intervention, as opposed to the traditional clinic.

The need for robust, evidence-based interventions for children is clear; the Mental Health Foundation and Office of Health Economics have found (2005) that 20% of children in the United Kingdom have a mental health problem in any given year, and about 10% at any one time. This equates to around three children in an average class. Even though we know that mental health problems are one of the key barriers to well-being, studies suggest that only a quarter of children affected by a mental health problem access specialist help (Green et al., 2005).

Alongside and including those children with a diagnosable mental health disorder are those who have been exposed to relational trauma and loss and, as a consequence, to toxic levels of stress. The CDC-Kaiser Permanente Adverse Childhood Experiences (ACE) Study explored the link between childhood exposure to a selection of adverse, or traumatic, experiences (including abuse, neglect, parental substance abuse) and a significantly increased risk of suffering chronic physical, social, and emotional problems in later life (Felitti et al., 1998). Numerous studies, including the Burke Harris (2018) research have explored the impact of ACEs on children's developing brain and nervous system. This suggests that some children respond to the overwhelming experience of trauma with volatile behaviour, hyperactivity, and hypervigilance. Their stress response system, or sympathetic nervous system, are stuck in fight or flight mode, sometimes long after the traumatic event has ended. Other children, whose parasympathetic nervous system dominates, may present as withdrawn or dazed as their body's survival strategy is linked to a freeze or dissociative response. Whatever the survival strategy, the implications for children's educational outcomes are profound: children identified as having been impacted by three ACEs (such as having been physically abused) are three times more likely to experience academic failure. Those with four ACEs are more than 33 times more likely to have behaviour problems (Hunt et al., 2017).

However, the picture is not hopeless and exposure to ACEs does not have to lead to a bleak, inevitable conclusion. With timely interventions, such as therapy provided by an integrative child psychotherapist, the impacts of difficult childhood experiences and emerging mental health problems can be mitigated.

A growing body of evidence maps the efficacy of the work in schools to do just this. For example, Daniunaite et al. (2015) found a significant reduction in psychological distress in primary school children after completing play-based therapy in school. Lee et al. (2009) found that after participating in school-based therapeutic interventions, "… children's social and emotional behaviour, as perceived by their teachers and parents, was improved."

The practical arguments for therapy to take place in schools are clear. First, most children attend school on a regular basis. There is, of course, a small but significant number of children who are not attending school due to home schooling, exclusion, or other reasons. Considering access to therapy for these children is also important but not within the scope of this chapter. Schools are often at the heart of communities where families have established relationships with staff over time. For many children and families, school is a trusted setting and so some of the obstacles that might otherwise prevent access to therapy can be overcome. This includes practical obstacles, such as the logistics of parents and carers taking children out of school to attend therapy, as well as psychological obstacles, such as the stigma that can be associated with accessing mental health services. The school environment itself can also be a setting that is difficult for some children, such as those who struggle with social anxiety or who find peer relationships challenging. For these children, locating the therapy in the school setting may have an added benefit.

This is not the case for all children and families, and there are certainly some who find it difficult to access in-school services. This might be because of difficult experiences in the parents' own childhood or because families want to keep their struggles quite separate from the school environment. In these cases, if they are available, other community-based services will be more appropriate.

Despite government investment, Child and Adolescent Mental Health Services (CAMHS) are significantly oversubscribed, waiting lists are long, and many of the children that parents and schools identify as struggling would not meet the threshold to access support. While resources are also limited in any school system, services embedded in these settings have the advantage of being able to respond earlier to children's needs before their difficulties increase. Decisions about referring to therapy can be made by adults who know children and their families, and children do not need to be taken out of their day-to-day routine to leave school and attend outside services. Indeed, school-based services tend to have a higher take-up than other services and there is evidence that young people are more likely to access school-based services when compared to others (O'Brien et al., 2015).

Highgate Primary School

Highgate Primary School is a mixed state school in a leafy part of North London. While nestled in an affluent part of town, the school's intake represents a wider social range than might be expected by its setting. The school prides itself as inclusive and this is reflected in the fact it shares a site and closely partners with Blanche Neville School for Deaf Children. The school has a high proportion of children who speak an additional language with more than forty languages spoken within the school. The school site also features a family centre. Originally run as part of the national Sure Start programme, the school took over its running when the government funding was cut. Today the family centre offers midwife appointments, breastfeeding clinics, and mother and baby groups.

In 2014, the school leadership had ambitions to put the emotional development of children at the heart of the school's ethos. The clinical manager had originally been employed to offer one-to-one counselling sessions to children but had realised quickly the need throughout the school was greater than one person could cater for. Consequently, her role had expanded to include school-wide pastoral care. With the enthusiastic support of the head teacher and the board of governors, the clinical manager approached the Institute for Arts in Therapy and Education to offer a training placement in the school. This began a continuing and fruitful relationship between the two organisations. The head teacher and the governors were positive, as well as appropriately tentative, about developing a therapeutic service. They deemed that success would be measured by the difference it made to some of the most vulnerable children in the school.

As an established member of the school community, the clinical manager had developed trusted relationships with staff, students, and parents which prepared the ground for the therapeutic work. She had even rallied the parent school association to fund the play and arts materials for the new therapy room.

Getting support for a therapeutic service from school leadership and the wider community is crucial in determining its success. The process can be compared to the therapeutic alliance that must be developed with parents, even when therapy is only with the child. Parents must develop a relationship with the therapist and accept therapy as a helpful intervention, so as to create the "holding environment" in which therapeutic change can take place (Winnicott, 1971). When the environmental conditions are there, the establishment of a clear framework for the therapy will enable the work to happen.

Establishing the frame

When a therapist begins working in a school, they must be mindful of the system they are entering and how they, and therapy itself, are perceived by that system. The world of education and the world of psychotherapy each have rules, cultures, and ways of doing things that are highly valued and well established. Expectations of how children engage with adults in each system are different. It is inevitable that at times there will be tension between teachers and psychotherapists as aims and methods, though overlapping, may conflict. But with respect and good communication in both directions, conflicts can be worked through to ensure that children's needs are put at the centre of policies and decisions.

Therapists take great care to communicate clearly to children what therapy is: we have contracts that make explicit what the rules and expectations are, for example, that the play materials must stay in the room. We are reflective and curious about any reactions a child might have to our boundary setting, and use our words, images, or play to help make sense of any feelings that arise as a result of them. In a similar way, we must also take the time to make the boundaries and expectations of therapy clear to the school staff and the other children in the school.

This is what we set out to do when I and my fellow trainee presented to the whole staff on an INSET day in our first term in Highgate Primary.

We explained the kinds of children who might benefit from therapy and made clear issues of confidentiality and the nature of feedback and support we would offer staff members.

It is fundamental to the therapeutic endeavour that sessions are confidential; that children can trust their therapist with their thoughts and feelings. This must be aligned with safeguarding policies, and the limits to confidentiality to keep children safe will always be communicated to them in an age appropriate way. A school's need to safeguard children who often have complex family backgrounds means that there is already a common understanding that the designated safeguarding lead holds confidential information about children and families, and shares this carefully with members of staff on a "need to know basis".

Apart from this, teachers and support staff talk openly about much of the day to day business of the classroom: teaching is a collaborative affair and staff teams work together, monitoring children's progress, responding to challenges, and offering support when it is needed. The school day is a busy one, and this often necessitates a certain urgency in communication. At times, the staffroom can be a forum of mutual support, a place to escape the intense pressure of the day over a cup of tea and a biscuit, and somewhere to vent about a particularly challenging lesson, breaktime, or conversation with a parent.

It is important that the therapist is warm and approachable in the staffroom and builds relationships with colleagues that encourage collaboration. However, therapists need to make clear that they must stand apart from these more informal conversations about children and that they will never divulge information from sessions other than for safeguarding purposes. We must hold the boundary firmly, not speaking about a child in the corridors and being careful about what we say in the staffroom, while not appearing to be obstructive or defensive to a well-meaning member of staff. It can feel like a tricky balancing act to get this right, especially when therapy or the therapist is new. Careful attention should be given to setting the tone and language of responses right and the therapist's supervision can be invaluable here. This becomes much easier when clear processes for all aspects of the service are established and shared among staff including how and when the therapist will communicate with staff. Within this framework, the teacher and therapist can develop a working relationship that will support the child outside the therapy room.

The clinical manager was responsible for holding the therapeutic service at Highgate Primary School. In other settings this link person might be the special educational needs co-ordinator (SENCo) or a senior teacher. It is particularly important that this person has a therapeutic background or at least a thorough understanding of psychotherapy and counselling.

The clinical manager at Highgate Primary School had a comprehensive knowledge of children and their families and was a constant daily presence in the school. This meant she was able to act as a bridge of communication between school staff and therapists, passing on important information in either direction.

The framework of the service, built collaboratively between the clinical manager, the therapists, and school staff clearly delineated roles and responsibilities including, but not limited to:

- The timing and structure of therapy sessions around the school day
- Communication channels between the therapist and children, teachers, and parents
- Time frames for regular parent and teacher meetings with the therapist
- Administrative aspects such as record keeping, impact monitoring
- Safeguarding policy and procedures
- Practical aspects including locking the therapy room and replenishing arts materials.

The day-to-day running of a service requires that the clinical manager is a consistent, reliable presence who becomes what Bowlby described as a "secure base" (1988). He or she must clearly and firmly hold the boundaries of the therapeutic frame, while demonstrating a reflective capacity regarding the emotional processes that occur. Highgate Primary School's clinical manager had a counselling background which helped her to remain curious about challenges or relationships that became strained. Her soothing, regulated responses contained the emotional processes of children, therapists, school staff, and families. She was able to provide emotional support and empathy within appropriate boundaries.

As she was the designated safeguarding lead, the clinical manager was able to hold in mind children's stories and ensure that vulnerable children were accessing support at the right time. Her understanding of psychotherapy meant she could help families understand the process of therapy and therefore commit to it fully. It also meant that the tricky moments when safeguarding concerns arose during therapy were handled with sensitivity so as to ensure all steps were taken to safeguard the child while protecting the therapeutic relationship.

At Highgate, we felt it was important that within this clear frame there remained a degree of flexibility. In some instances, the clinical manager would "hold" the relationship with the parents, managing all aspects of communication and acting as a link between the therapist and the family. For other cases, the therapist would communicate directly with parents and develop a therapeutic relationship through regular parent meetings. The aim was to provide the most helpful and suitable support that met both the child's and the parents' needs. Fundamental to this approach was the importance of developing a team around a child, consisting of the family, therapist, and teacher.

In some cases, other professionals became part of that team, for example a social worker or medical professional. A key part of the clinical manager's role at Highgate Primary was supporting appropriate collaboration between members of this team. For example, after careful consideration with the child and parents, I attended child protection meetings where I was able to represent the voice of the child. In another instance I was invited to provide a therapeutic perspective when professionals were making decisions about aspects of a child's care.

When there was a mental health or neurodevelopmental query, the team approach meant that families could be supported in understanding the process of a referral to CAMHS or other specialist services. Key to this was helping parents to have realistic expectations about time frames and the type of support offered. It was important that parents had the team alongside them, helping to negotiate and make sense of assessments, diagnoses, and treatments their child was offered.

The clinical manager's role in the management of an in-school service is fundamental. Each day they work hard to hold the therapeutic frame, to maintain relationships with all involved in the service, and to thoughtfully respond to emotional processes while putting the needs of children first. The therapist and the clinical manager have the important joint task of ensuring that the therapy in the room can take place in a way that is safe and boundaried.

The therapist in the school

A school-based therapist's role is different from a therapist in a more traditional clinic in which the child will come each week at the designated appointment time and this is usually the only contact the child has with the therapist. A school therapist is part of the school community in which the child participates every day. Children may see the therapist in the corridors at break times and may notice the therapist interacting with other children or members of staff. It is the therapist's responsibility to be mindful of this, thinking carefully about how they are involved in the school and how their presence may be interpreted by those children with whom they are working.

The therapy room is not an airtight container. Despite this the therapist must demonstrate that they can hold the therapeutic frame, they do not break confidence, and they respect the child's wishes. For example, I might ask a child how they would like me to react if we meet outside the therapy room. Some might say that they are happy for us to exchange a smile, others may want to pretend they don't know me. The feelings that can be evoked outside the therapy room may provide rich material for discussion within the therapy session.

Working with the clinical manager, and with my supervisor, I sometimes had to make tricky decisions about referrals that were complicated by the fact that the service was based in the school. For example, I was asked to see another child in the class of an existing client. Issues of sibling rivalry and deep feelings of jealousy may be roused in both children and we may have decided that it was not appropriate to start working with the second child. This would be an easier decision when there is a team of therapists in a school able to take on the second child. In other instances, even after careful consideration, it may be necessary for that second child to be seen by the same therapist. Therapists must accept that they cannot meet every need of the child perfectly—just as a parent cannot—and there are times when they may decide to go ahead with a less than perfect decision such as this. In such a situation it is crucial that the therapist understands and discusses both children's reactions to having to share their therapist.

At Highgate Primary School, the head teacher was always very generous in inviting the therapeutic team to events in the school calendar. We were welcomed to become part of the school community and this helped us to develop warm and friendly relationships with our colleagues. This can be an important way of preventing therapists from becoming a shadowy presence existing only behind the closed door of the therapy room; however, we must be thoughtful about what is appropriate. For example, attending an event where a client's parents are also attending may not be. At Highgate, I and my fellow therapists would try to be gracious in these instances, explaining why we might have to decline some invitations and enthusiastically accepting others when it was more appropriate.

Rupture and repair

At Highgate Primary School, similarly to any other school-based therapy service, even once the service was up and running there were difficult moments when the integrity of the frame was challenged or, despite good intentions, errors occurred which negatively impacted on the therapy. Part of what helped the service succeed was a willingness to learn from mistakes and an awareness, by the therapists and school leaders, to resist the pull to be reactive, defensive, or despairing when conflict arose—even though at times it was very tempting to be all three!

Some difficult moments included:

- *The closed door*—During a therapy session, the closed door creates a boundary between the therapy and the rest of the world. Behind that door, at a particular time each week, is a special, co-created space between a child and a therapist. In a school, a closed door does not have the same meaning and although there was an enormous sign on the therapy room door, stating in bold letters "Session in progress—Do not disturb", in those first months there were many moments when someone would knock on the door, or actually open it, in the middle of a session.
- *Using the room*—In a school where space is at a premium, the therapy room, which is well stocked with play and art resources, feels like a precious asset. I was surprised to find a teaching assistant sitting at the table in the therapy room with a sobbing girl when I arrived ready to start a session with a child. The teaching assistant was desperate to find a space to comfort the child and was delighted to see the door unlocked when she was looking for a quiet spot.

- *Resources*—As therapists we know that ensuring consistency in the room is important. We take great care to ensure that, as far as possible, we provide an unchanging space for children each week and appreciate that some of the play materials take on significant symbolic meaning for children. Imagine my dismay when I saw a group of children sitting at a table playing with the sand tray miniatures during wet play.
- *Missing sessions*—One day I arrived at the classroom door to pick up a child to be told by a teacher that the child had an important piece of work to complete and so wouldn't be able to come to the session. On another occasion, I went to collect a child to be told he was on a school trip. This was on a day when I had come into school especially for that session and I knew that that particular child's attachment needs meant that unexpected breaks in the therapy provoked very difficult feelings.
- *Use of language*—Play and joy are part of therapy and there can be great delight in the therapeutic relationship. But therapy is also a place for pain and hurt, for disappointment, fear, and terror. It can then feel jarring if a teacher waves off the therapist and a child with a big smile shouting, "Have fun!"

From a clinician's point of view, moments such as these can have an enormous impact on the therapeutic relationship with the child. However, from a well-intentioned, busy teacher's perspective, they may represent a simple misunderstanding or a moment of opportunism.

Mis-attunements and ruptures are a part of therapy, just as they are a part of all other relationships. When they happen in the room, therapists work through them with a child. For example, if a door is abruptly opened or knocked during a child's session, we might notice their reaction—do they become dysregulated, angry, adaptive, or withdrawn? We might invite the child to show us in the sand tray how it felt to find another child in the room during their "special time". Perhaps they feel abandoned by the therapist after a missed session, or feel full of fury when a special miniature is lost from the therapy room. The play, stories, and feelings that arise may help us understand the child's inner world, their attachment style, and the way they make sense of their feelings. Exploring these moments with a regulated, sensitive therapist can provide helpful insight into some of the most important aspects of the child's experiences and the reparation that follows can be important in facilitating therapeutic development.

Yet we do all we can to avoid such impingements on a child's therapy. Moments of mis-attunement will always happen within the therapeutic relationship and while the therapist will use them as they arise, our role as the "secure base" for the child means that, whenever possible, we provide a safe, secure, and predictable therapy space each week. When incidents like the moments above happen, it can be extremely frustrating for the therapist. Yet, more often than not, it is caused by a lack of awareness rather than any malice—how could that person possibly know that the rules of the therapy room are different unless someone tells them?

The therapist knows that the very particular boundaries around the therapy room are there for very specific therapeutic reasons which put the child's experience at the heart. We are much more likely to have compliance to these boundaries if we help the wider staff team understand these reasons. After all, remembering to inform a therapist about a school trip might be the last item on a very long list of things that a teacher needs to do on a given day and if we want it to be prioritised, that teacher needs to understand the difference it would make to a child if a therapist can carefully prepare them for interruptions in the sessions.

My experience at Highgate Primary helped me realise that the staff were not trying to be difficult in these moments. In the unusual instance that a staff member has been obstructive, consciously or unconsciously, then as therapists we can model how to hold boundaries in a calm and clear way, demonstrating that we can remain in a reflective adult state. It is helpful to hold in mind Porges's "open and engaged" way of being (2017) as we manage conflict in a healthy, productive way. Helping someone "get therapy" does not happen through lecturing or telling a staff member off, but by understanding their point of view, explaining our own perspective, and thinking together about how to address problems as they happen. We might need to go to our clinical supervisor, the clinical manager, or a fellow therapist to vent frustrations and be supported to facilitate productive conversations when difficulties arise.

Empathy and reflective thinking—working with teachers

This way of being can be applied to all aspects of the professional relationships we develop with teaching and support staff. At Highgate, if one were working closely with the child, before beginning therapy the therapist would meet the teacher and teaching assistant. Together they would share a picture of the child and their needs as well as working out logistics such as session timings, the way in which the child would be collected for therapy, and arrangements for further meetings to discuss the child.

The relationship children have with their teachers is extremely important—they spend 190 days a year in the classroom with them, compared to the therapist's one hour a week! The therapist hopes to develop a reflective, collaborative relationship with the teacher so they in turn can support the child in the classroom and enable them to learn and thrive.

Being a teacher is a rewarding yet demanding role and it is important that the therapist understands this. In their annual teacher Wellbeing Index, Education Support Partnerships found that 72% of all educational professionals described themselves as stressed, with this rising to 84% of senior leaders (2019). The current school system puts urgent requirements on staff's energy and attention; they might be considering children's SATS scores, attendance figures, the achievement of disadvantaged learners, learners with additional needs or those who have English as an additional language, as well as the special needs of the most able children in their class. Support staff who work with some of the most vulnerable children with the most complex needs are often given the least amount of training or remuneration for their roles!

When we have the opportunity to collaborate with teaching staff we must first understand the complexity of their roles and demonstrate this understanding. Siegel and Hartzell describe the importance that a person feels "felt" in relationships (2003). This is the experience of another person demonstrating a real understanding of our thoughts and feelings and letting themselves be impacted by them without being overwhelmed. By empathising with school staff, within appropriate boundaries, we can help them feel seen, heard, and understood and this can build a trusting foundation for collaborative work to follow. At Highgate Primary, the head teacher decided to offer counselling sessions to staff members who needed it. This was an important step in helping staff feel supported, and helped the community accept and value therapy.

During regular teacher meetings, the therapist hopes to create a reflective space in which the adults can be curious about the child in therapy, thinking deeply about the concerns that have led to the child being referred. The therapist does not discuss what happened in the therapy, but may share key themes or ask pertinent questions about how the child is in the classroom or playground. The therapist may empathise with how hard it might be for the teacher to support the child. The teacher and therapist will think together about what is working well and what is still a struggle. Together, the therapist and teacher wonder about how the child's experiences in school, at home, and within their past might be impacting on their present relationships. For example, they will think about how an impending transition or change in the child's life, such as a move to a new school, a close friend leaving, or a severe family conflict may trigger a reaction based on their history of trauma and loss. The therapist may include psycho-education to deepen the teacher's understanding and inform interventions to support the child. For example, the teacher and therapist may think together about a child who is frequently being punished for breaking the rules during playtimes. They might consider how the child's particular developmental needs, or their experiences of events in their past, may impact on how they perceive and experience the environment of the playground.

Siegel describes that when people are managing well and thriving in their lives, they are existing within an optimal zone of arousal (1999). When in this "window" they are neither over- nor under-aroused and the level of stress that they are experiencing is "tolerable". They can work, play, learn, and stay in relationship with those around them. When they are pushed outside this window, exposed to stressors that are intolerable to their stress response system, the body responds by becoming over-aroused (going into fight or flight mode) or under-aroused (shutting down in freeze mode). It would be expected that a child's "window of tolerance" is wide enough so that day to day school life would be manageable and not cause over- or under-arousal. If a child has a stressful experience, for example an argument with a friend or missing a football penalty, this might push them outside their "window of tolerance", temporarily causing their stress response system to become activated (sending them into a fight, flight, or freeze response); but they would be able to be soothed and calmed, perhaps with the help of friends or trusted adults, and would return to manageable levels of arousal within a reasonable time frame.

However, if a child is exposed to prolonged or repeated levels of toxic stress (for example when experiencing ACEs) or has particular developmental needs, their "window of tolerance" becomes much narrower. The stress response system will then be triggered much more easily and take longer to return to optimal functioning.

When the teacher and therapist are considering the child who frequently acts out in the playground, it might be helpful to consider their behaviour alongside Siegel's theory. They might consider together that perhaps the child's "window of tolerance" is very narrow and the hustle and bustle of the playground causes an overaction of the child's sympathetic nervous system leading to the dysregulated behaviour that is getting them into trouble. By sharing the theory, the team can consider the neuroscientific processes that are underpinning the child's behaviour and the school staff may revise the current strategy for this child. Instead of repeatedly punishing him for not coping in circumstances he simply does not have the skills to manage because of his narrow window of tolerance, the therapist and teacher may think of alternative strategies that will engage the child's parasympathetic nervous system, helping to develop his capacity to cope in smaller, more manageable steps. For example, the therapist may share that one way of widening the window of tolerance is through the development of trusting relationships and so the child may be supervised to spend breaks in a quieter part of the school with a friend or playing more structured games with a key adult. In time, perhaps the teacher will be able to pair the child up with a "buddy" from an older year in the school or have an allocated key adult who the child can turn to if things become difficult in the playground. Such strategies gradually increase the child's window of tolerance thereby enabling them to engage in positive peer relationships at a rate that is manageable for them.

Some teachers or support staff may have this knowledge already and the therapist's role may be to provide a space and time for the teacher and therapist to discuss relevant theory together. Importantly, the aim of these meetings is for the teacher to feel better equipped to support the child through their collaborative relationship and providing strategies that respond to the child's psychological needs. The feedback from teachers also provides invaluable information for the therapist to take back to the therapy room.

Therapists are often helpful in discussing those children who find it hardest to develop relationships with adults and peers in school. Children with a troubled past sometimes provoke powerful and uncomfortable emotional responses in those around them and they may actively reject relationships—pushing away the committed teachers and support staff who want to help them. It can be helpful for school staff to think with a therapist in order to make sense of these difficult and defensive responses. A child can reject meaningful relationships for fear of being deeply hurt or disappointed in the relationship. Also, Bomber writes about a rejecting child:

> His resistance to having a meaningful relationship with a teacher, a mentor, or a teaching assistant and so on, is grounded upon his solid belief that he does not deserve one, that he is not capable of one: while at the same time, being terrified of trying to form one and only failing again.
>
> (2007, p. 18)

It can be so tiring and disheartening when a child does not respond to a teacher's efforts, day after day, week after week. There are children who seem to reject all support that is offered to them, or who create problems wherever they go, or who make the adults around them feel incompetent as professionals. And yet these are the children who most need these adults to understand them, to hold them in mind and respond with an appropriate balance of nurture and boundaries. A therapist can be helpful in "translating" such behaviours in terms of the child's history of trauma, their relational challenges, or developmental needs. Perhaps most importantly, the staff around that child need to have the insight into the child's experience so as to continue to empathise with him or her even in the most trying of circumstances. When teachers have the right support from the therapist, they can continue to support that child with hope, generosity, warm-heartedness, and understanding.

The therapist may also be able to respond to particular concerns that teachers have about their wider class. For example, a teacher noticed a difficult dynamic emerging in a friendship group resulting in lots of arguments. We thought together about the children involved; their individual needs as well as the recurrent difficulties that the group seemed to be experiencing. I sought parents' permission and arranged a regular weekly session with the group to take place over a half term. Our sessions had a clear structure and we used creative arts to facilitate reflections and encourage open communication. The meetings were themed around aspects identified by the teacher and in response to the group members' suggestions and included managing conflict and kindness. The children's parents and teacher reported that tensions were noticeably reduced, and while friendships did continue to shift over the rest of the academic year, the children had a wider emotional vocabulary and capacity to manage these challenges and also they described being more satisfied with their friendships.

There can be a pressure on therapists to "fix" children, and part of the therapist's role may be helping the adults have realistic expectations about what the child's changes will actually look like. Increasing eye contact at the beginning of the school day or asking for help in a classroom may be outward indicators of small but significant changes in the child's internal world. For children with relational difficulties, it may take some time to trust the therapist and the healing can take a long time. Indeed, there are some times when there are significant bumps in the road to recovery and the child's presenting behaviour may appear to be getting worse. For example, previously suppressed rage may bubble up to the surface as a child begins processing something from their past or faces an academic task too difficult to master. The therapist will be helping parents, teachers, and caregivers to make sense of these processes—explaining that these may be stages in the child's longer-term psychological healing. The team around the child are then able to stay hopeful and responsive to the child's changing needs, to spot green shoots of hope, and continue to put in the thought, care, and empathy the child requires from others.

Dealing with the unconscious processes

It is important that a therapist considers how they, and therapy, are perceived in a school. Indeed, it is important that we also consider the unconscious processes that might be happening within the school setting as the therapeutic service is set up. Luxmore describes how the therapist can be both the idealised object of hope and the object of envy and resentment (2014) for school staff—often at the same time! So a frazzled teacher who is struggling to cope with a child's behaviour may make a referral for therapy. Some teachers might pin their hopes on the therapy to address all the challenges the child presents. In the same breath, they might sigh with envy as the therapist takes this child for fifty minutes of "play" when they are left dealing with the other twenty-nine students all demanding their time and energy. In this instance the teacher might simultaneously hope that we succeed in "fixing" the child whilst at the same time wishing we fail. The therapist might face an uncomfortable and confusing set of feelings. Their training equips them to remain reflective and not reactive in the face of this. They must receive the teacher's feelings in a calm, warm, and regulated way and understand them more fully in individual supervision.

Therapists must also consider what they themselves project onto their roles and the school they are working in. When starting in an education setting, the therapist needs to have deeply understood their own relationship with schools before they step into the staffroom, perhaps for the first time since they were a student or a parent. What ideas, values, emotional reactions do they bring from their past experiences to their present role? Without awareness of this they might find themselves caught in a reactive pattern of thoughts, feelings, and behaviour which will inhibit their ability to work in service of children. Perhaps they are often triggered into an anti-authoritarian stance that was familiar in their adolescence. They might find themselves with an urge to rebel against "the system" and frequently take the child's side against the adults. Or when in a school setting, trainee therapists may notice that they regress and act like the adaptive child they learnt to be when they were young, nodding and following the lead of the adults unquestioningly. In either extreme, and the myriad of other variations, if the therapist is lacking awareness of these patterns, they risk losing sight of the child and their needs. It may be that these need to be addressed in the therapist's own therapy or supervision.

Working with the head teacher

To ensure that a therapeutic service is effective, the therapist has to be working in two directions—from the bottom up *and* the top down. Our therapeutic work with children is the essence of our role. Week after week in the therapy room, we get our hands dirty, do the hard graft, and hope to make a difference to children's lives. Establishing a therapeutic service in a school is the bottom-up work. To ensure the survival of this service, we also need to think about the top-down aspect in our relationship with the head teacher.

Head teachers are key figures: they lead from the front, establishing the vision and setting the emotional tone for the whole school. In the case of Highgate Primary School, the head had already expressed a commitment to the emotional development of children and had embedded inclusion amongst the school's principles. The school website described an ambition that "every child in our school, especially those who might be considered vulnerable or troubled, fulfil their potential". The act of inviting therapists into the school community reflected a hope in therapy as a tool to help reach this ambition.

Schools are complex organisations and head teachers deal with an incredibly heavy daily load. The main task is children's learning but in order to facilitate this the head manages a diverse team of students, parents, and staff who have a range of ever-changing and, at times, competing needs. The head must also manage the demands of Ofsted and the Department for Education, balance the budget, recruit staff, deal with complex safeguarding issues, and maintain links with local authorities. Because the buck ultimately stops with the head, if the infant toilets are leaking, the website has crashed, and there is a fight in the playground at breaktime, the head may be urgently pulled in all these directions at once!

In the midst of this busyness, therapists in schools must try to foster a relationship with the head teacher. At Highgate, the head promoted an open door policy and I would make a point of making contact with him whenever I could. While the structure of the therapeutic frame meant that the day to day running of the service did not involve him, it was important that my face became a familiar one for him and for all the senior leadership team. Through our interactions I hoped to demonstrate my warmth, professionalism, and commitment to the children with whom I was working. I aimed to offer my reflective capacity to think about challenging moments in the school day and be an advocate for children when it was needed.

Therapists can support head teachers through regular reporting. For school leaders to build a case for having a therapy service, they need something more than anecdotal evidence. Regular reports should include statistics about the number of children who have been supported by a therapy service, a summary of the nature of referrals that protects the children's need for confidentiality, significant therapeutic successes, and any challenges the service faces. These reports should include analysis of currently used outcome measures, such as the strengths and difficulties questionnaire (Goodman, 2001). Therapists communicating in this way de-mystify what is happening in therapy, provide regular opportunities to reflect on children's progress, and notice emerging patterns in the therapeutic endeavours. Producing a report provides a forum for key stakeholders—the senior leadership team, the pastoral team, the school governors—to discuss the future of the therapy service.

Whole school change

Over time, the clinician and school staff's careful collaboration in thinking about the children can spread beyond the therapy room. Teachers, parents, therapists, and school leaders can work together to form a "therapeutic web" considering all the children's needs (Perry, 2008, p. 46), thereby creating a culture where children's emotional needs are central. The Highgate Primary School website summarises this approach:

> We believe that for children to thrive emotionally a holistic approach is required, relying not just on the individual act of therapy but with an open and congruent working alliance between parents, staff and relevant professionals.

The therapeutic stance held by the integrative child psychotherapist places relationships at the heart. While there will always be an insufficient number of therapists to support every child who might benefit from therapy, even at Highgate Primary where there is a thriving therapeutic service, all adults working with children have the capacity to have meaningful relationships with children that meet their relational needs and therefore help them to thrive. Part of the therapist's role in a school is to share their knowledge and experience regarding children, but the therapist can also model a way of being that is truly relational and share a way of thinking about children that can complement and enhance school staff's existing expertise.

If they work together, the two worlds of education and psychotherapy can create an environment in which children can thrive.

Highgate Primary six years on: a whole school approach

Six years after my clinical placement at Highgate Primary began, the therapeutic service continues to thrive. The school includes a team of trainee and qualified therapists, counsellors, well-being practitioners, and play therapists. At any given time approximately 10% of students are being supported by the therapeutic team through individual or group sessions. The school has well-established links with the Institute for Arts in Therapy and Education and other training organisations. In 2019, the school was awarded a Children In Need grant to fund a drama therapist to work across Highgate Primary School and Blanch Neville School for Deaf Children three days a week for three years.

A wide range of children are supported by therapy, not just the children whose challenging behaviour in class draws attention to their struggles. Those quiet children who internalise their conflicts and depressed children who might otherwise pass under the radar are also recognised as needing support. The school has adopted a proactive approach and encourages parents and children to identify problems early.

Because the therapeutic service is embedded across the school, any shame about asking for help and receiving support has been reduced. The classroom "worry boxes", playground mentors, and talking buddies are practical demonstrations of how Highgate has become a "talking school". They are components of a pastoral system that holds the needs of the whole school community, working closely with the safeguarding and special educational needs team to identify those who require support. This system can be characterised by strong, caring, and long-term professional networks supporting all children and staff.

The school takes pride in the fact that it approaches education in its broadest sense—putting well-being and emotional development alongside academic achievement. This is reflected in all aspects of the school including the school values, the parent handbook, and the school policies. The school offers a wide range of activities to enrich the curriculum, creating what Raine and colleagues described as an enriched environment that benefits children's neural development (2001). These include the school's allotment for planting vegetables, forest school sessions, and the thriving Mandarin language department.

In 2017 Ofsted inspectors commented that Highgate is "a truly inclusive school where pupils' personal development is as important as their academic achievement … Relationships between staff and pupils are warm, creating an atmosphere of openness and trust. As one parent says, 'They treat every child as an individual.'"

Conclusion

Developing a therapeutic service in a school takes time. All members of the community—teaching and support staff, school leaders and therapists—must be committed to the process. The example of Highgate Primary School demonstrates the collaboration that is required to create a "holding environment" (Winnicott, 1964) so that a therapy service can run effectively. The integrative child psychotherapist recognises that their knowledge, skills, and experience can support change, not only for the child in therapy, but across the school community. This is achieved when the therapist develops trusted, robust, and reflective relationships with the children and adults they encounter. In doing so their therapeutic approach permeates throughout the school. Through repeated moments of connection, the therapist hopes to demonstrate their empathy, reliability, warmth, and dedication. This builds relationships within the service and across the school which mean that children are held in the minds and hearts of the adults who support them. Hopefully, this is felt by all the children and it is this that enables them to learn, heal, and grow.

References

Bion, W. R. (1962). *Learning from Experience*. 8th edn. London: Karnac, 2007.

Bomber, M. (2007). *Inside I'm Hurting: Practical Strategies for Supporting Children with Attachment Difficulties in School*. London: Worth.

Bowlby, J. (1988). *A Secure Base: Clinical Applications of Attachment Theory*. Abingdon, UK: Routledge.

Brindle, D. (2017, November 29). Guardian Public Service Awards 2017: Congratulations to all our winners. *The Guardian*.

Burke Harris, N. (2018). *The Deepest Well: Healing the Long-Term Effects of Childhood Adversity*. London: Pan Macmillan.

Daniunaite, A., Cooper, M., & Forster, T. (2015). Counselling in UK primary schools: Outcomes and predictors of change. *Counselling and Psychotherapy Research*, *15*(4): 251–261.

Education Support Partnerships (2019). *Teacher Wellbeing Index 2019*. Available at: https://educationsupport.org.uk/sites/default/files/teacher_wellbeing_index_2019.pdf (last accessed June 1, 2020).

Felitti, J., Anda, R., Nordenburg, D., Williamson, D., Spitz, A., Edwards, V., Koss, M., & Marks, J. (1998). Relationship of childhood abuse and household dysfunction to many of the leading causes of death in adults: The Adverse Childhood Experiences (ACE) study. *American Journal of Preventive Medicine*, *14*(4): 245–258.

Goodman, R. (2001). Psychometric properties of the strengths and difficulties questionnaire. *Journal of the American Academy of Child and Adolescent Psychiatry*, *40*(11): 1337–1345.

Green, H., McGinnity, A., Meltzer, H., Ford, T., & Goodman, R. (2005). *Mental Health of Children and Young People in Great Britain, 2004*. London: Office for National Statistics.

Hunt, T. K., Slack, K. S., & Berger, L. M. (2017). Adverse childhood experiences and behavioural problems in middle childhood. *Child Abuse and Neglect*, *67*: 391–402.

Lee, R. C., Tiley, C. E., & White, J. E. (2009). The Place2Be: Measuring the effectiveness of a primary school-based therapeutic intervention in England and Scotland. *Counselling and Psychotherapy Research: Linking Research with Practice*, *9*(3): 151–159.

Luxmore, N. (2014). *School Counsellors Working with Young People and Staff*. London: Jessica Kingsley.

Mental Health Foundation, & Office of Health Economics (2005). *Lifetime Impacts: Childhood and Adolescent Mental Health, Understanding the Lifetime Impacts*. London: Mental Health Foundation.

O'Brien, S., Greatley, A., & Meek, L. (2015). *The Mentally Healthy Society: The Report of the Taskforce on Mental Health in Society*. Discussion paper. London: The Labour Party.

Perry, B. (2008). *The Boy Who Was Raised as a Dog and Other Stories from a Child Psychiatrist's Notebook: What Traumatized Children Can Teach Us about Loss, Love and Healing.* New York: Basic Books.

Porges, S. (2017). *The Pocket Guide to the Polyvagal Theory: The Transformative Power of Feeling Safe.* London: W. W. Norton.

Raine, A., Venables, P., Dalaies, C., Mellingen, K., Reynolds, C., & Mednick, S. (2001). Early educational and health enrichment at 3–5 years is associated with increased autonomic and central nervous system arousal and orienting at age 11 years: Evidence from the Mauritius Child Health Project. *Psychophysiology, 38*(2): 254–266.

Siegel, D. J. (1999). *The Developing Mind, How Relationships and the Brain Interact to Shape Who We Are.* London: Guilford.

Siegel, D. J., & Hartzell, M. (2003). *Parenting from the Inside Out.* London: Penguin.

Winnicott, D. W. (1964). *The Child, the Family and the Outside World.* London: Penguin.

Winnicott, D. W. (1971). *Playing and Reality.* 4th edn. London: Tavistock.

CHAPTER 14

Empathising with the defences through the use of arts and metaphor

Clair Lewoski

Introduction

Working with defences seems central to how we find a way to the child or adolescent through child psychotherapy. Frequently young people are referred to us when their defences or coping strategies are no longer serving them well. The child who had experienced profound neglect finds they cannot stop stealing even when they now receive good care. The child who had been overly compliant now finds their relationships with peers are marred by being dominated by others. The adolescent who had tried not to worry their parents with their own worries develops an increasing array of somatic symptoms.

In this chapter, I wish to explore how we conceptualise defences from an integrative point of view, as well as how we might work with them.

Brief historical context of working with defences in child psychotherapy

The question of the nature of defences and how to work with them was a central question in the development of psychoanalytic child psychotherapy. During the "Controversial Discussions" (Holder, 2017) the two pioneers of psychoanalytic child psychotherapy debated whether it was the defence itself that should be analysed, or the anxiety which the defence was seeking to protect the child from. Anna Freud asserted the need to analyse the defence, on the basis that the ego needed to be shored up in the child; whereas Melanie Klein argued from her clinical experience that children experienced great relief when she analysed their core anxiety.

This polarisation in technique between the Kleinian and Freudian approaches is one which is not so apparent now in psychoanalytic child psychotherapy. Certainly when one considers the work of Anne Alvarez (2012), one can see her tailoring technique to the level of analytic work called for in the moment as being congruent with Anna Freud's ideas of the necessity of strengthening ego defences (1936); even though Alvarez delineates her approach using Kleinian language and concepts.

Alvarez's work has consistently argued that for many children, defences feel an urgent necessity and have to be understood as the child's often desperate way of trying to preserve or establish their ego functioning. This feels very much in tune with Anna Freud's experiences during World War II at the Hampstead War Nurseries, where she worked with many severely traumatised children. We have to remember that for some children their defences are their only way of managing and may feel a matter of life and death. Both Alvarez and Anna Freud recognise the fragility of some children's defences and that we need to adjust our technique accordingly.

Moving towards an integrative approach—a view from attachment theory and clinical practice

For the integrative practitioner, although we may draw upon psychoanalytic child psychotherapy's rich history in working with defences, we also now have the benefit of attachment research and attachment-based clinical work to also inform our practice. As Jeremy Holmes (2001) has argued, attachment-based practice sees defences more relationally and interpersonally, rather than keeping to the purely classical psychoanalytic, intrapsychic focus. An interpersonal perspective on defences considers how the child uses their defences to relate to others and not just to themselves and how these may have been built up gradually through relational experiences since infancy. Hence, attachment styles can be viewed as forms of defence the individual has found necessary to develop, in order to cope with or manage their key attachment relationships. Thus, the child who minimises their worries in order to not worry their parents may have found this is the best way of eliciting caregiving behaviour from their parent and that to seek direct support might in fact lead to the opposite.

One form of attachment based clinical practice which offers a technical approach to defences and which recognises the fragility of the child is Dyadic Developmental Psychotherapy. Daniel Hughes, the originator of the Dyadic Developmental Psychotherapy model states: "… when the child does not have to defend his experience, he can explore it openly" (2007).

Hughes's curious, playful, and most significantly, empathic therapeutic stance approaches defences in such a way that the child may feel safe enough to explore his experience with the therapist, rather than defend against it. Attachment theory and neurobiology have taught us that the child feeling safe in our sessions is paramount and not to be taken for granted (Van der Kolk, 2014). As their therapist, we are a psychobiological regulator of the child, and if we wish to help them explore their experience less defensively, then they will need to feel emotionally regulated. Empathy and compassion are key to emotional regulation, as the work of Stephen Porges (2012), Daniel Siegel (2010), and Paul Gilbert (2010) have demonstrated. More recently mentalization work with children and their families, which has strong roots in attachment clinical research (Fonagy et al., 2004), has echoed Hughes's therapeutic stance, seeing that an empathic, playful, and not knowing curiosity on the part of the therapist may facilitate affect regulation and therefore the capacity to mentalize one's experience (Midgley et al., 2017).

For me, it therefore feels that a marrying of the psychoanalytic with attachment informed practice creates a stance where one is "empathising with the defence". This means there is the psychoanalytic understanding from Anna Freud, Melanie Klein, and post-Kleinians, such as Anne Alvarez, concerning the unconscious processes at work in the internal world, combined with an understanding of how these defences have been shaped by relational patterns. The therapeutic *technique* employed to "work with the defence" is one that is informed by attachment theory

and research, which places the interpersonal relationship with the therapist at the centre.

In practice this means we may need to tiptoe up to the defence
(Lanyado, 2003) *with empathy and consider the interpersonal context of the*
therapeutic relationship in which we are addressing the defence. Through
mentalizing our client, holding their mind in our mind and conveying
this empathically through our understanding of why they may need the
defence, we may avoid the potential dysregulation aroused by approaching the defence. The very act of naming or discussing a defence may be
enough to highly dysregulate some emotionally fragile clients. Instead, it
is hoped that through our empathy for their defence, our clients may feel
we are tiptoeing respectfully up to it. This is vital, for as stated by Vaillant
(1992) we must: "Never try to challenge a defence unless you have the
time, love and patience to share responsibility for the consequences."

We therefore begin by empathising with the need for the defence,
focusing upon this first before any attempt is made to reach the core
anxiety it may be protecting. In this way perhaps we are taking heed of

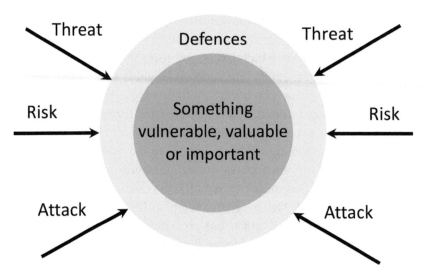

Figure 14.1 A conceptualisation of defences after Davy and Cross (2004)

Anna Freud's position on defences in her seminal work, *The Ego and the Mechanisms of Defence* (1936), echoed by Alvarez. For some children this may be a gateway to then thinking with them about the core anxiety or psychic pain that they are trying to eschew; for others just empathising with the nature of the defence itself is the work. We can look at these two approaches diagrammatically (see Figure 14.1), drawing upon Davy and Cross's (2004) conceptualisation of a defence.

From the diagram it is possible to see how a defence implies three elements:

1. Something vulnerable/painful (which maybe important or valuable), which may be at risk
2. Something which poses a threat/risk/attack
3. A *defence* which can mitigate or remove the apparent risk by mediating the relationship between the other two elements.

When thinking about what poses a threat or an attack, this may be something that arises intrapsychically within the client or it may be something originating in the external world. Usually it will be about the relationship between the external world and the internal world. This is why knowing about the child's external world context is essential in order to inform how we might work with the defence. I will refer to this again later in reference to a case example.

As an integrative child psychotherapist, we can therefore work with defence empathically through either empathising with the defence itself or by empathising with the anxiety, vulnerability, or psychic pain it may be defending against (see Figure 14.2).

For example, to an autistic child with learning difficulties, we may empathise with their need to show us all the complicated words they can now write, rather than focus on the core anxiety of feeling how much they don't know compared to their peers.

So one might say, "How good it feels to be the one who knows so much. You really want me to see what you know and how good that feels." (Empathising with the defence.)

Rather than, "I see you trying very hard to practise your spelling and I am wondering if it feels very hard sometimes to learn things?" (The core anxiety of the feeling of not knowing.)

Working with Defences

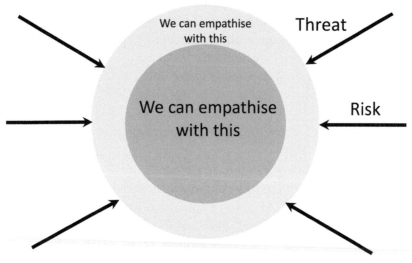

Figure 14.2 Working with defences using empathy

We may take this tiptoeing approach for many children with social and communication problems who experience high levels of anxiety and very fragile egos and senses of self, such as what Alvarez describes as working at the "vitalising level" (2012). The first response respectfully tiptoes up to the defence with empathy; the second, though possibly very true and helpful for a more emotionally robust child, may not be bearable to this child at this time without an ensuing sense of hopelessness and feeling like they are psychically crumbling.

A question may emerge, however, as to whether we always need to empathise with the defence first, or is there ever a case when we could directly empathise with the core anxiety? To make this decision we need to think what the child can bear at this time and what is likely to be the most growth enhancing intervention. For some children, they may very much need us to think about their core anxieties and they may experience a great relief in finding someone who can bear these anxieties with them, very much as Klein argued (1935). For others, they may need us to "shore up" their fragile defences, so that they can manage better being in relationship to themselves and to others. This is where Alvarez's work is so helpful, as she enables us to think about where a child or adolescent may be in relation to the depressive or paranoid–schizoid positions and that we may need to adjust our linguistic approach to the defence appropriately (see Alvarez, 2012 for more detailed discussions).

A young adolescent for example, who had spent several years in a very supportive and stable foster placement and several years in therapy, may need her therapist to acknowledge her very present and real anxieties about her foster carer seeking special guardianship and to not do so may leave her feeling alone with her understandable worries. She may need her therapist to say: "My guess is that you feel excited about the special guardianship process? But I also wonder if you're worried how your birth mum might feel that you want to stay with your foster carer long term? I am wondering if you are worried about her feeling upset by this and what she might say?"

For this young person, her capacity to tolerate a direct approach to her core anxieties is a testimony to her more robust sense of self, no doubt greatly helped by her secure relationship with her foster carer and her long-term relationship with her therapist. One can also see from the tentative language used ("my guess/I wonder") that her therapist is trying to empathise and co-create her experience with her in a curious and not knowing way. The cognitive capacity of this particular young adolescent is also a factor into what degree she is able to process, mentalize, and therefore tolerate these deeply painful and conflicting aspects of her experience. Crucially, this means the therapist can intervene at what Alvarez (2012) calls the "explanatory level" of intervention where more than one thought can be held in mind (wanting to stay with the foster carer *and* the fear rejection as a result) and the client is not so far from the depressive position that she can tolerate the ambivalent feelings this presents her with.

The earlier client, however, with a much more fragile ego, may not be able to bear knowing yet that his need to boast to his therapist about what he can spell may be an omnipotent defence against frequently feeling the one who so often feels he does not know. We see something similar in children who need to be the powerful one or the monster in the sessions so that the therapist can carry the feelings of being the scared, small, and vulnerable one instead. Alvarez might say these children are more deeply in the paranoid–schizoid position and therefore cannot bear to hear about their vulnerability yet, without it provoking an increased sense of fragility. As Alvarez states, a different "grammar" is needed to approach his defence, such as, "You're feeling so powerful … as if nobody can defeat or scare you."

One may question as to whether this simply colludes with his omnipotent defence and reinforces it? I would say that if one takes a developmental approach one might see this as necessary and to think about timing. The therapist might aim eventually to be able to think with him about the reason for his need for the defence, but it requires a stepped approach which does not rob him of a currently much-needed coping strategy.

If we now consider how we use the arts to work with defences, we will see how they offer us such a stepped approach.

Working with the arts

Until now we have been considering how we work verbally with defences. Yet as integrative child psychotherapists we also have the resources of arts media and play that we can utilise. Using the arts may be one of the most helpful ways in which we can work with defences. Working with arts media enables us to:

1. Tiptoe up to defences
2. Psycho-educate our clients about their use of defences
3. Portray the defence and the core anxiety simultaneously and empathically
4. Empower our clients in how they feel about their defences and co-create new coping strategies.

Any arts media can be used—sand tray, puppets, clay, musical instruments, drawing, movement. Some therapists use a puppet which is able to comment on and think out loud about children's defences. For example,

Therapist: [*speaking to the puppet in front of the child*] It seems really hard for Amy to talk to us today, she seems sad. I wonder what's making her sad?

Puppet: [*therapist pretending to be the puppet talking back to therapist*] Yeah she does seem sad. I wonder if anything happened at the weekend? I know sometimes when she sees her dad she can feel sad about having to say goodbye to him.

This approach is direct in that the therapist is stating a reason for the child not wanting to talk/seeming sad. It is slightly more indirect than the therapist talking directly to Amy. It gives Amy the option to not reply, which if offered as a verbal interpretation by the therapist may have felt more confrontational. An even more indirect way, with a more "tiptoeing" technique might be to say:

Puppet: [*"talking" to therapist in front of child*] I am feeling really sad today. I just don't feel like talking much.
Therapist: [*talking back to puppet*] Oh gosh … feeling so sad you don't feel like talking … I guess I am wondering if something has made you feel sad?
Puppet: Yeah … I had a sad weekend …
Therapist: A sad weekend …?
Amy: [*addressing puppet*] Me too. I had a sad weekend too.
Puppet: Really? What happened at your weekend?
Amy: I saw my dad …
Puppet: Saw your dad …
Amy: Yeah … he has the new baby … I wanted us to play football … but we had to stay home with the baby … we always used to play football when he lived with me and mum.
Puppet: Oh … so tough … to have to share you dad now … missing him and those special times you used to have. No wonder you feel sad.
Amy: Yeah … I really do miss him.

By displacing the possible defence and core anxiety onto the puppet, it allows the child to see their feelings represented at a safe distance, which may make these feelings feel more manageable through being externalised and "owned" by someone else.

These two examples show how we can use the arts to try to reach the right emotional distance for the client to be able to explore their defence and the core anxiety beneath it. The arts offer us an invaluable tool when working with defences, as they can help us titrate a digestible dose of thinking and feeling in the client. One way of considering this is through the concept of "aesthetic distance", which is used in the arts therapies when thinking about how to work with the arts for maximum therapeutic effect (see Landy, 1983). Aesthetic distance is achieved when the client is able to think and feel deeply simultaneously. I think of it as being rather like "mentalized affectivity" (Fonagy et al., 2004), which is being able to have a feeling and think about it at the same time. This does not mean that the client may not express strong emotions such as anger or grief when the defence is worked with, but there is some capacity either within themselves or in their relation to us that allows some thinking to go alongside. This is vital so that they do not feel they are drowning in overwhelming feelings, even if that means we are the ones doing the thinking for them at that moment.

Conversely, we may wish to help our clients not be so detached and intellectual in their approach to thinking about their defences that they are cut off from feeling. The arts can help our clients think about their defences or core pain while remaining in touch with feeling. The safety of the metaphor provided by the arts may mean a client can allow themselves to feel deeply without cognitively censoring their experience. As drama therapist Sue Jennings has stated, through the distance of the metaphor one can actually come closer to one's affective experience (1998). This may be crucial in our work with clients who present with a more avoidant attachment and tend to privilege cognitive over affective processing (Crittenden et al., 2014).

I will now present some case examples to illustrate how images and words can be used together to convey our empathy and to help a child reach the right distance emotionally and cognitively in relation to their defence or core anxiety/pain. The method I present is an adaptation of Margot Sunderland's "big empathy" drawings (see Sunderland, 2015).

Amil—an example of using "big empathy" drawing to work with defences

Unlike with the example previously cited of Amy, who was able to acknowledge the pain of missing her father and so was more accessible and less defended, with nine-year-old Amil the therapist needs to take a more oblique approach. Amil too had experienced his parents' separation at the age of three and the subsequent erratic contact with his birth father. Amil, however, has a well-established coping style or defence, of walling off his pain of missing his father, through becoming angry and aggressive towards others both at home and school. The therapist therefore needs to draw upon using the arts and metaphor in order to tiptoe up to Amil's core pain. To achieve the right distance from the defence and the pain it protects, the first step the therapist needs to take is to empathise with the defence itself.

Figure 14.3 shows an attempt to tiptoe up to Amil's defence of aggression. The images themselves are quite potent and may not look like tiptoeing but they are introduced as "Sometimes when people get angry they feel …" Note how there is no reference to Amil feeling these. He has the option to choose any of the images or none of them. The hope is that perhaps one may resonate, and he may feel "felt" by his therapist without having to own the feelings consciously or directly. The images below could also be hand drawn by the therapist using a whiteboard and giving Amil the opportunity to change them in any way. Saying to a child, "Is there anything you want to change or add … I might not have this

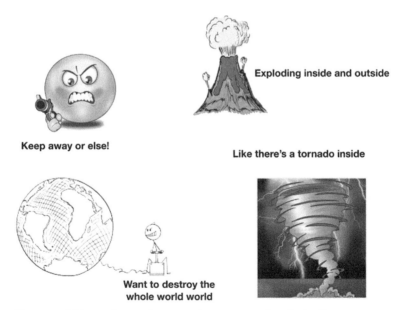

Figure 14.3 "Sometimes when people get angry they feel …"

right," enables the child to show the therapist if something has resonated by adding words or changing the image. This may provide more information which the therapist can then empathise with. It also allows them to wipe out an image if they feel it is "wrong" or is "too much", in a way that is impossible to do with spoken words. If a child chooses to wipe out an image on a whiteboard it might well be that it has resonated deeply, but they are letting us know they are not ready to explore this openly with us and this must be respected.

If trust has built in the therapeutic relationship and Amil has allowed himself to own his angry feelings in the presence of his therapist, there is then the opportunity to link the defence to the core pain of his loss. The therapist can draw another big empathy drawing (Figure 14.4).

Figure 14.4 A big empathy drawing

An alternative potential big empathy drawing is shown in Figure 14.5. The second image is more direct as it is a stick image of Amil showing the anger that the outside world sees, while concealing the pain and sadness inside. At this point there does not have to be direct linking to Amil's life data and his relationship with his father. The therapist may stay with the feelings themselves and how they relate to each other (e.g. one helping to

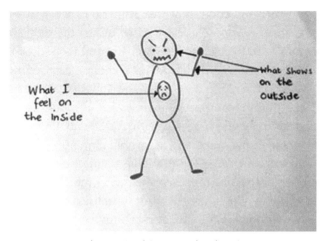

Figure 14.5 An alternative big empathy drawing

manage another more painful feeling) without trying to make that link. It is about observing closely the child's emotional response which we can attune to through our own somatic countertransference and the child's non-verbal communications. The first image of the wall around the heart can be emotionally distanced further through writing "building a wall around the heart", where the therapist talks about sometimes "some people" build a wall around the heart, without attributing that to Amil. If Amil is ready, he may then allow further exploration of ways in which he has constructed a wall around his heart. Our final aim would be that he would eventually allow exploration through our empathy for the pain of his loss and through enabling him to bring together his thinking and feeling about his father, to no longer need to use the "wall of anger and aggression".

Hopefully it is possible to see the "unpolished" nature of the hand drawn images. Children are much more likely to engage in communicating back through big empathy drawings if they feel there is no need to be "artistic" in their response. The therapist can model how this form of drawing on the whiteboard is a playful space where the aim is communication, not an artistic product. Whole conversations can be had on the whiteboard, where talking directly about an issue feels too difficult but the playful space of co-creating a conversation through a mixture of drawings, symbols, metaphors, and words feels less challenging.

Digital images can be useful if working online, as they can be saved in such a way as to enable them to be edited: the child then can delete or add text to them. Big empathy drawings are often done in the moment of the session with the child; however, sometimes what we are trying to communicate is so sensitive and in need of just the right words and images, we may wish to practise it beforehand and then "do it live" with the child when the timing is right. Digital images can be prepared in advance and again offered to the child at the right time. "The right time" may be a long time in coming. Sometimes I find I have images in my mind to share with a child long before they are ready to use them. This is part of our containing space, where we hold onto projections from the child until they may be ready to metabolise them.

For some children like Amil, even after many months of therapy they may still struggle to allow their therapist to tiptoe up to the pain in the ways already described. For some, it may only be through their transference to us that we will gain access to working with their defences. So, for Amil, it may be that much of his anger and aggression becomes constellated within the therapy relationship where feelings of loss, abandonment, and rage in relation to us may be alive and available for exploration. In which case, we may use big empathy drawings to describe what we feel might be happening between us. The wall around the heart might equally apply to how Amil is relating to us as well as to his father and may thus signify something of his attachment style as an interpersonal defence. It may be safer, however, to consider these feelings in relation to us, where we may hold less emotional valency than his father.

Contextualising defences

I have deliberately given the reader little or no contextual information regarding Amil and his external world, so as to focus on technique. However, no defence mechanism or coping strategy develops in isolation of an external world context. In fact, as Crittenden et al. (2014) argue, our defences are the best solution we may have found for managing our particular life contexts. Imagine now, if Amil were a refugee from Afghanistan. Imagine if he were one of the only children of colour in his primary school and community. Imagine if Amil and siblings lived in a community with high unemployment and poor housing. Imagine if Amil's mother worked very long hours trying to support Amil and his brothers. Imagine if she had had to do this since she separated from Amil's father who had been the main wage earner. Imagine if Amil's mother had to rely on a range of neighbours for ad hoc care of Amil. Does this alter how we may now view Amil's anger and aggression at school and at home? How might we view Amil's experience of his loss of his father now? His loss of his mother's availability? We use the term "defences" and I have maintained that throughout this chapter as it is a term still used within child psychotherapy literature, but we need to make sure we do not see these as simply innate to the child; thus Amil's "coping strategies" may make absolute sense given the struggles his family has faced. Amil has much to feel rageful about. His rage is not simply an intrapsychic process to protect him from his pain of loss. This rage may be being displaced or projected out onto safe figures at school and mother at home, but we must consider what this rage communicates of Amil's experience before we can approach it with him. The big empathy drawings shown here in response to Amil are bite-sized, hopefully digestible nuggets which can be offered to Amil as we gradually co-create the meaning together of his anger and pain. They may touch just one aspect of his experience. We must be prepared to think about race, class, culture, social and economic factors, ethnicity, religion, gender, sexuality, ability/disability—the social graces (Burnham, 2012), if we are to truly meet the child before us, and we may need different techniques with which to do this. We cannot maintain a purely intrapsychic focus. As stated by Frank Lowe (2014) in reference to adult psychotherapy: "This perspective [*purely intrapsychic*] assumes, erroneously, that there is no relationship between the external world and the internal world of the individual and that issues of race, culture, class, or sexuality are not vibrant aspects of the internal world that affect our feelings, fantasies, perceptions, identities and relationships."

The Power Threat Meaning Framework outlined by Johnstone and Boyle et al. (2018) is a meta theory which supports Lowe's view. It seeks to describe human distress in contextual terms and asks four key questions:

- What has happened to you? (How has **Power** operated in your life?)
- How did it affect you? (What kind of **Threat** does this pose?)
- What sense did you make of it? (What is the **Meaning** of these situations and experiences to you?)
- What did you have to do to survive? (What kinds of **Threat Response** are you using?)

We can see from these questions how defences are re-conceptualised as responses to threats to power and the power an individual has is inextricably shaped by the context in which they find themselves socially, economically, and politically. Those with diminished social and cultural "capital" due to inequality, discrimination, marginalisation, deprivation, and social injustice will inevitably find that they experience more threats to their sense of power than those holding more power. Being a child and a dependent obviously confers less power. As opposed to a medical model which asks, "What is wrong with you?" the question we should be asking is, "What has happened to you—that has led to you managing in this way?" This should reference the context in which this has happened.

When working with defences, our formulation about their meaning will naturally influence how we then empathise with them and make sense of them with our clients, as briefly illustrated with reference to Amil above. We therefore need a formulation which sees and understands the many strands shaping a particular defence and the meaning or function it serves for the client. Ultimately, our work with defences is about co-creating a narrative which helps a young person to make sense of how they arrived at the place they are now; how they have come to cope and perhaps survive in this way.

Working with therapeutic stories

For some children, it may be that the safety provided by metaphor is needed much more and that talking in any way directly about their external world or life data feels too threatening or intrusive. In these cases, we may consider writing a therapeutic story on behalf of the child, which speaks to the child's defences and core pain or anxiety, but does so through the metaphor of a story. I shall not describe here how to go about constructing a therapeutic story, as Sunderland has done this thoroughly elsewhere and I would advise the reader to consult her *Using Storytelling as a Therapeutic Tool with Children* (2017). Instead I provide an example.

Therapeutic story

Once upon a time there was a girl called Goldilocks who had become friends with three bears. She loved visiting the three bears and playing with them. She loved playing hide and seek. She loved hiding behind their big treasure chest. She would then surprise them when they found her by saying "BOO!" really loudly! She loved playing in their garden, where they would play tag while jumping on the stepping stones. Goldilocks loved this game as she could balance the best on the stepping stones and she never fell off them. Playing with the bears gave her the loveliest, warmest, and happiest together feelings inside and being with the bears made her feel full up of such wonderful safe feelings that she wished these feelings would never go away.

Then one day when the Goldilocks and the three bears had just finished playing tag on the stepping stones, the three bears said, "Let's go in and have some fizzy lemonade! All that running about has made us thirsty." Goldilocks was just about to follow them when she noticed one of the stepping stones. It looked so shiny and pretty and when she looked at it, it made her smile both on the outside and on the inside, as she thought of all the wonderful happy memories she had of balancing on the pretty stone while she played with the bears. And then, before she knew it, she had slipped the shiny stone in her pocket!

"Now I can always have the soft, warm together feelings with me!" she thought.

Just then the bears called her in for her lemonade. Goldilocks kept the stone hidden and went and drank her lemonade. Yet all the time she was drinking it she felt worried the bears would see she had their shiny stepping stone in her pocket. She suddenly felt bad for taking it but she also felt like she so desperately wanted to keep the warm, happy together feelings with her that she couldn't bring herself to put it back.

From then on, every time Goldilocks went to play at the bears' house, before she left, she always secretly took something of theirs with her. She didn't think the bears had noticed and she loved having the shiny things from their house. But instead of giving her the warm, happy together feelings inside, she was beginning to feel more and more worried and more and more guilty. She didn't know what to do: she was in a bit of a pickle.

Then one day baby bear said, "Let's play tag on the stepping stones!" "Yeah!!" said mummy and daddy bear. "Come on, Goldilocks!" But Goldilocks suddenly became very worried.

"Oh no! They will see all of the stepping stones have gone—then they might think it is me who has taken them, and they might get so cross they might not ever want to see me again! I couldn't bear that," she thought.

She slowly followed the bears into the garden and she found them looking very confused.

"Where are all the stepping stones?" said daddy bear.

"I don't know," said mummy bear.

"Someone has taken them," said baby bear. "And now we can't play our game!" he said sounding so disappointed.

Goldilocks felt very guilty as she hated seeing her bear friends looking so confused and unhappy.

She took a deep breath and said, "It was me. I took them." There was silence as Goldilocks looked at the ground, worrying what the bears would now do.

Then one by one the bears came over to her and gave her a bear hug.

"We know you took them, Goldilocks, because we know you love being with us and those stones remind you of our together feelings."

Goldilocks looked at her bear friends and said, "I thought having your things would help me keep those together feelings inside me for when I am not with you, but instead I have just felt worried and guilty. I didn't know how to tell you how I felt or how to give your things back."

The bears smiled at Goldilocks and gave her an even bigger bear squeeze saying it was all okay now, as she had told them and they had forgiven her.

And so the next day, Goldilocks went to the bears' house and she went out into the garden and put back the stepping stones one by one. And when she had finished her bear friends were there waiting for her.

"Shall we play tag on the stepping stones, Goldilocks?" said baby bear, smiling.

"You bet!" she said and she began chasing her bear friends as she lightly jumped from stone to stone.

In this story we can see how Goldilocks struggles to hold on to the "warm, together" feelings she feels when she is not with her friends, the three bears. The pain of being apart from them and the feeling of loss leads to her stealing from them in the hope she may take literally the together feelings with her with their possessions, the precious stones. We can see the empathy for Goldilocks via the three bears who understand the emotional communication of her stealing, much as the therapist feels for the client who steals from the room as a way to manage breaks between sessions. Directly talking to a child about stealing from the therapy room may be experienced as too confrontative and shaming. Using the metaphor of the story and the empathy conveyed through it hopefully provides the child with a route to be able to work through this with their therapist more openly.

The story can be told using sand tray figures or puppets to enliven the telling of the story but to also root it in the metaphor. In response, children may choose to link it to their life data or the therapist may sense the story has acted as a bridge to talking about an issue, such as the stealing illustrated here. However, it may be that no links are explicitly made to the child's external or internal world but that the story becomes a transitional object (Winnicott, 1951) which is left to resonate on an unconscious level, where it can facilitate change in the psyche much as Jennings described as a process of "through distance [of the metaphor] I come closer [to my feelings]" (1998, p. 117). Therapeutic stories are often helpful when the child has reached an impasse in therapy or an impasse in relation to their struggles with their defences.

Conclusion

In this chapter I hope to have provided a window into working integratively with defences. My intention has been to show the range of ways in which an integrative child psychotherapist can work with defences and to do so in a way that is respectful of what the client is able to manage. I have stressed the importance of timing and titrating an intervention and how the use of metaphor and the arts enable us to do this. I have not discussed in detail working through the transference as a way to address defences, as I believe many psychoanalytic child psychotherapists have done this very well elsewhere (see, for example, Alvarez, 2012; Lanyado & Horne, 2007). Instead I hope I have been able to convey an integrative perspective which values its broad heritage.

The focus in this chapter has been primarily upon technique. I have referred to the significance of considering context when making a formulation about the meaning or function of a defence, but I would point the reader to the work of Johnstone and Boyle, et al. (2018) for a depth discussion of responses to emotional distress.

References

Alvarez, A. (2012). *The Thinking Heart. Three Levels of Psychoanalytic Work with Disturbed Children*. London: Routledge.

Burnham, J. (2012). Developments in social GRRRAAACCEEESSS: Visible-invisible and voiced and un-voiced. In: I.-B. Krause (Ed.), *Culture and Reflexivity in Systemic Psychotherapy. Mutual Perspectives*. London: Karnac.

Crittenden, P., Dallos, R., Landini, A., & Kozlowska, K. (2014). *Attachment and Family Therapy*. London: Open University Press.

Davy, J., & Cross, M. (2004). *Barriers, Defences and Resistance*. London: Open University Press.

Fonagy, P., Gergely, G., Jurist, E. L., & Target, M. (2004). *Affect Regulation, Mentalization and the Development of the Self*. London: Routledge.

Freud, A. (1936). *The Ego and the Mechanisms of Defence* London: Routledge, 1992.

Gilbert, P. (2010). Compassion Focused Therapy: Distinctive Features. London: Routledge.

Holder, A. (2017). *Anna Freud, Melanie Klein, and the Psychoanalysis of Children and Adolescents*. London: Routledge.

Holmes, J. (2001). *The Search for The Secure Base: Attachment Theory and Psychotherapy*. London: Routledge.

Hughes, D. (2007). *Attachment Focused Family Therapy*. New York: W. W. Norton.

Jennings, S. (1998). *Introduction to Dramatherapy*. London: Jessica Kingsley.

Johnstone, L., & Boyle, M., with Cromby, J., Dillon, J., Harper, D., Kinderman, P., Longden, E., Pilgrim, D., & Read, J. (2018). *The Power Threat Meaning Framework: Overview*. Leicester, UK: British Psychological Society.

Klein, M. (1935). *The Psychoanalysis of Children*. London: Hogarth.

Landy, R. (1983). Use of distancing in dramatherapy. *Arts in Psychotherapy*, *10*(3): 175–185.

Lanyado, M. (2003). *The Presence of the Therapist: Treating Childhood Trauma*. London: Routledge.

Lanyado, M., & Horne, A. (2007). *A Question of Technique: Independent Psychoanalytic Approaches with Children and Adolescents*. London: Routledge.

Lowe, F. (2014). *Thinking Space. Promoting Thinking about Race, Culture and Diversity in Psychotherapy and Beyond*. Tavisock Series. London: Karnac.

Midgley, N., Ensink, K., Lindqvist, K., Malberg, N., & Muller, N. (2017). *Mentalization-Based Treatment for Children: A Time-Limited Approach*. Washington, DC: American Psychological Association.

Porges, S. (2012). The science of compassion: Origins, measures, and interventions. Available at: https://youtube.com/watch?v=MYXa_BX2cE8 (last accessed February 1, 2021).

Siegel, D. (2010). *The Mindful Therapist: A Clinician's Guide to Mindsight and Neural Integration*. New York: W. W. Norton.

Sunderland, M. (2015). *Conversations that Matter. Talking with Children and Teenagers in Ways that Help*. Broadway: Worth.

Sunderland, M. (2017). *Using Storytelling as a Therapeutic Tool with Children*. London: Routledge.

Vaillant, G. (1992). *Ego Mechanisms of Defense: A Guide for Clinicians and Researchers*. Washington, DC: American Psychiatric Press.

Van der Kolk, B. (2014). *The Body Keeps the Score: Mind, Brain and Body in the Transformation of Trauma*. New York: Penguin.

Winnicott, D. W. (1951). Transitional objects and transitional phenomena. In: *Collected Papers: Through Paediatrics to Psycho-analysis* (pp. 229–242). London: Karnac, 1984.

CHAPTER 15

Finding and nurturing the gold: an integrative approach to working with an adopted adolescent and her parent

Roz Read

Introduction

Over the years I have developed archetypes for giving meaning to the different roles that I bring in my work as a therapist when working with adopted children and their parents. Here in this chapter, I attempt to illustrate some of the ways in which a trainee might approach their work with adopted children and their parents using a clinical example of therapeutic work with a fifteen-year-old adopted adolescent.

I am employed part-time as a therapist within a small multidisciplinary team working exclusively with adopted and other permanently placed children and their parents. The model of therapy places a strong emphasis on using the arts, developmental play, body-based interventions, and narrative techniques underpinned by a research-based and neuroscientific understanding of developmental trauma and attachment. While I integrate these tools in my method, the main treatment model I use is Dyadic Developmental Psychotherapy (DDP); this is a specialist therapy created by Dan Hughes in the 1980s (Hughes et al., 2019) for children and their families who have experienced neglect and abuse in their birth families and suffered from significant developmental trauma. I have also had additional trainings in dissociation and EMDR (Eye Movement Desensitisation and Reprocessing). Occasionally the work will include individual sessions with children, but usually it takes the form of family work with children and parents together. Adopted children and their parents have unique challenges and working integratively in this context means that I can develop a framework that is flexible enough to meet the needs of the individual children and families that I'm serving.

Every therapist has a story

In my interview for my first post as a child psychotherapist in adoption, I was asked what it was that drew me to working in the field of adoption. It was a good question. Rarely are we drawn to working with complex trauma for purely altruistic reasons. I reached for different answers. I knew I had a preference for working within a team and that I was drawn to helping children and adolescents within their families, but I couldn't really answer the question. It wasn't until my mother was dying some twenty years later that I finally found the answer. My mother, while she hadn't been adopted, had suffered multiple separations from her own parents and was raised in her early years by extended family. Of course, the story was hazily familiar to me growing up but the significance of this developmental trauma didn't really "click" until the moment I was about to lose her. By then I had helped many adopted children process their losses, and now faced with the reality of losing my own mother, I began to take on a fresh perspective. I realised then that these "ghosts in the nursery ... from the unremembered past of the parents" (Fraiberg et al., 1975, p. 387), felt during my own childhood and attachment relationship with her, had left their imprint.

This has gone some way to explain the resonances I have felt within the field of adoption and why I have a found a home here in my therapeutic work. Like most therapists, I am seeking to understand something about my own history. The *wounded healer* is the first archetype relevant to this work.

The midwife

The second archetype is the *midwife*. The midwife facilitates the giving birth of something new. In this case, it's the helping to forge new attachment bonds between parent and child.

As an integrative child psychotherapist, I have been trained to think about *transference*, the usually unconscious process by which we transfer significant attachment relationships from the past onto others in the present. When working with adoption, there are multiple, complex transferences to take into account: the child's transference onto the adoptive mother which might carry abuse and neglect. This is an important one to understand and work with; both to encourage the parent to understand and so bear it, as well as to help the child drop the filter that hinders their trust in their adoptive parent. There are also the parents' transferences onto me of their own parents and the child's transference onto me as a strange, new person. Perhaps I could, in fantasy, adopt them or have the power to move them to a new family. Traditionally in psychotherapy, transference would be interpreted to help deepen understanding and can strengthen attachment. But here my ultimate aim is to be a trusted facilitator who can provide enough safety so that truthful encounters between parent and child can happen. This is where the real work is done. Not with the therapist, but with the relationship between parent and child. So instead, I mainly make a "silent interpretation", sometimes voiced as recognising the child's anxiety about whether I will like them, whether I will understand their worries and muddles, and help them feel happier in their adoptive family. This then informs how I work with the parent–child interaction.

In this way the midwife is a good image for one of the roles I take on in this kind of work. A midwife accompanies a mother and baby as they meet one another in the real world. Their task is complete once the new pairing is safely made. In adoption, the attachment relationship may begin when older but the journey is similar; it is not without risk and can potentially be dangerous and even life threatening. Here, the midwife provides containment, experience, knowledge, and is there as a guide as they meet one another in moment-by-moment connective experiences.

The alchemist

The third archetype is that of an *alchemist*. Developing a parent and child's attachment relationship is like alchemy: finding the base elements and working with them in such a way that these raw ingredients can be re-formed into the gold of a deepening attachment. "The alchemy of the transformational process turns emotional suffering into resilience and wellbeing: first, through accessing and processing emotional experience to completion, and then, through *metaprocessing* the emergent trans-formational experience" (Fosha, 2013). During a session, I take some-thing that has happened in the week which is broken and not working very well, and together we take it apart, sift through the details, and look at it together, including the full emotional impact, before putting it back into a story with new meanings that becomes something valu-able. I'm aiming to help a child make links and to start to be interested in and curious in the motivations of others, and so to shift assumptions of how the world works. This can be in very small ways, but over time as the iron turns into gold, reflective capacity or mentalizing begins to develop along with a more secure attachment (Fonagy et al., 2016). The process is creative, experimental, emotional, and spontaneous: working in the moment, and drawing past and present together to co-create new meanings and make sense of experiences. Hughes describes this process of conversation as "affective-reflective dialogue" (Hughes et al., 2019). These conversations happen within an overarching relational stance of PACE (an acronym that stands for playfulness, acceptance, curiosity, and empathy) shared by both therapist and parent, which forms the basis of DDP (Hughes et al., 2019).

The archivist

The final archetype is that of an *archivist*. When working with adopted children, it is unfortunately far too common to have insufficient details about their early life. Sometimes we are lucky enough to have access to local authority records that give a flavour of what life might have been like, but with increasing pressure to protect personal data and infor-mation, this is becoming less common. It seems incredibly unfair to the children who were there at the time (and to their adoptive parents who are caring for them now) that they don't have all the information available. Even so, we can hypothesise: sorting through the facts and meanings, preserving key information, and imagining into how those experiences might have felt. Children help by remembering small fragments and these details are pulled together to draw a picture of what life may have been like. Developing a coherent narrative, a story around what happened and leads to where one is now, helps to develop an integrated sense of self as in, "I know who I am, where I came from, and how I came to be here." Trauma has a way of creating rigidity in thinking (Perry, 2002), and the stories that children may have told themselves at the time frequently need to be addressed and revised. DDP is at heart a way of co-creating new stories (Hughes et al., 2019, p. 240) to aid healing through providing new meanings to past experiences. "From these jagged stories of shame and terror that arose from relational trauma, DDP is creating stories of connection, strength and resilience" (Hughes et al., 2019, p. 7).

The following shows how these archetypes of *midwife*, *alchemist*, and *archivist* fit together in a long-term piece of clinical work with a fifteen-year-old young woman and her adoptive mother.

A case: Aisling

Aisling, aged fifteen, was the youngest of a group of siblings all adopted together. Aisling's history was typical of the many children today who are adopted through the care system. She suffered neglect, physical, sexual, and emotional abuse, and had had multiple moves before her adoption at five years old. Aisling and her adoptive mother were not close and a mental health crisis eventually led to her referral for therapy.

Early on in the work, I experimented with keeping Aisling's mother in the room. Usually with adolescents they like to have a more independent space, but in adoption I'm still building the attachment while paradoxically also conscious that an adolescent in brain and body is pressing for individuation. We developed a pattern of beginning with a sharing of the week and highlighting an interaction between them which we would explore together.

In this dialogue taken from a session, Aisling and her mother had had an argument on their way to therapy and nearly didn't make it.

The argument had started over changes happening at home that meant her mother's attention had needed to shift towards her siblings. As we thought about this together, and meanings were made about how painful it was to have felt the loss, we got to the stage of making repair. For many adopted children, if they don't yet have a coherent narrative about their own past traumatic experiences, it can be difficult to know where to start. But it is crucial to do so if they are to build a more secure attachment relationship with their adoptive parents. Here, I use a technique developed by Hughes (2011, p. 63) as "speaking for the child"—a way of leading the child into an exploration of their internal world. This isn't about putting words into children's mouths so much as making a bridge for the child to speak to the parent themselves. Permission from both the child and the parent is important, as is safety, trust, and my own thorough understanding of the history. I speak about what I know. It arises out of the therapeutic relationship, and knowing how to pitch it and when to go in is one of the most risky things I can do. Cues are taken from the child and I step out in a titrated way. Sometimes the step is too great and the child is not yet ready, so tiny steps need to be taken backwards and forwards. It's important that both the child and the parent are comfortable. At the beginning of this vignette, Aisling and I speak together to try to draw out the complexity of what she is thinking and feeling. The mother is listening to us before I draw her in and speak for Aisling.

Speaking for the child

Therapist: How are you doing? You look quite sad actually. But I think you might still be angry. Maybe a little bit less? Your Mum is looking at you. [*Aisling nods*] But you can't quite bring yourself to look at her yet. This is the bit that isn't so easy for you. How do you reconnect? How do you do it? It's a tough one. Would you like to be the first to speak? [*silence*] Would you like some help? [*silence*] Shall I have a go? [*silence*]

Aisling: Well … yeah.

Therapist: I take that as a yes—thank you. Okay, I'll have a go. [*pause*] *Mum, help me.**

---

* I have used italic font to delineate where I speak for Aisling.

Aisling: For what?

Therapist: *I'm stuck over here.*

Aisling: I'm not ready to let it go. I'm still pissed off.

Therapist: *I'm still pissed off with you.*

Aisling: Yeah.

Therapist: *Not ready to let go of my anger just yet. So I might need you to hold on just a bit longer. Don't give up on me. I love you really.*

Aisling: Never said I hate you.

Therapist: *Never said I hate you so I must love you really. Wait for me.*

Aisling: Just don't touch me.

Therapist: *Otherwise I might punch you.*

Aisling: In the face.

Therapist: Yup.

Aisling: I don't want Costa with you either Mum.

Therapist: *Because I'm that cross with you.*

Aisling: Don't want to sit down and have chit chat.

Therapist: *So don't be offended if I'm still cross. Or rather, do be offended because I want you to feel something. But we will move on from this.* [*pause*] Okay, it's your turn, Mum.

Mum: Aisling, I know you're angry with me. I can really see that. And actually, I'm really pleased that you've been able to tell me and show me how angry you are. And I am really sorry that I caused you hurt and pain.

Aisling: Again!

Mum: Again. I'm really sorry. And I'll be here when you're ready. Because I love you and I will always love you. And I know you well enough not to try to touch you. You'll be able to show me when you're ready.

Therapist: *Yup, don't think I want that Costa yet Mum just because you said that.*

Mum: Oh I got that loud and clear.

Aisling: [*silence*]

Therapist: *Just wait for me.*

Mum: I'll always wait for you. Whatever happens, today, next week, throughout your life Aisling. I'll always be waiting. Because now we've fallen in love as mother and daughter, nothing will ever shatter that … we will always get back to normal and I will always wait. [*pause*] You look so sad.

Therapist: Mmm.

    Mum: I have a scooping sense.

Therapist: *Don't touch me, Mum.*

    Mum: I'm not going to touch you. I just want to let you know that I
           see. I see how sad you are. I feel how sad you are.

    Aisling: [*silence*]

The mother's words were beautiful. Working in this way highlights how crucial it is to work with the parents, to help them be part of the therapeutic process. I can only go as far as I can with the safety of the parent, and building this requires much work. My relationship is not just with the child, but with the dyad. Aisling was punishing her mother, giving her the "silent treatment" before she could be nice to her again. My role here was to work out some way to help them connect and find one another, even while still full of feeling. Sometimes this means reminding the child of what they have.

For adopted children, who have suffered so many losses, love can feel transitory. My words offered a scaffolding to Aisling's own words— either more or less. Reflecting on this piece now, perhaps I might have added a summary at the end, that when her mother has said those words about falling in love and that she was really sorry, there was nothing more to add. It's important that there shouldn't be an expectation of saying, "… and I love you too." Aisling had a lot to be angry about, and her mother was letting her know that she knew that.

As therapists we're in charge of the ending, and sometimes, especially when working with these delicate pieces of affective-reflective dialogue, there can be an urgency in the therapist to make it right. The healer within the therapist pushes for something before the child is ready. All the same, having a way of ending this process contains it. When working with trauma, there needs to be a balance of acknowledging reality while also keeping a hope burning for something different. A summary would have helped, such as, "Sometimes when you don't say very much, so much is happening. Your Mum has said things that deep down you need to know. It's believing it that is hard. You might need to hear these words many times."

Therapy sessions are small times in a child's life. Ultimately, I'm looking for the work to happen when I'm not there, when the connections are happening outside and the therapy begins to shrink to a small part of a child's life so it's become integrated inside them. Aisling and her mother would often go for a coffee following our sessions, and that combined with the travelling back and forth provided space to reflect together. Many times, cycles begun in therapy would be completed just after and the mother would text me to say a further insight had been made, or they had found a way of connecting again. In this way, the process is about helping children learn how to safely reach out themselves; to know what to do and manage the accompanying fear. We start as a therapist getting something going with the parent's help, then the parent takes over and then finally, the child starts something off that isn't based so much on anger but on curiosity; they're now trying to work something out for themselves.

Just over a year later, I began to see such a shift with Aisling as in the following session, where she started making links herself.

Aisling and her mother arrived sitting at opposite ends of the sofa. A text before the session told me that they had not seen one another all week. The atmosphere was tense. Usually when this happens, I invite the parent to let me know the story in a matter-of-fact way in front of the child. The aim is to have a shared understanding so that we could then work with it. Her mother said that Aisling had been out every night.

As her mother explained to me what happened, she said that she had gone into her bedroom in the evening to say goodnight and plan that the next morning they would be alone in the house so they could spend some time together. In the morning, the mother went to wake her, and Aisling grunted irritably from under the covers and the mother took that as a message that she wanted to be left alone. In the evening Aisling got angry with her mother saying, "You said you were going to wake me and we were going to spend some time together!" The evening ended in a row. Unpicking this became the content of the next session.

"We missed each other"

Therapist: So does that make sense with your Mum as well, why you
          were angry with her?
  Aisling: Mmm?

Therapist: I'm trying to piece it together in terms of when you then saw your Mum. You had an argument with her. You shouted at her last night.

Aisling: Oh, last night.

Therapist: I was thinking that—

Mum: Aisling came home Tuesday night and I put her to bed and I said, "I'll wake you in the morning and we'll spend some time together." And when I went into her room the next morning, she grunted and turned over and I took it as a message to leave her be. It was just Aisling and me in the house yesterday. She was in her dressing gown for the rest of the day and I took that as a message to *"leave me alone"*.

Aisling: No!! [*starts coughing loudly and trying to interrupt*]

Therapist: Just hear your Mum out.

Mum: I took that as a message from Aisling: *"Leave me alone."* I was there, I was available. But then last night Aisling was really angry with me because she said, "You said you would wake me! And we were going to spend some time together!"

Therapist: Ahh! So you realised!

Aisling: But at the same time she said I didn't wake up when she came in my room! But I heard her outside talking!

Mum: I didn't go back in until later.

Therapist: Aisling—your Mum is in the middle of a story and she's about to say something about herself. [*to the mother*] Go on.

Mum: I realised that we had just missed each other and I was angry with myself because it was like—I should have done more to try and get through that "Go away"—

Aisling: You say "Go away!" You're being rude and horrible!

Mum: No, no, no, no! Aisling I didn't say any of that!

Therapist: Aisling, listen to your Mum. You're not listening to what she is saying.

Mum: It was what I was feeling. Not what you were doing. I was feeling that you were saying, "Go away! I don't want to spend time with you." And I was angry with myself because I didn't recognise the real message.

Therapist: Which was?

Mum: Which was, "*Mum, I need you.*" And I needed to just get past that "Go away" message to get through to what Aisling really needed.

Therapist: *And I'm feeling miserable …*

Mum: "*And I need you to hang on to me.*" I think the reason why I was angry with myself was because yesterday morning for whatever reason I was feeling too—whatever—to see past that. I wasn't feeling robust enough. Does that make sense?

Therapist: Ahh. So what was going on for you, Mum? Help Aisling understand that. Because she isn't likely to know what you were feeling.

Aisling: I was like … I woke up and you didn't try waking me up cos you didn't want us to spend the morning together.

Therapist: Right.

Aisling: And I was ready to come downstairs and if you were to make the slightest comment about it, I was ready to say, "Well, you didn't wake me up!"

Therapist: Ohh!

Aisling: The last thing you said to me was, "I'll wake you up in the morning so we can spend some time together."

Therapist: Aww. You missed each other!

Mum: We just missed each other! But you know what the great thing is, Roz?

Therapist: You're talking about it now.

Mum: She let me know last night!

Therapist: Oh, did she?

Mum: But she let me know last night. So I was able to buy the Doritos and the salsa and leave them on the pillow and say, "Aisling, we missed each other yesterday."

Therapist: Ahh. Lovely, lovely.

Mum: But I've got it now.

Therapist: And when you missed her, help Aisling understand what you were feeling cos she obviously didn't get you right either. So tell Aisling what you were feeling.

Aisling: So when she came in, I didn't register it.

Therapist: No, I'm not talking about that. I'm talking about—you need to know what was going on for Mum. We know what was happening for you because you explained it, but you need to know what was going on for Mum. So what was going on for you, Mum?

Mum: I just … we hadn't really spoken since we finished here last Friday. Aisling was very angry with me, wouldn't come to Costa. And at one point she said, "I'm going to wait here!" [*Mum folds her arms grumpily with a frown*] And I thought, do I go to Costa? Or wait? But we decided to go home and she stormed off and we travelled separately.

Aisling: She started yelling at me on the escalator …

Mum: I wasn't!

Aisling: People were looking at me on the escalator, in the eye. And I thought I'm not going to be publicly humiliated by you and so I said goodbye!

Mum: Aisling—I'm still explaining Wednesday to you …

Aisling: [*tries to interrupt*]

Therapist: Mum—just a little bracket here. When you explain it, Aisling might be reacting a bit to the "grrr". [*folding arms and frowning*]

Mum: Oh, Okay.

Therapist: It's a little bit touching into her shame. You might need to just temper that.

Mum: Oh, was I?

Therapist: That's what she's reacting to. She's very sensitive about how you might do that.

Mum: Oh, I'm sorry. I didn't mean to do that. Did I do that?

Therapist: I'm not saying it to shame you either! I'm just saying it because she will make more of it than you intend her to. So it distracts from the story which she needs to hear.

Mum: [*turning softly to Aisling*] We had all of that going on. And I know when you left on Monday, we weren't connected in the way that we had experienced before. And then something happened on Monday. And I thought what is going on? And I was so worried about you and worried about upsetting you. And sometimes it feels like I don't know what to do. I don't know what to do! [*Mum becomes tearful*] It was my "I don't know what to do" that stopped me on Wednesday.

Aisling: No—I feel bad now. Because when I was with my ex, I didn't know what to do and when he was acting all psycho I felt useless. And it makes you feel bad. And you haven't even done anything. Can't do much. And they're just angry with you. I know it doesn't feel very nice.

Therapist: That's lovely Aisling. You've made that connection with what Mum is saying.

Aisling: No—Mum—all the time I sit there and I'm like, I don't know how she does it when I'm being like—horrible—when I know I can be. Must feel like you're always on the edge.

Mum: No. It doesn't always feel like that. But I'm fighting the urge to rescue you. To scoop you up. To wrap you up. To keep you safe. And I know I can't.

Therapist: And I think that's lovely. And I think Aisling did need to know that. You said it so beautifully, Mum. And I think it's lovely for you Aisling—I've not heard you do that before, which is immediately make an association with what Mum is talking about with something from your own experience. And now you're both talking very intimately. It's really beautiful to listen to and watch. Very intimate. This is love.

Reading this through, it would be easy to see that somehow I had controlled the trajectory of the session. There are many, many threads that could be taken up but it's important in this case to keep everyone to one simple track so that a process can be completed. When completed, this is integrated and other links made; the sense can be felt in the body. Some interruptions are important but sometimes an animated boundary, as shown above, is a way of pushing through the many deflections. Control issues are a familiar behavioural pattern in adopted children who understandably struggle to feel the good intent in those entrusted to look after them. Not recognising this and not dealing with it head-on by maintaining one's authority as a therapist can mean the therapy never gets anywhere. Of course, this can only be done after understanding how to build "cues of safety" (Porges, 2017, p. 50) that can be returned to when the autonomic nervous system threatens to move into overwhelm.

By this stage, Aisling did trust me so I could risk halting the deflections more directly.

At a deeper level, which we returned to many times in our work together, the dialogue reveals the painful expectation in Aisling that her mother would have understood her communication when she grunted from under the covers. The longing she felt inside to be understood and welcomed in that moment of waking had its origins in her neglectful history. Underneath Aisling's rejecting behaviours of "go away" was the opposite longing to have her mother push past these defences. What is also revealed is how incredibly difficult it is for adoptive parents without help and support to recognise the meanings behind these rejections and to be persistent. These daily interactions are rich with potential to strengthen attachments and find meaning and this is why it becomes so important to use the therapy to unpack them in this way for both parents and children.

Working with dissociation: the "five-hour brain"

Alongside working with the attachment relationship between Aisling and her mother, we were also working with the developmental trauma and the resultant dissociation in a multilayered treatment. In the context of Aisling's developing attachment to her adoptive mother, it would then become safer to look at the trauma, and as the trauma was processed, it in turn would become safer to draw closer to her adoptive mother. The two processes are worked with in tandem. As Herman states, "There is no single, efficacious 'magic bullet' for the traumatic syndromes" (1997, p. 156).

Dissociation in adopted children has often been overlooked but more has been understood about its significance in recent years (Silberg, 2013; Wieland, 2011). It makes sense with very young children, when faced with extreme trauma that they cannot run away from or fight, and often at the hands of people close to them, that they would dissociate. Dissociation acts like a buffer; an involuntary way for a baby or young child to protect themselves by creating a distance from unbearable, overwhelming circumstances around them that threaten their very survival. We all have the capacity to daydream from birth, but trauma takes this to a whole new realm. Faced with terrifying violence and shouting around them, a young child might focus on a favourite toy—something that helps them to escape from their present reality. This toy becomes a helpful "part", taking on a life of its own in the child's imagination, becoming a hero and saving the day. Aisling focused on pictures in a catalogue of happy families and would imagine jumping into this ideal world to escape from where she was. She also developed other "parts" which gradually became known during our work together.

Right from our first session together, Aisling was clear that she didn't want to use any art materials; but she did agree to draw her brain. I showed Aisling an iPad app of the human brain, pointing out the different regions. Psycho-education and explaining some of the neurobiology around the brain in a very simple and basic way helps children recognise that it's not their fault that they find life a struggle. Instead, there are "muddles" in their brain (Marks, 2011, p. 92) and therapy can help make their brains "*stronger*". This idea helps motivate children without pathologising them; after all, it must be a clever brain that can work out how to dissociate in order to manage extreme trauma.

Having explored the brain a little, I suggested that Aisling draw what she thought was her own brain. I'm often amazed at how children know that there is something "not quite working" with their brain and how accurately they draw it. The first drawing Aisling did was drawn so faintly in yellow that the writing could hardly be seen, bringing to mind a dissociative quality (Figure 15.1). She described her brain as being like a computer that could only store information for five hours, so that whatever happened during the day at school she would later completely forget. A large part of her brain was "memory that I can't remember", and the remainder "mixed feelings—angry but sad underneath everywhere". She had a tiny corner that was happiness, but even then, it was about reassuring everyone else that she was happy when she wasn't really.

From here, I drew her awareness to her body, where she noticed comfortable spots and ranges of temperature. Her body tended to shift states very quickly, common in developmental trauma (Levine, 1997), but she found walking around the room and moving her legs and arms opened her up to talk more.

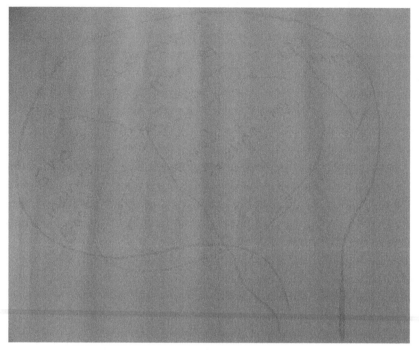

Figure 15.1 Aisling's first drawing of her brain

I soon got to experience for myself how Aisling's "five-hour brain" worked. The early sessions were marked by a thick, heavy dissociation that felt like a pea-souper in the room. Aisling herself would arrive looking different for every session, with different hair, make-up, style of clothes, voice, and way of holding her body that suggested different ages. These were the multiple "parts" of her that helped her survive various traumatic events. I would find myself constantly moving to try to stay awake—the tiredness being a common countertransference when there is dissociation. Movement helped shift the energy in my body but I still found it hard to think. Sometimes the fog would lift but sometimes it would remain there throughout. Sometimes when it lifted, a hostile, potentially violent "part" of Aisling would be exposed and I did have sessions which finished suddenly with shouting and angry slamming of doors while walking out. At least once, I did a session over the phone while the mother put the loudspeaker on in the car so that my voice could be heard. Aisling was silent but her mother's descriptions helped me track what was happening and whether my interventions were being helpful. Sometimes I sent emails to Aisling, particularly in the breaks, and many times I emailed and texted the mother out of hours to support the transitions around the work. However, throughout all of this, Aisling showed her own resilience and very rarely missed a session, returning the following week supported by her willing mother. Her engagement, even if it was difficult, told me that she was getting something even if I was not always sure at the time what it was.

Towards the end of our first year of work together, I asked Aisling to draw her brain again. This second drawing was a great deal richer than the first and noticeably, the "five-hour brain" had become smaller (Figure 15.2). Some of the dissociative "parts" had begun to make themselves known in our work together as we began to understand how they had developed at various stages in Aisling's early life to help her survive unbearable experiences. We were at the beginning of understanding their stories and why they had come to live within Aisling. A level of "co-consciousness" between the parts was also developing so that the dissociation was lessening. Different parts were becoming aware that there were others within a system.

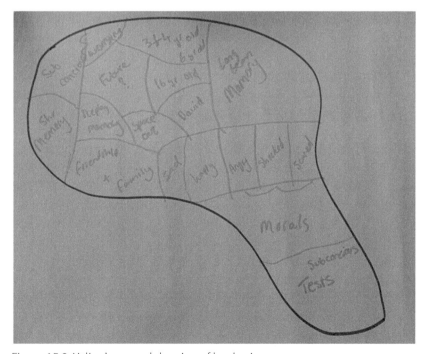

Figure 15.2 Aisling's second drawing of her brain

In one session, Aisling recounted a dream she had had in the week of how a man had pushed her into a car boot and driven her to a garden centre where they met a woman and two children aged three and six. The woman disappeared and the man put magnets into the hands of all three children and wrapped them around a pole. The three-year-old managed to get out and went to call for help. People came from a cake shop and the man was scared off. The dream ends with Aisling in tears and praising what the three-year-old did. Through the dream two important "parts" who had helped Aisling survive had been identified. As we explored the dream together, how young she was, and what a responsibility she had taken upon herself while so young, Aisling began to realise the inappropriateness of the three-year-old part's role and said that she needed to be "relieved of her duties". Furthermore, Aisling began to realise that neither the three-year-old nor the six-year-old parts were aware that they had been adopted. This is relatively common in adopted children with dissociation, where younger parts may be "frozen in time by the trauma and may be unaware of the existence of the adoptive parents" (Marks, 2011, p. 102).

Together we devised a drama to work with these parts. We found cushions and a teddy bear to represent the three-year-old part and buried it under some cushions with Aisling saying she was "trapped because of fear". Aisling felt she would like to be her sixteen-year-old self who would help bring the three-year-old part to her adoptive mother. Together we planned how the drama would unfold: Aisling would take the bear, wrapped in a soft blanket, and present it to her mother. The mother was asked to sit on the sofa and it was explained that, "Three-year-old Aisling was trapped and needed rescuing." Aisling collected the bear and carried it in the blanket and then questioned her mother: "Will you look after her and keep her safe? Will you love her? Adopt her?" The mother took the bear into her arms, and movingly reassured the three-year-old part that she was wanted and loved. It's important to note here that I didn't work directly with the younger parts myself; my role was to support Aisling in caring for her own parts—this ultimately is what helps support integration.

After two years, Aisling drew another more colourful brain (Figure 15.3). The dissociation was becoming better understood, a complex system was being revealed, and a level of co-consciousness was happening with the parts of Aisling becoming more aware of the others with different ages and functions. After she had completed the new drawing, we would look at the older ones and these served to encourage her that more was becoming known. Over time, Aisling developed her own strategies for managing her different parts when they were clamouring for attention by saying, "Hey, guys" as a way of calling them all together.

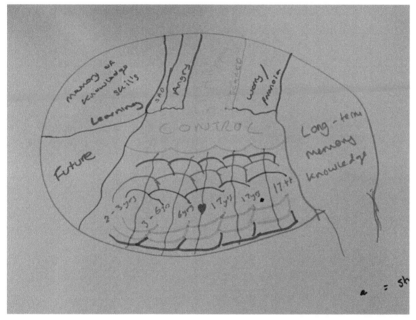

Figure 15.3 Aisling's third drawing of her brain

Aisling had always been aware of various bodily symptoms that over time we realised were connected to her different "parts". For instance, with one "part", she would have more painful hips and pelvic area and this helped us have an understanding of who was particularly active. Aisling would often want to take her shoes off and curl up on the sofa in the therapy room under a soft blanket, allowing her body which held so much trauma to relax.

In one session, Aisling described herself as struggling all week because she had been hearing "all the parts inside talking all at once and making a lot of noise and I can't shut them up".

She drew a picture of herself as having layers, drawing another image inside and then further images on the outside (Figure 15.4). Around her was "electricity". She described how the bodily sensation was in her bowel and drew rings around that area, but when she had finished the drawing, we realised that she had drawn the centre on the bowel of the one that was her, but around the genitals of the little "part" inside her. This drawing became significant in her understanding of how the trauma of her sexual abuse had been somatised in her body. Here her "drawing hand" had been able to give clues from the non-declarative memory system in her brain. We had discovered that not all the "parts" knew, but some did,

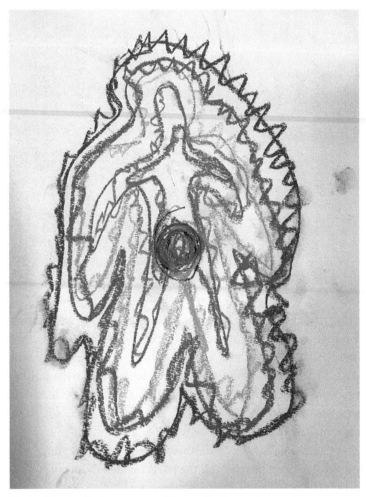

Figure 15.4 Aisling's drawing of the activation in her body

and the drawing hand that had not been forbidden to speak revealed more (Magagna, 2012, p. 130).

Adoptive families need more than just the therapist; they need a team around them and so the work included other important elements which I've not included here. The "team around the family" (TAF) is something of a cliché, but when it really works, it has potential to be the transformative space that Bion (1962) had in mind with "the container–contained". Part of the system includes supervision in the different models, bringing them together in a way that ensures quality and coherence, so that it doesn't become a mess. In concentric circles with Aisling at the heart, then her parents, then me, my colleagues, and then finally the enveloping of the wider professional system around everyone, it offered an arousal to soothing cycle of a thinking and understanding space.

The work with Aisling ended a few years ago. But when preparing this chapter, I asked Aisling if there was anything she wanted to say, reflecting back on her therapy. Using a metaphor, she said, "My brain was a jigsaw all jumbled up in a box, and therapy with Roz was like putting it out on a table looking at every piece individually and putting it back together in the right order. I put the puzzle together because in that room she gave me the courage and safety to look at every piece from every angle. That really helped me."

Conclusion

The "parts" of Aisling stepped forward to lead at various points depending on the presence and the nature of the trauma. In a similar way, the various "parts" of me as archetypes step forward therapeutically depending upon which therapeutic challenges and goals are present in the moment. Over many years in therapy, I have learnt about the various parts of me so that I have become aware of their qualities, roles, and usefulness. Likewise, successful therapy brings awareness and eventual integration to the client's various parts.

Working integratively means that the therapist is not confined by one particular theory or a given framework through which to see their client, but instead works in a uniquely creative way to bring different theories together into a congruent whole. This means that the therapist can address the individual needs of a client and at the same time draw upon the range of theories and tools that are most relevant to them. All of this has a context within the history and experiences of the therapist, their strengths and passions, that can contribute meaning to the work. In this chapter I have attempted to show how I have integrated using the arts, DDP, and the body with an understanding of attachment, trauma, and dissociation to help a developmentally traumatised adolescent. The archetypes of "wounded healer", "midwife", "alchemist", and "archivist" are just some of the images that reflect the approach of an integrative child psychotherapist when they work with children and families. Of course, one is not limited to just these; the beauty of this work is that other therapists may develop their own.

References

Bion, W. R. (1962). *Learning from Experience.* London: Heinemann.

Fonagy, P., Luyten, P., Allison, E., & Campbell, C. (2016). Reconciling psycho-analytic ideas with attachment theory. In: J. Cassidy & P. R. Shaver (Eds.), *Handbook of Attachment*, 3rd edn. (pp. 780–804). New York: Guilford.

Fosha, D. (2013). A heaven in a wild flower: Self, dissociation, and treatment in the context of the neurobiological core self. *Psychoanalytic Enquiry: A Topical Journal for Mental Health Professionals*, 33: 496–523.

Fraiberg, S., Adelson, E., & Shapiro, V. (1975). Ghosts in the nursery: A psycho-analytic approach to the problems of impaired infant–mother relationships. *Journal of the American Academy of Child Psychiatry, 14*(1): 387–421.

Herman, J. (1997). *Trauma and Recovery.* New York: Basic Books.

Hughes, D. A. (2011). *Attachment-Focused Family Therapy Workbook.* New York: W. W. Norton.

Hughes, D. A., Golding, K. S., & Hudson, J. (2019). *Healing Relational Trauma with Attachment-Focused Interventions: Dyadic Developmental Psychotherapy with Children and Families.* New York: W. W. Norton.

Levine, P. (1997). *Waking the Tiger—Healing Trauma: The Innate Capacity to Transform Overwhelming Experiences.* Berkeley, CA: North Atlantic.

Magagna, J. (Ed.) (2012). *The Silent Child: Communication Without Words.* London: Karnac.

Marks, R. (2011). Jason (7 years old)—expressing past neglect and abuse: Two-week intensive therapy for an adopted child with dissociation. In: S. Wieland (Ed.), *Dissociation in Traumatised Children and Adolescents*, 2nd edn. (pp. 89–134). New York: Routledge.

Perry, B. (2002). Childhood experience and the expression of genetic potential: What childhood neglect tells us about nature and nurture. *Brain and Mind*, 3: 79–100.

Porges, S. W. (2017). *The Pocket Guide to The Polyvagal Theory: The Transforming Power of Feeling Safe*. New York: W. W. Norton.

Silberg, J. L. (2013). *The Child Survivor: Healing Developmental Trauma and Dissociation*. New York: Routledge.

Wieland, S. (Ed.) (2011). *Dissociation in Traumatized Children and Adolescents: Theory and Clinical Interventions*, 2nd edn. New York: Routledge, 2015.

CHAPTER 16

Developing a "cradle of concern" using transference and countertransference in therapy and supervision

Jeanne Magagna

Introduction

One might say that there is a triangular relationship existing between supervisor, trainee therapist, and the child in therapy. The supervisory process involving the supervisor and trainee therapist's unconscious and conscious interactions both affects the child–therapist relationship and is affected by it. As the trainee brings the child–therapist interaction alive in the session, the supervisor receives the unprocessed aspects of the therapy session and by holding the feelings aroused within and in discussion with the trainee, lends a deeper understanding to the child's internal and external relationships. In this way a "cradle of concern" for the child's emotional life and the trainee therapist's development occurs.

In providing a suitable supervisory setting, the supervisor needs to arrange a regular and fixed supervision time with preparation for super- vision breaks that either therapist or supervisor might arrange. Inevita- bly, because there is a transference relationship existing between these two people, cancellations and illness can cause disruptions and some- times impediments to the ongoing work between therapist and child and also between therapist and supervisor; therefore, preparations for breaks in therapy and in supervision are also important.

The aim of supervision

The therapist brings a detailed process recording of the child and their verbal and non-verbal interaction. In the IATE training this is often accompanied by audio recording of the session. The supervisor's task is to create, through receptive, tolerant, non-critical understanding of all that the supervisee brings to the supervision, a containing atmosphere promoting security, respect, and confidentiality. The therapist is given the opportunity to freely associate to the therapeutic interaction between herself and the child. Through this process a "cradle of concern" involving conscious and unconscious processes of interaction between trainee therapist and supervisor is created. As a supervisor, I hope the therapist remembers the session and the child's non-verbal activities rather than simply bringing a transcript and audio recording to supervision. Generally, after the IATE training is completed, therapists prefer to alternate between bringing audio recordings of sessions and doing a process recording through memory of the session. Both methods are very helpful in gaining understanding of the moment to moment emotional tone and atmosphere of the therapy session.

Using what the trainee has learned through infant observation, it is important that they note the child's tone, volume, gentleness or forcefulness when playing with toys, and the openness or closed-up qualities of the child's eyes/body/hands. In a collaborative way, the supervisory pair recognise, tolerate, and explore the child–therapist interaction while simultaneously the supervisor, through use of the countertransference, gains understanding of the trainee's pattern of relating to the child's feelings and anxieties.

Between supervisions

I always suggest that if something very serious arises with regard to child protection, abuse, serious self-harm, or suicidal ideation, then rather than wait till the next supervision my supervisees should contact me. I do this to ensure that the child is protected and that the supervisee is supported in relating effectively and responsibly to the situation. This is particularly important for trainee psychotherapists whose anxiety may become too intense if they are unsupported in a difficult work setting.

Sometimes, when the therapist writes notes for the supervision, imaginary conversations with the child or dreams about the child may arise. These imaginary situations may be a means of surfacing unconscious positive or negative countertransference experiences with the child. These imaginary conversations or dreams can be important in understanding the session more fully. In group supervisions it may also be useful for the supervisee to undertake role playing through speaking the child's words to feel more fully what the child is experiencing and transferring onto the relationship with the therapist.

Repairing therapeutic ruptures

One of the tasks of a training supervision is to discover ways of recognising and repairing ruptures in the triangular relationship existing between the child, the therapist, and the supervisor. Ruptures in the relationship between supervisor and therapist can promote a sense of inadequacy in the therapist who then may find it difficult to receive and contain the child's feelings of inadequacy. Because the supervisor is required to write a report on the therapist, in the initial stages of supervision the therapist's anxiety about not being "good enough" can interfere with thinking alongside the supervisor about the psychotherapy session being discussed. The trainee's anxieties involved in learning new ways of being can be somewhat mitigated by the supervisor inspiring curiosity and interest in the child's emotional experience while being with the therapist. For example, it is very facilitating to note how the therapist's understanding of the child's anxieties has helped a child to offer a spontaneous thought or engage in an activity which deepens the discourse.

> Six-year-old Johnny, who was very aggressive to other children, begins a session playing with dinosaurs that kill, torture, and eat. When the therapist talks about how it seems that the child feels he has to attack in the strange new therapy room, Johnny ends the session by saying that the dinosaur is so scary and evil because he has to protect the small and weak. With the supervisor's encouragement the therapist becomes interested and emotionally impacted by how her understanding has enabled Johnny to move beyond his initial narrative of fighting dinosaurs needed

for protection. Thus the supervisor and therapist can mutually consider what the child may be taking with him as he leaves the therapy session.

Ruptures sometimes occur in therapy when the therapist is directing the child with a prearranged activity or superimposing her own structure rather than receiving the child's unconscious discourse and trying to follow and respond to the freely flowing unconscious feelings and anxieties which are portrayed in the transference relationship through the child's conversation and activities.

> On one occasion, six-year-old Johnny wanted the therapist to hold the teddy and monkey and have them speak to each other. The therapist suggested that Johnny take the teddy which could speak with the monkey which she would hold. It seemed that, for the child, the teddy and monkey represented the parents and thus the therapist's intervention created a different script, a more oedipal script, with the child speaking to a parent. Johnny didn't like this for his unconscious narrative about the internal parents' quarrel was disrupted.

Perhaps it is helpful for the therapist to realise that although ruptures in the therapeutic alliance can contribute to poor outcomes if unresolved, the successful repair of ruptures actually promotes more progress in the child's development. Eubanks et al. (2018) provide some general guidelines for supervisors to help the therapist to recognise negative transferences which may promote ruptures in the therapy. These include the supervisor helping the therapist to:

- Realise that initially both child and therapist will have unconscious fears and hopes of cure and understand that the therapist's important task is simply to deeply understand the child's verbal and non-verbalised emotions.
- Attune to therapeutic ruptures evidenced by the child's withdrawal, dissatisfaction, or appeasement of the therapist.

> Six-year-old Johnny's introjected early childhood experience of his mother leaving him for six days with an unfamiliar babysitter

left him fearing the therapist would unexpectedly leave him (represented by a toy lamb) "starving for six days".

- Receive and empathise with the child's expression of negative feelings towards the therapist.
- Explore the child's fear of expressing more concrete reasons for complaining about the relationship.
- Accept responsibility for one's own part, linked with the therapist's countertransference difficulties such as denying the child's hurt, fear, aggression, or dependency, which may promote the child's withdrawal or confrontation.
- Link ruptures in the therapy to the child's internalised pattern of relating to people while simultaneously being prepared to look at how the therapist might be disappointing and hurting the child, projecting one's own pathology into the child or not noticing that the child is too fragile to explore such intense feelings so quickly.

It is not all simply transference of the child's negative feelings towards internalised figures that contributes to ruptures in the therapeutic alliance; obviously, the therapist's behaviour has an influence on what the child feels.

Psychotherapy research consistently demonstrates that the quality of the therapeutic alliance is one of the better predictors of outcome across a range of different treatments as well as across a range of varying experiences as a therapist (Horvath et al., 2011). The therapeutic alliance is based on the healthy part of the child and the therapist collaborating to help the child develop the capacity to hold emotions, and lend understanding to them through introjection of the therapeutic "cradle of concern" developing between child and therapist.

Understanding the transference

When meeting a child, one may become aware through the child's body posture that the child is having an important experience of the therapist before the therapist actually says more than a hello. Is the child relaxed or stiff? Are the child's hands clenched, moving, or still? Are the child's eyes looking directly at the therapist or are the eyes cast downwards? How is the child's mouth: still or nervously moving, or closed firmly shut or lip being held by the teeth? Although each time upon initiating a therapeutic encounter the therapist is "the same person" more or less, each child may greet the therapist with a different non-verbalised communication regarding how the therapist is being experienced at that very moment in time. This non-verbal communication needs to continue to be empathically received and understood by the therapist when greeting the child entering the therapy session and then tracked throughout the encounter with the child.

The temptation is to rush to create a therapeutic alliance with the child so that the child is not anxious in one's presence. But to do so misses a very important signal regarding how the child is feeling inside in relation to internalised family figures which are projected onto the new therapist. These internalised family figures are not simply the child's external family members; the internalised family figures consist of the important people in the child's life transformed by the child's projections of love and hate and transferred onto the relationship with the therapist. A child who feels more securely attached to internally containing parental figures will appear less anxious in meeting the therapist, a stranger. Conversely, another child who has not experienced security, and in relating to emotionally volatile, disturbed, and traumatised parental figures who were not able sufficiently to contain the child's anxieties, may defend himself through withdrawal. Or he may do as six-year-old Johnny did in the first session, as he walked around the room like a mechanical toy repeating that he was a "piggy", a "killer".

Regardless of what seems appropriate for the child to hear in relation to the child's transference of internalised parental figures onto the therapist, the therapist will be experiencing the child's transference. Sigmund Freud (1912b, 1914g) thought what is called "the transference" was an obstacle to therapy at times, but later he realised that understanding the person's transference relationship and its richness in relation to the therapist moment to moment in the therapy, was an extremely important aspect of effecting therapeutic transformation.

Donald Meltzer in his book *The Psychoanalytic Process* (1967) describes developments in the therapy involving consideration of transference and countertransference experiences. *In the first moment*, Meltzer describes the therapist being "the toilet breast", as the child rids the self of unwanted aspects of his experience and projects them into the therapist for the therapist to feel the child's feelings.

When six-year-old Johnny, with his reputation for hitting other children, arrived in the therapy room saying he was "a killer" and couldn't wait to be "a bad fifteen-year-old", the therapist was filled with concern.

In the second moment, the therapist in the countertransference experiences the feelings projected into herself. This is often the moment when the therapist may say aloud or to herself a type of *analyst-centred interpretation* (Steiner, 1994) such as:

- I am to feel what it is like to feel threatened.
- I am to feel the unloved one.
- I am to feel the helpless one.
- I am to feel the angry one.
- I am to know what it is like to feel useless.
- I am to feel the confused one.

In the third moment, the child experiences how the therapist receives the projections of feeling without criticism, without feeling persecuted and defensive, without being driven to enact something in the session that has been projected into the therapist. In other words, the child finds relief when the therapist receives the projected feelings and gives them meaning without criticism.

Six-year-old Johnny finds some relief when the therapist tries to understand him as he builds gallows, makes a noose, and tries to hang a monkey puppet. The severity of the superego prompting repression is mitigated by the therapist's non-punitive, accepting, empathic way of receiving and thinking about the child's feelings. Hopefully this experience of being contained by the therapist is then introjected by the child.

The difficulty arrives when there is misattunement between therapist and child or when the end of the session arrives or a therapy holiday occurs. Of course, if the child is feeling persecuted by the therapeutic encounters, the child will feel relieved to have a break from therapy; however, if there is a positive transference to the therapist, the child's hostile feelings threaten to damage the goodness of the introjected therapist. This is when the child might subsequently have nightmares of frightening animals, burglars, or ghosts linked with hostile feelings turning the good therapist into a frightening nightmare figure. As a consequence the child may have difficulty returning to therapy and may require the support of teachers and/or parents to meet the therapist again.

Gradually through the therapeutic process a child will have sufficiently introjected a containing therapist to be less possessive of the therapist's time and generously allow the therapist to have a life with others without so much hurt and anger. Over time, through introjecting the emotionally containing therapist, the child develops security in the relationship with the therapist. Gradually, from this internal secure base, the child is further able to receive, explore, and lend understanding to his own emotional experiences.

> In a later therapy session six-year-old Johnny again starts questioning how his caterpillar is going to live in a tent without his mother for six days. He is beginning to explore aspects of his own development which was marked by separation from his mother, an experience revived in the transference to his therapist as the session is about to end.

Betty Joseph (1985), suggested that all that a child brings to therapy is tinged with the transference relationship to the therapist. This implies that stories about life outside the therapy, stories from the past, present, and future, can be understood also through understanding the unconscious internalised family relationships colouring aspects of the child's stories or play that are connected to the child's relationship to the therapist. Here are some examples:

> Seven-year-old Stephen is making a plasticene pizza with cheese upon it. As one little piece of cheese was hastily put on the pizza, the therapist commented on how it had jumped onto the pizza. Speaking as the cheese, Stephen, said, "Eat me. I hate my family." The therapist, understanding that Stephen wished that the therapist "eat", that is empathically receive, his communication, spoke to the cheese: "Why do you hate your family?" Stephen, speaking for the cheese replied, "They hurt my feelings."

In this session, the last one before the summer break, Stephen in the positive transference was turning to the therapist, via the cheese, to express the conflictual relationship he had with his mother and grandmother which he was usually terrified to reveal. Simultaneously, he is also expressing his negative transference of both his infantile hurt and anger towards the therapist for leaving him in his difficult family for the long summer break. It was important for the therapist to gather some of the intensity of both Stephen's negative and positive feelings into his transference relationship with her.

The therapist also transfers aspects of his/her internal world onto the child. One is looking at what kind of unconscious relationship exists moment to moment between the therapist and the child. The therapist has to struggle to understand and not become defended against the powerful feelings that they experience towards the child. The child's urgent non-verbal communications projected into the therapist are those that the child is not yet able to put into symbolic form. The child's communication beyond words is that which requires reception and understanding by the therapist (Heimann, 1956). If one can bring alive again and contain the child's feelings within a relationship that have been deeply defended against or only fleetingly experienced, the therapist can enable the child to integrate split off aspects of the self. "Regardless of the frequency of transference interpretation the therapist is using their understanding of the transference/countertransference process to guide all their responses, verbal and nonverbal to the patient" (Lanyado, 1989, p. 86).

Two possible kinds of negative transference

First, fencing against the threat of the therapist's attack on the omnipotent self

A nine-year-old anorectic, Alice knew that initially to have feelings meant to be overwhelmed by feelings. She had no internal psychic structure to contain her disturbing feelings and hence she could not or did not want to think or talk about feelings. She insisted that she was identified with a grown-up, unfeeling, omnipotent part that was not subject to feelings such as jealousy of other children or wish to have her mother all to herself.

In the countertransference the therapist felt what it was to be trapped, paralysed, with very little notion of how to make a connection with the child in Alice. First, she hostilely told the therapist to "shut up" and covered her ears. She was being hostile, its intensity a negative transference. But it is aggression from the omnipotent self, *the only protector* she had, which is being used to protect herself from so much trauma that she has experienced. But then she drew a picture (Figure 16.1).

Figure 16.1 Trapped girl

Through this drawing she helped the therapist to understand how confined her vulnerable self was in relation to her powerful omnipotent self. It was now painful to experience the sense of confinement of "the little vulnerable child in Alice". This omnipotent self kept Alice away from intimacy with the therapist but also often kept Alice disconnected from "the little child in her". Her vulnerable self was barely visible.

Traumatised children, such as Alice, are threatened by dependency on the therapist, because people whom they should have been able to trust have been unreliable, hurtful, or unavailable to such an extent that the very sensitive child's hostility to them has rendered them internally useless as a source of containment and security. Both the therapist and I, the supervisor, felt it painful to experience "the little vulnerable child" held captive by the omnipotent self.

Second, negative transference of the hurt, disappointed, and angry self

Another negative transference is the child's hurt and then fury with the therapist for being a disappointment, for ending a session, for having rules so that the child can't have an endless supply of paint or paper (representing the therapist's love), for having a holiday, or for not being sufficiently attuned to the child's emotional state.

Part of the child's negativity to the therapist is linked with the therapist's own denied aspects of herself which might prompt mis-attunement in the relationship. However, the child's negativity is intensified by his relationship with the mis-attuned internal figures onto whom the child has projected hostility. In other words, an internal drama becomes externalised and enmeshed with the present *moment-to-moment drama* between child and the therapist.

> Nine-year-old Alice is beginning to get in touch with the possibility of depending on both the therapist and her parents. The therapist worried about how Alice would experience depending on her and then experiencing her Christmas holiday departure at such a vulnerable moment. She lets the therapist know when she determinedly states: "If I were really courageous, I would really cut myself. That would really be the way to get the attention of

people." She adds, "How can I make anyone worry about me?" Alice plaintively tells the therapist that the therapist feels so far away when she is out of the session.

She fears that the therapist's mind is so similar to hers ("out of sight, out of mind") that she will slide out of the therapist's mind if she doesn't evoke extreme anxiety in her. Some of this fear of losing her grip on the therapist is linked with the hostility directed to the therapist's internalised image because she is leaving her for the Christmas holiday. In her rage Alice experienced the therapist internally as a "thick-skinned thoughtless therapist", impervious to her needs. Alice feels she has to scream out for help in order to break through the therapist's "thick skin". She ensures that she makes a penetrating impact on the therapist by making threats to self-harm. Perhaps she unconsciously hopes that, if she threatens, thus thrusting anxiety about her safety onto the therapist, she will control the therapist through positioning herself permanently in her mind during the Christmas holidays.

> When the therapist returns from holiday, nine-year-old Alice is furious. She walks out of the first session and then won't return for the next one. When she returns for the third session she says, "I feel really bad about myself. I have a very angry, nasty side. I am worried everyone will reject me for having it." She states she has been angry with the therapist since the previous week. Reluctantly she does come after a second missed session and tells the therapist, "You feel different to me now that you have come back. I don't like how you are. I don't like how much I dislike you."

It feels as though the therapist has become a noxious therapist filled with projections of her hostility. After the Christmas holiday Alice is less reliant on the "omnipotent destructive" (Rosenfeld, 1987) part of her personality. As a result, Alice is becoming more dependent on the therapist. Once she can trust the therapist she feels safer to be angry directly towards her. She is angry about being overlooked, about not having her specific needs as an individual being taken into account.

Another example of negative transference

Younger children, like seven-year-old Max, may show their negative feelings to the therapist through their hands. The hostile feelings towards the therapist contain a transference of all the ongoing hostility in relation to the internalised family figures. Here we see Max when the therapist didn't arrive bringing a new toy which he had wanted her to buy:

> Just after the half-term school holidays, Max arrived, quickly looked at the toys, and demanded, "Where is the Superman doll I wanted?" Max then grabbed some plasticene, threw it on the table hard, picked it up, pummelled it on the table and then threw it towards the therapist's feet in frustration. Max is owning his anger about his thwarted wish to have more concrete signs of the therapist's affection and remembrance of him when they were apart and more consistent containment of his sense of deprivation and frustration. He also wants her to help him feel a strong, resilient boy.

Other aspects of the child's negative transference in the therapist–child interaction can arrive because the child does not have an internal psychic structure for bearing hurt, distress, frustration, and all the unprocessed frustrated and hostile feelings are projected into the therapist. For instance:

> Sarah, aged six, triumphantly pushed the whole doll's house filled with furniture and dolls onto the floor and then hid under the table in the therapy room.

There was a sense that having attacked the doll family and house Sarah feared the therapist's retribution. The therapist's way of relating non-punitively but firmly, in an emotionally containing way to the negative transference, is one of the keys to helping the child introject "containing internal parental figures" to receive and consider her anger and resulting persecutory anxieties. These containing internal parental figures can then mitigate the harshness of the cruel superego creating anxiety when one has hostile feelings.

The positive transference

As the relationship with the therapist deepens, the child may think of the therapy room as a "home-base" and begin to feel trust and dependence on the therapist's capacity to understand the child's anxieties and feelings.

> This occurs when seven-year-old Jane told her therapist that on a different day she had seen the door of the therapy room open and crept inside only to find that she didn't see her toys. She added that she thought someone, probably the last child the therapist had seen, had put them away somewhere. After further discussion Jane told the therapist she wanted to be in the therapy room every day or maybe at midnight.

Here one sees that, in the light of the positive transference, Jane's dependency on the therapist initially fosters possessiveness, a feeling of interference by other children in the therapist's mind, and a wish to have "the night-time therapist" who is reserved for relationships with other adults (Meltzer, 1967).

Use of the countertransference as a base for understanding

The use of the therapist's countertransference is the main therapeutic method in work with a child. Much of our understanding of the transference comes through how we are affected by what the child brings to the session. This is what is given the name "the countertransference".

Understanding the *countertransference* is crucial, for the therapist's experiences of the child go beyond the child's conscious words and obvious themes in the child's play. The countertransference experience holds the unsymbolised sensations and experiences still held in the non-declarative, non-verbal part of the child's memory.

Use of the countertransference is linked to Bion's (1962) psychoanalytic approach and the research into therapeutic effectiveness described by Allan Schore (2002). Using the countertransference involves closely observing, receiving, experiencing, and considering non-verbalised experiences present in the bodily states, pictorial images, gestures, actions and play, tone, rhythm, volume and velocity in speaking both in the self and the child. Joseph (1985) says the therapist can be looking not only at what the child says, but can focus on how the child is affecting the therapist, "alongside and beyond what he is saying". In this way the child has the opportunity to recover and develop infantile aspects of the psychological and physical self that need understanding and repair. By this means the child can discover their potential for intimacy with themselves and others, their hopes and desires, their capacity for learning and work, and psychological understanding of themselves and others.

The application of Bick's (1968) observational approach of empathic attunement to the minute aspects of the non-verbal dialogue between child and therapist is considered by Schore (2002) to be the first point of therapeutic action. Two years of weekly infant observation seminars enable trainee therapists to be more fully attuned to non-verbal communication of the children in therapy. Also, many children are naturally specifically attuned to non-verbal aspects of the therapist's relationship with them (Perry et al., 1995). Lewis (1992) points out that the therapist's use of his bodily countertransference is especially involved in the reception of right-brain to right-brain transferential projections of split-off parts of the self and this mechanism specifically mediates defensive projective identification. Friedman and Lavender (1997) conclude that the therapist's discomforting bodily signals are necessary somatic markers triggered by his perception of the projective identification. Both the psychological and physical holding in the countertransference are crucial for therapeutic progress to occur (Muir, 1993).

The therapist usually finds ways of "mirroring" the child, but in order to transform the child's distress the therapist must go "beyond mirroring" (Schore, 2002). More than the clinician's verbalisations, it is his non-verbal activity—the therapist's physical containment of the child's disavowed experience—that needs to *precede* verbal processing (Dosamantes, 2002, p. 362). It is this spontaneous emotional pre-attunement, which constitutes a conversation between limbic systems, a conversation between the therapist's inner experiences and the child's non-verbal bodily postures and experiences. Emotional pre-attunement links with what is described by neuroscience literature (Buck, 1994, p. 266) as a biologically based communication system. It is this that creates the safe holding environment (Davis & Hadiks, 1994) promoting transformation of the personality.

More crucially, research suggests that if the therapist blocks the negatively balanced somatic markers—for example, by defensively shifting out of the right-brain intuitive state into a left-brain intellectual state—he cuts off his empathic connection to his own pain, and therefore to the child's. The therapist must by necessity act as an interactive affective regulator for the child in order for therapeutic transformation to occur (Schore, 2002). If the therapist becomes too overwhelmed by the projection of bad states of mind into him, the child becomes disorganised and can often feel criticised. Transformation takes place through projective identification, through the effective use of the countertransference, creating a transitional space in which mental pain, hopelessness, despair, and flickerings of hope can be explored authentically.

Also, the acceptance, consideration, and verbalisation of one's countertransference responses to the child's primitive experiences, including sensations and movement or stillness of his body, have been essential particularly before an inhibited child can put these experiences into a symbolic form through play, drawing, dreams, or words. It is very helpful to attend closely to one's own bodily experiences (Damasio, 1999) while closely observing and patiently experiencing the child through use of the countertransference, before making interpretations either verbally or silently to oneself. I do believe that *a silent interpretation* affects the therapist's whole vocal and bodily demeanour in relation to the child.

When the therapist feels too great a wish for an obvious response from the child, the child experiences this as intrusively demanding and withdraws from the relationship. In these situations, when the therapist becomes too worried about making something "therapeutic" happen and being seen as "a good, successful therapist", a persecutory situation occurs. When a child is "in retreat" the therapist needs to move from a persecutory demand for "something to occur". The therapist can attempt to lessen questioning the child and instead use their countertransference to accept, understand, and describe the communication present in their countertransference experience during a particular moment in the session. Through the therapist's mentalization process, the child begins to trust the therapist and there is a lessening of the need to hold onto primitive projections of the omnipotent self which prevents emotional intimacy with parts of the self and significant others. Modulation of emotional states and good self-esteem occur through internalisation and identification with the good, mentalizing internalised parents, represented by the therapist, and developed in the therapy (Bateman & Fonagy, 2004). This permits an integration of the child's body and psychological self. Internalisation of the therapist's state of mind enables a child to develop a "cradle of concern" facilitating the development of a process of mentalization (Bateman & Fonagy, 2004).

Countertransference feelings can often feel disturbing, overwhelming, or embarrassing, yet therapeutic research suggests that it is vitally important for the therapist to use their countertransference experience *or felt sense* to initiate an explicit exploration of something that's being unconsciously enacted in the therapeutic relationship. For this reason it is important to provide an opportunity in supervision for the therapist to describe countertransference experiences and with the supervisor's help to use them as a basis for understanding the therapist–child relationship. It is perhaps likely that the greater the child's emotional disturbance, the more frequently the therapist will experience intense feelings of being overwhelmed, disorganised, helpless, and frustrated. One supervisor I had, Donald Meltzer, said to me, "Unless you *feel* the child's acute disturbance the child will never make progress." By this he is implying that the therapist must truly be "at-one-with-the-child", having a moment of deep communion, a shared emotional experience *before putting the experience into words.*

In supervision I have found it helpful to stop section by section of the transcript of the session and then develop more detailed observation of verbal and non-verbal communication to understand the meaning of the intense feelings being experienced. I feel it is very important to look at what preceded a particular theme to understand how the child is gaining more awareness or protecting the self through various defences.

> In approaching the end of the fourth session, six-year-old Johnny began to describe a very hungry kitten who was left by the mother cat to starve in the desert for six days. It was obvious that now Johnny was losing some of his previous fierce exterior and becoming vulnerable as he began to trust the therapist and she became aware of how valuable she was to him.

Noting the transference to the therapist as the session approaches the ending is extremely important, for it helps one understand the hurt, frightened, angry, possessive feelings which may become temporary impediments to introjecting a good, emotionally containing therapist.

The supervisor's emotional and bodily countertransference experiences also require attention as the child–therapist encounter unfolds. For example, as a supervisor, I am aware of a soporific sensation when denial of the negative transference permeates a session being presented. It can be very hard for a therapist, and sometimes the supervisor, to accept and acknowledge the full weight of the child's infantile transference of being hurt and cross with the therapist either for leaving him between sessions, during half-term and longer holidays, or for mis-attuning with the child within the session.

> Near the end of a session six-year-old Johnny talks about the gases wanting to get out of his bottom and he subsequently runs to the loo to pee. When the therapist fails to acknowledge his hurt and aggression towards her, Johnny escalates his aggressive stance by portraying a tsunami hitting the monkey representing the therapist. The therapist found it difficult to accept the full weight of the child's hostility and fear, and as a supervisor I temporarily denied the full impact of the child's aggression and resulting terror. A kind of emotional impasse could then have occurred in the child's therapy had the countertransference not eventually been fully experienced by both therapist and supervisor.

Two of many countertransference conflicts

I shall now address in detail only two of the many countertransference issues that arise during therapy. These are the child's silence and the child's aggressiveness.

The child's silence

Problems in the countertransference occur frequently when the child is "in retreat", fearing intrusion and feeling that no one can be trusted.

> One non-speaking eight-year-old child, Sarah, who didn't want to see the therapist, but who eventually put her thoughts into verbal communication said, "I'd like to be a rabbit and I would like to run away and hide … I would be in my burrow and I would be thinking, 'Oh no. People. I don't want to be near them.' "

Here the therapist has one aspect of the countertransference, the protective self that feels the therapist is an intruder. Simultaneously though, the therapist needs to experience that underneath her sense of being rejected lies the child's wish to be understood. Later the child mentioned above said, "I wish I had spoken."

It is fairly unusual for children to ask to see a therapist. Instead, a teacher, parent, or doctor has usually recommended that the child have therapy. Some severely traumatised children hide "in their rabbit hole" and don't play, draw, or speak. This is when the therapist often experiences difficult countertransference issues (Magagna, 2012). As a therapist one may skip this issue of silence as unimportant and simply fill the patient's silence by asking interesting questions which often are greeted by more silence or reluctantly spoken one-word answers. This gives a clue that questioning the child is simply persecutory and should suggest to the therapist that a different approach is important. One silent child, eleven-year-old Ellen, left her first therapist saying, "Her questions were just too intrusive." The therapist needs to have a dialogue within herself to find meaning in the non-verbal communications of the child.

The meaning of the child's silence varies from moment to moment and can only be understood through receiving and understanding the child's projective identification communications through use of the countertransference. Sometimes one can simply go through a transcript and underline the child's non-moving silence, or the child's inaudible speaking, preventing the therapist from hearing, and try to discover what has happened just before the inaudible speech or silence occurred. The therapist's task is to continually try to understand who the child is being and what the therapist is feeling and supposed to be feeling in the role into which the child has thrust her. In what way is she in the child's dramas? What is the script? It is important for the therapist to carefully note her bodily/emotional countertransference experience in relation to the child's bodily gestures of hands, feet, body and her facial expressions as well as the general emotional atmosphere.

Here is a description of the therapist's encounters with nine-year-old anorectic Alice at the beginning of therapy when Alice isn't speaking.

Don't touch

When Alice is filled with intense feelings she sometimes has turned to not speaking as a way of protecting herself from feeling too much before she can bear it. She has attempted self-harm when she felt too much. She is holding herself together physically and emotionally in a protective way through her silence. She doesn't trust the therapist. At times when the therapist describes this to Alice, Alice blurts out the problem saying things such as, "I feel miserable at school" or "Nobody at home understands me" or "When I feel unhappy I just can't eat." The therapist needs a gentle, empathic voice on these occasions.

You're useless

At other times though, when Alice purses her lips, goes "Tch" and acts superior to the therapist as if saying, "You almost never get it right," she is into her omnipotent combative soldier self which is silencing the therapist. The therapist is to feel small, unimportant, and useless.

> Alice's sessions were reduced from twice to once a week. When this reduction was being discussed, Alice spent two months frequently unconsciously or consciously abandoning the therapist through silence to project her feeling that the therapist was abandoning her.

I want you to understand without my having to speak

At times Alice was visibly distressed, having argued with her brothers or mother just before the session. When Alice is in an emotionally intimate posture, the therapist feels she has permission to describe Alice's feelings. On those occasions the therapist's understanding words were often greeted by Alice's talking with her or by her drawing animals mothering their young babies as a way of showing her appreciation of the therapist.

Can you allow me to be separate?

Since Alice had a mother who was very enmeshed with her, Alice needed to know that the therapist could be different from her and that Alice could have a separate mental space. Plying her with too many questions would simply lead her to feel that she was forced to exist in the sessions to please the intrusive therapist, to help her feel she was a successful therapist. After one silence Alice complains, "It irritates me when people feel they can be successful in getting me to eat, acting like it had nothing to do with me and how I feel." Alice needed to know the therapist could bear her existing independently in the silence without intruding into her, without the therapist needing to be "successful" in feeding her with her words. Bion's (1967) statement about the importance about working "without desire" certainly rang true at this moment.

Alice's psychic retreat has been described, but what about the therapist's countertransference in response to the child's silence? That is a far greater problem than the child's silence.

Here are three dangers in the countertransference which at times threatened the therapeutic alliance which the therapist was attempting to maintain with Alice:

- *Boredom*, when the therapist felt useless and rejected by her.
- *Intrusiveness*, when the therapist's curiosity about what she was feeling became too intense, the therapist restrained herself completely.
- *The desire to placate* which occurred at times when Alice was furious. This placation was linked with the therapist's temptation to project her own anger into Alice and then feel her anger to be overwhelming.

Sometimes, when Alice was curled up against the radiator saying nothing, the therapist could become bored, sleepy, or silent in a passive way. In supervision the therapist, who was embarrassed by having to bring the sessions to a training supervision, discovered that sometimes she was taking revenge on Alice for her continual withdrawal and abandonment. Obviously, at this moment the therapist's feelings about bringing a silent child to supervision are interfering with the therapy. Sometimes though, through her own therapy, the therapist realised that her boredom arrived because she was defending against unconscious feelings of being useless or rejected.

Feeling anxious the therapist sometimes misinterpreted Alice's feelings by stating what she believed Alice might be feeling in the silence. Each time the therapist did this Alice would let the therapist know it was a controlling intrusion by making remarks such as, "Don't tell me what I feel" or "Don't read into my mind." At the same time it is essential for the therapist to speak at times during the silence, otherwise the child feels the therapist is starving her, depriving her of an understanding therapist. However, the wording of the therapist's understanding is crucial. Alice's feelings are often not available to her for they were split off and projected into the therapist. At these times she would feel it was false if the therapist was talking about Alice having a feeling. It was much better if the therapist talked about the feelings projected into the therapist and now existing in the therapist or "in the room" without suggesting that Alice was consciously intending to project the feelings. In these situations the therapist might say, "It looks like I can never get things right," or "I guess I am to know what it is to be alone and lonely." Alice needed to know that the therapist was never accusing her or feeling persecuted or controlled by her silence. She needed to know the therapist was simply trying to understand *the present moment*.

At times the therapist found herself to be too submissive to the omnipotent part of Alice because she felt the risk that Alice could persuade her parents to stop her private therapy or starve herself. At other times the therapist could feel her voice assuming a too friendly or too gentle style which felt like a pacifier rather than a food for thought about Alice's situation. Luckily, the child sometimes corrects the therapist's errors. For example, Alice would say, "Don't treat me like a two-year-old!" The therapist's tone of voice had to be firm and strong in the silence when Alice's hard omnipotent self was prominent. Otherwise she felt the therapist was weak and colluding with her attempts to humiliate the therapist. Meltzer (1994) in "Temperature and distance" describes ways of attuning vocally as well as linguistically to different aspects of the child as they are presented.

Various other countertransference problems in the therapist may impede progress in the therapeutic encounter. Mentioned below are some of those described by Sandler et al. (1992).

Placation and denial in the face of aggression

As mentioned earlier, if the therapist has not sufficiently integrated her own aggression into her personality she may simply deny some of the child's negative transference. Or she may find herself placating the child, trying to avoid gathering the child's hostility into the transference with her, because she has not resolved her own conflicts due to her own aggression. Also, she may split off her infantile aggression, project it into the child, and become frightened of the overwhelming nature of the child's aggression coupled with her own projected aggression. In all three of these situations the child is not having an experience that his or her "hostile feelings" can be accepted and understood in a non-critical way. The child does not have a "sturdy object" into which the child can project. Somatic complaints, nightmares, and placatory gestures sometimes arise in a child existing in such repeated impasses in the relationship with the therapist.

Accepting the idealised transference for too long

Early in therapy, splitting making the therapist the idealised good therapist might temporarily be necessary to internalise sufficient good experiences to deal with the negative feelings (Alvarez, 1992). Nevertheless, it would be important eventually for the child to feel sufficiently safe to bring his disappointment, his hurt, his anger, his rage, and his possessiveness to the therapist.

Sometimes though, children need to experience positive transference and countertransference sufficiently long enough to be sure that the therapist won't stop the therapy or dislike them if they bring their hostile feelings into the relationship. Sometimes the positive transference arrives when the child feels the therapist fully accepts both his loving and hating feelings. Maybe the child requires adequate experience of the positive transference and countertransference to continue to come to therapy and to develop an intimate relationship with the therapist.

Initially in therapy with a child there can be "a split in the transference" just as there is in early infancy when the mother is experienced as wonderfully good one moment or terribly bad if she has been absent for too long or has left the baby calling out for her for too long.

An ill-treated child could potentially feel extreme relief in meeting a non-parent who is receptive to him. Initially he may feel so grateful that he may idealise the therapist and be afraid that any negative feelings would damage the relationship. In order to integrate bad impulses the child needs first to develop a sense of a good containing object. Both Rosenfeld (1987, p. 271) and Alvarez (1992, p. 126) suggest that it is important not to break down the idealisation too quickly with "very vulnerable", severely traumatised, and/or deprived children who need to idealise the analyst in order to create a benign atmosphere. Alvarez (1992, p. 121) goes on to say of idealisation that patients whose capacity for bright hope is severely undeveloped should not be constantly reminded of the very despair and anxiety that they are finally managing to overcome.

> When a severely depressed ten-year-old girl, Nina, was not attending school, but said she wanted to be a therapist like her therapist, the therapist did not swoop in to look at all her problems that could prevent her from doing so. The therapist allowed Nina to hold onto the hope that she could get out from under "the cloud of despair" that had permeated her life for years.

On the other hand, having repeated sessions where only an idealising relationship with the therapist exists, the risk is that the child's negative feelings about being left by the therapist can permeate all other relationships leaving all the severe conflicts "outside the therapy" in relationships with teachers, peers, parents, and siblings. Therefore it is incumbent upon the therapist to gradually gather all the transference feelings from internalised relationships being reactivated in the therapy and when separated from the therapist.

There is a constant debate about how much should an interpretation be spoken to the child and how much an interpretation should be "*a silent interpretation*" within the therapist, based on the countertransference, regarding what is happening within the relationship. Perhaps most important is the therapist's emotional stance in relation to the patient. Bowlby (1988) places emphasis on the therapist's role as a trusted companion for his client in the latter's exploration of himself and his experiences with the advocation that the client tells the therapist what he knows about his experiences.

Looking at pain prematurely

Mentioning the child's history of trauma in relationship with others can create an exposure and danger which leaves the child shattered with pain and shock or very highly defended. There is a big debate between therapists regarding whether or not, during initial meetings, the therapist should tell the child that one knows their traumatic story. These different views may both be valid, but I hold to the view that first the child's trusting relationship with the therapist needs to be established

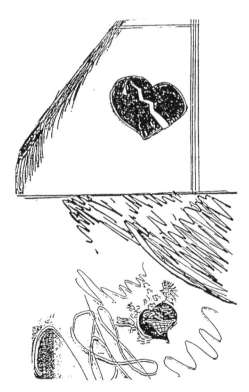

Figure 16.2 The people dancing on the broken heart

in order that the child can feel the upsetting feelings which arise can be "held" and contained. Below one sees how two therapists have learned this the hard way.

> The therapist made the mistake of going too deeply, talking about how nine-year-old Alice might miss time with her during the holidays rather than the therapist discussing how Alice could hold onto the therapy during the holidays. In response Alice drew a picture (Figure 16.2).

Through this drawing Alice showed how, when the therapist touched her hidden hurt feelings prematurely, her sense of a painful emotional experience, her loss represented by a broken heart was quickly transformed into a laughing heart covered with dancers. Until there is sufficient containment of the feelings projected into the therapist, and until there is sufficient accessibility to the child's true feelings, the manic, omnipotent part, the dancers, the laughing and perhaps mocking face quickly arrive to protect the broken heart. The therapist and child may still talk

Figure 16.3 Big hand, big feet girl

about the child having a feeling, but the child will simply be talking about a feeling without being connected to it. Therapeutic progress will certainly not occur in this way.

> On another occasion when the therapist talked about Alice's intense feelings too quickly rather than addressing Alice's more *mature self*, wondering how Alice could "hold on to the therapist and wait for the next meeting", Alice drew a picture (Figure 16.3).

Here Alice depicts how her impulses to suffocate, strangle, break, and throw objects, or to run away from home, take her over her more *mature self*. Once she is more in touch with her feelings and has a normal appetite for living her life, the repressed feelings burst out in an uncontained way and tend to overwhelm herself. The therapist needed to gauge how to work more slowly with her barely repressed feelings.

On the other hand, some IATE therapists have found it useful to follow Margot Sunderland's (2015) technique of gently telling the child's story using figures in the sand tray suggesting, "This is what I know about you." The story is told simply in a straightforward way and then the child is asked to change anything in the story that the child feels is incorrect. This technique is met with various responses depending on the therapist's timing in the session and how emotionally secure a child is. Here is one situation with a traumatised child where the technique of "telling the child's story" perhaps could have been used later in the therapy:

> The therapist showed six-year-old Johnny with the characters in the sand tray how she knew that his parents now lived in two separate houses. She told him gently that this may have created feelings of disappointment, hurt, sadness, and anger, feelings she wanted to understand with him. As the therapist spoke, Johnny's muscles stiffened and he turned his back to the therapist.

Here, like Alice, Johnny is psychologically and physically retreating when, in one of the initial therapy sessions, the therapist discussed his child's traumatic past history.

I would like to suggest that ideally the therapist follows the child's unconscious narrative expressed through play, drawing, or words. The child's internalised drama will reveal itself if the therapist is emotionally available and understanding. Talking to the child involves waiting momentarily, in a state of reverie, to allow thoughts to be borne within oneself intuitively rather than hanging on to repetitious thoughts, already-formed thoughts from a previous supervision, and plans suggested in classes and textbooks. Also it is important not to necessarily attach oneself to the first thought that forces itself, perhaps defensively, into one's mind. Infant observation, during which the observer closely observes the details of interaction using the counterransference experiences to understand, while not making verbal interpretations, is the ideal training ground for therapeutic work. Using the countertransference involves the therapist in being aware of creating an emotional space for thoughts to arise when one's mind is

> ... still and still moving
> Into another intensity
> For further union, a deeper communion.
>
> T. S. Eliot, "East Coker", 1940

Conclusion

The therapist's own therapy as well as the experience of supervision should enable one to sustain aroused feelings and allow interventions to spontaneously arise from within. If the therapist tries to work without consulting his own *felt experience* the child becomes disturbed and the interventions are poor. Various research findings suggest that good therapeutic outcome is correlated with a high frequency of interventions making conscious the transference to the therapist of the child's internal object relationships (Malan, 1995) and Davanloo (2001). This chapter therefore suggests that the most therapeutic "cradle of concern" is built through both the therapist and the supervisor utilising notions of transference and countertransference when trying to understand the child's, therapist's, and supervisor's emotional experiences in *the present moment.*

References

Alvarez, A. (1992). *Live Company. Psychoanalytic Psychotherapy with Autistic, Borderline, Deprived and Abused Children.* London: Routledge.

Bateman, A. W., & Fonagy, P. (2004). *Psychotherapy for Borderline Personality Disorder.* Oxford: Oxford University Press.

Bick, E. (1968). Notes on infant observation in psychoanalytic training. *International Journal of Psychoanalysis, 45*: 558–560.

Bion, W. R. (1962). A theory of thinking. In: *Second Thoughts: Selected Papers on Psycho-Analysis* (pp. 110–119). London: Heinemann, 1967.

Bion, W. R. (1967). Notes on memory and desire. *Psychoanalytic Forum, 2*(3): 272–273, 279–280.

Bowlby, J. (1988). *A Secure Base.* London: Taylor & Francis.

Buck, R. (1994). The neuropsychology of communication: Spontaneous and symbolic aspects. *Journal of Pragmatics, 22*: 265–278.

Damasio, A. (1999). *The Feeling of What Happens in the Body and Emotion in the Making of Consciousness.* London: Vintage.

Davanloo, H. (2001). *Intensive Short-Term Dynamic Psychotherapy: Selected Papers of Habib Davanloo.* Chichester, UK: John Wiley.

Davis, M., & Hadiks, D. (1994). Nonverbal aspects of therapist attunement. *Journal of Clinical Psychology, 50*(3): 393–405.

Dosamantes, E. (1992). The intersubjective relationship between therapist and patient: A key to understanding denied and denigrated aspects of the patient's self. *Arts in Psychotherapy, 19*(5): 359–365.

Eliot, T. S. (1940). *East Coker: Four Quartets.* In: *T. S. Eliot: The Complete Poems and Plays* (p 183). London: Faber & Faber, 1969.

Eubanks, C. F., Muran J. C., & Safran, J. D. (2018). Alliance, rupture, repair: A meta-analysis. *Psychology, 55*(4): 508–519.

Freud, S. (1912b). The dynamics of transference. *S. E., 12*: 97–108. London: Hogarth.

Freud, S. (1914g). Remembering, repeating and working–through (further recommendations on the technique of psycho-analysis, II). *S. E., 14*: 121–145. London: Hogarth.

Friedman, N., & Lavender, J. (1997). On receiving the patient's transference: The symbolizing and desymbolizing countertransference. *Journal of the American Psychoanalytic Association, 43* (19): 79–103.

Heimann, P. (1956). Dynamics of transference. *International Journal of Psychoanalysis, 37*: 303–310.

Horvath, A. O., Del Re, A. C., Flückiger, C., & Symonds, D. (2011). Alliance in individual psychotherapy. *Psychotherapy, 48*: 9–16.

Joseph, B. (1985). Transference: The total situation. *International Journal of Psychoanalysis, 66*: 447–454.

Lanyado, M. (1989). Variations on the theme of transference & countertransference in the treatment of a ten year old boy. *Journal of Child Psychotherapy, 15*(2): 85–101.

Lewis, P. P. (1992). The creative arts in transference/countertransference relationships. *Arts in Psychotherapy, 19*: 317–323.

Magagna, J. (Ed.) (2012). *The Silent Child: Communication without Words.* London: Karnac.

Malan, D. H. (1995). *Individual Psychotherapy and the Science of Psychodynamics.* London: Hodder Arnold.

Meltzer, D. (1967). *The Psychoanalytic Process:* London: Heinemann Medical.

Meltzer, D. (1977). Personal communication.

Meltzer, D. (1994). Temperature and distance. In: A. Hahn (Ed.), *Sincerity and Other Works.* London: Karnac.

Muir, R. C. (1993). Transpersonal processes: A bridge between object relations and attachment theory in normal and psychopathological development. *British Journal of Medical Psychology, 68*: 243–257.

Perry, B. D., Pollard, R. A., Blakley, T. L., Baker, W. L., & Vigilante, D. (1995). Childhood trauma, the neurobiology of adaptation and "use-dependent" development of the brain: How "states" become "traits". *Journal of Infant Mental Health, 16*(4): 271–291.

Rosenfeld, H. (1987). *Impasse and Interpretation.* London: Routledge.

Sandler, J., Holder, A., Dare, C., & Dreher, A. U. (1992). *The Patient and the Analyst.* London: Karnac.

Schore, A. (2002). Clinical implications of a psychoneurobiological model of projective identification. In: S. Alhanati (Ed.), *Primitive Mental States. Volume II.* London: Karnac.

Steiner, J. (1994). Problems of psychoanalytic technique: Patient centred and analyst centred interpretations. In: *Psychic Retreats: Pathological Organizations in Psychic, Neurotic and Borderline Patients.* London: Routledge.

Sunderland, M. (2015). *Conversations that Matter.* Broadway, UK: Worth.

Index